The
Point Is

Also by Lee Eisenberg

Breaking Eighty:
A Journey Through the Nine Fairways of Hell

The Number:
What Do You Need for the Rest of Your Life,
and What Will It Cost?

Shoptimism:
Why the American Consumer Will Keep On Buying
No Matter What

The Point Is

Making Sense of Birth, Death,
and Everything in Between

LEE EISENBERG

TWELVE

NEW YORK   BOSTON

Twelve
Hachette Book Group
1290 Avenue of the Americas
New York, NY 10104
twelvebooks.com
twitter.com/twelvebooks

First Edition: February 2016

Twelve is an imprint of Grand Central Publishing.
The Twelve name and logo are trademarks of Hachette Book Group, Inc.

The publisher is not responsible for websites (or their content) that are not owned by the publisher.

Bertrand Russell's dedication to his wife Edith originally appeared in *The Autobiography of Bertrand Russell, Volume 1*, published by George Allen and Unwin Ltd., 1967. Reprinted with the permission of Taylor and Francis.

The Meaning in Life Questionnaire appeared in the *Journal of Counseling Psychology* 53, no. 1 (2006), 80–93, and is reprinted with the kind permission of Michael F. Steger.

The Purpose in Life Test was developed by Joseph C. Crumbaugh and Leonard T. Maholick, psychologists at the Bradley Center Inc., Columbus, Georgia. It was introduced in a paper titled "An Experimental Study in Existentialism: The Psychometric Approach to Frankl's Concept of Noogenic Neurosis," then published in the *Journal of Clinical Psychology* 20 (April 1964), 200–207.

The Death Attitude Profile-Revised: A Multidimensional Measure of Attitudes Towards Death was developed by P. T. P. Wong, G. T. Reker, and G. Gesser, and appeared in R. A. Neimeyer (ed.), *Death Anxiety Handbook: Research, Instrumentation, and Application* (Washington, DC: Taylor and Francis, 1994). Reprinted by permission of the authors.

Library of Congress Cataloging-in-Publication Data

Names: Eisenberg, Lee, 1946– author.
Title: The point is : making sense of birth, death, and everything in between / Lee Eisenberg.
Description: First edition. | New York : Twelve, [2016]
Identifiers: LCCN 2015039133 | ISBN 9781455550463 (hardcover) | ISBN 9781478979111 (audio download) | ISBN 9781478964797 (audio cd) | ISBN 9781455550470 (ebook)
Subjects: LCSH: Life. | Conduct of life.
Classification: LCC BD431 .E4195 2016 | DDC 128—dc23 LC record available at http://lccn.loc.gov/2015039133

Printed in the United States of America

RRD-C

10 9 8 7 6 5 4 3 2 1

In memory of my parents,
Eve and George

We invent fictions in order to live somehow the many lives we would like to lead when we barely have one at our disposal.

—Mario Vargas Llosa, upon being awarded the
Nobel Prize in Literature, 2010

Contents

PART III

The End

Introduction

One summer a couple of years ago, my wife, Linda, and I rented a house for several weeks in a small town on Long Island. Being there would allow us to catch up with people we don't see often enough. Experts say that close personal ties—family, friends, community—are fundamental to achieving a meaningful life. Given that we happen to live in Chicago, we now and then have to get on a plane to connect with these relationships. Most of our friends are in the East. Our kids, Ned and Katherine, both in their twenties and on their own, live in Brooklyn. The plan was for the kids to come out to Long Island and spend a few weekends.

The house sat on a quiet street, a short stroll to the center of the village, a ten-minute bike ride to the beach. There was, however, an old country graveyard right around the corner, an unexpected bonus. When I walked through the cemetery's iron gates for the first time, I realized I'd never visited a graveyard when there wasn't a grim reason to be there.

From day one the graveyard became part of my daily routine. Every morning after breakfast I went over there to jog, concerned at first that tromping through in Nikes and gym shorts was ill-mannered. I made certain to keep to the unpaved lanes separating the plots—a good thing, too, because I later came across this warning in "A Curse Against

Elegies," a poem by Anne Sexton: "Take your foot out of the graveyard, / they are busy being dead."

It's been said that to focus on life we must deprive death of its strangeness. Partly because middle age had swiftly come and gone, partly because summer arrives with long shadows, and mostly because I had a book to write, that became my daytime assignment during those weeks on Long Island: deprive death of its strangeness. After my morning run, I would close myself off in a small spare bedroom with a pile of books that have never made it onto anyone's summer-reading list: *The Denial of Death*; *Death and the Rebirth of Psychology*; *Life Against Death*; *How We Die*; *Staring at the Sun: Overcoming the Terror of Death*; *Being Mortal: Medicine and What Matters in the End*. Sounds grim, but it actually wasn't too bad. I've had worse getaways, such as the time in Scotland when a babysitter hired to look after our son challenged me to a round of golf. Our boy was only two. So was the babysitter's handicap. She mercilessly wiped the gorse with me.

When my workday was over, I'd restack the books about death and dying and return to the cemetery to unwind. I never once saw another living soul there. Everyone was still busy being dead. I would wander aimlessly until dusk fell. Here was a giant anthology of life stories, every genre imaginable, two hundred years' worth, each story distinctly different from all the others. And yet, as if by some ingenious narrative sleight of hand—even a director like Robert Altman couldn't have pulled it off—every last story ended up in exactly the same place, this old country graveyard.

It's no exaggeration to say that I've got stories on the brain. I always have, actually. For a big slice of my career, nearly twenty years of it at *Esquire*, I've been up to the eyeballs in stories, fiction and nonfiction, commissioning them, celebrating them when they clicked, mourning them when they fizzled. Later on, I was paid to think about how I could apply storytelling to everything from enriching a school curriculum (at an education start-up) to explaining the wonders of a high-tech down-filled jacket (at a catalog company).

Some of my best friends are stories. Just the other night at a dinner party, I glanced around the table and realized I was in the company of a soap opera, a farce, a chick flick, and an incessantly chatty shaggy dog story with no clue as to where it was going. The farce and the chick flick drank too much, the soap opera sobbed a little, the shaggy dog went on and on. But it turned out to be a surprisingly pleasant evening—though between you and me there were times I thought it would be better to be home in bed with a good book.

You have your life story, I have mine. The people around the table had theirs, and so did everyone in the old country graveyard. Our stories are us. Each is unique. Even if the events, relationships, and characters in your story were exactly the same as those in mine, our stories would be very different. If we spent every day of our lives welded at the hip, they'd still be different because we'd remember things differently.

To be absolutely clear: I'm not talking about the version of a life story either of us might put down on paper. I'm talking about the story you know like the back of your hand, the complete, unabridged account of how you and I came to be here at this very moment, me typing this, you sitting there with a book or e-reader. You know exactly how your story begins and whether it's gone uphill or downhill. You know whether it's sad or happy. You know which parts are interesting and which put you to sleep. You know the events and characters you'd delete if you possibly could. The story begins with your earliest memories and unfolds from there: your hopes and fears are included in the story; your victories and disappointments; your love affairs won and lost. Every secret of yours is there. So are your dreams, the ones you remember. It's quite the saga, isn't it?

But here's the kicker: your story remains an enduring mystery story because there's one thing you *don't* know and you may not *want* to know even if you could—how and where the story ends. And there's another thing you'd give almost anything *to* know:

Is there any point to it?

That's what this book is about.

Now, obviously, the point of existence is a vast ocean of a topic. Clearly, some boundaries are in order. What the book won't try to do is convert you to (or from) any faith or spiritual quest. Far be it from me. If you choose to see God's plan in every arachnid, fine. I also won't try to replace your values with my values. If you insist on believing that shopping for shopping's sake is what it takes to fill the human soul with sufficient purpose, I may not applaud you, but it's your life story and I wish you well.

What this book *will* try to do is offer a different perspective on how our life stories come to be, one that applies to every man, woman, and child alive or as yet unborn. And it will do its best to explain what it takes for a life story to add up to something meaningful, even endure into the future.

Bold claims, I know, especially these days. Once upon a time, we paid dutiful attention to certain stories we could hitch our personal story *to*. Ancient myths and fairy tales cued us to life's unpredictability. They instilled courage and imagination in young minds. And of course there's the Greatest Story Ever Told. It's a big and sprawling story, brimming with lessons and warnings. It lays out the difference between right and wrong. It offers chapter and verse on how to overcome obstacles and suffering. It boasts a colorful cast of thousands. At the center of the sweeping plot, there's an all-knowing leading character, possessed of unparalleled wisdom and power. A story on such scale offers a mere mortal's story a leg up. It nails down where and how one's own story begins and what happens after the story's over. It doesn't dillydally over what the human purpose is, it comes right out and says what it is: it's to follow the commands laid down in the story.

And yet when I talk to people, most seem to be saying that they're flying blind. They're making up their life stories as they go along. For instance:

A twenty-six-year-old, a grad student in criminal justice, says she thinks about the point of her life story only on Sundays when in church, otherwise gives it little thought. "An overwhelming concept," she says.

A woman in her mid-thirties, a social worker, says she tries not to think about the point. She deals with mental and critical illness in children from morning till night.

A man in his late fifties—he retired early, moved to a warmer climate, now regrets it—wishes he were busier. "The trick is not to waste days," he says.

A widower engaged to a woman he met on a dating site says, "At the end of the day, the only thing I'll think about on my deathbed will be the people I knew and loved. I don't think it's more complicated than that, though it might be."

Is it so bad that the great old universal stories are no longer in play?

"It's not easy to build a life for yourself with no model whatsoever," said Joseph Campbell, who didn't mince words when it came to the wisdom to be gained from reading mythological stories. Without a model, he said, we're lost in a labyrinth, groping our way through our life story as if no one's ever lived a life story before. The problem with our stories today, Campbell said, is that too few of us have a "deep sense of being present" in them.

But it doesn't have to be this way.

The
Point Is

PART I

The Beginning

No story has power, nor will it last, unless we feel in ourselves that it is true and true of us.

—John Steinbeck, *East of Eden*

1   *Meet the Scribbler*

Right now you have company upstairs. There's a little storywriter nestled in the fissures of your brain, a writer-in-residence, a compulsive scribbler. If it helps you to conjure such a fantastical idea, imagine a diminutive scribe in a teeny-tiny Aeron chair, sitting there with pen, pencil, or proportionately sized laptop. If things aren't going well for you at the moment—lousy relationship, dead-end job, no job—there may be other items on your storywriter's desk: a whiskey bottle or a packet of pills.

Your storywriter is at work on an assignment of indefinite duration: take your memories and mold them into chapters, the so-called chapters of your life. Some chapters are necessarily long and irksome—maybe a misguided career choice or an exploratory consultation with a doctor that turned into ten years of twice-a-week treatment sessions. Other chapters are short and adventurous—the summer you drove across the country or that delirious week on Tobago (or was it Trinidad?) with whatsisname. Still other chapters that seemed important at the time may now strike you as utterly forgettable. First marriages are a classic case.

Long or short, riveting or not, the chapters eventually thicken into an overall plot. You may find yourself thinking of this plot in terms of bunches of chapters clumped together. One woman, for instance, said she divides her overall story into three distinct clumps. Part I: "Childhood." Part II: "Motherhood." Part III: "My Time." Throughout the plot, however you bunch the chapters, minor and major characters make entrances and exits. Some characters you remember in great detail; others are hazy. An English teacher would refer to them as "flat" characters (sketchily detailed) or "round" characters (fully developed). Naturally, some flat characters you've known have been fat, while some round characters were skinny. Flat or round, fat or skinny, a given character can remain in your life story for a day, a week, a year, many years, through sickness and health, till death do you part. Some characters outlive the story itself, others don't. Quite a few characters simply fall off the face of the earth, though occasionally you can stalk them successfully on Facebook.

This process of shaping memories into chapters has been going on since you were three or so. I say "three or so" because that's when we typically start collecting and keeping memories for the long term. Memory and story making go hand in hand. But once settled in, your storywriter scribbles silently in the background, the way certain software programs run. The work is nonstop: 24/7, 365 days a year, for as long as you live or until your memories vanish, at which point the story's over.

Now, you can think of your personal scribe as a playwright, screenwriter, ghostwriter, it doesn't matter. He may be a she if you're a he and vice versa. (I'll use them interchangeably throughout.) Or he/she can be a transgender, cross-dressing storywriter. Think Jan Morris or Janet Mock, only much, much smaller.

As for personal appearance or quirky habits, none of that matters, either. Writers have license to be peculiar. Yours may be as eccentric as Goethe, who craved the smell of rotten apples when he sat down to write, and in fact kept a few decomposing under the lid of his writing desk. W. H. Auden guzzled tea nonstop. James Joyce wrote with a crayon on scraps of cardboard. It takes all kinds. Many writers, though, do fit a mold. They "live through oscillating self-doubt and mild paranoia, the rival temptations of vanity and self-pity," wrote Julian Barnes in an essay titled "Literary Executions."

I realize that some of you may not like the idea of a self-doubting, too-clever-by-half narcissist living inside. Some of us don't like houseguests, period. Others aren't at ease around "creative types." If it will help you keep an open mind about the scribbler upstairs, feel free to think of your storywriter as one who can hold her own in a corporate environment. She's your Chief Subjective Well-Being Officer—with a pen. But whether you think of her as a scruffy bohemian or Chief Well-Being Officer, your life story starts and ends with this person. By arranging your memories into chapters, she can make your life seem coherent and meaningful. Or not.

I know, some of you are *still* incredulous. How could anyone get anything done working in such ridiculously tight quarters? Not a problem. Zadie Smith favors a small room with the blinds drawn to keep the light out, which would make the fissures of the brain quite accommodating, don't you think?

Some of you remain unconvinced. You may be thinking, yes, I really did spend time in an old country graveyard, but that's as far as it goes. There's no storywriter in the attic. No Aeron chair, laptop, cluttered desk with a drawer full of rotting apples. No THERE'S A CHANCE THIS COULD BE VODKA coffee mug. No ashtray with stale butts and a framed photo of you at age three or so wearing a Davy Crockett cap. Or a tutu. Or a Davy Crockett cap and a tutu, if your writer-in-residence is of blended orientation.

You're probably thinking the storywriter's a half-baked metaphor for something not nearly so exotic and now that we're under way I'll promptly axe her from the book. And you'd be half right about that. The scribbler *is* a metaphor. But she's a metaphor who's not going anywhere. Metaphors serve a purpose, in life as well as in stories. "Metaphors," says Milan Kundera in *The Unbearable Lightness of Being*, "are not to be trifled with. A single metaphor can give birth to love." If a single metaphor can do that, then a metaphor can account for how our life stories come to be.

I first started thinking about the scribbler one night while leafing through an old paperback collection of *Paris Review* interviews. Martin Amis, former bad boy of British letters, now a ruminative, middle-aged dad, was asked whether he thought "ego and self-confidence" mattered to a writer. (No eye rolls, please.) "If I die tomorrow," Amis answered, "at least my children ... will have a very good idea of what I was like, of what my mind was like, because they will be able to read my books. So maybe there is an immortalizing principle at work even if it's just for your children. Even if they've forgotten you physically, they could never say that they didn't know what their father was like."

I was intrigued by this idea that the stories writers write live on in others, and therefore the writer himself lives on in a way. Okay, I wondered, then what about the rest of us? We've been compiling our own *internal* stories for as long as we can remember. Why exactly do we do that? Why do we unthink-ingly turn events and relationships into distinct chapters; come up with reasons for why this or that thing happened; label something a "turning point"; impart motives to char-acters who come and go throughout our lives? Is it to give ourselves and others, as Amis said, an idea of who we really are? Is it how we bring *ourselves* to life? And is there some "immortalizing principle at work," as Amis put it? That's when it hit me. We all have a little "writer" inside. An even tinier Martin Amis!

The thought got me Googling around to see whether I could push the idea any further. I tried "Life stories." "Immor-tality." "Legacy." My willy-nilly search eventually landed on a YouTube video of a boyish-looking professor and a lecture he gave about a book he'd recently written—*George W. Bush and the Redemptive Dream: A Psychological Portrait*. It was part of a series of lectures that addressed a common theme, explained the professor who introduced the speaker. The series had to do with how we "construct self-identity" in the hope we'll find some meaning in life.

Given that George W. Bush's psychobiography isn't cen-tral to the story here, I'll skip over the particulars of the talk. But as a side note, knowing what I know now, it's interest-ing to think about what W's upstairs storyteller makes of his patron. Whenever asked about the disastrous foray into Iraq, Bush likes to say his legacy is out of his hands; it's a job for future historians. The Decider will let others decide. And yet when Bush is asked why, after leaving the White House, he started painting portraits of himself shaving and taking a bath, he says it's because he wants "to leave something behind." There's an immortalizing principle at work. If the paintings do the trick, then mission accomplished.

The lecturer on the video, Dan P. McAdams, gave an engaging performance, offering keen insights into Bush's makeup. So I looked him up. It turned out he was the director of something called the Foley Center for the Study of Lives at Northwestern University, just up the road from our Chicago apartment. He's a highly regarded narrative psychologist, a so-called personologist, a term I'd never heard before.

I ordered a couple of McAdams's books. They lay out what he calls "a life-story model of identity," which, academic jargon aside, seemed to be just what I was looking for. The model describes how, beginning in adolescence, we think of our life as an ever-evolving *narrative*. The narrative enables us to link our "reconstructed past"—how we remember things, accurately or not—with our "imagined future." McAdams observes that redemption, for example, is a dominant theme in many American life stories: we like to think of ourselves as rising from nowhere, recovering from setbacks, fulfilling our inner destiny. Pick up a newspaper or magazine or current autobiography; go to People.com or any other celebrity site; turn on a reality show or a Diane Sawyer special; or simply open your eyes in the morning. You'll be witness to a bounty of high-profile redemption tales: politicians, athletes, movie stars, desperate housewives who've been down long enough that it's starting to look up. Monica Lewinsky, for instance, is currently on a multiyear, national Redemption Tour. It kicked off with a 2014 first-person confessional in *Vanity Fair* ("Shame and Survival"); was followed by a TED talk ("The Price of Shame"); and is now playing out in a venue near you as Lewinsky participates in antibullying workshops around the country. It's where her life story stands now and she's sticking to it.

Whether the theme is "Look how far I've come," or "I

want to leave the world better off than I found it," or "I need to put my hidden talent to better use," or "Sometimes I feel like a motherless child," whatever the refrain, the narrative we create about ourselves amounts to a "personal myth," McAdams says. We draw on our personal myth to make sense of ourselves. It points to where we've been and where we'd like to wind up. Coherent or muddled, everyone's personal myth is distinct from all others, notwithstanding that there may be common themes. McAdams says that as a kid his personal myth dreamed of playing shortstop for the Cubs. Mine dreamed of playing second base for the Phillies. His personal myth apparently had a better arm than mine. Neither of our young personal myths made it to the big leagues, which is why we now have thoroughly revised personal myths.

Believing that I'd stumbled upon credible support for the idea that we each have a little writer upstairs whose job is to construct our personal myth, I e-mailed McAdams and asked whether we could get together. I said that I was working on a book idea that was still a little raggedy (I probably said "formative") but that it seemed to dovetail with the work he was doing. He graciously agreed to meet at Peet's Coffee across from the Northwestern campus. There we chatted amiably about the field of narrative psychology. He told me about his early influences and described the kind of research he and his students were doing. There's extensive fieldwork involved, interviews with people about how their life stories are unfolding. Before we parted, he gave me suggestions for further study. Those books and papers provided more than enough evidence to think the scribbler notion wasn't nearly as cracked as it sounds.

- One's life story, or personal myth, is ever changing. The story evolves. You and I are thus at all times *works in progress*. It's not easy being a work in progress. Being a work in progress can be unnerving, especially in middle age. "The road to hell is paved with works in progress," said Philip Roth, declining to write about his then current work in progress for the *New York Times*.

- Without our life stories, we'd be lost in time and space, and who wants that? Psychologists say that each of us is born, thankfully, with a "narrating mind." (Narrating mind, a little writer upstairs, call it what you will.) Our life stories are the vehicles that enable us to draw a connection between who we were, who we are, and who we wish to be. The question of "who I am" presupposes "who will I be," as one academic put it. Real writers have been onto this idea for a long time. "Our being consists not in what it is already, but in what it is not yet," wrote the Spanish essayist José Ortega y Gasset.

- Making a story of our life enables us to organize scattered events into a single whole that has a beginning, middle, and end, says Donald Polkinghorne, a prominent figure in the field. The sequence is vital. When a story—movie, book, play, life story—lacks a perceptible beginning, middle, and end, we get grouchy and perplexed. The story comes across as incoherent or incomplete.

- Storytelling and storywriting are elemental. Stories are what "make us human," I read over and over again. By now I've lost count of all the things I've run across that make us human. Knowing that we're going to die makes us human. It used to be said that cooking makes us human, though recent studies show that a chimp will hold off eating a raw slice of sweet potato if he thinks a cooked slice may be on the way. But it's fair to say stories *do* make us human. "Our lives are ceaselessly intertwined…with the stories…we dream or imagine or would like to tell," Polkinghorne writes. "All these stories are reworked in the story of our own lives which we narrate to ourselves in an episodic, sometimes semiconscious, virtually uninterrupted monologue." Which is a perfect if overly elaborate description of what the scribbler's up there to accomplish.

Granted, the books and papers I perused offered nothing that hinted at the existence of a bearded inner-sanctum loner in horn-rims and a carpal-tunnel brace on his wrist. Nor did they say there's *no* such creature. Those who study life stories admit they don't have all the answers. Maybe they should spend more time with real writers, who cite chapter and verse on how life is one big, fat, occasionally juicy, often dull, not very predictable, now and then meaningful *story*.

Dostoevsky: "How could you live and have no story to tell?"

Julian Barnes, in his novel *The Sense of an Ending*: "How often do we tell our own life story? How often do we adjust, embellish, make sly cuts? And the longer life goes on, the fewer are those around to challenge our account, to remind us that our life is not our life, merely the story we have told about our life. Told to others, but—mainly—to ourselves."

And consider what Joan Didion says in *The Year of Magical Thinking*, which she wrote—was *compelled* to write—after the death of her husband of forty years, John Gregory Dunne: "This [book] is my attempt to make sense of the period that followed, weeks and then months that cut loose any fixed idea I had ever had about death, about illness, about probability and luck, about good fortune and bad, about marriage and children and memory, about grief, about the ways in which people do and do not deal with the fact that life ends, about the shallowness of sanity, about life itself."

To make sense of the unfathomable, Didion says, she had to write a version of herself as yet unwritten. Years before, she published a collection of pieces titled *We Tell Ourselves Stories in Order to Live*. It comes down to this: your life, my life, Joan Didion's life, anyone's life, will feel "meaningful" to us only if our storywriter can take the flotsam and jetsam stashed upstairs and artfully hammer it into narrative submission.

2   *Inside the Memory Factory*

It didn't take long for me to grasp how it all comes down to the memories we keep. The life stories we maintain inside are wondrous in their complexity and degree of detail. But whether they're "true" or not depends on whether the memories are "true." Are they true? Yes and no. There's historical truth and *narrative* truth. It's not that we *lie* to ourselves, it's that memories are slippery. Events and relationships get bigger and smaller, more and less important in a life story over time. We're sure that certain things happened that in fact never happened. "Life is not what one lived, but what one remembers and how one remembers it," wrote Gabriel García Márquez in his autobiography, *Living to Tell the Tale*.

True or not, the memories pile up. We traffic in memories so naturally that it's easy to forget the sheer number of them that must be uploaded into whatever miraculous filing system your writer-in-residence draws on to build your ever-lengthening life story.

It's nothing short of astounding when you think about how effortlessly we fling memories around. If, say, you and I meet in a bar and introduce ourselves, we quickly start cherry-picking from our vast memory archive to give each other a sense of who we are or who we'd like the other to think we are. We introduce ourselves, then begin exchanging chunks of our respective life stories—"evolving stories of self," as narrative psychologists call them.

Let's say I'm chattier than you are, so I take the lead. Maybe I'd open up with only a small, specific cut of my evolving story of self, a goofball part, such as how years ago I had a regrettable encounter with Susan Sarandon, who got furious with me even though it wasn't my fault. I wouldn't share the anecdote just to name-drop—well, maybe to some extent. I'd share it because it's a fairly embarrassing, self-deprecating sliver of my evolving story of self that people get a kick out of, especially over drinks. A narrative psychologist might say that the reason I occasionally dust off the old chestnut is because it does a good job of reflecting my current personal myth—i.e., I'm kind of a cool guy but also a nebbish. Maybe after another drink I'd share a torrent of excerpts from my evolving story of self, perhaps a good deal more than you wanted to know or could bear listening to. How I grew up in Philadelphia in a redbrick row house with a small front yard and a tiny concrete patio under a green-and-orange-striped awning; how my bedroom walls were covered in wallpaper with cowboys on it and festooned with collegiate pennants; how in high school I was sentenced to ten detentions for taking exactly one step beyond the grounds to buy a soft pretzel from a food truck; how eventually I came to get a really cool job in New York City, though it required me to swallow my pride; how, when, and where, many years later, I met Linda, and this or that about Ned and Katherine; some inside stuff about how the Rotisserie League got started and how it gave way to fantasy sports, and how, like fools, we didn't make any money from it; how it happened that we now live in Chicago; warmhearted remembrances of my dogs Corky (mutt) and Woody (vizsla). Even if I bent your ear off for a couple of hours you'd still be getting a snippet of the full story of my evolving self.

By our third or fourth drink—by the way, you'd also be telling me about your life, or you'd be trying to—it's possible that I'd have drilled down to such minor bits of personal lint as why and when I had myself tattooed—small dolphin, left shoulder—long before it was fashionable for nontattoo types to have tattoos, and made further fashionable because the artist who put it there also tattooed Janis Joplin; my ten favorite Philadelphia Eagles of all time; or the two recurrent dreams I had as a child: a priest driving a school bus who kept trying to run me over; and E.S., a girl I knew in the second grade, spotting me in the subway and I wasn't wearing pants.

Sooner rather than later, having been battered with so many bits and pieces of my evolving story of self, you'd remember you were late for an appointment and reach for the check. You'd have learned an immense amount about me. But it wouldn't amount to even a minuscular *fraction* of what the writer upstairs has access to.

Here's my theory on that. At some point early on, we grant our storywriters top-drawer security clearances: VIP, backstage, inner sanctum, eyes only, Category One. The permissions provide a writer-in-residence with unfettered access to what cognitive scientists refer to as our "autobiographical memory." As a result of this extraordinary access, nobody else comes close to knowing as much about us, not even the NSA, not even Google. Parents, spouses, partners, kids, siblings, former lovers, therapists, priests, friends, neighbors, and folks in the office know varying amounts of your evolving story of self. Some know the truth (more or less), others a whitewashed version. Your writer-in-residence knows *everything*. Were she ever to turn on you, go off the deep end as writers have been known to do, she'd be highly dangerous. You'd be unimaginably exposed. No online identity hack has ever come close to the emotional rack and ruin the writer-in-residence could leave in her wake. Knowing your memories— yes, even *that* one—is just the tip of the iceberg. She knows your fears, and in some respects knows them *better* than you do because *she's* not in denial. She's up-to-date on your latest longings. She knows who's been important in your life and who hasn't, even though you pretended otherwise. She knows when you've been ecstatic and when you were bereft, even if you concealed your emotions skillfully.

How do we, how does the scribbler, keep it all straight? What's the process? How do our memories get archived, retrieved, returned to storage, revised over time, deleted, recovered from the trash in a pinch? While science is still working on how we manage to do all that, we've come a long way since Descartes, whose seventeenth-century notion of how we manufacture memories was even wackier than my scribbler theory. The pineal gland, Descartes said, serves as the center of human consciousness. "Animal spirits" on the surface of the gland create patterns or impressions that result in images of that which is no longer right before our eyes.

Flash forward to now. Great strides have been made. Forget the pineal gland. Neuropsychiatrist Eric Kandel won a Nobel Prize a few years ago for his "discoveries concerning signal transduction in the nervous system," a major breakthrough in our understanding of how brain cells operate. He arrived at it in an amazing way—by examining electrical synapses in slimy, oversized sea slugs. Our own neural activity (which can also be sluggish) takes place in distinct areas of the brain, depending on the type of memory. For example, memories of things fast and furious, such as the night you totaled your father's Buick, flicker around the amygdala. Highly charged, sexy memories, too. Neuroscientists say such memories may return with no apparent warning, in "flashbulb" fashion. The writer-in-residence needs to be careful when drawing on these memories, as they're often wildly inaccurate.

In any case, major progress has been made on how it all works, with so much more to come over the next decades. Francis Crick, who codiscovered the double helix, predicted that as early as 2030 we'll have a full understanding of how the brain generates consciousness. I don't know about you, but I don't have time to wait until then. Which is why, and for now, I choose to imagine that there may be a little bitty person sitting on an exercise ball in front of a monitor, or some other simple way to picture it. She punches up memories with the touch of a keystroke, then edits individual memories or strips of memories the way a film editor cuts a movie. Using a Photoshop-type program, she can crop and retouch memories at will.

Scientists will push back on this, of course. Memories, they say, aren't at all like snapshots or video clips. The story of your life, cognitive psychologists insist, is made up of images and perceptions that are "figurative and creative," not "literal imprints of factual events." Indeed, the entire storywriter-upstairs hypothesis runs into a brick wall when subjected to scientific scrutiny. It isn't that brain researchers and molecular biologists deny the importance of life stories. On the contrary. Narrative formation is "the inescapable frame of the human experience," says a neurologist at UCLA.

But scientists will be scientists. They demand evidence that can be tested and verified, and to date nothing resembling a storywriter has been observed hanging out up there. Whenever a scientist surveys the brain with any of the usually reliable neuroimaging devices, whenever a brain surgeon pops open a skull for direct eyeballing, what they see is a three-pound mass of jelly packed with a hundred billion neurons. No Aeron chair. No laptop. No yellow legal pads or index cards. No drafts on whether or not there's an afterlife. No paperweight in the shape of Maslow's pyramid. No trace of coffee grounds, spliffs, booze, or little green pills. No evidence that a scruffy writer's been within body odor of the remarkable three-pound mass of jelly.

But just because nobody's yet found any tangible evidence, it doesn't mean a scribbler *isn't* up there, ingeniously concealed. (As I've said, this is a really small person, even in Doc Martens.) For now, though, let's call a truce. I won't suggest that the surgeon have his eyes tested or whine that the fMRI machine's on the fritz. Only a fool or a religious fundamentalist (sometimes one and the same) would bet against the scientific breakthroughs that lie ahead. The day will come when we'll have a very good idea of how "a three-pound mass of jelly that you can hold in your palm is able to imagine angels, contemplate the meaning of infinity, and even question its own place in the cosmos," as neuroscientist V. S. Ramachandran eloquently put it.

In the end, we'll applaud the progress but may not like where it takes us. Personally, I prefer to believe that our most important and cherished memories *are* literally true and accurate. Those memories are me. Yours are you. So long as we retain them in precise, glorious detail, we'll remain who we want to be. Push too hard on whether our important memories are or aren't literal imprints and you start questioning whether we are, in fact, who we think we are. Personally, I'd rather not go there.

If there's one thing we can all agree on about memories, it's that they're frequently far from accurate. Some people speculate that once you retrieve a memory it's no longer the same memory. It's a new memory of an old memory. Others will tell you that what we think of as a memory isn't even a memory. It's an actual *experience* we live through again and again. Each time we remember something we construct the experience anew.

Whatever our memories are or aren't, wherever and however they're stored, they're shifty. In a book about autobiographical memory, John Kotre describes how over time memories have a way of rewriting what passes for reality. Good people in our past grow into better people; bad people regress into worse people; a baby bass balloons into a lunker. Kotre tells of how we commonly say we "always did this" and "never did that" when in fact we never did this and always did that. But we're not really lying, are we? For instance, I've told people that when I was a kid I was always the youngest to make a sports team. Yet because I was young and a shrimp I never got to play much, always rode the bench. I honestly believe that's true. But if you ran an intensive background check on my athletic career at Camp Arthur in the Poconos, and then you delved into my participation in pickup teams at school or around the neighborhood, you'd find precisely *one* instance of my being the youngest to make a team (at Camp Arthur, for the record). Then why do I say that I was *always* the youngest to make the team but never played? Because it helps define me in the present. I'd like you to understand that I was athletic but not *that* athletic.

Another example: I'll swear up and down that I *never once* cheated in school. And I really, truly believe I never did. But I'm also reasonably sure there were times in elementary school when I must have glanced over at Jeannie Malamud's paper. (Jeannie was a genius, never got anything wrong.) Why have I erased any memory of glancing over? John Kotre quotes a developmental psychologist who reminds us that "once a caterpillar becomes a butterfly, it doesn't remember being a caterpillar; it remembers being a little butterfly." In my own mind, I'm a fully grown ethical person and honestly don't remember ever being a little thief.

The storywriter upstairs isn't out to spread falsehoods by doctoring our memories. She's merely doing what she can to create a story that's coherent and consistent. She jiggles memories, playing up some, downplaying others, such that they don't contradict each other or muddy the overall theme. If you're currently stuck in a lousy job because you flunked out of school, the memory of all the dope you smoked may by now have given way to the memory of your mother saying you were one of those students who doesn't do well in a traditional classroom setting. Or you may clearly remember how your now ex-wife said she needed her space and have no recollection of all the times she asked you to please stop chewing with your mouth open. The scribbler's only trying to help when she allows certain memories to take precedence over others.

"Every act of perception is to some degree an act of creation, and every act of memory is to some degree an act of imagination," suggests Gerald M. Edelman, a Nobel Prize–winning biologist. Writers know that, without having to take a science course. "When it comes to the past, *everyone* writes fiction," says a character in Stephen King's *Joyland*. Perhaps that's too strong. If you ask me, life stories are more like nonfiction novels.

There's a lot of talk these days about how our memories are under siege, which if true presents a grave challenge to keeping our life stories straight. Technology's making us stupid, some fret. The concern is that now that we're all packing search engines in our pockets, we don't need to remember as much as we used to. Why remember something if we can simply Google it? Not to use it is to lose it. Our memories are thus atrophying, some worry.

That's one reason to be nervous. Another is that some believe that our "transactive memory systems" are becoming extinct. A transactive memory system is when two or more people draw on a shared memory archive. If one person doesn't know or can't recall something, there's someone else around to fill the void. Once upon a time, that's how we remembered a lot of things. The first line of inquiry was to query another human being. The late Jean Stafford, who in her waning years reviewed books for *Esquire*, told me how great it was to have someone in the house—her husband, journalist A. J. Liebling, also a terrific writer—who knew everything about everything. Whenever Stafford needed a piece of information for a story she was working on, she'd walk over to the foot of the stairs and holler up: "Hey, Joe! What's such-and-such or who was so-and-so?" The answer came thundering down.

Back in the day, the interface was person to person, not person to Siri. What one person couldn't remember, someone else in the transactive memory system could. Your mother and father holding memories of you comprised a small-scale transactive memory system. Multiple generations of a family living in close proximity and maintaining daily contact, pooling their memories, preserving those memories through the telling of stories, added up to a more extensive transactive memory system. You don't know? Ask Pawpaw. (But ask loudly.)

Trouble is, we no longer live within shouting distance of multiple generations. We also no longer live in tribes, a tribe being an even larger transactive memory system than a family. We do live in *brand* tribes, but I doubt that my fellow Mac users can tell me where exactly in Belorussia my mother's side of the family hails from. Other than "somewhere in Russia" in the case of my mother's side, "somewhere in Austria" in the case of my father's, I have no idea where I come from. I wish I did. It would make my life story far more meaningful if I could place it in a longer-term historical context. If, say, I knew that someone in my bloodline had fought valiantly against the invading Mongol hordes, it would make me feel more—more *what*? Connected to time's infinite arc, or something like that. Arthur Schopenhauer said, "To our amazement we suddenly exist, after having for countless millennia not existed; in a short while we will again not exist, also for countless millennia. That cannot be right, says the heart." If I knew I dated back to the ancient steppes, I might feel less like I'm just breezing through. But there's no one left to ask. The only recourse is to go online, which I've done. Genealogy sites don't reveal much, so I'm reduced to gathering crumbs of information I run across in history books and biographies of those who were decidedly *not* relatives of mine. Hitler and Stalin, for example. Thanks to books about their life stories,

I *assume* that my father's family wound up in Austria at the end of the nineteenth century as part of the mass migrations of Jews who fled there from Russia, Hungary, and the Balkans. It's a start. As for my mother's side, I still don't know whether her people came from Minsk or Pinsk, though I at least know where Minsk and Pinsk are, thanks to Google Maps.

It's only fair, however, to say that technology giveth and taketh. Cuts both ways. It may induce atrophy but it also jars memories loose. The other day I decided to listen to the score from Richard Rodgers's *Victory at Sea*, a TV series that ran in the early fifties on NBC. My father and I never missed an episode; in retrospect, a highly meaningful bonding experience. Thanks to technology, I found it on Spotify in just a couple of clicks. The *instant* the overture—"The Song of the High Seas"—came on, I was conveyed (convoyed?) immediately back to Whitaker Avenue in Philly. I saw the tuning knobs of the Philco TV in the living room. I saw the pull-down ceiling light in the little breakfast room, with the egg-shaped thing that adjusted the cord, the same fixture my father installed the day of his first heart attack. I saw our canary, Tweetie, pecking at the cuttlebone in the cage that stood in a corner of the room. All it took were the opening bars of *Victory at Sea*, which were right there at my fingertips.

3   *Authorized and Unabridged*

E. M. Forster, whose *Howards End* has been called one of the best-structured novels in English, wrote that we start life with an experience we forget and end with an experience we anticipate but don't understand. He also defined a written story as "a narrative of events arranged in their time sequence." The same generally applies to your life story. Your life story is a narrative made up of memories arranged in a time sequence.

Compiling an internal life story arranged in a time sequence is no mean task. Unlike a real writer, your writer-in-residence can't just make shit up. She can't pluck interesting characters out of thin air. She can't move the story back and forth across centuries. She can't throw in a talking pig the way a magical realist can. Or set loose a homicidal Martian the way a science fiction author can. The writer upstairs must make do with what memories are available. And while the scribbler can and will take reasonable liberties with your memories, she must color within the lines of what seems to have actually happened. Unlike a real writer, the writer upstairs can't snap her fingers and pull off some corny stunt at the end, a cheap trick such as the leading character waking from a bad dream and living happily ever after. But your life story does have to add up fundamentally, pay off in some way. Otherwise, what's the point?

To get a sense of how your story came to be, let's imagine it in book form. I'm not the first to come up with that idea, nor will I be the last. Thinking of our life story in terms of a book lulls us into thinking that it won't fall apart at the seams. Thus reassured, let's further imagine that your book starts out with entirely blank pages. Why blank? Because you haven't yet "stepped into the light," to borrow a phrase from neuroscientist Antonio Damasio, who likens the switching on of the knowing mind to the moment an actor steps from the semidarkness of the wings and suddenly encounters stage lights and the audience.

Philosophers and scientists have differing perspectives on how blank you really were when you started out. Some theories are more simpatico than not with the scribbler hypothesis, so of course I'm partial to those. Philosopher John Locke famously said that we start out with utterly blank pages, with no preconceived notions. The newborn's mind is like blank paper, "void of all characters." "How comes it to be furnished?" Locke asked. In a word, through *experience*. We live and we learn.

Other great minds offer alternative theories on whether we're born entirely blank or come with certain standard or optional mental equipment. Linguist Noam Chomsky theorized that we come factory equipped with a sort of motherboard, a preinstalled "Language Acquisition Device." Think of it as located in a microscopic IT closet adjacent to where the scribbler works. The metaphorical motherboard allows us to decode grammatical structure, which in turn enables us to understand and create stories. Since then, Chomsky's advanced the idea that there's something akin to a universal grammar (no matter that English doesn't sound remotely like Liki, which about five people on a small Indonesian island speak). The scribbler theory remains neutral on the matter of how we come to have a capacity for language. We just do and we must if we're to have any idea of who we are.

But back to your imaginary book: On the front cover there's a photo of a beautiful baby, sweet and chubby, with a newborn's beanie (pink or blue, you choose) on its cherubic little head. The baby's you, of course. Well, you but not really you, not as far as your current "self" is concerned. The baby will evolve *into* that you, the "you" you think you are today. But even though you're something well short of *you*, you've already weathered an "existential crisis," the first of many, said psychologist Rollo May. What crisis was that? You could have just as easily *not* been born. But you were, so crisis averted. Having weathered the ordeal, said May, you've taken the first step toward creating your own personal myth. It has all the earmarks of a classic myth. You're destined to confront obstacles and suffering. You're primed to seek truth and purpose. In this sense, you've started out in good company, May said, really no different from Moses when he was found floating in the bulrushes or Jesus as he lay in the manger. But, hey, no pressure.

The key thing is that you now *exist*, your existence confirmed by a birth certificate signed by the county clerk. You may or may not have a name just yet. When you finally do get one, it could be the same name as that of a living or deceased family member, whose life story will, in a sense, live on as a result. Whatever your name, your existence may be further documented by a commemorative certificate featuring a pair of inky prints that affirm you have two small feet. Those feet are of no use at this stage. You're not going anywhere on your own, and won't for a good long while. You're as helpless as any suckling in the animal kingdom, more helpless than most. You're not yet equipped to collect memories. You can't string together even a couple of primitive belches to form the simplest of sentences. You're far from ready to take on the world. But you are cute, and make for a most appealing cover baby.

Above your beyond-adorable face on the cover is the imaginary book's title. Compulsive editor that I am, I dithered over a good working title for us to use—nothing fancy, nothing smart-assed, we're not talking the old *Esquire* here. I was going to go with *Me: A Life*, but that struck me as too generic and flat. *The Life and Death of the Enduring Self* was better, but after staring at it, I decided that it sounded a little, well, grandiloquent. And the "death" part bothered me a bit. So I tweaked it as follows, which is good enough for our purposes:

TIMES   MY
THE LIFE AND ~~DEATH~~ OF ~~THE~~ ENDURING SELF

Our title in place, the pages are now ready to be filled. Let's work together on it. What should come first? A book editor will tell you that a prologue is usually a good idea. It tees everything up, provides useful context. So take a moment to think about where, how, and when the story of your life really begins. It's not an idle question. How you conjure your pre-story can have a definite bearing on what you expect the ultimate point of your life to be. If you believe there's something mystical about how your life story began, that's one thing.

It's another if you believe the cosmos isn't all that mysterious. Bereft of anything better, you could always use your prologue simply to note that your life story began with conception, a random collision, an infinitesimal bump—not even a fender bender—near the ampulla-isthmic junction.

Some of you, however, may feel that conception doesn't reach back nearly far enough, doesn't do your life story justice. You'd use the prologue to expound on how your life story began long before the tiny collision that occurred, for all you know, in a motel room or the backseat of a Nash Rambler. You might feel obliged to use your initial pages to acknowledge and praise the *true* author of your life story, Our Author who art in heaven.

Others of you wouldn't be caught dead with a prologue like that. You kneel to science, not the supernatural. So you might want to use the front matter to explain how your life story began with a subatomic particle that somehow burst into what we think of as the cosmos. Something explosive, in any event. After the spark or whatever it was, one thing then led to another, ending with that baby mug on the cover. Still others might wish to use the prologue to underscore how neither you nor anyone else has the vaguest idea of how or why anyone's life story begins. We're each a Cosmic Orphan, anthropologist Loren Eiseley said, plopped into a universe through which we wander aimlessly, a thought bubble hovering above our head. Inside the bubble, a question: WHO AM I? There may even be a few of you who'd use the front matter to say, Sure, I have a name, birth certificate, and I'll eventually have a Social Security number, driver's license, passport, and eventually an AARP membership card, but there's really *no* me. Or *everyone's* me. Or I'm a tiny bit of everybody else, my so-called life story rising to nothing more than a narrative neutrino embedded in an endless saga titled *The Life of Every Human Being Who Ever Walked the Earth.*

Your life story can begin with whatever prologue makes you happy and is consistent with a chosen belief system, if any. Let's just agree that the life story each of us is *able to remember* begins with our earliest memories, which happen to kick in when our capacity to understand and create stories kicks in, memories and stories being inextricably linked.

But what if you're a crusty contrarian? What if you don't want to write a life story *at all*? "We begin in the madness of carnal desire [and] end in the dissolution of all of our parts and the musty stench of corpses," wrote Schopenhauer, philosophically as gloomy as ever. Why even bother to write a life story if that's how empty life is? *Because we have no choice*, that's why. We're compelled to write a story of our life even though we never asked for that life. We simply must. Which is why, anatomically, there's that small patch of space reserved in the skull for something or someone to arrange our memories into the chapters that comprise the plot. *Is there any point to that?* We won't know for certain until the pages in our imagined book are mostly filled, and with any luck, that won't be for a very long time. "Let us wait for the page proof," replied Vladimir Nabokov when asked what the meaning of life was.

4 *First Jottings*

In *The Stories We Live By: Personal Myths and the Making of the Self*, Dan McAdams says that on day one of his developmental psychology class he gives his students an unusual assignment: write a hypothetical magazine article about your first day outside the womb. Terrific idea! I thought when I read that. I would have used the assignment for real back when I was editing *Esquire*. I would have called up a writer and asked him or her to take a whack at such a piece. Philip Roth would have been perfect, would've knocked it out of the park.

Truman Capote? Better still! Capote would have been intrigued by the thought of describing exactly what transpired in the hours after 3 p.m. on September 30, 1924, at the Touro Infirmary in New Orleans. Had Capote accepted and handed in the assigned piece—delivery was always a big if with him—I'm sure his account would have been unforgettable and more than a little Southern Gothic. Truman's mother, Lillie Mae, never wanted the baby, but she waited too long to get a safe abortion. His father, Arch, *did* want a child, but he was an entirely untrustworthy, smooth-talking hustler in bottle-thick glasses, the makings of a great character in any delivery room. Lillie Mae and Arch were quite the pair, not exactly June and Ward Cleaver. Capote's biggest childhood fear was that he'd be abandoned, so I'm sure he would have cooked up a harrowing depiction of his first day on earth. I'm equally convinced he'd have sworn on a stack of Bibles that every last detail was rendered *precisely* as it happened.

The fact is, the story of your life—as you remember it—doesn't start on day one. If you think you really remember back to when you were a newborn and then a toddler, you don't. Even Saint Augustine, inarguably closer to God than you or me, freely admitted that he couldn't remember his first few years, came right out and said so in his *Confessions*.

The same goes for the rest of us. Over the first couple of years we actually do collect some memories, but they evaporate for reasons no one fully understands. We think we remember events from those earliest days and months because our brain makes memories out of what our parents, grandparents, and older siblings tell us later on. Photos in old albums also have a way of leaping out of their self-adhesive corners to become what we insist are real memories. There are other explanations as well: your writer-in-residence has her dates confused; you have an overactive imagination; you're under the influence of a controlled substance.

Even though no memories are being stored, a dim awareness of "self" begins to develop prior to your first birthday. This rudimentary "self" isn't much of a self; it's a vest-pocket self, clueless that one day it could turn into a full-blown self that's pitiable and self-loathing, though let's certainly hope not. Your fledgling self expresses itself whenever you share your "subjective feelings" with a caregiver. Your subjective self is thus able to communicate but not via language. For example, you smile, which in turn prompts your mom's face to gleam with unbridled delight, a moment she cherishes for the rest of her life, though you deserve little credit for it.

Within a year or so, the self you'll come to know as *you* will finally begin developing in earnest. One day it'll dawn on you that you have a body. You'll begin exploring its most out-of-the-way parts. A human mind (in waiting) atop a creaturely bottom? How can that possibly be? If you asked yourself that, wondered about the apparent disconnect between your humanness and creatureliness, it would have marked the very first time you groped instinctively at what the point of your existence was.

As I've mentioned, it's not until we reach three or so that the life stories we remember slip into gear. Very slowly at first. It's around now that your bright-eyed and bushy-tailed writer-in-residence shows up for work, albeit haphazardly. Too small for the Aeron chair, she'll scribble while curled up on a bean bag (for all I know). Now is when your love of stories, your need for stories, grabs hold. You awake one day and you're hooked, a story junkie. "A child's need for stories is as fundamental as his need for food," says novelist Paul Auster.

If you're a parent, I'm sure you've experienced how your kids quickly developed their insatiable appetite for stories. How many nights did your three-year-old browbeat you into reading and rereading *Goodnight Moon* when all you wanted to do was slug down apple martinis and binge-watch *Downton Abbey* or *House of Cards*? We remain story junkies from beginning to end. "We are told stories as children to help us bridge the abyss between waking and sleeping," John

Cheever wrote. "We tell stories to our own children for the same purpose. When I find myself in danger—caught on a stuck ski-lift in a blizzard—I immediately start telling myself stories. I tell myself stories when I am in pain and I expect as I lay dying I will be telling myself a story in a struggle to make some link between the quick and the defunct."

It's also now, when we're three or so, that we start creating stories. A story can be extraordinarily brief. Margaret Atwood, one of a number of writers invited by *Wired* magazine to compose a short story using only six words, turned out a classic, right up there with *Madame Bovary*: "Longed for him. Got him. Shit." Any toddler, upwards of a hundred billion neurons already straining at the bit, can create a story using only *three* words: "Me go poo." "Me go poo" is the story a three-year-old can and inevitably will tell more than once before he moves on to a higher level of narrative construction. "Me go poo" may sound primitive, but it fulfills the criteria scholars say define a legitimate story:

1. There's a protagonist (in this case, "me").
2. There's statement of a goal or desire ("to poo" or "have pooed").
3. There's an overt action relating to that goal or desire (will go/did go), which leads to the attainment or non-attainment of said goal or desire, which is to poo.

You and your writer-in-residence are now on your way to a storied future. From here on out, stories will not only entertain you, they will explain you to others and to yourself. Your life story will be how you'll "self-continue," narrative psychologists say. As long as your memories flow freely, you're in business. But if something happens to disturb memory flow, you'll have trouble self-continuing. Disorientation and worse—complete loss of identity—can result.

Even though our earliest autobiographical memories are highly suspect ("islands in the sea of oblivion," a novelist called them), there are those who are convinced that they hold enormous significance. Our early memories are neither accidental nor inconsequential. Alfred Adler, whose close relationship with Freud dissolved into bitter acrimony—pioneering psychoanalysts have difficulty playing nicely in the sandbox—believed that our earliest recollections reflect a fundamental view of life that we carry with us for the long haul. Early memories, Adler said, contribute to a "guiding fiction" that persists all the way through *The Life and Times of My Enduring Self.* The memories we designate our "earliest" are the beginning of our private autobiography.

As if sporting an Alfred Adler mustache and pince-nez, I went around asking people to share some early memories with me. Only last week I asked a friend to tell me hers. She's a well-adjusted, successful journalist, a loving wife and mother. Without missing a beat, she recalled how when she was six months old she was trapped in a tent with an angry, hissing snake. Not possible, I told her. You've just settled on that as a subjective starting point of the guiding fiction otherwise known as you, I explained. She was adamant, however, claiming to remember the snake as if it had hissed at her the day before yesterday. (Freud, of course, would have had an absolute field day with the snake.) Adler would say that even if the hissing snake memory was entirely "fancied," the memory is fundamental to how my friend is trying to satisfy a need or quell an insecurity. He might propose that she *made the snake* her first memory so that her life story would have nowhere to go but up. Conversely, I read in one of McAdams's books that if your self-selected "first memory" is suspiciously joyful, it could be that you've *made it* your first memory to set your life story up as a fall from grace.

My daughter, Katherine, a poised young professional woman, said her earliest memory is of peeing in a swimming pool while wearing a white bathing suit with garden vegetables printed on it. I'd be curious to know what Adler would do with that.

An old friend of mine—a woman who's led a satisfied life despite some harrowing blips (house fire, rare tropical parasite picked up in the Caribbean)—reports this early memory: "My grandpa was dying in our apartment. I was little more than three, and my parents sent me to stay with second cousins. After dinner every night, the dad, a psychiatrist, would haul me over his shoulder, pick up the garbage from the kitchen, take me to the backyard and say: 'I'm going to dump you with the garbage.' I remember screaming and kicking and being terrified every night. After that, whenever we'd leave home, I'd leave half a glass of milk in the kitchen, or a game half played in my bedroom, figuring my parents would have to bring me home so I could finish it."

Early memories are often highly cinematic. Do we amp them up for effect? Ronald Reagan had not one but *two* rip-roaring first memories, which he recalled on separate occasions. One was of nearly being crushed beneath the wheels of a freight train on a hot summer day in Galesburg, Illinois. The other was of being taken to view a passenger steamer that had capsized on the Chicago River, killing more than eight hundred people.

Even though you didn't ask, here's one of my earliest

memories, as accurately as I remember it: My mother has taken me on a shopping trip downtown. We've had lunch at the Horn & Hardart Automat, which is where we usually went, the long-gone place where you inserted nickels into slots that opened little glass cubbies with your favorite food inside, in my case a tongue sandwich on a kaiser roll. After lunch we walk over to one of the big Philadelphia department stores—John Wanamaker, Strawbridge & Clothier, it doesn't matter, they're also gone. Leading me by my left hand, my mother steps onto an escalator going up. Because I'm daydreaming or distracted, or lagging behind whining that I'm bored or tired or hungry even though I just ate a tongue sandwich followed by chocolate pudding, I accidentally put my left foot on the stair my mother's on, leaving my right on the stair below. As the stairs edge apart I find myself getting split up the middle, a tiny human wishbone. Behind me, a man in a suit tries to help out. He grabs my free hand. My mother yells for him to let go, which he promptly does, then she hoists me up to safety.

Though I remember all this playing out in super-slow motion, I'm sure the terror lasted at most a couple of seconds. No big deal. What's odd, though, is that the escalator memory keeps returning in unexpected ways. It rises out of nowhere, or nowhere I can easily trace. Neuroscientists say a memory is "recorded" in a highly specific pattern of neural activity. Show me something that elicits the same neural activity and my brain will comply by coughing up the escalator memory. Occasionally, however, the escalator memory is brought back for a reason I halfway understand. Maybe it's a "screen memory," as Freud called it, a childhood memory that stands for a later event. The escalator memory flashed through my head when I first saw the scene in *Goldfinger* where Sean Connery is strapped to a table and an industrial laser moves horrifyingly up between Bond's legs, headed straight for his crotch.

It also wouldn't surprise me in the least if the escalator memory fills the final frames before my screen goes to black. One grief expert says that a person's deceased mother often makes a cameo in a last-minute highlight reel. It's not uncommon to envision "hands passionately reaching upward to some unseen force." As on an escalator, maybe? Very Rosebud, no?

The pages of *The Life and Times of My Enduring Self* begin filling up quickly by the time we move into grade school. "I know I was writing stories when I was five. I don't know what I did before that. Just loafed, I suppose," P. G. Wodehouse, at ninety-one, told an interviewer. By first grade the loafing's over, at least for the young scribe upstairs. As your early self begins to round into shape, the scribbler turns it up a notch. He'll start rank ordering certain memories. Some will get priority status. It's a good bet that some of these select memories will relate to a subject I've managed to avoid almost entirely till now.

I haven't dwelled on death for a few reasons. Why risk turning this into a downer before I have to? I've also minimized the subject because it isn't yet a big deal in one's life story. It'll blossom, if that's the right word, soon enough. In those weeks I was holed up in the house by the graveyard, I came across a long paper published a hundred years ago in the *American Journal of Psychology*. The author was G. Stanley Hall, a major figure in the early days of the field, a pioneer of childhood psychology who among his other accomplishments brought the word "adolescence" into mainstream use. Hall devoted a good portion of the paper to how young children instinctively react when encountering death for the first time—such as when they see a corpse at a viewing, a dead family member, for example. Hall described how a very young child is taken aback when he feels how cold to the touch a dead person is. Or when he's met by an "immobility of face and body" instead of the prompt and tender response he always expected from the departed uncle or aunt. "There is no answering kiss, hug, pat or smile," Hall wrote. "[Often] the half-opened eyes are noticed with awe. The pallor, shroud, and especially coffin are often focused on fetishistically. [The] infant who has been permitted such scenes often turns away, perhaps almost convulsively, to whomever holds it, as if in fright."

Do you remember your first run-in with a dead something? I do. I'm supposing it couldn't have been long after the escalator incident. We are in Atlantic City. I'm running on the beach, focused on something else, something very much alive, probably the ice cream man pushing one of those carts with bells on it. (The sound of those bells was once the sweetest music in the world, though now the incessant ringing drives me crazy as I squint into my Kindle on the beach by Lake Michigan.) Anyway, according to the old memory, I'm sprinting across the sand as fast as my chubby little legs will carry me when I nearly step on a festering fish carcass, eyes plucked out, scary looking and disgusting. I stop and stare, so transfixed I even forget about the Creamsicle. My mother runs over, wagging her finger, and drags me away. She points to the dead fish and tells me I am never, *ever*, to go near anything like that again.

I'm assuming that the writer upstairs tagged the dead-fish memory as notable, filing it away as a moment that could have some later significance in the larger story. Memories are fluid. "An event may be extraneous and irrelevant to one episode, but important for understanding another," says a narrative psychologist. How do I now see the dead-fish memory? My mother was protecting me from mortal danger, much the way a mother bear, deer, or duck looks out for her cub, fawn, or duckling. She was shielding me physically and emotionally, not so much from the rotting fish as from the terror of death.

Shielded temporarily, that is. In *Staring at the Sun*, Irvin D. Yalom, the noted psychotherapist who has long studied death anxieties, describes how our fear of death waxes and wanes throughout one's life cycle. As children, even as the scribbler's doodling our earliest chapters, we catch our "first glimmerings of mortality . . . in dead leaves, insects and pets, disappearing grandparents, endless acres of cemetery tombstones"—the significance of which our parents are disinclined to enlighten us. We barely give death a further thought until we reach puberty. After that—well, these days, anyway—it seems like it's all death all the time: video games, horror movies, the whole ball of wax. My kids have lived through successive death-infused *genres*: Death Pop, Death Rock, Death Rap. Their iTunes libraries are stocked with Death Row label releases. There's an emcee who calls himself Necro (né Ron Braunstein, a.k.a. The Sexorcist and Mad Mooney), whose playlist includes tracks by Flatlinerz and Gravediggaz. In my day, "Tell Laura I Love Her" and "Teen Angel" were about as cadaverous as pop music got. But creepy nonetheless. We were more innocent then, it's reasonable to conclude.

How much do you remember from back when? Is the early part of *The Life and Times of My Enduring Self* fairly sketchy?

As kids we have no idea what we'll remember and why, nor do we get any better at predicting whether twenty years from now we'll remember something that happened yesterday. In his novel *Norwegian Wood*, Haruki Murakami tells of a day in a meadow that he vividly remembers eighteen years after the fact. In the moment he didn't give a damn about it, his mind was elsewhere. Some of us, in fact, remember *nothing*, episodically speaking. It's called "severely deficient autobiographical memory," or SDAM. Those who suffer from SDAM remember facts and figures, and that's about it. A sixty-year-old so afflicted told a writer from *New York* magazine: "I used to be really interested in photographs of me as a child—I would often get them out and look through them. And, evidently, one black-and-white photo showed me at three or four, sitting on a tricycle between my two brothers, wearing a pink dress. I happened to be looking at it with my mom and said something about my pink dress, and she said, 'Oh, no, it was a yellow dress.' I was really upset—here that was one of my embellishments to one of my childhood stories that I now had to change."

As for my own preadolescent chapters, beyond the escalator incident and the dead fish on the beach, there aren't a slew of memories rattling around up there. But there are some. Most have to do with my father. I follow him around like a puppy. We go fishing off a falling-down pier at the Jersey Shore. *Carl's Pier*—I just this second remembered that, hadn't thought of the name in decades. We keep the flounders (we call them "doormats") we haul up, throw back sea robins and blowfish. We're both wearing cotton pants with elastic waists known as "hobby jeans." Mine were blue, his were green. Hobby jeans were popular in the fifties, advertised as "perfect for fishing, gardening, boating, golf, painting, shop, or hobby work, washing the car, puttering around the house or just relaxing comfortably!" (The ad copy I had to look up.)

On fall Saturdays my father takes me to Franklin Field, where we watch the University of Pennsylvania (his school, mine, my sister's, my kids', we practically bleed Red and Blue), once a football powerhouse. Week after week, the Quakers are thrashed mercilessly by the Notre Dames of the world. The whole family attends the annual Thanksgiving Day game against Cornell. My mother and sister Barbara, she's five years older than me, wear yellow chrysanthemums pinned to their coats. From earlier in the season, I still have an impotent BEAT NAVY button pinned to my jacket.

I mostly daydream through elementary school. Scant memories of all that. I'm a safety patrolman with a silver Automobile Association of America badge on a white shoulder belt. (I'll eventually make sergeant—hold your applause.) My tonsils are removed. I remember what I see as the ether knocks me out (can conjure the smell of it, too): a black-and-white checkerboard spinning furiously down into a black hole. I associate it with *Alice in Wonderland*.

Then comes a detailed subchapter in that long-ago early part of the story. My father takes the family on a trip to California, where he's to attend a medical convention. I seem to retain more vivid memories of this week than of any other event prior to the age of thirteen. I'm sure you have memories like that as well, and it wouldn't be surprising if they have something to do with travel. Going places rouses the senses. The day before we leave, I'm given a few dollars to buy a week's supply of Pez, several comic books, and an issue of *Sport* magazine with a cover featuring Ted Kluszewski, the immense Cincinnati Reds first baseman whose biceps were so huge he had to cut the sleeves off his jersey. We leave Philly on the Pennsylvania Railroad, stopping in Chicago for a couple of days. We see a movie, *The Student Prince*, about which I remember nothing other than how sappy it was. The following day we drive north on Lake Shore Drive to the Northwestern campus in Evanston, where my father has a meeting. (We surely pass *directly* below the apartment Linda and I now live in and where I'm typing this. Part of me thinks I was drawn to this building because of that serendipitous drive-by, a connection to the past).

The next leg of the journey seems literally imprinted. We head west on the streamlined Super Chief, the new, all-Pullman train. We barrel through Colorado, New Mexico, Arizona. Real live Indians (as they were called) greet us at scheduled stops, selling turquoise jewelry and souvenirs spread out on colorful blankets. My parents buy me a cheap wooden peace pipe. On the bowl there's a decal of a chief in a headdress. I think I still have it, though I can't find it. Trust me, though, there's a chief in a headdress on the bowl. In fact, I'm pretty sure every detail of the foregoing is true, though on reflection I wouldn't swear it was Ted Kluszewski on the cover of *Sport*. It could have been Sam Snead. I'm dead certain it wasn't Ted Kazanski, who couldn't hit his way out of a paper bag, let alone make the cover of *Sport*.

Oh, and another memory from around that time. One day I'm on my bike and forget to duck as I pedal under a set of wooden stairs. I gash open my scalp. Frantically, my mother puts a dish towel over the wound and hurries me over to a doctor who lives in the neighborhood. Not any doctor, our family doctor. It's dinnertime. He opens the door, still chewing. Rather than let us in, even for a quick determination of whether the injury might be fatal, he tells us to go to an emergency room for stitches. This is the right advice, but I still wonder whether finishing his dinner didn't have something to do with it. Doctors were supposed to be gods, remember those days? Now, for the first time, I realize doctors have feet of clay, just like the rest of us. A few stitches and I'm home again. An intimation of mortality? Of course not. The worst part is going to school with a thick white bandage on top of a partially shaved dome. Embarrassing. Sidelined temporarily, I'm not allowed to play touch football in the street. For a week or so I sit on the stoop, watching my friends go at it. I wait for the afternoon paper, which is tossed my way by a kid on a bike, a canvas bag slung across his scrawny chest.

That I was reading the paper at that age signifies nothing: no precocious curiosity about world events that would later lure me into the Peace Corps and the deep satisfaction of doing my part on behalf of the developing world by teaching English in a village in Vanuatu. Nothing remotely that meaningful. I only looked at the sports and comics sections. But to reach those sections you had to thumb through a page or two that listed—in tiny type, signaling that the news couldn't be all that important—"Births, Marriages, and Deaths." At ten or eleven I had absolutely no interest in deaths, births, *or* marriages. Who does at that age? But I remember those pages even now. There's even a specific image I associate with them, not literally imprinted I'm sure, but for some unfathomable reason inserted retroactively. I see a granny in glasses with tightly curled gray hair, ancient looking though it wouldn't surprise me if she was all of sixty-four—which, come to think of it, wasn't so young back then. Women weren't expected to live beyond their early seventies. The blurry snapshot was probably taken at a Christmas get-together, with nieces, nephews, brothers, and sisters snipped out of the frame.

Accompanying the printed photo was a little note. It went something like this—I'm making it up, but it's close enough:

> No one knows how much we miss you, life has never been the same. In our hearts your memory lingers, sweetly tender, fond and true. There is not a day, dear mother/grandma/Gladys, that we do not think of you.

At the time, those messages struck me as icky but not at all sad; exactly the reverse of how they strike me now. I'd forgotten the granny and those pages with all the little type until something I read not long ago brought it all back. I came across a small paperback titled *On the Meaning of Life*. It was written in the 1930s by historian Will Durant. He observed that "hidden away in the small type of our daily press, under the captions of 'Births,' 'Marriages' and 'Deaths,' is the essential history of mankind." Everything else, Durant said, is "ornament."

What do you make of that? Sounds good, doesn't it? The meaning of life is that we're born, we make babies, we die. Is *that* the point? If it is the point, it makes you wonder why we overthink everything, spend too much time working on philosophical puzzles about the unanswerable, even as the fundamental purpose of existence is staring us in the face. We're born, we marry, we die. Isn't that pretty much *it*?

5   A God-Shaped Hole

When social scientists go into the field to collect our life stories, they follow an established protocol. If you agree to an interview, you're told that the session will last about two hours. "This is an interview about the story of your life," they explain. "As social scientists we are interested in hearing your story, including parts of the past as you remember them and the future as you imagine it." Then they assure you that it won't be a therapy session. As researchers, they tell you, they collect life stories in order to understand the different ways we live our lives and how we reach an understanding of who we are. You're then asked to imagine a book, just as we're doing here. You're informed that the interview will cover select scenes and chapters in this book. We don't need to know everything, the interviewer says, we'll just focus on a few "key things." Included among the key things are eight events the interviewer may refer to as "nuclear episodes"— "nuclear" in the sense that they're central to your personal myth. Nuclear events include a positive and a negative childhood memory; a "wisdom event"; a vivid adult memory; a high point and a low point; a spiritual experience; and a turning point. A turning point, the interviewer says, is an episode in which you underwent a significant change in self-understanding. It isn't necessary to realize that an event's a turning point when it happens, only in retrospect. There is no right or wrong answer to what is or isn't a turning point, you'll be told, nor is there a correct or incorrect answer to any of the other questions you'll be asked during the interview. So try to relax for the next couple of hours. Let the good and the bad times roll.

While the life-story interview protocol calls for sharing only a single turning point, we all have more than one turning point in the story of our evolving selves. Most written stories of any length have more than one, too. Enroll in a screen-writing course and you'll hear right off the bat that every good movie (every bad one as well) consists of three acts and x-number of turning points peppered throughout those acts. Five isn't uncommon. These are strategically placed in the plot to signal an opportunity; a change of plan; a point of no return; a ratcheting up of conflict; an "all-is-lost" moment; and a final turning point that usually sets up a triumphant, happy resolution, Hollywood being Hollywood.

Our lives, I've now come to understand, are apparently built on the screenplay model, though they don't often end as happily as Hollywood movies. If tonight you sneaked into my bedroom, jostled me out of a deep sleep, and told me to rattle off the major turning points in my life, I'd immediately tick off the twist of fate that got me my first job; my marrying Linda; the birth of each of my kids; and the turning point that preceded all of the above, which I'll tell you about in a minute. There—the minimum five turning points needed for my life to qualify as a movie script—not that there's a Lee Eisenberg biopic coming any time soon. You could list your five turning points if I woke *you* in the middle of night. (In fact, why not take a second and identify them now?) Having listed our respective five, if you and I kept the conversation going we'd surely be able to come up with numerous other turning points of varying significance. The right or wrong undergraduate major. The right or wrong doctor's diagnosis. The right or wrong weather the day this or that was supposed to happen. The right or wrong decision to go to bed with someone. The right or wrong thing you said at the right or wrong moment. The day we found someone or lost someone.

"When with the benefit of hindsight one begins to search one's past for such 'turning points,' one is apt to start seeing them everywhere," wrote Kazuo Ishiguro in his appropriately titled novel *The Remains of the Day*.

Here's that left-unsaid turning point, the one that came first. It's a perfectly beautiful fall day, October 26, a Monday, a few months after the summer I was the youngest boy to make the softball team at Camp Arthur, though as I said, I didn't see much game time. I'm thirteen. It's right after school. My scalp is by now healed and I'm playing touch football in the street in front of our house. The curb's lined with fallen leaves. Even now I can hear them crunch. I can smell them. I can see the paving stones that line the curb, the concrete steps leading up to our front door. Combining a memory of something that happened with a memory of *where* it happened yields details of surprising clarity, memory scientists say. It's like a dream or a movie. Memory researchers also say the reason we remember a certain occasion in extraordinary detail is because a given narrative requires it. This particular memory validates both of those theories.

My mother, indescribably distraught (Munch's *Scream* comes to mind, *not* a literal imprint), opens the screen door and yells for me to come in. I run up the steps. Even before I reach the landing, she tells me my father is dead. What I don't remember is whether she actually used the word "dead." It could have been "gone." I'm sure it wasn't "passed away." It was most definitely not "gone to his eternal rest." After she says my father is "dead" or "gone," and probably not aware she's even addressing me, she cries out a medical term, or what I take to be a medical term because it sounds like one. For years, whenever the scribbler pushed the memory of that day back to the surface, I tried to recapture the exact words she used, running the audio over and over through my head as if through an analyzer in a sound lab. One day I finally figured it out. *Myocardial infarction.* "He's had a myocardial infarction," she said, as if whomever she was speaking to would understand.

When did you first lose an important person in your life? How does the occasion currently read in your version of *The Life and Times of My Enduring Self*? Was it a turning point? Were you angry? Bewildered? Overwhelmed? Did you cry and cry?

Angry, bewildered, and overwhelmed though I was, I don't remember crying very much. My mother made it even harder to cry because she kept telling me that crying would "let the hurt out." I'm pretty sure I remember those exact words. They're imprinted, but not literally. Was I too existentially confused to cry? Maybe. It was utterly astonishing to me that anyone could be alive today and banished to oblivion the next. I'm sure that thought has occurred to you as well. I remember staring at my father's Longines Wittnauer wristwatch, which I've kept in a box on my dresser ever since, never once winding it in all these years. When my mother wasn't around, I'd tiptoe into my parents' bedroom and stare into my father's closet, looking at his suits, dumbstruck at the idea that he'd never wear them again. A few months later, my mother donated the suits to Goodwill. The thought that others would be wearing them was beyond bizarre.

I remember only a little bit about the funeral. It's not that I've repressed the rest. The scribbler hasn't flattened, smoothed, or squashed my memories of the event. I'd remember much more if I'd been there. Instead, the scribe and I were sealed off by ourselves in a side room. "I want you to remember him the way he was," my mother said on the way to the service. Recently I read Thomas Merton's account of the day his mother was buried—he was a few years younger than me, eight or nine. He, too, was denied entry to the funeral: "Everything about sickness and death was more or less kept hidden from me, because consideration of these things might make a child morbid." Well, yeah, but chances are a child who loses a parent will become a tad morbid whether or not he's lucky enough to attend the funeral.

On the other hand, maybe my mother was right. A man in his late sixties said in an interview that his mother had died twenty years earlier. She went swiftly, barely a month after she was diagnosed. He confessed that he continues to be "haunted by her face in the coffin." So, yes, perhaps my mother was onto something, that I'd only remember my father dead, not how we went fishing or to football games, all of which I'm happy to remember. I also recall my father from snapshots and home movies, which is not the same as remembering him when he was alive, but still. In her classic essay on photography, Susan Sontag said that all photographs are *memento mori*: "Precisely by slicing out this moment and freezing it, all photographs testify to time's relentless melt."

That works for me. Now, whenever I look at a photograph of my father, I'm not so much looking at him as staring at time's relentless melt.

Here's another memory from that turning point. After the funeral, everyone comes back to our house. The mirrors are covered with black fabric; there are folding chairs in the living room; the dining room table is groaning under a mountain of cold cuts and pound cake. My aunt Ruth comes over and pinches me on the cheek. That pinch, by the way, feels powerfully imprinted—Ruth was a strong woman. The two of us then act out that old movie scene cliché. Aunt Ruth leans down and tells me I'm now the man of the household and it's my job to take care of my mother. Instead of saying what I feel like saying—that I'm scared shitless—I respond the way every kid does in that lame movie scene. I nod and mumble solemnly that I'll do my best. Dan McAdams would most definitely view that response as an attempt to launch a personal myth around a young man determined to show courage in the face of adversity.

In the days that follow, I'm convinced that my father will suddenly reappear in ghostly guise. This may be the only chapter in my edition of *The Life and Times of My Enduring Self* with anything close to supernatural overtones. Stephen Hawking once told Charlie Rose that he regards the afterlife to be "a fairy story for people that are afraid of the dark." Though I had no fear of the dark to begin with, the idea that my father, much as I longed to see him, would show up in my room in the middle of the night is an excellent reason *to* fear the dark. Before going to sleep, I check under my bed. At school, I half expect to glance up in the schoolyard to see an apparition peering out from behind a tree, smoking a Benson

& Hedges even though he was ordered to quit after his first heart attack.

For the next eleven months, twice a day, before school and after, my grandfather drives me to a nearby synagogue where I recite the *Kaddish*, the traditional Hebrew memorial prayer. While my grandparents are observant, my immediate family is not. I am under no pressure to endure this torture, but I have no other meaningful way to express devotion to my father. I suppose it was an act of penance, though I couldn't tell you for what.

There are at most about a dozen old men who attend these sunrise and sunset services. It's a social event, gives them something to do, gets them out of the house. I remember their faces quite well, or think I do. All are in their seventies or older, wizened and disturbingly cold looking, or so they appeared to me then. I have never felt more exposed and out of place. They don't say ten words to me. They just stare. I'm sure they feel compassion, but it comes across as forbidding and harsh. The service, which lasts about forty minutes, is entirely in Hebrew. By then I can haltingly read Hebrew, but needless to say I have no clue as to what the words mean. Within a week, I know the mourner's prayer by heart; that is, I can recite it phonetically from memory. I take no part in the service other than to stand up and recite:

Yisgadal v'yiskadash sh'mei rabbaw (Amen)
B'allmaw dee v'raw chir'usei
v'yamlich malchusei, b'chayeichon, uv'yomeichon,
uv'chayei d'chol beis yisroel,
ba'agawlaw u'vizman kawriv, v'imru: Amen...

On it goes for another twenty-four lines.

When the eleven torturous months are finally over, I feel some small satisfaction that I made the effort, put in the time, endured the stares. I disliked everything about it, but I'd honored my father as best I could. Today I'm ambivalent about the whole experience. "What do I have in common with Jews?" Kafka wrote in a diary. "I have hardly anything in common with myself and should stand very quietly in a corner, content that I can breathe."

Why am I telling you all this? About my not crying, Aunt Ruth's pinch, the covered mirrors, checking under the bed for my father's ghost? Yes, it's good to air difficult memories. There's research to prove it, plenty of studies. They start off with instructions like this:

> *I would like for you to write about your very deepest thoughts about an extremely important issue that has affected you and your life. In your writing, I'd like you to really let go and explore your very deepest emotions. You might tie your topic to your relationships with others, including your parents, lovers, friends, or relatives; to your past, your present, or your future; or to who you have been, who you would like to be, or who you are now. Don't worry about spelling, sentence structure, or grammar. The only rule is that once you begin writing, continue to do so until your time is up.*

In the allotted time—fifteen minutes a day, say, for three or four days—participants are expected to write about lost loves, deaths, and personal failures. And guess what? The researchers report a variety of mental and physical benefits, including improved immune function, less emotional anxiety or depression, even quicker reemployment following job loss. Routinely writing about *anything* has been shown to improve memory capacity. Why does writing about a difficult time make you feel better? No one's altogether sure, though a long-standing theory holds that letting go on paper lessens inhibition, inhibition being a source of stress.

But that's not why I told you about the death of my father. I wasn't looking to throw off inhibitions. Nor was I trolling for sympathy. I shared these memories to make a point about turning points. Years after a pivotal event, a scribbler will often revisit and reinterpret the role it played in the overall story. The death of a parent, as devastating as that event is, can turn out to be a growth experience. Or a wake-up call. Or it can turn a life story into an irreversible nightmare. At the time, you just don't know. All I knew then was that in the blink of an eye there was a giant hole in our family, as gaping as any "God-shaped hole," a concept favored by those who believe that it takes something as big and majestically contoured as God to fill the emptiness of existence. I hadn't realized there were such holes before. Now I did. My father's death was the turning point that changed how I measured life. "It is the decease of the father which opens the prospect of one's own end, and affords an unobstructed view of the undug but awaiting grave that says 'you're next,'" Christopher Hitchens wrote in his memoir, *Hitch-22*.

It was also a turning point for the writer upstairs. He understood for the first time that the gig wasn't all fun and games. That he wasn't up there to write bullshit, throw memories at the wall to see which of them would stick in the extended plot. He was up there, as yours is up there, to pay attention and write a coherent story that (as E. M. Forster said) begins with something we don't remember and ends with something we anticipate but don't understand.

As for the scribbler *and* me, we now had a rough sense of what the page count would likely be. There'd be just enough pages for what I'd come to think of as a novella, but not enough for a doorstop novel. There'd be pages enough to take me through my late forties, which is not only when my father died but his two brothers as well. The scribbler and I knew squat about genetics or actuarial tables. All we knew was what my father had often said during the three years between his first heart attack and the Monday morning myocardial infarction that killed him. He was a scientist to his bones, was recognized in his field, and taught at a top-tier medical school. He knew what he was talking about. Medicine and science, he remarked now and then, could work formidable wonders, "but it all comes down to the hand you're dealt," he said.

I remember—honestly, I do remember—taking out pencil and paper. I did some basic arithmetic. Assuming I'd been dealt the same crappy hand as my father and my two uncles, I wouldn't be around to ring in the year 2000. That's when everyone would surely be zipping to work in business suits with jet packs strapped to their backs. Nuclear-powered cars. Two-way, picture-phone wristwatches. Robomaids and vac-ubots. It was a bummer to think I'd never get to have babies with Annette Funicello and live happily ever after in a house with a robomaid and a vacubot.

6 *Is the Beginning Important?*

As we prepare to move from the beginning to the middle of the story, it's reasonable to wonder: How much do the early chapters in *The Life and Times of My Enduring Self* determine what happens in the middle and the end?

Some will tell you the beginning has everything to do with what happens in the middle and the end. Saint Ignatius Loyola: "Give me a child until he is seven, and I will show you the man." Not so fast, with all due respect. Those who rely not on faith but on long-term data will tell you that nothing's set in stone when you're seven years old. It's nature, nurture, and dumb luck.

By way of longitudinal example: In 1938, the Department of Hygiene at Harvard launched what became known as the Grant Study. It would be an ambitious long-term probe into how life stories unfold. Funding for the project came from W. T. Grant, the five-and-dime magnate, himself a tenth-grade dropout. Grant saw the study as an opportunity to predict what makes for a reliable long-term store manager. Researchers would track men over the course of their entire lives, from Harvard Yard to the graveyard. The goal was to document how "the stress of modern pressures" affects one's overall well-being.

Two hundred and sixty-eight student guinea pigs (all male) volunteered to take part in the study. Each was screened physically and psychologically. Those with problematic health histories, or current or potential medical risks, or men who showed signs of academic deficiencies were booted out. The authors of the study insisted that the guinea pigs be as robust as possible. Longer lives would yield richer data. Accordingly, twice as many muscular mesomorphs made the cut as skinny runts and pudgy marshmallows. The participants' life stories were then tracked in meticulous detail through extensive self-reporting and periodic interviews. Nearly eight decades later, the study is still running, albeit with a severely reduced number of guinea pigs.

Some of the subjects, as you might imagine, went on to flourish while others flamed out. Everyone went through life's wringer. Their bodily functions peaked within ten years of the project's launch. By age forty, they started shrinking a half inch per decade; by fifty, their taste buds were faltering; by sixty, they required three times more light to read by than when they were students cramming at Widener Library. Blood vessels stiffened. Brain volume decreased. By seventy, many were unable to make out high-pitched consonants such as k, t, and p, and were complaining that their wives, kids, and bridge partners were all mumbling. Marriages and careers fell apart, often more than once. Colleagues and loved ones bit the dust. There were wars and economic calamities to cope with. Many lives were shattered by excessive drinking. But for a writer upstairs, that's not the worst of it. The worst can be expressed in the nicest-sounding but dirtiest words a scribbler will ever hear: "Benign senescent forgetfulness."

In one of his essays, Somerset Maugham observed, "What makes old age hard to bear is not a failing of one's faculties, mental and physical, but the burden of our memories." Give me a break! the writer-in-residence all but cries out. What makes old age hard to bear is loss of memory. Loss of memory equals loss of *self*.

Based on the results of the Grant Study, and with all due respect to Saint Ignatius Loyola, what a boy of seven needs if he's likely to turn out okay is a warm and loving relationship with his parents. Give a boy of seven a warm and loving relationship with his mother and the Grant Study will show you a man more likely to have a more successful career than one who grew up without a mother. Or a mother who was cold and disinterested. Give him a warm and loving relationship with a father and the study will show you a man who was less likely to suffer from anxiety and more likely to enjoy his geriatric years.

But there are no guarantees even with warm and loving early chapters in *The Life and Times of My Enduring Self*. Many of the Harvard guinea pigs' stories were fated from the beginning. "Sleeper effects" from childhood were identified. Some sleeper effects had a positive impact on the story—a remembered encounter with an inspiring teacher, or a young love affair warmly remembered. Some sleeper effects worked in reverse. They haunted the story line—the predisposition for alcohol abuse or depression. We're all at risk. A damaging sleeper effect can flare up out of nowhere and torpedo the plot just when we're getting to what's supposed to be a really good part of the story.

PART II

The Middle

Maybe all I can do is hope to wind up with the right regrets.

—A character in Arthur Miller's *The Ride Down Mt. Morgan*

7   *Beware the Elbow*

Established in the mid-nineteenth century, the old country graveyard is home to tombstones that go back a century earlier, marking remains relocated from an overcrowded neighboring cemetery. Wandering up and down the paths, I marveled at the trove of great stories that had found their way here, a golden treasury of finished stories, no longer works in progress.

There are tales of valor. A Revolutionary War casualty along with his five wives. An eighteen-year-old seaman third class killed in combat in the South Pacific; and his father, a US Army corporal who survived campaigns in China, Burma, and India. The father died at age ninety-five, outliving his son by over half a century. A lieutenant corporal, US Marines, winner of the Navy Cross and Purple Heart in Operation Iraqi Freedom, killed in action at age twenty. A dozen or so military challenge coins sit atop his black marble headstone.

There are tragedies at sea. Whaling captains and crew members who perished in storms, their tumultuous ends honored by a memorial in the form of a broken ship's mast ("Entombed in the ocean, they live in our memory").

There are love stories. PARTNERS FOREVER is chiseled across a tombstone. On the left side, a man's name and dates.

On the right, another man's name but as yet no dates. George Balanchine, the ballet master, is buried not far from that stone. Not far from Balanchine is Alexandra Danilova, the celebrated ballerina who went to school with him in St. Petersburg. They lived for seven years as woman and husband, never marrying because Balanchine was married to somebody else.

There are family sagas. Massive monuments pay stolid tribute to patriarchs, while matriarchs get short shrift, simply their names and dates on unprepossessing slabs. Surrounding many parents' markers are itty-bitty stones, some just small rocks reading BOY or GIRL. They were babies who died at childbirth or not long after. It was customary not to name children till there was reasonable assurance they'd survive smallpox or cholera. In the town records there's an epitaph for one who didn't make it: "A bud on earth will bloom in heaven." If you're a believer, to bloom in heaven is point enough. For others, blooming in heaven is beside the point. Was the child's time *on earth* well rewarded? *That's* the point, according to Tom Stoppard. In a play of his, *Shipwreck*, Stoppard wrote: "[The death] of a child has no more meaning than the death of armies, of nations. Was the child happy while he lived? That is a proper question, the only question."

There are tragedies of pathos and despair. Spalding Gray, the author and monologist, lies silently here. Two months after he disappeared, suspected of jumping off the Staten Island Ferry, Gray's body washed up along the East River in New York City. His tombstone reads AN AMERICAN ORIGINAL, TROUBLED, INNER-DIRECTED AND CAN-NOT TYPE.

There are forgotten stories. Weathered rocks with neither a date nor a full name, brown stones not much bigger than a pumpernickel. S.E.N. rests next to C.T.N., who in turn rests next to FATHER, 1884, & MOTHER. Whether these stones were kept deliberately spare out of humble intent or because carvers charged by the word are answers lost to history.

And I was surprised to discover a series of stories I'd known personally, some better than others: journalist Nelson Algren; editor Clay Felker; novelist William Gaddis, whose books run close to a thousand pages but whose tablet is inscribed with only his dates and a single word: PAPA. And there's Bob Sklar, who taught film history at NYU, was thoughtful and soft-spoken, a good friend and one of the founding fathers of Rotisserie League Baseball.

Before they ended up here, the stories in the graveyard had moved every which way. Some had gotten better as they went along, others slid in reverse—"Boats against the current, borne back ceaselessly into the past," the final words of *The Great Gatsby*, and the line engraved under Bob Sklar's name and dates.

Many of the stories in the graveyard carry illustrations: olive branches, anchors, horseshoes, cherubs, lilies, columns, crosses, poppies, doves, hourglasses, shells, mermaids, roses, snakes. Plots are also garnished with what narrative psychologists refer to as "objects of reminiscence": toy cars, beach toys, costume jewelry, tchotchkes bequeathed by family and friends. Me? I'd be pleased with a fountain pen, a mini–fly rod, a tiny baseball bat, the kind you get in a gumball machine. A few CDs would be warmly received. *Sinatra at the Sands. Ahmad Jamal at the Penthouse*, the first LP I ever bought. Anything Thelonious Monk, I'm not picky.

I trust I haven't given you the impression that the writer upstairs serves as an ink-stained guardian angel who keeps your life story reliably pointed in the right direction from beginning to end. Not everyone has a literary heavyweight up there, and even the best authors lose their way. "I write one page of masterpiece to ninety pages of shit. I try and put the shit in the wastebasket," Hemingway wrote to someone who'd asked about the secret of his success.

It's often the middle of the story when trouble arises. The middle of any story presents a stern test for even the most accomplished author. The middle's hazardous. The middle's where a plot goes to unravel. It's where characters are prone to fall apart. I can't tell you how many times I ran into middle-muddle back when I was at *Esquire*. A writer, often a highly praised and generously paid writer, one who should have known better, would hand in a piece that started off like gangbusters. The first third was confident, even electric. Then, without warning, a faint tremor rattled off the page. An irrelevant reference. A paragraph inserted for no apparent reason. *Huh?* The wobbles intensified from there as the ground shifted from under the story, and after another page or two you knew you had a reclamation project on your hands.

The editors on staff had a shorthand way of referring to the troublesome midsection of a story. We called it the "elbow." I'm not sure how that got started. I may have said it one day and it caught on. After that, when an article or short story circulated, there'd be comments such as "weak elbow," "the elbow sucks," or "brilliant until you get to the fucking elbow."

The reason a piece of writing often falls apart at the elbow is that the writer sat down at the typewriter with a ton of great material and started pounding away, in love with his own voice. He hadn't bothered to think very hard about the point of the story. How it might build to a satisfying conclusion. Say the story's about Leo DiCaprio. Okay, *what* about Leo DiCaprio? The writer wasn't sure what about Leo DiCaprio. This minor detail went unnoticed—the prose was deft, it swept you along—until the story made it to the middle, where it swerved, sometimes stalled, just the way many careers and marriages swerve and stall when they make it to the middle. What an online writing coach says about writing a story also applies to writing a life story: "The middle has to do more than just fill up the space between beginning and end. It should be a time of 'rising conflict' where the protagonist is tested up to (and often beyond) the limits of his ability."

Because there isn't universal agreement about when the middle of a life story starts and when it ends, let's not fuss over it. It's when a leading character's "no longer young but not yet old," as some researchers define it. It's when our focus shifts from "time since birth" to "time to live," a gerontologist will say. If that's still too vague, let's leave it that midlife begins at forty and ends at sixty. For many, this stretch equates to twenty years of bad road. E. L. Doctorow once compared writing to driving a car in the fog. You can see only as far as your headlights but eventually you get where you're going. For the writer upstairs, getting through midlife can be like typing at night without a desk lamp. And you may or may not get to where you'd like to go.

If you're currently of a certain age, midlife or older, you grew up primed to be apprehensive about the middle of your life story. An almost certain cataclysm loomed. You hit the Big Four-O and all hell breaks loose. Your spouse is boring. Your kids have devolved into irredeemable louts. Your career's dead in the water. A full set of these sorry symptoms can still be found on Dr. Phil's website. In no particular order of anguish: You lament goals not achieved. You obsess over your appearance. You hanker for adventure. You wonder why you ever married her (him). You feel hopelessly tied down. You're consumed with nostalgia. Sound eerily familiar? To me, too. If these be the hallmarks of the classic middle-age crisis, mine's been on low-to-high simmer since my late twenties.

Still, I confess I was doubly spooked when news broke of a male menopause. By age fifty, I read in a magazine, my hormone production would tank, my head would bald, my sexual vigor would diminish, my parents would die. My friends would be clutching at their chests as our collective past floated by in a haze of hopes not realized, opportunities not grasped, potentials not realized, men or women not bedded. Looking to the future, all I'd see was my own mortality.

According to a raft of magazine articles and books in the seventies and eighties, our all-but-guaranteed rendezvous with menopausal doom fits neatly into one or another "human life course" model. Depending on the template, the human life course is composed of a series of ages, stages, phases, seasons, or passages. It's comforting, isn't it, to look at life this way? It doesn't seem quite so unruly if there's a schematic that explains life from A to Z. There's nothing new about our search for a blueprint that satisfies. One night on a business trip, marooned at an airport hotel due to a canceled flight, I ordered a pizza and settled in to listen to a Joseph Campbell lecture on Dante's four ages of man. (It was either that or the gentleman's club across the road.) Campbell clearly relished Dante's take on the human life course. There are four extended chapters. The first, which Dante called "adolescence," is all about personal growth. We learn how to conduct ourselves with good manners, speak courteously, and so on. It gets us to our mid-twenties. The second stage, which Campbell refers to as "maturity," spans the next two decades, age thirty-five being the critical midpoint. Now it's all about "doing our job," as Campbell puts it. We apply what we've learned in adolescence to transforming the world around us. We exercise courage, love, loyalty, "our knightly virtues," in other words. Forty-five to seventy is "old age." The task now is to give advice, impart wisdom and justice, be generous and affable to those around us. Finally, we reach the fourth stage, "senility" or "decline" or "decrepitude"—they've all been applied. Now is when we look back on our life with gratitude and look forward to "going home." These four stages correspond to the daily transit of the sun: morning, afternoon, evening, and nightfall.

Shakespeare offered an alternative scenario in the immortal "All the World's a Stage" soliloquy. We go from Baby ("puking in the nurse's arms") to Schoolboy ("creeping like [a] snail / Unwillingly to school") to Lover ("sighing like [a] furnace") to Soldier ("quick in quarrel") to Justice (wise and with "fair round belly") to Old Guy (shriveled and shrunken) to Really Old Guy, a helpless, debilitated bag of bones ("Sans teeth, sans eyes, sans taste, sans everything").

In the 1970s and 1980s, psychologists stepped up to put the kibosh on all this poetic folderol. Forget the evocative metaphors, bring on some hard data. Magazines, newspapers, and self-help books feasted on a groaning board of studies purporting to illuminate what Yale professor Daniel J. Levinson called one of the best-kept secrets in our society and "probably in human history"—"the concrete character of adult life." How best to nail it down? By chartering a multidisciplinary team of psychologists, psychiatrists, and sociologists—no poets or philosophers need apply. Under Levinson's lead, the social scientists analyzed the testimony of forty men ranging in age from late afternoon to slightly later afternoon (Dante Standard Time). The study, documented in a book called *The Seasons of a Man's Life*, focused on what many judge to be a less-than-representative sampling of guys. All forty men lived in the Northeast Corridor. Six of the forty happened to be novelists. That alone gives me pause. Martin Amis says novelists are a breed apart. They have two ways of talking about themselves: either they feign false modesty or they indulge their inner egomaniac, viewing one another as "blind worms in a ditch, slithering pointlessly around, getting nowhere." From *them* we're going to extrapolate the answer to one of the best-kept secrets in human history?

Methodological objections notwithstanding, the research findings generated plenty of media attention. Lots of juicy stuff to run with. In the preface to *Seasons*, Levinson notes that "middle age activates our deepest anxieties about decline and dying." He decries how "overly negative imagery of old age adds greatly to the burden of middle age." By the time a guy reaches his late thirties, he's a lost lamb, reckoning with how well he's fared in becoming his own man. With the precision of an expert arborist who's carefully counted the rings on a tree stump, and based on the limited sample of men who all live in the Northeast Corridor, Levinson says the most challenging midlife transition ordinarily begins at age forty or forty-one and lasts five years or so: "We doubt that a true Mid-life transition can begin before age 38 or after 43." While some men manage to escape the ravages of the elbow, the large majority—80 percent—have evidenced "tumultuous struggles within the self and with the external world." They must straddle the "polarities" of being Young/Old, Masculine/Feminine, Destructive/Creative, and Attached/Separate.

It took almost twenty years, but Daniel Levinson went on to publish *The Seasons of a Woman's Life*, a better-late-than-never acknowledgment that half the human race also has a life cycle to plow through. In his preface to the women's book, Levinson explains, not altogether convincingly, that he started with men mostly out of a desire to understand his own adult development. He offers an apology for the many centuries science has held fast to a male-centered view of adult life. Now, however, "a gender revolution" is under way, the result being a breakdown of the division of labor "between female homemaker and the male provisioner." Women are living longer, devoting proportionately less time to a "domestic career." The divorce rate further reinforces their need for job skills that will allow them to take care of themselves. A homemaker who makes it to the "Mid-Life Transition," her early forties, typically suffers through a "rock bottom" marital experience: a relationship that's likely to be arid and stagnant, with infrequent sex, usually at her initiative, Levinson observes. A woman's self-interest now has to be served through personal struggle and individual development. This requires her to ask "with greater urgency than ever before: Who am I? What is most important to me? How will I try to live in the next season of my life?" Chilling questions. "They raise the possibility of drastic, frightening changes in a self and a life structure that...are not readily altered." "Every season has its own time, although it is part of and colored by the whole," Levinson writes. "No season is intrinsically better or more important than any other." The changing of the seasons, the transitions between all of them, are stormy.

Transitioning into the *midlife* season is especially harrowing, replete with depression, anxiety, and the urge to take "manic flight."

While there were conceptual differences among the modern human-life-course models, a common denominator was the presumption that each successive stage augurs a changing pattern of behavior. Psychiatrist Roger Gould saw a fundamental push-pull at work between and within each stage. It's what Levinson referred to as a "polarity"—opposing tendencies or conditions. We're being tugged back to the "safety" of our childhood while at the same time drawn forward by our need to be "autonomous"—in control of our own destiny. When we get to our late thirties or early forties, our kids (whom we've probably screwed up by now) have reached adolescence and are beyond our remedial grasp. We've become useless as parents. Our careers are likewise *meh*, beyond salvation. "We stand naked and exposed, toe to toe with life. Our naiveté is lost forever," wrote Gould in *Transformations*. The challenge is how to move forward, how to "grow."

The most popular human-life-course book proved to be Gail Sheehy's *Passages*, which leaned heavily on both Gould's and Levinson's theories. Gould thought Sheehy leaned *too* heavily, suing her for plagiarism before agreeing to an out-of-court settlement. Amid the legal battles, the book sat atop bestseller lists for years and even today is promoted as a "humane, widescreen view of adulthood [that] speaks eloquently to men and women, to couples and singles, to 'wunderkinds' and late bloomers, to careerists and homemakers.... [The] only book that brings together a coherent vision of the passages we must all take through the Twenties, Thirties, and Forties toward what is potentially the best of life." Still, a river of fear runs through it: "There is nobody to keep you safe.There is nobody who will not ever leave you."

But before anyone jumps to the conclusion that fear-mongering the human life course was little more than trumped-up sensationalizing to sell books and newspapers, consider three case studies I've chosen from among many qualifying ones. Two involve towering figures who shaped Western civilization and whose midlife stories must bear serious consideration. The third was a lamentable shmuck who lived on Peapod Lane in suburban Connecticut.

Midlife Crisis Exhibit A is an 1884 essay by Leo Tolstoy. It's titled *A Confession*, though it's tempting to refer to it as "Tolstoy's Complaint."

Writing shortly before he turned fifty, the Russian master confessed to discomfiting fits of anxiety. When he was younger, everything was on the ascendance: "My muscles were growing and strengthening, my memory was being enriched, my capacity to think and understand was increasing, I was growing and developing." As long as the trajectory was moving in the right direction, Tolstoy tried to convince himself that there was order to the universe, confident he'd discover a "universal law in which I should find the solution of the question of my life."

Then, in the midst of a career already burnished by success—by now he'd written *Anna Karenina* and *War and*

Peace—and even though Tolstoy was blessed with a loving family and sufficient rubles to be more than comfortable, things came unhinged: "Something very strange began to happen to me. At first I began having moments of bewilderment, when my life would come to a halt, as if I did not know how to live or what to do; I would lose my presence of mind and fall into a state of depression. But this passed, and I continued to live as before. Then the moments of bewilderment recurred more frequently, and they always took the same form. Whenever my life came to a halt, the questions would arise: Why? And what next?"

Driving at night in the fog, Tolstoy had run out of gas in the middle of midlife. He was fifty-one. Why, and what's next? he asked. Death is what's next. The more Tolstoy ruminated over his inevitable demise, the more he fretted that life was little more than "a stupid and spiteful joke." How does one respond to such emptiness? Tolstoy studied how his "narrow circle of equals," people like himself (educated, comfortable enough) were wrestling with the problem. He observed that we deal with our sorry predicament in one of four ways. To paraphrase:

1. *We keep ourselves ignorant.* We try not to think too hard about the point. What we haven't figured out won't keep us up at night.
2. *We eat, drink, merry our way to the end.* It's how the Most Interesting Man in the World is dealing with late middle age. By staying thirsty, my friend.
3. *We do the only brave and honorable thing: take gun, knife, pills, or exhaust pipe to the problem.* Tolstoy said he could not bring himself to take this step, but we all know of those who could and did. A former

neighbor of ours swallowed a bottle of pills then leaped off the old Tappan Zee Bridge. Whether in his case it was an act of philosophical, midlife courage, or a response to mounting debt, or a stroke of insanity, or all of the above, is a matter of interpretation.

4. *We have no better solution than to live out our days in zoned-out uselessness, waiting for the final buzzer.* Here's where Tolstoy regretfully placed himself.

It wasn't as if Tolstoy hadn't already searched high and low for a better answer. Over the years he'd looked for the point "amid the gleams of mathematical and experimental science." He found no satisfying answer there. He'd also looked to philosophy for solace, concluding that Socrates, King Solomon, and Buddha all viewed life as but the lounge act for the Grim Reaper, the eternal headliner. From Schopenhauer all he got was "the passage into Nothingness is the only good in life." Borscht, *cold* borscht, for the soul. Undaunted, Tolstoy didn't zip around on a Vespa, hitting on Crimean hotties half his age. Instead, he pondered the essence of Christ's teachings, weighing them against how the church had exploited the scriptures in order to feather its own nave. He concluded that each of us is *already* invested with the essential teachings of Christ; that the purpose of life on earth is to serve not our lower animal nature but the power to which our higher nature recognizes its kinship with the Gospels, as Tolstoy scholar Ernest J. Simmons interprets the awakening. The point is to use that power to do good. This awareness is not lost on everyone, Tolstoy realized, only on some of us. The teachings are alive and well in the souls of honest, common working folk.

"In contrast with what I had seen in our circle," Tolstoy

wrote, "where the whole of life is passed in idleness, amusement, and dissatisfaction, I saw that the whole life of these people was passed in heavy labour, and that they were content with life. [They] accepted illness and sorrow without any perplexity or opposition, and with a quiet and firm conviction that all is good. In contradistinction to us, who the wiser we are the less we understand the meaning of life, and see some evil irony in the fact that we suffer and die, these folk live and suffer, and they approach death and suffering with tranquility."

Tolstoy thus found his calling by reimagining the restorative power of faith. He didn't genuflect back to the orthodoxy of his earlier religious upbringing. He didn't launch a megachurch in the Russian sunbelt. He rediscovered in the Gospels the answers he was seeking. They lay in plainspoken precepts: rein in anger and lust; be kind to all men. He spent his remaining three decades as a Christian anarchist, preaching austerity, believing wholly in the Ten Commandments while holding the established church and authoritarian state in equal contempt. In this way, Tolstoy hit upon the elusive point and nipped his midlife crisis before it doomed what remained of his story.

Midlife Crisis Exhibit B: Had Tolstoy booked a therapy session with Carl Jung, he'd have heard a very different explanation for what was roiling his Russian soul in midlife. In his late thirties, Jung himself struggled mightily through his own major crisis. "A constant state of tension," as he described it. He suffered hallucinations, heard voices in his head, imagined blocks of stone raining down from above. Thunderstorms raged, episodes so severe he relied on yoga exercises to keep his emotions in check. "I stood helpless before an alien world;

everything in it seemed difficult and incomprehensible," Jung wrote in *Memories, Dreams, and Reflections*.

Having sampled midlife hell, and strongly influenced by Hinduism, Jung formulated his own map to the human life course. Like Dante's, Jung's scheme extends from morning to night. In the early hours, we exist as a "problem for others," our job eventually being to cobble together an ego. In the afternoon, it's to cope with conscious problems such as declaring independence from our parents and making a go of working, mating, and raising a family. In the evening hours when we reach old age, we "descend again into that condition where...we once more become something of a problem for others." Life in the mid- to late afternoon is particularly unsettling. Jung observed that there was a dramatic rise in depression among patients when they entered their forties, particularly for men. Neurotic traits buried from childhood often resurface—what the Grant Study referred to as "sleeper effects."

What's going on here, Jung said, is a standoff with one's unconscious. Like the sun, we grow weaker in the afternoon. We sense something's missing. It's akin to separation anxiety, but from what or whom? From the who we *used to be*, the who we were earlier in the day. We long for our former strength and effectiveness. We miss being Nurturer in Chief, Chief Family Medical Officer, Master or Mistress of the Family Universe. We feel less potent at the office and in the sack. Now is when daddy, having attained power and influence at work, feels increasingly feeble. He shimmies into jeans too skinny for someone his age. He so desperately wants it to be morning again that he can't keep his sunrise boner in his pants. A stay-at-home mom, no longer with kids at home, reasserts her authority as best she can. She turns into what Joseph Campbell uncharitably mansplained was a "power monster," a harridan who won't let her paunchy spouse snack in the media room lest he drip ketchup on the recliner.

What do you do to quell this aching longing for the you who used to be? How do you shuck off the lethargy and gloom? Accept it, Jung said. Come midlife, you need to acknowledge that the younger you wasn't built to last. Yet we assume otherwise, don't we? Studies show that we typically believe that the we we are now will be the we we'll always be. Psychologists call this "the end of history illusion." One of the authors of such a study, Daniel T. Gilbert, said that "At every age we think we're having the last laugh, and at every age we're wrong." It's useless to try to reclaim the old you, according to Jung. The old you can't be resurrected by anything so banal as sleeping with younger partners, or by overimbibing or undergoing cosmetic face work. Nor, Jung wrote (giving the fish eye to his mentor Freud), will you make peace with your old self by lying on a couch and obsessing over what demons lurk in your unconscious past. Instead, you must find a pathway to the core of your being, discover the *true self* that lies within. The only way forward is *individuation*. We need to try to make ourselves *whole*.

In Jungian terms, thus does midlife trigger an archetypal crisis. Murray Stein, a leading Jungian psychoanalyst, describes it this way: "You wake up one day and you're unexpectedly out of gas...the sweet milk of achievement is sour...the old patterns of coping and acting pinch your feet. The ability to prize your favorite objects—your 'works': children, possessions, power positions, accomplishments—has been stolen, and you are left wondering what happened last night? Where did it go?"

*   *   *

Midlife Crisis Exhibit C: There was a time in my lifetime when everywhere you turned you saw your future diminishing in front of your soon-to-be-failing eyes—you saw it in books, movies, *New Yorker* cartoons. The most depressing preview of what lay in store was Joseph Heller's 1974 novel, *Something Happened*. The blackest of comedies, it chronicles the wretched existence of Bob Slocum, middle-aged basket case. When Heller conceived the plot, his previous work, *Catch-22*, was already out but had not yet caught on. He had no clue as to what he'd do next. Then, one day as he brooded on his Fire Island deck, the plot details and the story's leading character came to him in a flash. It then took Heller a dozen difficult years to finish the book, the whole of his fearful forties and beyond.

A friend of mine, a veteran book editor, considers *Something Happened* "the best novel of the last half of the twentieth century." But he says he hasn't had the nerve to look at it since it came out, he was that bummed the first time through. I hadn't gone back to it either, not until I was researching midlife and forced myself to reread the book.

Strictly speaking, I realized this time around, it isn't midlife per se that turns a well-adjusted human being into a contemptible, cowardly jerk. Bob Slocum was always a contemptible, cowardly jerk, afraid of the dark from the day he was born, fearful that he would open his eyes and it would *still* be dark. Midlife, however, has loosened his screws even further. Slocum misses being young, fears getting old, disparages his colleagues (of whom he's terrified), finds promiscuous sex with younger women less pleasurable than it's cracked up to be. He daydreams about divorcing his wife but is overwhelmed by the mechanics of filing for a divorce. At the dinner table each night, his teenage daughter taunts and ridicules him. His prepubescent son "wants to cast me away and leave me behind for reasons he won't give me." It gets even worse. A third child, born with brain damage, is a social embarrassment. This is not an admirable person, it's clear from page one. Anyone who's read the book will remember the immortal opening lines: "I get the willies when I see closed doors... the sight of a closed door is... enough to make me dread that something horrible is happening behind it, something that is going to affect me adversely." The dreadful "something" that happens happens at the very end of the story, which I won't give away. In between, and relentlessly so, Bob Slocum's midlife doesn't amount to an existential hill of beans. Writing in the *New York Times Book Review*, Kurt Vonnegut referred to Slocum's predicament as a "written-to-death situation"—that situation being existential angst in general, life at the perilous elbow in particular.

Tolstoy found his way out of midlife darkness through the unfettered teachings of Jesus. Jung found his way via the pathway to individuation. Slocum, too, sees a speck of light at the end of midlife's dark tunnel: "I know at last what I want to be when I grow up," he says. "When I grow up I want to be a little boy." In other words, Slocum misses the person he used to be, exactly what Jung had warned us about. "I miss the forsaken child," Slocum says.

Just a couple of years after *Something Happened* appeared, another something happened, according to Tom Wolfe. It was a cultural shift that wasn't remotely anticipated or alluded to once in the 569 pages of Heller's grim but hilarious novel. Bob Slocum's suburban neighbors made a mad dash for daylight. However they could pull it off, they were determined to get *whole*. In his zeitgeist-defining essay "The Me Decade," Wolfe chortled over how every Tom, Dick, and Harriet in the suburbs was working to reboot by emulating affluent seekers such as those pictured in *Bob & Carol & Ted & Alice*, who *in turn* were following in the barefootsteps of hippie communalists. Middle-class dunderheads were leaving hearth and kin to make solitary pilgrimages to the Wailing Wall or Konark Sun Temple. Or they were spending their weekends getting Rolfed; or being indoctrinated into est or Arica. It was, in Wolfe's view, the start of the "Third Great Awakening" in American spiritual history.

What everyone had awakened *to* was how easy it was to remake, remodel, elevate, or otherwise transform one's existing self into a more enlightened and *whole* human being. Everyone suddenly felt entitled to write their own ending to the well-worn Clairol slogan: "If I have only one life, let me live it as a blonde!" Just take out "blonde" and fill in the blank you wanted to be: Free spirit? Transcendental meditator? Primal screamer? Moonie? Nowhere in the long essay does Wolfe mention what lay at the core of all this questing—the search for a meaningful life story.

With the benefit of hindsight, we may take a more considered view of the Me Decade. It was the start of the American "Soul Rush," in the words of Marion Goldman, a professor of religion. It was the dawn of the age of "spiritual privilege." Suddenly, we could mix and match ideas and traditions from all over the world and throughout history to try to find some semblance of spiritual fulfillment. And there was quite a smorgasbord out there to sample: Zen, yoga, tai chi, African drumming, workshops on integrating the mind, body, spirit, and psyche. When I was a kid, all we had on the spirituality menu was a *shul* on the one hand, and on the other, a

downtown Russian-style bathhouse, the *shvitz*, a dank labyrinth of rooms reeking of pine-scented disinfectant, where for
a little extra you could pay a husky Eastern European attendant to pummel your back with a *yenik* of palm fronds.

The great Soul Rush began in California—where else?
Ground zero was the Esalen Institute in Big Sur; yes, the
place that inspired the shooting location for Don Draper's
mountaintop epiphany, the one that made him (more or less)
whole in the final episode. The national media had a field day
with Esalen back then: nudity in the coed hot tubs; mind-
bending trips fueled by LSD; ego-blasting encounter groups
with uncontrolled hugging and weeping. Esalen was easy
to make fun of. But in fact, Esalen's magical hot springs fed
directly into the mainstream, bringing the New Age along
with it. Back in the day at *Esquire*, George Leonard, one
of Esalen's early apostles, wrote regular features under the
rubric "Ultimate Fitness." He applied his mastery of aikido—
George was a black belt—to improving not just a yuppie's
physical condition, but clarifying his mind and enhancing his
spirit in the process. It's called realizing our *human potential*. Esalen was where the pioneers of humanistic psychology
gathered for symposia that emphasized the primacy of *personal growth*. Esalen incubated the notion that each of us has
an inalienable right to find spiritual and emotional satisfaction *without* having to set foot in a traditional house of worship. Big Sur was its own church. It was here at Esalen that
a new religion was born: "the religion of *no* religion." You
could baptize yourself in a spiritual hot tub filled with leading-
edge psychologists, futurists, mystics, and philosophers, from
Abraham Maslow to Aldous Huxley to Alan Watts. And on
any given day, run into a familiar face in the dining lodge—
Dyan Cannon and Cary Grant, Jane Fonda, etc.

It was, and still is, easy to punch holes in Esalen. It was male-dominated, pulsing with erotic and psychedelic avails, all comprehensively documented in Jeffrey J. Kripal's mostly reverent history of Esalen. There was psychodrama aplenty. Gestalt psychologist Fritz Perls, an Esalen fixture, traveled to Hollywood, where he led a poolside encounter session at Jennifer Jones's home. Natalie Wood was assigned the "hot seat." Frustrated in his attempts to pry loose anything that amounted to a closely guarded secret (*gestalt* denotes a whole that's more than the sum of its parts, so you can't hold anything back), Perls lost it, calling Wood "a spoiled brat" and attempted to put her on his knee for a good spanking. Rushing to her defense, Roddy McDowall offered to fight Perls. Wood stalked out of the party without saying ciao. Not long after, according to George Leonard's account, the same thing, minus the spanking, happened between Perls and Tuesday Weld.

As part of my research, and with Linda along to protect me from evil shamans hiding among the giant redwoods, I signed up for a workshop at Esalen. The hope was to gain a deeper, more holistic understanding of the Esalen mystique. I'd been curious about the place ever since Leonard started writing for *Esquire*. Though it's evolved over the years—it's in part a corporate conference center now—my expectations ran high, and in many ways Esalen delivered on them. You really do find yourself slipping into "being mode." There's not a more spectacular beautiful place on earth: the ocean crashing against the rocks, the seabirds, seals, sunsets, they're all timelessly breathtaking. The coed hot springs are exactly as advertised. They leave a body wholer than ever. The workshop itself? Well, let's put it this way: not my cup of oolong. The facilitator of the week-long session opened the agenda by slipping on a red clown's nose and a rainbow-colored Afro wig. He then performed a pantomime—not my favorite form of performance art—which I was too unenlightened or impatient to comprehend. We were then handed cards with animals printed on them (I was a beaver, Linda was a squirrel, if memory serves). We were instructed to hold our card to our forehead without looking at it—a variation on what binge-drinking frat boys call the "forehead idiot game." We were invited to roam the room to find the only other person with the same creature on his or her head.

It was then that I decided that my week-long plunge into wholeness would be better served by trekking the incomparable cliffs and forests of Big Sur. At night when we returned from those hikes, I read Henry Miller's memoir of his years living along the jagged coastline. This was decades before there was Esalen and a religion of no religion. No, that's not right. Before there was *Esalen*. A religion of no religion had been in place for a very long time. Every morning, Miller writes in *Big Sur and the Oranges of Hieronymus Bosch*, he opened his cabin door and raised his hand in benediction. He blessed the trees, the birds, the dogs, the cats. He blessed the flowers, the pomegranates, the thorny cactus. He blessed men and women everywhere. "An inviting land, but hard to conquer," Miller said of Big Sur. It was "the face of the earth as the Creator intended it to look."

Meanwhile, back in the real world and living in the now, it's reasonable for us to wonder: Did our growing awareness of our own potential, our quest for wholeness, our adoption of a religion of no religion, reduce the severity of what we used to think of as the "midlife crisis"? Or was there *never* a generalizable midlife curse to begin with, Tolstoy, Jung, and Bob Slocum's considerable traumas notwithstanding?

Whatever happened, as Dan McAdams observes, by the end of the 1980s we were no longer moaning about our middle-age crisis, we were cracking jokes about it, telling ourselves to enjoy the fun because sooner rather than later life would return to normal. Are we that much more enlightened and sure of ourselves now? Is it our daily use of homeopathic eyedrops that did the trick? Our disciplined insistence on sustainable seafood? Our ten minutes of Hatha each morning? Have we been narcotized by digital technology? Has a new generation of antidepressants put a lid on the midlife blues? Or was there really *no such thing* as a generalizable midlife crisis embedded in the universal human life course?

The fact is, hardly anybody today refers to the midlife crisis with the same foreboding as they did back in Bob Slocum's day. Indeed, numerous studies over the past couple of decades reached the conclusion that midlife itself has little to do with whatever torment we're feeling in our forties and fifties. A paper in the journal *Gerontology* reminds us that twenty-five-year-old men also buy red sports cars. If, in my early forties, I *did* set new goals for myself, it was because I'd either succeeded in, failed at, or gotten tired of my old goals. It takes a while to even have goals, after all. At twenty-five I didn't have any, so what was to reset?

Simply stated, there's "no evidence for specific changes in personality due to age," one extensive midlife survey concluded. "What changes...are your roles and the issues that matter most to you. People may think their personality has changed as they age, but it is their habits that change, their vigor and health, their responsibilities and circumstances— not their basic personality." The report noted that if you're reasonably content and emotionally together at twenty-five, you'll be reasonably content and emotionally together a few decades later. Indeed, studies show that in many professional fields one's forties are our most productive decade. They point to how seniors look back on their forties and fifties as their most fondly recalled chapters. "The stereotype that people become cranky and rigid as they age does not hold up," one study said. How we feel about our life story depends on the *day*, not the season.

But some studies have turned up tantalizing gender differences. Women in midlife become "less guilty about aggressive and egocentric impulses." About time! Men grow "more receptive to affiliative and nurturant promptings." About time for that, too! Men more commonly take stock of their accomplishments and attempt to map out fresh goals. Why more men than women? Women, a researcher speculates, are by nature more "self-reflective" *throughout* their lives. So, reading between the lines, it doesn't come as such a swift kick in the groin to discover that life doesn't always deliver on its promises.

8   *Interlude: Other Voices*

Throughout this project I opened conversations with a diverse group of men and women who were willing to answer intimate questions about how their life stories were playing out. I wasn't after stories of operatic dimension, lives wracked with unusual distress or graced with saintly purpose. These were ordinary people who ranged from twenty-somethings to seniors. As far as I know, no one was filthy rich or destitute. No one was famous. There's little reason to think any of them will be remembered a hundred years from now. I mostly wanted a reality check on how we think of our life as a story, with chapters, characters, turning points, a beginning, a middle, and, sooner or later, an end.

A few people I talked to were leery of my snooping into other people's life stories. It was a dicey business, they admonished. Who died and made me Plutarch? A friend looked at me cross-eyed when I told him I was working on a book about what the point was. Like Oscar and Felix, we've been bickering about anything and everything for decades, going back to when we were young editors in New York City. My Oscar can be nettlesome. (His wife, only half kiddingly, says her tombstone will read "I Lie Corrected.") But Oscar is uncommonly astute, and I value his counsel. And it's not as if there's a sage under every lamppost. In fact, I just typed "sage" into the Craigslist search box and it returned exactly one result—a Chicago party planner.

"You're talking about the meaning of life, right?" Oscar asked. "That's 'the point' you're referring to?"

I nodded, bracing for the controlled aggression I've come to know and love. Oscar advised me to be extra careful. He said not everyone has the "luxury"—adequate time or means—to go looking for what life's point is, as if access to the answer is reserved for the top 1 percent, akin to copping a Hamptons beach-parking sticker. He said readers with kids to raise and/or aging parents who require care, those working double shifts or who can't find jobs, people who don't live in New York or L.A., billions everywhere who devoutly believe in a supreme being, all these and others were primed to be pissed off at someone like me mucking around "the point." Not only that, Oscar continued, clearly looking to fire another missile, I'd had a career that wasn't "typical" and would strike many as hard to relate to.

I was tempted to push back but held my tongue. The older I get, the more inclined I am to let things go. Who has time to spar? In younger days I would have launched into a sermon on how finding meaning isn't a luxury. How there are studies that show that those who struggle to find purpose suffer from a broad range of emotional disorders, phobias, and substance abuse, up and down the socioeconomic ladder. That finding meaning can be *more* challenging for those who are reasonably comfortable—more choices, distractions, superficial wants that scramble priorities. How throughout history it didn't matter if you were rich or poor, a pharaoh or Neanderthal, you faced the same bleak abyss. Surveys indicate that *personal attachments* are the prime determinants of life satisfaction, far surer predictors than income, age, gender, race, or GPA. As for my career, Oscar and I both know it's been more erratic than calculated, built on a lucky break that happened when I was too young to know what I was doing. But no, my life's not "typical." I was going to ask him whose is, but checked myself there as well.

I thanked Oscar for his feedback and concern. I told him I'd be mindful. And that I'd make sure to say loud and clear how grateful I am—*I'm grateful!*—that I now could take the time to figure out why I'm here, why any of us are here.

Oscar and I then had a brief spat over something I don't exactly remember, but I'm sure it was existentially pressing— e.g., who was the better horn player, Lester Young or Coleman Hawkins?

Unbowed, I plowed ahead and engaged complete strangers on matters of life, death, and meaning. Saying nothing about any scribbler upstairs, I prodded them with questions such as these:

Do you ever think about the so-called meaning of life?

A man in his mid-sixties said that he does all the time. He and his wife have taken to reading aloud to each other. When you read serious fiction, he said, you're always contending with what matters in life. (That answer earned a gold star in my book.)

Looking back on your life, what's been the least meaningful chapter?

A woman in her fifties said it was the four years she'd spent working as a lawyer. "Dehumanizing—fifty-hour workweeks and systematic pressure to obtain billable hours."

If your life story were to be narrated, whose voice would you like to hear read it?

A woman in her mid-twenties said Joseph Campbell, explaining that she likes to think of her life in mythological terms, as a kind of journey.

When you were growing up, was there a particular character in a book you identified with?

A woman in her early thirties mentioned a book called *The Road to Damietta* by Scott O'Dell. She said it's about a young girl who falls in love with Saint Francis, renounces her possessions, cuts off her hair, and ministers to lepers in order to remain close to Francis. She'd found the point.

Where do you think your story will go from here—in five years or in ten?

A man in his late fifties said he doesn't have a bucket list, then shifted into talking about his sons. One's in his late twenties, the other in his early thirties. The man worries that they're floundering professionally, so if he did have a bucket list, it would consist of doing something to help his sons figure things out.

What, if anything, would you like to outlive you?

"My daughter," said a man in his forties. "I can't think of anything else."

Talk to me about time. How conscious are you of it?

A woman in late midlife said that technology's causing her to be "hyperfocused," but not on anything she thinks is worth focusing on. She said this is the first time in her life she routinely loses track of time. It's not the dreaded onset, she was quick to clarify. It's all those cable channels with nothing worth watching. It's TMZ, YouTube, Facebook, Pinterest, the Yahoo! News page. The result, if you ask me, is that we pay what's been called "continuous partial attention" to everything and full attention to little or nothing. I read somewhere that people fifty and older spend an average of about thirty hours a week online. Assuming you have twenty years left to live, you'll spend a full three and a half of those years checking stock quotes and pinning photos of holiday sweaters.

Most people seemed flattered to be asked questions like the ones above. As they became more comfortable, they'd admit to a host of *coulda's* and *shoulda's*. And *woulda*, had not *x*, *y*, or *z* gotten in the way: Went to the wrong school. Did what my parents wanted. (Or didn't listen to my parents, and for once they were right.) Had mouths to feed, what else could I do? Was young and foolish. Didn't have the guts. Had I only known then what I know now.

These cascading *woulda's* and *shoulda's* came as no surprise. I'd heard them all before. Some years ago, I wrote a book about why many of us confuse money with what really matters, carrying on a tortured relationship with money that lasts over the human life course. Money drives families apart; screws up priorities; befogs the point. One of the takeaways was that we're not altogether sure *what* money's good for. Or we think it allows for "the abstract satisfaction of every wish," as Schopenhauer said.

To help readers put money in its proper place, I included an exercise I borrowed from a financial adviser. It asks that you imagine you have only twenty-four hours to live—so think hard about "Who you did not get to be" and "What you did not get to do." You'd think, wouldn't you, that there'd be a huge number of different answers to "Who did you not get to be?" and "What did you not get to do?" But there aren't. Our answers fall into a handful of categories: Didn't give enough back. Didn't make peace with a loved one. Worked too hard. Wasn't creative enough.

The interviewees for this book echoed those answers. A

good many of the *woulda's* and *shoulda's* were connected to a perceived untapped talent of some sort. "I wasn't creative enough," basically. A middle-aged woman told me she still fantasizes about being the lead singer in a rock band. A middle-aged man secretly thinks he's the second coming of Johnny Cash. Someone else is trying to reclaim a passion for painting that's been dormant since college. A good friend's auditing a course in journal writing.

As for what traveling through the elbow specifically sounds like, here's what some people said:

A soon-to-be midlifer, on the road to a PhD, says she's experiencing the most disappointing chapter of her life. She wishes she'd never started down the academic path. Almost from the beginning she realized she'd make a mistake but "didn't have the courage to risk being perceived as a failure." What she didn't anticipate, she says, was how "useless an experience" her thesis would turn out to be. Useless as far as any knowledge it's generating. *Hopelessly* useless as far as getting a job goes. She's been looking for a job for a year and a half. She says if she could turn the clock back she'd pursue an MBA. "I'm feeling overqualified and completely lacking in basic skills," she reports.

One man, fifty years old, an accountant who lives in a midsized midwestern city, goes on and on about how happy he is at work. Career satisfaction, however, isn't doing much for the rest of his life. He says he knows "happiness comes from the inside" and yet he has talked repeatedly to a friend, a plastic surgeon, about getting a hair transplant. He keeps putting it off. "It might change people's perception of me," he says, "but inside I'd still be the same."

A fifty-year-old woman, born in the United States and

now living abroad, longs for "the writing life." After earning a graduate degree in English Lit, she took a job in the corporate world, eventually married, and had three kids. The birth of the first she regards as the most meaningful chapter of her life. During her maternity leave she started a novel, then worked on the book for the next decade. It was eventually published after numerous rejections. With children still at home, she says she's able to write only occasionally, a book review now and then. She yearns to do more. She says had she known then what she knows now, she'd have started writing when she was right out of school, when there was so much more time. She wishes she'd pushed herself harder, had been more "tenacious and confident." It wasn't procrastination that did her in, she said, something more "insidious and detrimental." She didn't think she was "any good," so she held back.

A man in his mid-forties, living in Northern California, talks glowingly about how much his parents, a museum director and a curator, loved their careers. Their jobs were also their hobbies, he says, which is the ideal. Their personal passions carried right through the weekend, when they enjoyed going to auctions and restoring furniture together. He says he regrets having spent most of his own career in a corporate setting, where he built his "work muscles at the expense of his play muscles."

A woman only now approaching the elbow lives in the Northeast and spent two years counseling victims of sex abuse in the military. She says she found the job frustrating because of how little progress is being made to confront the issue, which is widespread. Just "a lot of noise in the media," she says. She's currently working for a nonprofit devoted to women's health issues, a mission she's passionate about but the job doesn't allow for "personal expression"; she's tethered to official talking points. Recently she stopped drinking, which "had gotten to be a problem." Moving into midlife marks a clear-cut pivot point, she says. When we're past our twenties, she believes, we need to assume full responsibility for the choices we make.

A woman in her late forties with a run of health problems—Crohn's disease, a misdiagnosed glandular condition followed by two strokes—says she's lucky to have a good relationship with her husband, knock wood, who's there to take care of her. Things are as good as can be expected, she says.

An insurance broker in Virginia, mid-sixties, recounts various personal misfortunes, concluding: "They made me aware of life's impermanence—that anything can happen at any time." He tells me he was drawn to Buddhist teachings in the hope they'd help him cope with adversities yet to come.

Now and then in a conversation, I'd reach back for the high, hard heat and throw out the $64,000 question:

The point. The meaning of your life. Do you ever think about that?

A few people grew peevish, exactly what Oscar had warned would happen. They said they were too busy surviving to gaze at their navels. Indeed. The real wealth of 90 percent of American families has been declining for years. Single parents and working couples struggle to find enough time to spend with their kids. Millions of middle-agers are woefully short of having what it takes to retire.

"What do you mean, 'the point'?" one woman demanded. When I explained, she reacted as if I'd said I was compiling a guide to artisanal cheeses. "Oh," she exclaimed in a startlingly loud voice. "The meaning of life! How *timely*!"

She was spot-on. The point *is* timely. It's been timely since time began. I held my fire, though. I could have mentioned that the point was timely for Adam and Eve the instant they bit into the apple. It was timely back when we wrote with sticks and stones, when anonymous Mesopotamians carved *The Epic of Gilgamesh* onto a clay slab: "The life you seek, you will never find." It was timely when Lao Tzu calligraphed the *Tao Te Ching* ("Heaven and earth are not sentimental; they regard all things as dispensable"). It was timely for the Greeks, who, if they made it out of infancy alive, went on to live almost as long as we do. It was timely when Christ returned to show us the Way. It was no less timely two millennia later when Nietzsche announced that God was dead: "Do we not feel the breath of empty space? How shall we comfort ourselves?" And timely when Bertrand Russell, philosopher/mathematician/activist/confirmed atheist, declared in his autobiography that the point was three things rolled together: love, because love relieves loneliness; knowledge, because knowledge enables us (in theory) to know how the universe works; empathy, because empathy allows us to hear the cries of pain of the oppressed in a world of poverty and pain. It was *still* timely when *Time* magazine reminded us that God was *still* dead on its famous 1966 cover. And it was as timely as ever two years after that when, on the very first page, the *Whole Earth Catalog* echoed what Nietzsche had said a century prior: "We are as gods, and might as well get good at it."

And it was timely when jazz critic Nat Hentoff (with his CAPS LOCK key evidently jammed) wrote a letter to bassist Charles Mingus. It was in reply to a letter the musician had written Hentoff on the kind of night "you're feeling the pain... and the larger questions that seem to have no answers loom up before your eyes":

FOR ME A MAN'S MEANING, THE REASON HE HAS TO KEEP ON LIVING, IS THAT WERE HE TO LIVE... THOUSANDS OF YEARS HE WOULD NEVER FULFILL ALL HIS POSSIBILITIES, NEVER COMMUNICATE OR CREATE ALL HE IS CAPABLE OF. SO HE MUST USE WHAT TIME HE HAS CREATING NOW FOR THE FUTURE AND UTILIZE THE PAST ONLY TO HELP THE FUTURE, NOT AS A RAZOR STROP FOR GUILTS AND FEARS THAT INHIBIT HIS VERY BEING. OR LIKE IT SAID AT THE END OF A LABOR UNION SONG I LIKED A LOT WHEN I WAS A KID: WHAT IT MEANS IS, TAKE IT EASY, BUT TAKE IT.

I DON'T KNOW IF THIS HAS MADE SENSE OR IS OF ANY USE BUT IT'S WHAT I THINK.

NAT.

But however timely the point was, is, and will always be, it's not so easily talked about. At dinner one night, I grilled a few friends about what makes their lives worth living. They were far more interested in assessing the pig's bladder and the other dozen small plates on the table. Looking to outflank them, I resorted to a familiar party game. If you were stranded on a desert island, what would get you through your isolation? My friends, let's face it, aren't a particularly representative focus group unless you're plumbing the psychographic proclivities of sardonic New York City gourmands in midlife. One of them, after thinking about what he'd need to fight off isolation and despair, said he'd pray that "eighteen pounds of marijuana" washed ashore. Another, looking gnomic, took mild exception, saying if there was booze on the island he'd opt for lansoprazole, a gastric-acid inhibitor. If there wasn't booze, then a generous supply of Wellbutrin, the widely prescribed antidepressant.

9   *Breathing Space*

With each passing day in midlife, the past grows longer, our future shorter. While we know precisely how long the past is, the length of the future's uncertain. Recently, a person I hired at *Esquire* fresh out of college dropped dead at age fifty-nine. Just a kid, right? Looking to the shrinking future, we may or may not have plans for what to do with it. Or our plan is to *have* a plan before it's too late. Or we may not even have that, in which case the present and future appear blank or bleak. Plans or no plans, the past will grow longer still, the future that much shorter. A zero-sum game. It explains why in midlife the writer-in-residence is restless as a cat, hungry to take the story in a viable new direction. "At 46 one must be a miser; only have time for essentials," Virginia Woolf wrote in her diary.

Okay, so maybe it's not an all-out *crisis*. But something's for sure going on.

An ex-pat living in Paris laments in an op-ed about how it feels to be a woman in her mid-forties who's marooned in "the world's epicenter of existentialism." She complains that waiters call her "Madam" without so much as an ironic wink. (*Ouch.*) She finds there are "no grown-ups anymore," everyone's just "winging it." If there's a bright side, it's that she no longer needs to pretend she likes jazz or feel inadequate that she doesn't know how to cook a leek. (Really—what's so hard about cooking a leek?)

Or maybe you're just feeling bad about your neck, as Nora Ephron did.

Or you're in your early forties and you know your marriage is decent and everyone's healthy but you hear yourself humming Peggy Lee's "Is That All There Is?" in the shower.

That rosy-cheeked baby on the cover of *The Life and Times of My Enduring Self*? All she required when that photo was snapped was food, warmth, and security. Eventually, we call out for more. Just as a baby needs food, Jung said, the human psyche cries out for meaning. Jung reckoned that fully a third of his patients suffered from nothing other than the perceived "senselessness and aimlessness" of their lives. And *every* patient over thirty-five, he said, borrowing from Hamlet, battled the sense that the world felt "weary, stale, flat, and unprofitable."

Meaning isn't a luxury. Meaning is crucial. We have a "*will* to meaning," Viktor E. Frankl declared. To be human is to live in three dimensions—the physical, the mental, and the spiritual. It's this spiritual dimension that compels us to seek answers to why we exist. Frankl is rightly celebrated for his extraordinary *Man's Search for Meaning*, which was originally published in the United States under the less-than-winning title *From Death-Camp to Existentialism*. The book, which I commend to you if you haven't read it, has by now sold in the tens of millions. It's not strictly speaking a memoir of the Holocaust, though Frankl's personal experiences in Nazi camps are sharply drawn and affecting. He uses the horrific setting to lay out the principles of what he called "logotherapy," an analytic framework for treating emotional issues and addiction. Among these principles is a need for "a defiant spirit," an insistence on finding purpose in the face of powerful challenges. On a grander scale, logotherapy (*logos*, the Greek word for "meaning") is a "complete blueprint for living and dying well," says psychologist Paul T. P. Wong. The concept is founded on the premise that life has meaning under all circumstances, even the most adverse, and that our principal motivation for living is finding the value and purpose in it. "Self-transcendence" is, at the core, connecting to something larger than yourself. This calls for continual self-improvement, cultivating faith, courage, and compassion.

How does one accomplish this, exactly? You won't find specific to-do lists in Frankl's writings. No ten easy steps. "[The] true meaning of life is to be discovered in the world rather than within man or his own psyche," Frankl wrote. The more you offer yourself to a cause or person you love, the closer you get to finding meaning in life. "To do the useful thing, to say the courageous thing, to contemplate the beautiful thing: that is enough for one man's life," as T. S. Eliot wrote. According to Frankl, you might find the useful, the courageous, the beautiful in nature or in art or in work, or by knowing at least one human being in all his or her uniqueness. And you will find it in overcoming suffering. What each of us needs, Frankl said, is "not a tensionless state but rather the striving and struggling for a worthwhile goal, a freely chosen task."

In another of his books, *The Doctor and the Soul*, which is more technical than *Man's Search for Meaning*, Frankl devotes a lengthy chapter to the meaning of work. Given its centrality in our lives, work commonly gets the credit and more often the blame for whether we deem our lives to be fulfilling. We spend a lot of time at work. Our self-worth is on the line. Frankl expounds on what's at stake. He distinguishes the social status or material rewards we derive from work from the degree of meaning a job offers. No occupation per se offers the road to salvation, he says. You can be a doctor or a nurse, both professions providing necessary and admirable services, but the meaning to be derived lies beyond making the right diagnoses and incisions, or drawing blood and cleaning wounds. These tasks, while important, won't satisfy the human spirit. "To practice all the arts of medicine is not to practice the art of medicine," Frankl says. The *art* of medicine is finding the right words to say to a patient. Now apply this to the modern doctor's predicament. Exhaustion and overwork, a young physician writes in the *Times*, are among the reasons doctors are twice as likely to commit suicide as nondoctors. There's not enough time to look for the right words, so the work lacks meaningfulness. Being the right *human being* is what counts, Frankl says. This applies to any trade, any job, white collar or blue, however menial.

Having *no* job can be cataclysmic. Unemployment leads directly to the Existential Vacuum, Frankl says. "The jobless man experiences the emptiness of his time as inner emptiness, as an emptiness of his consciousness. He feels useless because he is unoccupied. Having no work, he thinks life has no meaning." This is precisely the message Pope Francis delivered in 2015, when he issued his encyclical on the plight of the planet. Francis laments not only the environmental crisis that's been brought on by the rampant consumption of fossil fuels, he observes "how the orientation of the economy has favoured a kind of technological process in which the costs of production are reduced by laying off workers and replacing them with machines." Work, the pope declares, "is a necessity, part of the meaning of life on this earth, a path to growth."

Personally, I'm drawn to Frankl's contention that meaning

is to be found in our acts and deeds; in the degree to which we encounter and experience others; in how we overcome the challenges we face. But I'm presumptuous enough to add a crucial ingredient that Frankl and the pope overlooked—the need to make a *story* out of it all. We have a body and we have a brain, no argument there. Each is vital, obviously. The body and the brain allow us to live in the physical and the mental dimensions. They provide conclusive evidence (in the form of sensations and ideas) that yes, we do indeed exist. But neither the body nor the brain, if said brain lacks a narrative mechanism, can drive the story home to us. That's where our friend in the attic comes in. Until something (the scribbler) whips our physical sensations and mental capacities into a story, it won't make sense. This is clearly a process best managed in proximity to where our memories are housed—the brain. Which is why, thanks to hundreds of thousands of years of human evolution, the writer-in-residence resides *in* the brain and not elsewhere, such as the pyloric sphincter or an equally intolerable place to write.

The search for meaning, while fundamental, can wear a body down. Especially in midlife. One steel-gray afternoon, staring at a halfway-frozen Lake Michigan, I found myself thinking about my father's all-too-brief passage through the elbow. While I don't remember him as a melancholy person, certainly not a depressive, it occurred to me that my father would often gaze expressionlessly at nothing in particular. He was in early middle age, forty-three, with two young kids and a wife at home. He was living under the sword of heart disease at a time when there weren't the miracle drugs and surgical procedures we now take for granted.

Staring at the lake, I remembered that each week, on

Sunday night, right around the time the *Ed Sullivan Show* came on, my father heaved a sigh and said to no one in particular: "Well, back to the salt mines tomorrow." I was confused by that. He was a microbiologist, not a salt miner. He didn't tote a pickaxe to work, he carried a battered brown leather briefcase stuffed with notes for some journal article he was writing. On Saturday mornings, he'd often drive me down to his lab at the hospital, a crystal palace of beakers, funnels, and flasks. He delighted in showing me how microscopes worked. He fired up Bunsen burners to demonstrate chemical reactions. I remember the smell of the place—faintly metallic. He loved everything about his world and was recognized for his contributions to research. But maybe it wasn't enough. The weekly sigh, what was *that* all about?

Staring out at the lake, I made a connection. When Viktor Frankl proposed that the search for meaning is endemic, he wasn't saying that we necessarily sit around disconsolate all day. (Although some of us do.) But he did argue that the need for meaning plays gotcha. "The Sunday neurosis," Frankl called it. It settles in when the rush of a busy week subsides. The busier we are during the week, the faster we run, the harder we crash come Sunday. Joseph Heller's Bob Slocum suffered from it. "Sundays are deadly. Spare time is ruinous," he says midway through *Something Happened*. My father, otherwise never to be compared with the objectionable Slocum, had a case of it as well, I realized on that day by the lake. He'd been in overdrive his entire life. His parents had died young. Orphaned, he worked his way through high school and university while helping to support his younger brothers. He graduated from college at some ridiculously young age—nineteen? Failing to get into medical school thanks to the ethnic-quota system—at Yale, for example, the applications of Jewish students were clearly marked with an "H"—he earned an advanced degree in microbiology without breaking stride. He was kept out of the war so he could work on a new generation of antibiotics. He was thirty when my sister was born; thirty-five when I came along; forty-three when he wrote the book that my mother always kept prominently displayed, *Antimicrobial Therapy in Medical Practice*; forty-four when he suffered his first heart attack; forty-seven when he died. He had barely made it to the elbow when he was heaving those Sunday sighs just as Ed Sullivan came on. Maybe what he needed was a time-out, a chance to regroup. Sitting there by the lake, I wondered if he'd been able to take a brief time-out it might have made a life-saving difference.

A thought then came to me: What if life, like a hockey game, was divided into three distinct periods? Biologists already think of the human life course that way. There are three distinct phases of growth: progressive, stable, regressive. In life-story terms, what if period one ended at age forty, period two at sixty, and period three ran to the bitter end? Now, here's the interesting part: What if there were two intermissions, as in a hockey game, one between the first and second periods, the other between the second and third? *Everyone*—rich or poor, salaried, hourly, or unemployed—would be eligible for these sabbaticals (not just tenured professors). Knowing that a hiatus was upcoming, you could plan for it long in advance, never incurring a lousy change fee if your sabbatical called for air travel. These intermissions would not be construed as vacations. They'd be working sessions, offsite retreats, at which you and the writer upstairs could stop, take a breath, and gain your bearings. The agenda? Three bullet points, that's it. They'd apply to both sabbatical number one and sabbatical number two:

- *Review* whether your life story's been meaningful so far.
- *Assess* whether it's meaningful at the moment.
- *Brainstorm* what it would take to keep it meaningful or make it meaningful before it's too late. In other words, figure out what it would take for you to die satisfied.

Imagine the difference it could have made had Tolstoy, Jung, or Bob Slocum been afforded the luxury of an offsite retreat before they turned forty. Imagine if Tony Soprano, Walter White, or Don Draper had had the benefit of a premidlife sabbatical. What if *you*, assuming you're now in midlife or beyond, had taken a sabbatical, given yourself an honest performance review, assessed whether your life was meaningful enough, and if not, devised a plan to do something about it, if and when circumstances allowed? And if financial circumstances didn't allow, you'd use the offsite to figure out how to make some changes, if only in attitude?

So let's imagine what such an offsite might be like. You're about to navigate the hazardous elbow. You and your scribbler are in a meeting room at a Courtyard Marriott. There's an easel holding a giant notepad, a box of colored markers, a tray of pastries on the table. Cell phone's in airplane mode. Imagine that the scribbler's gone golf-resort casual for the occasion: he's wearing a Tommy Bahama polo shirt and pleated Bermudas, dark ankle-length socks, fisherman's sandals, and a Tilley hat, which is not a good look for him.

If, like me, you've been forced to sit through an offsite or two, you're doubtless familiar with the drill. The presiding alpha dog, in this case you, steers the discussion from a seat closest to the doughnuts. A toady in the room, in this case it's your scribbler, "volunteers" to take notes on the giant pad, ripping off sheets as he goes, taping them up one by one on the walls around the room. It takes maybe two minutes before the agenda you came with—*Review! Assess! Brainstorm!*—is placed on hold. Why? Someone raises a question nobody's planned for but should have. It goes like this: I know we're here to try and get to the point, but don't you think we ought to know what the point actually *is* before we figure out how to get there? Whereupon you and the scribbler start throwing out possible answers to what the point actually is, the scribbler capturing them on the giant pad:

THE POINT IS . . .

FAITH? HOPE? CHARITY?

"BIRTHS, DEATHS, MARRIAGES?"

SUCCESS? ACHIEVEMENT? MAKING A DIFFERENCE?

LEGACY?

PROCREATION?

PERSONAL "GROWTH"?

GOD OR GODS ?

KINDNESS (DOING UNTO OTHERS, ETC.), COMPASSION?

KNOWLEDGE? WISDOM?

MONEY? FAME? GETTING LAID?

FAMILY? FRIENDS? COMMUNITY?

HUMOR?!

WORK (DOING WHAT YOU LOVE)?

ART (IN THE BROADEST SENSE)?

NATURE?

LOVE?

HAPPINESS? ☺

The scribbler, irritable over how things are dragging out—writers hate meetings like this—is inclined to go with happiness and the hell with it. He just wants to get out of there. The point is happiness. To be happy all the time. If he'd take a step back, however, he'd realize that trying to make a life story entirely about happiness is a one-way ticket to self-indulgence and disappointment. Happiness isn't a goal, it's an outcome. Happiness is a by-product of something else.

Thus do retreats go south. The goal is to leave "aligned," "strategically focused," "everyone on the same page." But nothing on the list taped to the wall makes it through the gauntlet. All it takes is for someone to piss on a given item and off it comes. Art? Too esoteric. God or gods? Divisive. Nature? What if you're allergic? The aim of the offsite is to leave with a takeaway grander than you could ever have come up with back at home. Sadly, that's not what usually happens. At offsites, it's been my experience, what usually happens is a reshuffling of what little you knew going in.

You look at the scribbler. He looks at you. An impasse. Okay, let's go at this from a different angle, you say finally. Would it help to know whose point we're talking about here? My current self's point? My ideal self's point? My true self's point? Whose sabbatical *is* this, anyway?

By the time we reach midlife, the storywriter isn't at all sure which of our assortment of selves she's working for. Let's not call it an identity *crisis*. Let's call it an identity *skirmish*, reserving the c-word for what you went through when you were a teenager and couldn't choose from among a raft of competing identities, or decide whether you even had an identity to start with.

According to narrative psychologists, we go through life testing out a multitude of selves. We slip in and out of them with no greater effort than it takes to change socks. It's a Western culture thing. A practicing Buddhist isn't concerned with which socks to wear, which self to be. He exists as a *no*-self. In Buddhist teachings, the self is more of a process than a who. Because the Buddhist no-self resides in eternity, it has a strikingly different relationship with fellow creatures and with the universe as a whole. The no-self is at one with the universe. We in the West, and especially when we're at Esalen, are attracted to this idea because it seems gentle and relaxing. But we find it hard to pull off. So instead, we keep changing in and out of selves in the hope that in one of them we'll feel somewhat closer to our fellow creatures and to the universe as a whole.

Who are these selves aspiring to be *the* self? Ulric Neisser, often referred to as the father of cognitive psychology, proposed that we consist of at least five selves woven together: a "private self," who lives deep within our inner experience ("I am me and you're not"); an "ecological self," who relates to its surrounding environment ("I am here at this place right now"); an "interpersonal self," who reveals itself in how it interacts with others ("I am here right now interfacing with you"); a "conceptual self," who belongs to a social or cultural category ("I'm a husband, an American, and I've been a puppet, a pauper, a pirate, a poet, a pawn, and a king"); and a "temporally extended self," the self we're concentrating on here, the self who lives in one's memory and projects itself into the future.

Multiple selves needn't signify schizophrenia. Venerable thinkers have defined us fundamentally as multiself organisms. In 1890, William James spoke of a "Self of selves."

Your body and your possessions are your *material* self. Your relationships are your *social* self. Your values represent your *spiritual* self. These component selves are at times in conflict, with one self or another making a power grab for whatever reason. Your spiritual self, for instance, may have a hard time living with your material self—as in, *$800 for a pair of Prada flip-flops is beyond egregious in light of the homeless woman on the corner, but screw it, I only live once, and life is short,* one self whispers in another's ear.

What happens in midlife, according to the scribbler theory, is that your Self of selves gets sick and tired of all the squabbling going on among its component selves. Your Self of selves wishes everyone could join hands and commit to a single *true* self. "It is common," linguist George Lakoff writes, "for people not to be satisfied with the kind of life they are leading. You may feel that your job is unrewarding or that your whole way of life is somehow not compatible with your judgment of what counts as living a rewarding life." Hence, your true self believes there's a great novel in you if you could only muster the time. Your true self would trade your MBA for a theological degree.

There are exceptions. Some people are fine with the self they are—abrasively so. "When I look at myself in the first grade and I look at myself now, I'm basically the same," said Donald Trump. Mark Cuban, NBA franchisee and billionaire provocateur, says he knows which self he is and wouldn't change it for the world. In a magazine profile, he declared, "When I come back I want to come back as me." (The piece, by the way, was titled "The Twelve-Year-Old Owner.") If you're lucky enough to be Trump's or Cuban's writer-in-residence, you've got a plum assignment. Your boss's self is so self-satisfied—he knows who he is, his story's his story and he's sticking to it—you can pretty much spend your afternoons at the gym.

Dan McAdams contends that the self you are at any given stage evolves out of an elaborate process. By nine or ten, we begin to understand that our needs and wants aren't always satisfied in the short term. We come to realize that goals and desires are addressed over time. We learn that we have motives, just as characters in stories have motives. We're motivated to love or be loved; to be powerful; to achieve. Our motives drive the creation of that "personal myth" described earlier, a story we create about ourselves, a one-of-a-kind story, a "detailed, conscious autobiographical narrative of one's past that is highly valued and presented to oneself and others as comprehensive and complete." So goes the textbook definition. It's through the development of a personal myth that each of us "discovers what is true and what is meaningful in life," McAdams says. We don't *find out* who we are via personal mythmaking. We *make* ourselves who we are. It's how, as Nick Carraway came to understand, James Gatz became "just the sort of Jay Gatsby that a seventeen-year-old boy would be likely to invent...." Gatsby was Gatz's personal myth writ large. He eventually self-destructed. And so did the man who conceived him. In *The Crack-Up*, his first-person *Esquire* account of his descent into booze, failure, and self-pity, the forty-year-old Scott Fitzgerald wrote: "So there was not an 'I' any more—not a basis on which I could organize my self-respect. [It] was strange to have no self—to be like a little boy left alone in a big house, who knew he could do anything he wanted to do, but found that there was nothing that he wanted to do—"

Creating a personal myth gives each of us a shot at setting out on a mythic-like journey. Now that I've been immersed in all this, I realize that I left Philadelphia in pursuit of something, but I'm not sure what. *Bliss?* as Joseph Campbell would have it, a deep sense of "doing what you absolutely must to be yourself"? This is, after all, mythology's first function—to evoke, as Campbell said, "a sense of grateful, affirmative awe before the monstrous mystery that is existence."

It's in the service of a personal myth that we try on so many different selves. Metamorphosis makes for a good story, always has. In the *Odyssey* men turn into pigs. Jekyll turns into Hyde. Kafka turns an ordinary salesman into a giant vermin. Gregor has no good explanation for the self he's become: not even a baby vermin, a fully mature specimen. In biology this is called the imago stage, the adult stage of a bug's life. Psychologists use imago to describe an idealized image of self, a mini-me, says McAdams, who "plays the main character in a segment of a person's life story." This character can come and go throughout the human life course: "I was the boy (or girl) who never got into trouble." "I'm the corporate executive playing out the American dream." Or, more simply, "I'm a clown," "I'm the athlete," "I'm the loyal friend." There's nothing wrong with being multiple imagoes at once, assuming they're not in conflict. To be "I'm the coolest dude in the room" and "I'm a hopeless nerd" doesn't always click. I know, I've tried it.

You might want to ask yourself which imago(es) *you* are at the moment. Currently I'd say I'm gyrating between Kindly Mentor, generous of spirit, and Irascible Curmudgeon, subscribing to Thomas Hobbes's philosophy that in life it's every man and woman for themselves, fighting if not for survival then at least for an affordable place to live in New York City or San Francisco. The Kindly Mentor imago seems more meaningful to me than the Irascible Curmudgeon, but sometimes it's hard to give up an imago you've bonded with.

Other people take an avid interest in how we're constructing our personal myths. There's no shortage of informed and uninformed commentators who prattle on with sincere or smug assurance about what's a meaningful personal myth and what isn't. They started buzzing around when you first embarked on your personal mythmaking, back in grade school. Expectations were hurled from every direction: do this, or do that, and you'll grow up to be the central character of a myth deemed to be socially worthwhile. The scribbler tries to keep up with all this unsolicited advice, but it would take a writers' *colony* of scribblers to capture the competing suggestions.

Whether you're a girl or a boy makes a difference in terms of the expectations others set for you. Even more so when Linda and I were growing up. Linda, never a reprobate, had her knuckles routinely rapped by her parochial-school nuns, not an especially good tactic in that they also hoped she'd find the personal myth of nunhood so alluring she'd one day join the flock. Later on, they urged her to bide her time as a demure, nicely groomed, celibate typist until she could secure a meaningful life via marriage and motherhood. Leave a mark? Not part of the expectation set. For me, it was the opposite. "Don't settle, you're better than that. Go to medical school!" It wasn't until recently that I understood how the nuns and my father were, in their separate ways, pushing their own "immortality formulas," as anthropologist Ernest Becker put it. Had Linda joined the order, she'd be endorsing the nuns' own reason to exist. Had I become a research scientist or a doctor, I'd validate my father's life purpose. The nuns and my father—can't imagine how else I could ever put them in the same sentence—would be passing off something of themselves *to* us and *through* us. Symbolic immortality, it's called.

But it wasn't in the cards, for them or for us. We went looking for our own what-matters. Linda broke from the church (quietly, no hair-on-fire rebellion), insisting on going off to a secular coed college. Then it was on to a corporate career, eventually marrying and bearing children, yes, but with an unredeemed apostate. As for me, I don't know the difference between *Staphylococcus aureus* and *Staphylococcus epidermidis*. There'd never be a *Godfather* moment, as in when Michael Corleone, tucked away in Italy for safekeeping, asks a local mafia chief to get a message to Don Corleone: "Tell my father I wish to be his son."

Our personal mythmaking accelerates when we hit adolescence. Mythic role models get tacked up on the bedroom wall. Che Guevara. Farah Fawcett. Tony Romo. Jennifer Lopez. (Not all in the same bedroom, of course.) As teenagers we begin to seek out personally meaningful answers to the Big Questions. What do I believe in? Who am I? Suddenly your scribbler's gone from having a low-stress day job inside an innocent kid to working overtime for a bizarro, sullen nutcase desperately trying on one self after another.

The plot eventually simmers down. By your twenties and early thirties, the scribbler has more or less found her groove and you've settled into a reasonably stable mythical drift. Although yours is a wholly individual personal myth—like fingerprints, no two personal myths are identical—your myth probably falls into one of a handful of classic genres, I gathered from one of McAdams's books: comedy, romance, tragedy, and irony. The first two suggest that yours is a mostly optimistic personal myth. Linda, for example, is living a romantic myth. I'm wedged somewhere between tragedy and irony.

While thinking of ourselves as personal myths can be fun and enlightening, it's important to recognize how attaching ourselves to the wrong mythic identity can have unfortunate consequences. I'll give you a personal example. The moral of the story is, had I not pushed back on the mythic identity I'd adopted in my teens, my life story would have turned out differently and not half so well. In fact, it could have turned out to be a fucking disaster.

The chapter goes like this: Nearing the end of my second year in grad school, I have no clue as to where I'm heading. Zero prospects. An issue of *Esquire* arrives in the mail. On the editor's page there's a notice saying the magazine is holding a contest. The winner will land an incredibly alluring job in New York as a junior editor. There are only two qualifications: you must be under twenty-five and be shameless enough to believe you have a "good sense of humor." If you're shameless enough to believe that, you're invited to rewrite certain elements of that particular issue.

I sit there thinking, Hey, I can do this. But for weeks I can't bring myself to enter the contest. Or the personal myth I'm attached to can't bring *itself* to. My existing mythic identity—Tragic Hero or Noble Failure, not sure which—refuses to concede that fate can once in a blue moon hand you a gift. It revels in the certainty that it will wind up writing inane advertising jingles and drinking itself to early liver disease after failing to write the great American novel. My mythic ID, in short, is too proud or fearful of failure to enter the bloody contest.

After a few weeks, however, an alternative mythic identity somehow manages to slip through an open window. It gags and binds the Noble Failure. I enter the contest and eventually get the job. A call to adventure, the start of a heroic journey, as Joseph Campbell might see it, though maybe I'm flattering myself.

10   *Paper and Dust*

There are any number of ways to reach out for a fresh personal myth in midlife. Thankfully, booking a meeting room at a Courtyard Marriott isn't one's only option. When the weather turned too cold for lakeside reveries, I tucked the scribbler in under a wool watch cap and off we went to a university library, where there are six hundred thousand square feet of vintage cultural artifacts quaintly known as books. If an offsite calls for defining "Meaningful Life," and if a monastery or ashram isn't within convenient reach, a university library might offer up ideas worth pondering. Yes, I could have done much of it online, but nothing beats the smell of "paper and dust and years," as George R. R. Martin describes a library in *A Clash of Kings*.

But where does one start? A sizable tranche of the millions of volumes in the building has *something* to offer on what the point is. Where best to roll up one's sleeves? The philosophy shelves? Anthropology? Biology? Physics? Art? Poetry? History? Archeology? Psychology? Nursing? A glutton for punishment, I set up base camp in the philosophy stacks, where I put my lumbar region at risk by sitting on a little rolling step stool, hunting for quarry to drag back to a six-by-six-foot study cell.

The ancient Greeks spent a lot of time thinking about the point. They had plenty of open-field running room. In search of clues, they reached for the moon. And the stars. And the anatomy of crustaceans. And the composition of matter. At the same time, they understood that the quickest route to an answer to what the point is—it's always the quickest route— was to do whatever the gods said. Make the right sacrifices and you'll be home free. Epicurus refused to buy into that solution. Instead, he warmed us to the possibility that the point of life is *pleasure*. Unfortunately, we ran more than a little too far with the invitation. Epicurus didn't mean that the point of life was filling out your fantasy football roster while scarfing Buffalo wings. Pleasure derived from leading a gentle and agreeable life in a fair garden, teaching, learning, and debating important matters. As for the wrath of the gods, nothing to sweat, Epicurus said. The gods don't rule the universe. Atomic structure accounts for everything: trees, rocks, living creatures. How lilies smell depends on how their atoms are hooked together. Atoms determine whether a stone is smooth or jagged. The *soul* is made up of atoms. After we die, our soul atoms disperse back into the universe's atomic pool, where they link up again with other atoms, perchance to attach themselves to atoms that once formed a horse or determined how a grape tasted.

Aristotle, for his part, viewed the point not in terms of pleasure but in terms of happiness—here again, though, not how we typically think of "happiness." Aristotle said happiness derives from gaining wisdom and knowledge, wisdom and knowledge being more meaningful than money or power or fame or the other things we routinely confuse with happiness.

In time, the world grew considerably more complicated

than even the knowledge-hungry, pleasure-loving Greeks could imagine. Eighty years ago, Will Durant wrote a popular book called *The Story of Philosophy*. I spent a few hours with it in the stacks. Durant laments how over the centuries Western philosophy (and religion) wilted in the face of scientific discovery. The telescope captured stars too numerous for man to count. Geology showed that the cosmos was billions of years old, not a scant couple of thousand. Biology uncovered an entire world within the cell. Physiology discovered "inexhaustible mystery" in every bodily organ. Psychology perceived deep mysteries in a single dream. The disciplines of anthropology and archeology and history proved that human history as we understood it had barely scratched the surface. The universe was composed of atoms, yes, the smallest unit imaginable until quarks, leptons, and bosons entered the picture.

"Human knowledge," Durant said, "had become too great for the human mind."

Leaving the Greeks to their gentle gardens, I mounted my rolling step-steed and moved to a new location in the stacks. I was curious to find out what *modern* philosophers have to say about what the point is. The current crop needs no convincing that knowledge is too great for the human mind. Today's philosophers grew up in a time of unparalleled scientific and technological advancements. They've lived their entire lives skirting one or the other or both chambers of the existential vacuum. There's the "terrestrial" chamber, in which existential upset is induced by genocide, religious extremism, nuclear threats, melting ice caps, and indestructible new viruses. Then there's the existential vacuum's "cosmic" chamber, where all evidence points to a world gone mad a long time ago. W. B. Yeats wrote: "Things fall apart; the centre cannot hold; / Mere anarchy is loosed upon the world." And Barack Obama (not quite rising to the rhetorical occasion) said: "The truth of the matter...is that the world has always been messy...we're just noticing now because of social media."

You'd think that finding a way to circumvent the existential vacuum is what would attract the best and brightest to modern philosophy. Think again. You take your life in your hands if, at the department's end-of-semester picnic, you dare use "meaning" and "life" in the same phrase without attaching a caveat, subclause, or stipulation. Philosopher Susan Wolf says in a lecture that a fresh-faced student who so much as inquires about "the meaning of life" is setting himself up for classroom shaming. The question annoys today's philosophers because they're hell-bent on ridding the field of ambiguity and obscurity. They hear the age-old question "What is the meaning of life?" as unintelligible. "When we ask the meaning of a word...we want to know what the word stands for, what it represents," Wolf explains. "But life is not part of a language....It is not clear how it could 'stand for' anything, nor to whom."

Philosophers also dislike the question because the only conceivable correct answer is..."God." If *God* exists, they concede, then there's an avowed purpose to life: to be fruitful and multiply, and so on. But answering "God" doesn't go down well with modern philosophers, 73 percent of whom, when polled, say they're atheists. So if they don't think about the point, what do today's academic philosophers think about all day? E. D. Klemke, editor of a widely cited anthology titled *The Meaning of Life*, says that when philosophers gather for symposia they present papers with titles such as

"Negative Existentials," "On Referring," "Parenthetical Verbs," and "Elementarism, Independence, and Ontology." So much for ridding the field of obscurity and ambiguity. It's enough to make you wonder whether this is what Plato had in mind when he offered up his immortal cave parable: Philosopher leaves cave. Sees world for what it really is, returns to cave. Everyone still staring at shadows on wall. Delivers lecture first night back: "Is Existence a Predicate?"

Susan Wolf and other dissidents propose that philosophers quit nitpicking and tap their ample reservoirs of logic and reason to have a go at what the point is. It's the least they can do. The rest of us need help figuring out what we should be doing with our lives, in midlife especially. Einstein told us that the man "who regards his own life and that of his fellow creatures as meaningless is not merely unfortunate but almost disqualified for life." A good place for philosophers to dig in, Wolf says, is to reach some agreement on what constitutes a meaning*less* life. She volunteers to get the ball rolling. Certain life stories are patently pointless: for instance, a life story we might call *Blob! The Nonadventures of a Human Sloth*, the slow-moving saga of a slacker who watches all-day reruns of *The People's Court*, engaging in little or no social interaction. It's a life story of "hazy passivity," says Wolf. Lack of engagement is destructive to body, mind, and spirit. Social ostracism, whether self-inflicted or imposed, has been shown to be physically and emotionally debilitating.

Another example of a pointless life story is one I'm tempted to title *Confessions of a Shopaholic*, but that's been done. So let's call it *Useless! How to Successfully Take Up Space and Fill Up Your Time Without Standing for Anything Other Than How You Look or How Much You're Worth*. The prevailing theme here is uselessness. You make money to make money, or partake in some other orgy of self-gratification that has no connection to anything beyond yourself. By way of illustration, Wolf cites the pig farmer who buys more land to grow more corn to feed more pigs to buy more land to grow more corn to feed more pigs. It's an amusing reference, but I have trouble with it. On the surface, it does look like the farmer is chasing his own tractor. Then, one morning over at the grain elevator, you find out that the farmer has five kids, and that college costs are rising at a rate in excess of the price of pigs *and* farmland. A conscientious dad, he figures his only solution is to grow more corn to feed more pigs, and at a clip faster than the cost of tuition's going up.

What's lacking in the lives of both blobs and the useless, Wolf says, is active involvement with something that holds "positive value." Positive *objective* value. Wolf understands that she is now tottering on a slippery slope. Who's to say what's of "positive objective value"? Nearly all of us will agree on a broad set of behaviors that qualify—loving unconditionally, giving generously to charity, doing something well that's worth doing. But there's a vast gray area. Taking videos of shepherds who marry their sheep may be meaningful to some. Are there no anthropologists who conduct longitudinal, ethnographic studies of shepherds who marry their sheep?

Wolf makes sure we understand that a "meaningful" life isn't always an admirable or moral life. I'm thinking of Edward Snowden. Meaningful life? Many of us would say yes, absolutely. Thanks to Snowden, we're having an overdue national debate on government overreach and the right to privacy. We've rolled back ill-conceived legislation as a direct result. To Dick Cheney, though, Snowden betrayed his country and put American lives at risk; ergo, Snowden's life is meaningfully traitorous.

A "meaningful life," Wolf reminds us, is not necessarily a happy life. Tchaikovsky is sometimes brought into the discussion at this juncture. Weeks following an ill-advised marriage, the composer waded into the icy Moscow River in the hope that he'd contract pneumonia and thus find a way out of his marital misery.

Finally, a meaningful life needn't be a celebrated life. We all know this, but Wolf reiterates it. You don't have to be a Madame Curie, or an Oskar Schindler, or even a Benedict Cumberbatch to live a meaningful life. Raising kids the right way is a project of profoundly positive, objective value, however thankless it may seem at times.

The scribbler and I credit Susan Wolf for at least trying. Her willingness to take a machete to these weeds gives college kids a definition they can chew on in freshman seminar: *A meaningful life is one that satisfies personal desires; connects to something beyond yourself; and results in something of objective, positive value.*

Is that it, then? Is that the point?

I tried, really did try, to buy into that definition. It touches the right bases and looks good on paper. But we don't live on paper. We live in our own stories. The stories need to move forward in a satisfying way. A Julian Barnes fictional character at midlife draws the distinction between "adding *on*" and "adding *up*." Until and unless we live out a *story* that over time connects our personal desires with something beyond ourselves and results in positive value, we won't feel that we're adding up. It'll just feel like an isolated chapter or two, not a full-length story you hope never ends.

11   *Who Needs Happiness?*

One of the nice things in theory about an offsite, and this is the last thing I'll say about offsites, is that you can take the giant sheets off the wall, roll them up, put a rubber band around them, then revisit your bright ideas at a later date. We always say we'll do that with those rolled-up sheets, but we almost never bother. We're too busy catching up with the e-mails we didn't reply to while at the offsite. But if we *were* to circle back to the sheets from our hypothetical sabbatical and we unfurled them for the people I interviewed for this book, three of the scribbled proposals would stand a chance of adoption. Each is an arguable reason we're here in the first place.

Let's start with "procreation," which is Linda's first choice. *Of course* it's the reason we're here: to keep the human race going. Having and/or raising kids is all-consuming and gratifying, and indeed repopulates the planet. Yes, it can be a heartache, but let's not get hung up on the so-called parenthood paradox—the more intensely one parents, the higher the incidence of stress and guilt. Let's also not get hung up on how we may not have done certain kids any favors by bringing them into existence. I'm not talking about whatever unfortunate physical inheritances we bestow. Genes also play a determinative role in whether a child turns out to be friendly, confident, and reliable, qualities essential to forming the solid social and romantic relationships that are at the heart of a meaningful life. Some of us, face it, aren't genetically coded to be warm, fuzzy, and outgoing. By passing less-than-endearing qualities along, are we condemning our offspring to long, lonely nights that add up to long, lonely chapters in their life stories?

When I ask unmarried twenty-somethings how they envision their lives five to ten years from now, women invariably see kids as central to any meaningful future, men less so. A national survey of millennials bears it out. Women exceed men by 10 to 20 percent when asked whether a successful marriage and being a good parent are among the most important things in life. But kids have a way of growing up. Then what? Those in midlife who've already procreated say they're scrambling to find an alternative investment. And what about those who don't want or can't have kids? Some of us aren't wired physically or temperamentally to have children. If procreation's the point, are lives lived without children pointless by definition? Meghan Daum, who edited a book about why people—okay, not people, writers—decide not to have kids, says those who take a pass "bear no worse psychological scars. . . . In fact, many of us devote quite a lot of energy to enriching the lives of other people's children, which in turn enriches our own lives." A contributor to the book, novelist Geoff Dyer, professes astonishment: "In a park, looking at smiling mothers and fathers strolling along with their adorable toddlers, I react like the pope confronted with a couple of gay men walking hand in hand: Where does it come from, this unnatural desire?"

*   *   *

Based on my conversations, other strong contenders for what the point is are "kindness" and "happiness." Of these, kindness—doing unto others—is far and away the most favored answer. "How would you like to be remembered?" I will ask.

"As loving, caring, thoughtful, as someone who was curious and inquisitive. And who wanted to help eradicate the kind of ignorance that marginalizes people."

"Only as someone who tried to improve the lives of those who knew him."

"First and foremost, as a kind person and a wonderful mother, who didn't realize in her youth how much being a mom would be a part of her life, and then how it became her career."

"As someone who was steadfast in her beliefs, but who also tried to have an open heart and endeavored to have difficult conversations even when they were tiring for all concerned."

One midlife respondent didn't care at all for the question. "It's not important how I'm remembered," he said. As for kindness, "I'd rather not live for others. Just do things for the right reasons."

Now and then, if someone scratches his head for a couple of minutes and can't think of a point, I'll prime the pump and ask how he feels about kindness. Yeah, of course, sure, kindness, absolutely, he'll reply. But I can tell the heart isn't in it. Kindness—what else is new? Do they think kindness is for wimps, as in the old Italian proverb: "So good that he's good for nothing?" But I invite even the most self-centered, ironically inclined millennial to do himself the supreme kindness of reading George Saunders's classic commencement address at Syracuse University (2013). Saunders recalled that the greatest regret of his life was not being kinder in the seventh grade to a small, shy girl, a new kid in school, who wore blue cat's-eye glasses and had a habit of chewing on a strand of her hair. Saunders confessed that he's been unable to forget how lonely she looked when teased or ignored—"eyes cast down, a little gut-kicked, as if, having just been reminded of her place in things, she was trying, as much as possible, to disappear." Then one day the girl moved away. Forty-two years later— smack in the middle of midlife—Saunders remains haunted by his failure of kindness.

The problem with "kindness" as the guiding universal theme of a well-wrought life story is that you're either kind enough or you're not. The scribbler can't simply wave a staff and canonize you Saint Mother Teresa. Not me, for sure. While I don't think of myself as an unkind person, some of my kindest accomplishments have been accidental. I can't claim credit, let alone build a guiding philosophy around them.

Years and years ago, on a flight from New York to Los Angeles, I apparently offered someone a piece of advice that changed her life forever. And for the good. I was completely unaware of this beneficence until a couple of years ago, when an e-mail arrived. It was from a woman whose name, Valarie, didn't ring a bell. She recalled that, back in the days when there were upstairs piano bars in 747s (those *were* the days), "our paths crossed several times as I was a flight attendant for American Airlines with an irrepressible urge to write. I had written six chapters of a novel and you told me that if I wanted an absolutely honest critique I should send you my first chapter." And so she did. And true to my word, I must have given her a brutally honest critique. Whatever I said it was more than enough, Valarie wrote, to keep her from writing anything for years. "It wasn't because you discouraged me. It was because you helped me realize how much I needed to grow as a writer before I could tackle something so big. As you said, it was especially ambitious—a woman trying to write a novel in the first-person POV of a gay man! Ha! No shit!"

I'd like to say that I knew exactly what I was doing. What I thought I was doing was anything but kind. In fact, it was kind of nasty. I wanted to keep the world safe from another self-deluded wannabe. But somehow it backfired into an act of kindness. Valarie spent the next fifteen years "learning how to write and raising a family," she told me in the e-mail. Today, she lives in a town in North Carolina, is a former newspaper columnist, and is at work on a novel, presumably (and hopefully) not written from the first-person POV of a gay man. Toward the end of her e-mail she said this: "Life is good and mostly easy in this wonderful Carolina town where I'm very much at home and am recognized by strangers when they hear my name. Just last week someone said, 'You're the writer?' It still feels so good to have realized a dream, to have reached a goal set at the tender age of twenty-seven, when I met you (my son's age now). All these words are to let you know you made a difference in my life—a positive, life-affirming difference. You helped me know that if writing was what I *had* to do, I had to learn how to do it better and keep at it until it was good enough. I truly don't know how I could have lived a full life without writing. Thank you for your words (wherever that letter is) . . . and for taking the time for me in 1980."

I actually grew a little misty when I read that. Ned and Katherine happened to be in town just then, and I showed them Valarie's e-mail, feeling as proud of myself as I've ever felt in my career.

It was clearly a one-off. Those who extend acts of kindness

even at enormous personal risk—harboring Jews from the Nazis, for instance—say it isn't a choice, it's just how it is. People like that perform no cost-benefit analysis before displaying extraordinary selflessness. "I did nothing unusual. Anyone would have done the same thing in my place," they say. Those who were highly altruistic during the war were highly altruistic before and after the war as well. Bestowing kindness at a high level is in their bone marrow.

Like every other proposed single-word reason to exist, "kindness" has built-in practical and philosophical drawbacks. If you live to be kind to others, the last thing you want is to hurt someone's feelings. Kindness can blow up in your face. The "ideal man," said Aristotle, believes that "to confer a kindness is a mark of superiority; to receive one, a mark of subordination." On top of that, if bestowing kindness is the one and only thing you live for, but if your heartfelt offers of boundless kindness are then refused, you'll be left with *nothing* to live for. This applies to all stand-alone reasons to live. Finding and maintaining meaning in life is no different from building a solid financial plan—diversify or suffer the consequences.

"Happiness" is the other contender that begs for serious consideration as a reason to live. Here again, it's not so simple. The baby on the cover of *My Enduring Self* may one day wrestle with a wicked trade-off: Do I want this story to be a *happy* life story or a *meaningful* life story? Maybe you've wrestled with it as well. You probably did if you weren't among the coolest, most popular kids in your high school class. Remember those nights when you sat alone in your bedroom, reading *A Separate Peace*, asking yourself whether, given the choice, you'd trade your brains and untapped talent for the good looks, clothes, and vacuous but happy social lives of the A-crowd? Does it have to be a trade-off? Can you not be deeply reflective *and* vibrate with day-to-day, simpleminded joy? Of course you can, up to a point. The pursuit of happiness and the pursuit of meaningfulness feed off each other. Roy F. Baumeister, a psychologist with long-standing curiosity about what distinguishes happiness and meaningfulness, has done a number of studies that show how happiness and meaningfulness overlap. But they also diverge.

For example, people who are inclined to say their story's a happy story are people who are happy because their material wants and needs are satisfied. *Stuff* makes them happy: a big, comfortable house, great vacations, a new outfit when they're feeling a little down. For them, money can purchase a feeling of provisional well-being. Those who consider their lives meaningful, however, know that money buys neither happiness nor can it be exchanged for additional meaningfulness. (To have little or no financial wherewithal works against both meaningfulness and happiness, but affects one's level of happiness more than it reduces one's sense of meaningfulness.) Paradoxically, Baumeister reports, a sense of meaningfulness is often associated with anxiety. This explains why, even though you were blue sitting up in your bedroom reading *A Separate Peace*, you may have felt a smidgen of pride. Believing that one's life is difficult correlates positively with a sense of meaningfulness, likely because adversity and suffering beg for a meaningful response. Baumeister suggests that the more we take on difficult challenges, the more likely it is we'll wind up disappointed. This doesn't make us happy, but it does leave us thinking we at least reached for something worthwhile.

As for whether it's better for a life story to be happy or meaningful, the A-crowd's lifestyle or yours, there's a small-arms war going on over that question. Facing off are so-called positive psychologists (PPs) versus existential psychologists (EPs). The PPs say happiness is the point. No, *meaning's* the point, the EPs counter. Uh-uh, the PPs reply, finding meaning is but one important component of achieving happiness along with others, such as experiencing positive emotions (warmth, comfort, pleasure); engagement with absorbing activity; maintaining solid relationships with others; and personal achievements.

And what do the EPs, their guiding light being Viktor Frankl, say to that? They say it's wrong, that meaning is the wellspring from which happiness flows. (The director of Harvard's Grant Study says that happiness is the cart and love is the horse, which works for me, too.) Happiness, according to the EPs, comes to those who are open to new experience; who live in the moment; who are creative and constructive. No meaning, no happiness. If you don't think your life story holds meaning, you'll feel dissatisfied, disengaged, anxious, helpless, and frustrated. And you'll be colossally bored.

Both camps only want the best for us, which causes them to lose patience with each other, sniping back and forth. Dispatches from the frontlines published in academic journals offer evidence that PPs think EPs are pessimistic and self-absorbed, harp on the negative and tragic, and are overly obsessed with death and dying. For their part, EPs think PPs are Pollyannas living in la-la land. They're sloughing off the enormity of moral quandaries and the effects of social injustice, making life sound too easy. When their underlying principles are whipped up into self-help books, it can sound suspiciously too easy (*Authentic Happiness: Using the New*

Positive Psychology to Realize Your Potential for Lasting Fulfillment).

The great thing about the scribbler theory is that it works equally well on both the positive and existential sides of the street. The mission is to write a life story that satisfies the leading character's goals. There is no one kind of story that fits the bill. What's important is that the story *pays off*. For you. So maybe it comes down to what type of story your writer-in-residence is best at. Mine happens to be drawn to the work of Kafka, Roth, and Edgar Allan Poe. EP-type stuff. Yours may be partial to up-with-people-type stories—*I think I can, I think I can!*—the kind vetted and recommended by the Oprah Book Club. One isn't inherently a better kind of story than the other.

The other night, a friend of Linda's turned the tables and started grilling me. She asked whether I had learned anything while working on this project. Had it changed me in any way? Ooh, good question! I thought. After a moment or two, I told her that like everyone else, I always said that what I want most for my kids is for them to be happy. And healthy, of course. Now, I told her, I'm not so sure about that. I then looked around and saw I'd gotten the attention of everyone else in the room. No, I said, trying desperately to recover, I obviously still want my kids to be healthy, but I no longer say I want them to be happy. Plenty more dark stares. Well, *of course* I want them to be happy. But, you know, not *happy* happy. Because if all they are is *happy* happy, then one day something will happen that'll make them unhappy. And as Viktor Frankl said, our culture doesn't think it's right or normal for anyone to be unhappy, which means my kids may begin to worry that there's something wrong with them, even though they have excellent reasons *to be* unhappy. They'll walk around feeling unhappier *still* because everyone will be wanting to know why they're so miserable. Which will make them unhappy squared...do you know what I mean?

No one seemed to know what I meant. Look, I said, it's a be-careful-what-you-wish-for kind of thing.

12   *The James Dean Story*

With the end coming into hazy view, we eventually reach the closing stretch of the elbow. Having made it down the long, winding road of midlife, it's only natural that we ask ourselves whether we're heading in the right direction. Is the story on track? Is it adding up as well as adding on?

Back when Kurt Vonnegut gave master classes in creative writing, he used chalk and a blackboard to illustrate how a story line can be plotted on a simple graph. He believed you could chart every story this way, from a Greek myth to *The Avengers: Age of Ultron*. The notion went back to when Vonnegut was a grad student in anthropology. He proposed a topic for his master's thesis that was quickly rejected "because it was simple and looked like too much fun," Vonnegut said.

Standing at the blackboard, Vonnegut drew two axes. The horizontal axis, marked "Beginning–End," denoted the plot of a story. The vertical axis, "G–I," denoted the degree to which the story's main character experienced good fortune (prosperity, health, and so on) or ill fortune (poverty, sickness, and so on). He then chose a story—he was partial to *Cinderella*—and plotted out the heroine's ups and downs over time. The graph reveals how things get better and better for Cinderella after her fairy godmother drops in to doll her up for the ball. The line on the graph *keeps* climbing as Cinderella turns heads when she gets to the party, dances with the prince, etc. Then, when the clock strikes twelve, Vonnegut's graph dramatically illustrates how Cinderella's good fortune plummets to earth with the vehemence of a major stock market crash. Vonnegut then drew a straight line to indicate how, in his words, Cinderella "poops along" for a while. But eventually, of course, the day comes when the prince knocks on Cinderella's door, the shoe fits, and Cinderella's good-fortune line rockets up and off the chart.

It's with a touch of wistfulness that I admit that I, too, was developing a primitive method for graphing stories. In fact, I thought I was blazing the trail. Mine wasn't concerned with written stories, however. Mine had to do with how we might graph our own *life stories*. I was all set to call it my exclusive "M (for Meaning)" graph when, a few weeks into development, I found evidence that others had gotten there before me. Not just Vonnegut. I discovered that philosopher Robert Nozick had laid out much the same notion as mine in an essay written thirty years ago: "Imagine graphing someone's total happiness through life; the amount of happiness is represented on the vertical axis, time on the horizontal one." My concept was similar. It consisted of a y-axis labeled "Meaningful" and an x-axis labeled "Time":

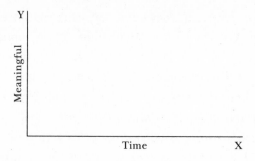

To test out the idea, I began putting down dots that denoted various satisfying events in my past. Drawing on these memories yielded a graphical representation of *The Life and Times of My Enduring Self.* I hopscotched through my grade school years, where there were just a couple of meaningful dots; then added a bunch of dots denoting satisfying things that happened in high school; then on to college, where the dots flew hot and heavy (lots of creative satisfaction in college, mainly having to do with an on-campus theater group). From there I dotted the early years at *Esquire*, a dizzying chapter with plenty of satisfying dots; then on through major and minor relationships, career successes and disappointments in my thirties; up to and through marriage to Linda, birth of my kids, all the way to now. It wound up looking like this:

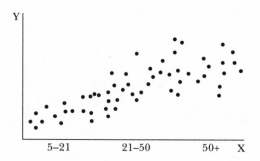

Pretty nifty, right? Am I sorry I wasn't first to the party? Not much. Ownership is unimportant. What's important is the takeaway. What matters in life isn't the sheer *number* of meaningful or happiness dots in one's life story graph, or even how high the dots reach on the y-axis. *What matters is whether the dots are moving in the right direction as a life story extends from the beginning to the middle to the final chapters.* Most of us, as Nozick observed, would willingly give up a little happiness in exchange for a narrative that moves in the right direction. A meaningful life story is a story that's *moving onward and upward.* Adding on *and* adding up along both axes.

Finnish philosopher Antti Kauppinen, picking up on many of the themes in Robert Nozick's essay, cites any number of others who argue that it's better to live an improving life than a deteriorating one, even if there's more absolute meaningfulness or happiness in the deteriorating one. It's the *shape of a life* that matters. A life story in which our satisfying chapters go from good to not-so-good is less satisfying than one in which our satisfying chapters go from not-so-good to good—even though there may be more satisfying dots in the story that goes from good to not-so-good. Scholars refer to this phenomenon as *bonum progressionis*—the progression of the parts can matter more than the sum of the parts.

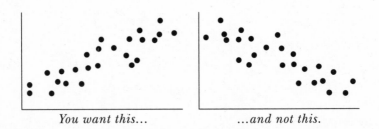

You want this...   *...and not this.*

A trajectory that moves in the right direction isn't usually dependent on a single source of ongoing satisfaction, such as a job. Some of us commit to long-term projects, most of us bounce from one thing to another. Taylor Branch, an old friend, is one of the former. He spent twenty-four years reporting and writing his three-volume history of the Martin Luther King Jr. era. His commitment was full-bore and nonstop. Taylor stretched his book advances as far as he could, taking a part-time job to help his family through the early years of the project. He continues to address King's legacy a dozen or so times a year in speaking engagements, focusing on "race as both a good and bad barometer of our democratic experiment." "So I'm a Johnny-one-note," Taylor says, "although to me it's a resonant note."

The majority of us, and I speak from personal experience, change jobs or careers multiple times, in which case new sets of goals need to be established if the right trajectory is to be maintained. Men or women who drop out of their careers to raise kids or pursue a personal passion are tasked with finding satisfaction in each successive chapter. Retirement, of course, presents its own special challenges—it's one thing to downshift, it's another to stall out.

When the end draws near and your days along the x-axis dwindle down to a precious few, the trajectory your dots are moving in counts for everything. A study conducted a number of years ago illustrates it nicely. The study was designed to determine whether we judge a good life story that ends abruptly more desirable than a not-quite-as-good life story that drags on. Is a shorter really good life more satisfying than a longer not-so-good life? Researchers presented a subject pool with a fictional life story of an unmarried woman who perishes suddenly and painlessly in a car crash. There are multiple versions of her life leading up to the tragic event. There's an extremely *happy* version in which she had a great job, enjoyed exciting vacations, and a wide network of friends. There's another version, a happy *enough* one, in which she had a reasonably okay life. And there's an *unhappy* version, in which she grew up depressed and angry, had a terrible job, no close friends, and spent her time watching TV (this was before the current "golden age," when TV wasn't worth watching). The study's participants were variously told that the fatal crash occurred when the woman was as young as twenty-five or as old as sixty, with a few ages in between. They were then asked to numerically rate how "desirable" the woman's life was. For both the younger and older participants in the study, *how things were going at the end* mattered significantly. An extremely happy life that's snuffed out near the moment of peak fulfillment was held to be preferable to an extremely happy life with just a few blah years tacked on at the end. Adding years to a wretched life was judged to be preferable if the additional years were not quite as wretched as what had come before.

Again—how things were going at the end was what mattered—in the abstract, anyway. Adding a mildly pleasant chapter to an extremely happy story doesn't make the story more appealing: "the James Dean Effect," the authors called it. At twenty-four, Dean had already achieved meteoric stardom the day he died on a California highway, crashing his brand-new Porsche 550 Spyder. Better to go out like Dean, the study's participants felt, than make a string of so-so movies, then die a couple of years later.

In the abstract. Most of us, if given a choice, would opt for additional years, even if it meant trading down from a Porsche to a Ford Fiesta. Of course we would. Why? Because you never know. Things could always turn around and get better for us. Looking back, though, when our story's over with, we might feel it would have been a better story had it ended earlier. I say that all the time about books and movies— they should have quit while they were ahead. In terms of a life story, there's only one good way to test the premise: conduct a survey in a place like the old country graveyard. "Given how things turned out, my good sir or madam, would you have preferred a shorter story, an earlier final curtain, when things were honky-dory? Or were the extra years worth the trouble and pain?" Only the dead can answer that question with full authority.

13   *How We Live On*

We've all read stories like the ones I just mentioned—where the plot wheezes out with a big chunk of pages still to go. As readers, we have a dilemma. There are two ways to go. We can soldier on, repeatedly stopping to decide whether the clump of remaining pages is worth our time and attention, or skip to the last page to see how things turn out, putting ourselves and the story out of our misery. The same applies to a life story. The trick is not to let *The Life and Times of My Enduring Self* turn into a downward-sloping slog when it reaches the last third. Robert Nozick, having come up with a simple way to plot happiness on a graph, likewise thought of a cool way to keep a life story from running out of steam.

It's surprisingly easy. You train yourself to think you're never more than halfway through a given run of chapters. For example, telling himself he wasn't quite halfway through life took Nozick happily up to the elbow, age forty. Plenty of time left to do good stuff. Five years later, Nozick told himself he was only halfway through his post-college work life. Still plenty of time left to do good stuff. At fifty, he was just halfway between college and the end. By the time he got to sixty, Nozick said, he'd have thought of something else he was halfway through. You see the point. The philosopher's clever trick doesn't add more pages to a life story. You don't get to live longer. What it does is provide a more manageable view of the time left in which you can do good stuff. It can help you choose which goals can be reasonably set and successfully achieved over the next designated run of pages. Right now, as I approach the elbow of this book, I'm beginning to think about what I'm going to do next. Probably another book, which I'd like to complete in no more than two or three years. After that, I'd like to do some traveling with Linda. In Nozick's terms, I'm telling myself I'm roughly halfway between the time I started this book and the time I will have written a couple of books and done some fun traveling. Notice that I haven't told myself anything about how many or how few pages there are to go in the overall story.

Nozick said there'd never come a time when he wouldn't be halfway through something or other. He died of cancer thirteen years after publishing his goalpost-shifting maneuver, his half-lives having been trimmed to an insupportable sliver. He was sixty-three.

The stretch between the age Nozick was when he died and the presumed end date for most of us (currently, just shy of eighty) calls for major readjustments. On the one hand, you get discounts at the movies and on buses and subways, and Uncle Sam pays your doctors. On the other hand, if it's not one aching joint, it's another. The Patriots' Tom Brady, then thirty-six, said that "you don't have to suck when you get older." Well, you really *do* kind of have to suck when you get older. Years ago at *Esquire*, we published a talked-about cover story called "How a Man Ages." The feature was a detailed, decade-by-decade accounting of many of the eventualities I listed earlier in connection with Harvard's Grant Study—deterioration from head to toe. From age sixty on, we're all too aware that these changes are happening to us; no need to read about them in a magazine. And yet most sixty-year-olds will say, in all innocence and candor, "But I don't *feel* old. I certainly don't *smell* old." (FTR, there is such a smell. In 2012, the Monell Chemical Senses Center conducted a study in which forty-one sniffers confirmed that there's a recognizable odor associated with age. "Elderly people have a discernible underarm odor," said Johan Lundström, a sensory neuroscientist. The good news is that it wasn't judged to be particularly unpleasant or especially intense. "However," Lundström added, rather gratuitously, "it is possible that other sources of body odors, such as skin or breath, may have different qualities.")

Some of us do what we can to convince ourselves that all is not lost as we shuffle toward the end of the x-axis. Until recently, I worked for a company that provided an extraordinary fringe benefit for vice presidents and above: an annual physical at the Mayo Clinic. In a single day, you had your blood and urine sampled; your chest X-rayed; your pulmonary function assessed; your bone density measured; your heart stress-tested; your skin examined for cancerous growths; your eyes examined; and, if the time had come, your colon scoped.

To be honest, I looked forward to the Mayo visit, where I could smugly congratulate myself that I wasn't sucking nearly as much as others my age. (No, it's not a competition, but you can't help comparing.) At Mayo, when you're called in for an ECG or a chest X-ray, you go in as part of a forced march with eight other males, all of them battle-scarred baby boomers. Everyone troops into a hall of changing-room stalls where you state your serial number, in this case your DOB. I was invariably five, sometimes ten, years older than the others in my platoon—but I looked pretty damn good, all things being relative. This alone made me feel frisky whenever at Mayo, so I flouted the rules. I ordered a martini or two the night before my blood work, even though the instruction sheet proscribed it *in italics*. When morning fasting was called for, I'd eat a banana anyway, haughty in the belief that a banana would go entirely undetected by even the most finely calibrated, advanced medical device, which in my case I'm not sick enough—not yet—to warrant. I enjoyed myself at Mayo, went from one test to another with a bounce in my step. I chatted up lab techs and receptionists with uncharacteristic *bonhomie*. At Mayo I almost felt like a kid again, even if, for all I know, I *did* smell a little.

When you get to be my age, when your life story's halfway between the birth of your kids and the end of the x-axis, or halfway between your first false-positive mammogram or PSA reading and the end point on the x-axis, there's a good possibility you'll start wondering where your story will go from there. How important is it that your story live on? Isadora Duncan believed it was incredibly important. The dancer said that she wanted to be remembered as a *legend*. Not so a lot of people I've talked to. "What's to live on?" they ask with a shrug. The story's a dud, they've already decided.

Others say it's a stupid question and that they don't give a rat's ass if their stories live on—when you're dead, you're dead. Unwittingly, they're channeling Franz Kafka. Why

Kafka? In an interview Philip Roth gave not long after he retired from writing, he talked about how one of his characters lived in accord with something Kafka, his literary hero, had said: *The meaning of life is that it stops.*

I wish the interviewer had followed up by asking Roth whether he personally agreed with that. And if he did agree that "the meaning of life is that it stops," was it not gratifying to think about how he'd keep on attracting new and admiring readers long after he's gone? That there was an immortalizing principle at work? That's what I would have asked. But the interviewer didn't pursue it. The two went on to talk about other things, such as how Roth had recently reread every single word of every book he'd ever written, thirty or so over a span of fifty years. "I wanted to see whether I'd wasted my time," Roth explained. The interviewer did follow up on that one. He asked Roth what the verdict was. In reply, Roth quoted another hero of his, boxer Joe Louis: "I did the best I could with what I had."

Bingo! I thought. "I did the best I could with what I had" is a sneaky good stab at what the ultimate point may be. Unlike most attempts to nail down life's purpose, "I did the best I could with what I had" is refreshingly concise, a mere ten words, just thirty-nine characters (with spaces). "I did the best I could with what I had" can thus fit handily on a tombstone and falls well within the limits of a routine tweet. Indeed, "I did the best I could with what I had" makes for a dandy final tweet.

As for "the meaning of life is that it stops," I kept turning the possibility over in my mind. It, too, is tweetable and would fit on a headstone. But it troubled me for reasons I couldn't quite figure out. Then, not long after I'd discovered the Roth interview, news came that Emory University had acquired thirty boxes of Flannery O'Connor's letters and assorted effects. The author of indelible collections of short stories, including "A Good Man Is Hard to Find" and "Everything That Rises Must Converge," O'Connor had died fifty years before, at age thirty-nine—right on the cusp of midlife, two years younger than Kafka was when he died. She'd never married, living her final thirteen years with her mother in Milledgeville, Georgia.

Included in the boxes now at Emory were leftover props from O'Connor's brief but illustrious life story. A hand-drawn children's book about a goose. A few old toys. Unpublished journals. A self-portrait taken in a mirror. More than six hundred letters to her mother. Would O'Connor be astonished to know that these letters and artifacts are so treasured today? Possibly. Throughout her life, however, she expressed doubt that anyone would ever be interested in her life story. "Lives spent between the house and the chicken yard do not make exciting copy," she once wrote.

Most of us say things like that, don't we? Our story's humdrum, what's to live on? Do we really mean it? Did O'Connor really mean it when she dismissed the possibility that anyone would ever be interested in the years she spent shuffling back and forth between the house and the chicken yard? There's reason to think she didn't really mean it. For in a journal entry written when she was twenty, O'Connor says: "It is a pity I can't receive my own letters. If they produce as much wholehearted approval at their destination as they do at their source, they should indeed be able to keep my memory alive and healthy."

What that suggests to me is that she really *did* care about whether her life story would live on. That her life story was *worthy* of living on. That even though *life* stops, a life *story* doesn't. Anyone care to argue? Kurt Vonnegut cared to argue. "If a person survives an ordinary span of sixty years or more," Vonnegut wrote in *Deadeye Dick*, "there is every chance that his or her life as a shapely story has ended and all that remains to be experienced is epilogue. Life is not over, but the story is."

Vonnegut had it ass-backward, in my opinion. He was being ornery and arch, perhaps at sixes and sevens with himself at that moment, for all we know adrift at the elbow.

Having reflected on it, I'm now convinced that as a guide to better living, "I did the best I could with what I had" beats "the meaning of life is that it stops." If everyone really believed that the meaning of life is that it stops, would we be kind to one another? Would we bother to try to save the whales, recycle bottles and cans? Would we vote in local elections? Would we ever reevaluate the choices we've made, let alone wish to correct certain mistakes before it's too late? Would we bother to start a business? Would we no longer regret missing our kids' soccer games even if we *had* started a business? Would we bother to care for and nurture our kids? Would we even bother to *have* kids?

The preceding fusillade of questions was chosen for a reason. When we care about the future of the planet, participate in the community, make time for kids, we do so not only because these are nice, socially admirable things to do, we do them because they're all activities that benefit those whose stories will outlive our own.

Think about it: if you set a child, yours or anyone else's, on the right road with the right values; if you raise funds to keep the local library open; if you start a children's theater in your town; if the company you founded creates good, long-term jobs; if you trade your oil-burning furnace for solar panels; if you're a scout leader or Big Brother or Sister; if you sponsor a child in Indonesia; if you teach a kid to fly fish and to always release the catch; if you do any of a limitless number of things in the name of the future, a part of your story will live on.

"Generativity" it's called, which is variously described as an urge, a need, a motive, a trait, an instinct, a drive. The term was coined by Erik Erikson in his 1950 groundbreaking work, *Childhood and Society*, the book that made him the most celebrated psychologist in America. He was featured on the cover of *Time*, invited to lead conferences at the White House, and was the therapist to whom the rich and powerful turned for professional counsel when their offspring showed disquieting emotional symptoms.

Erikson's own life story is odd and interesting unto itself. The short version goes like this: He was born in Germany in 1902. His mother, who was Danish, was abandoned by her first husband and never married Erik's biological father, a man whose identity remained murky. Erik was told that his true father had died shortly after he was born. When he was three—just when his memories and narrative capacity were kicking in—his mother married for propriety's sake a devout Jewish pediatrician named Homburger, who formally adopted Erik. Now the boy was Erik Homburger, Nordic in every respect, tall, blond, and blue-eyed, who had a "father" who was slight and had brown hair and eyes. Erik attended religious services at Dr. Homburger's synagogue, where congregation members, as well as classmates at school, referred to him as the *goy*. It didn't make for a firm early identity. In his early twenties, Erik took off for Vienna, dabbled as a painter, and taught art at a school where he met Freud and Freud's daughter Anna, under whom he studied psychoanalysis.

Within a few years, he met and married Joan Mowat Serson, a gifted Canadian student with identity issues of her own. They eventually made their way to America, where, with Joan's active collaboration, Erik would leave his mark on the history of developmental psychology, first as Erik Homburger and then, at age fifty-eight, as Erik Homburger Erikson, the new surname perhaps chosen to underscore the idea that if Erik was anyone's son he was his own—Erik's son. It's not for nothing that Erik Homburger Erikson became known as "the architect of identity."

In a memoir, Erikson's daughter Sue Erikson Bloland, the youngest of three siblings, describes an unhappy childhood in a blissful Northern California setting. Erikson was, by her account, "an awkward father," given to irritability but capable of shy affection. Socially, he was charming and widely admired. The family story was riven when a fourth child, Neil, was born with Down syndrome. Doctors said the boy had three years to live. While Joan was hospitalized following postbirth surgery, Erikson consulted two friends (one of whom was Margaret Mead) and unilaterally decided to place Neil in a special-care institution. Joan, who never even held the baby, wasn't consulted. The other kids were told the baby had died at birth. (Neil lived to be twenty-one.) It's reasonable to suppose that Erik Erikson wasn't crazy about this chapter of his story living on.

"We were not a family that ever talked about the things that hurt or angered us the most," Sue Erikson Bloland says in her memoir.

The concept of generativity is rooted in Erik Erikson's enduring contribution to developmental theory: the idea that the human developmental process doesn't screech to a halt at adolescence. We continue to evolve through eight "psycho-social stages." Erikson summarized the process as follows: "In youth you find out what you *care to do* and who you care to be....In young adulthood you learn whom you *care to be with*—at work and in private life....In adulthood, however, you learn to know what and whom you can *take care of*."

Each one of Erikson's eight developmental stages (some prefer "tasks" to "stages") carries an intrinsic challenge for our writers-in-residence. As infants, stage one, the task is to figure out what or whom to trust. Since the writer upstairs hasn't moved in yet, we need to figure this out for ourselves. Stages two through six have to do with gaining autonomy, finding a sense of purpose, forming solid relationships. Stage eight, the final stage, calls for us to reflect on our stories. It's during this last stage that the writer-in-residence may conclude that our life story's one of fulfillment and satisfaction; or, if we fail to resolve the earlier crises or tasks, bitter and full of regrets.

The penultimate stage, stage seven, is where generativity—not a great word but the best Erikson could come up with—comes into play. While there are no hard-and-fast rules for when Erikson's stages take place—they're not strictly successive, but rather meld into one another—stage seven is concentrated in midlife. At the elbow. It's when we ask ourselves, Who am I? And through our actions and values we answer: I am what survives me. Generativity is concern for, and taking care of, the next generation. It's passing something on. James Michener, who never had kids of his own, sent 150 of them through college. Generativity in action. If you send care packages, take part in breast cancer walkathons, mentor the disadvantaged, or would sooner go hungry than eat takeout that comes in a polystyrene box, you're being more generative than you may have realized.

Generativity pays dividends. Your story's better off for it. Donating blood, volunteering at a school, tending a community garden help satisfy your "need to be needed," Dan McAdams says. It also addresses your narrative's need for a "sense of an ending." You've done things for others, left the world a better place. A life story, one can argue, is hardly worth talking about if it lacks a healthy dose of generativity.

Caring for the next generation is also a terrific theme with which to self-promote. Pay attention, if you can bear it, to stump speeches and candidates' campaign autobiographies. Progressives' proposals to reduce greenhouse gases are for "our children's and their children's sake." Conservatives demand reduction in the national debt for "our children's and their children's sake." In a revised epilogue to her memoir *Hard Choices*, Hillary Clinton writes: "I'm more convinced than ever that our future in the twenty-first century depends on our ability to ensure that a child born in the hills of Appalachia or the Mississippi Delta or the Rio Grande Valley grows up with the same shot at success that Charlotte will," she says, referring to her granddaughter, who emerged just in time to be a key sound bite in the campaign to come.

The alternative to generativity, story-wise, is not nearly as appealing. Erikson called it "stagnation." Or "self-preoccupation." If your life story lacks a generative element, Dan McAdams's interviews show, it likely starts out with a psychological injury. Or there was no generative role model in the person of a parent, teacher, or other adult who demonstrated a personal connection to the future. The plot of a stagnant story doesn't move forward so much as revolve in vicious circles, says McAdams. It ends up as a life that's been lived chiefly in the moment. Those who lack the generative impulses indulge themselves as if they were their own children, Erikson declared.

In one of his books, *Outliving the Self*, John Kotre revisited Erikson's view of generativity in light of the social and cultural changes that had occurred in the three decades following Erikson's introduction of it. By then, we'd been through the contraception revolution, which resulted in more women putting off having kids or choosing never to have them. We were living longer, which in turn meant that even if we had kids, we were spending more years in the empty nest than at any time in history. Both developments meant that we were now living "biologically sterile" for a longer time than ever. The challenge, Kotre said, was figuring out how, in this new paradigm, we're to remain, in a figurative sense, "fertile." To help us figure that out, he outlined four distinct types of generativity: biological (the old standby—begetting and nursing offspring); parental (educating, disciplining, initiating those offspring); technical (mentoring, passing skills along to others); and cultural (contributing something new through art, science, technology, you name it).

Kotre also questioned some of Erikson's assumptions. Generative impulses are hardly confined to midlife, something Erikson had merely nodded at. My daughter, when she was a college sophomore, decided to major in Health and Society. Inspired by a museum exhibition, she saw an opportunity to put her passion for design to work in the field of global development. I can trace my own urge to leave something behind all the way back to when I was thirteen, suddenly aware that the clock had a way of running out with nary a two-minute warning.

Acting in a generative way isn't strictly altruistic. Some psychologists say that it stems in part from a desire to be "symbolically immortal." There's something to this. Yes, symbolic immortality is small beer compared to literal immortality. ("I don't want to achieve immortality through my works," said Woody Allen. "I want to achieve immortality through not dying.") But symbolic immortality is more reassuring than no immortality. *You* don't live on but some vestige of you does. Your story, or parts of the story, for instance. Generation to generation, the stories we hear, the stories we tell, and the stories we build upstairs commingle and live on indefinitely.

As I've said, having and caring for kids is the easiest and most natural way to strive for symbolic immortality. Well, at least the most natural. Your children, knowing your story, will pass bits of it along. Moreover, your genes will live on, which edges you to within a whisper of literal immortality. "Our death is not an end if we can live on in our children and the younger generation," Einstein wrote in a letter of consolation to the widow of a Dutch physicist. "For they are us, our bodies are only wilted leaves on the tree of life." "The point is to be a good ancestor," many have said, including Jonas Salk, who lived on not only through his own kids, but through his polio vaccine, which saved the lives of millions of other kids, giving them in turn an opportunity to seek symbolic immortality for themselves.

There are numerous other avenues to symbolic immortality. Putting something into the world that wasn't there before can act as a buffer against existential anxiety. Studies suggest that taking pride in, and being admired for, one's own good works suppresses, at least to some extent, one's anxieties about dying. Some say the drive for symbolic immortality is what art is all about, creativity in general: putting something into the world that wasn't there before. Stephen Sondheim's Georges Seurat memorably sings, "Look, I made a hat—where there never was a hat." Plato himself likened creativity to procreativity. He referred to creativity as the "pregnancy of the soul."

But there's a dark side to all this as well, John Kotre points out. A soul can be *so* pregnant, the drive to create so ferocious, that the artist becomes a self-possessed monster. *My* work will live on, but the rest of you can go to hell for all I care. In a probing analysis of Martha Graham's long career as one of our most influential choreographers, Susan A. Lee, a professor at Northwestern, cites evidence of how the so-called mother of modern dance was seen as a "bad mother" by young dancers in her corps. Graham was ungenerative in the extreme, notoriously demanding and cruel.

We take a million small steps toward making ourselves symbolically immortal, not that we're aware of our motives:

A friend in his seventies, an orthopedic surgeon no longer operating but now mentoring residents, is passing along his experience to others. His story will live on. (The doctor has also managed to hold on to his childhood collection of baseball cards these many years. They still give him pleasure, no more so than when he passes them on, one by one, to his ten-year-old grandson.)

A piano player—he's pushing eighty—shares his set with a musician in her twenties. His story will live on. When the young musician plays Johnny Mercer, Cole Porter, and Sammy Cahn tunes, the songwriters' stories live on. Same goes for when a Chinese American poet (Ha Jin) credits a Yiddish story-writer (Isaac Bashevis Singer) as his literary muse; Truman

Capote cites James Agee; J. K. Rowling acknowledges C. S. Lewis. Their stories live on.

Paul Kalanithi was a young neurosurgeon who in 2015 died of lung cancer at thirty-seven, a few months after his first child, a daughter named Cady, was born. Shortly before the end, Kalanithi wrote an essay in *Stanford Medicine* magazine, a powerfully moving reflection on generativity and symbolic immortality. It read in part:

> I hope I'll live long enough that she has some memory of me. Words have a longevity I do not. I had thought I could leave her a series of letters—but what would they really say? I don't know what this girl will be like when she is 15; I don't even know if she'll take to the nickname we've given her. There is perhaps only one thing to say to this infant, who is all future, overlapping briefly with me, whose life, barring the improbable, is all but past.
>
> That message is simple: When you come to one of the many moments in life when you must give an account of yourself, provide a ledger of what you have been, and done, and meant to the world, do not, I pray, discount that you filled a dying man's days with a sated joy, a joy unknown to me in all my prior years, a joy that does not hunger for more and more, but rests, satisfied....

The writer upstairs stands foursquare behind the nurturing of the next generation. Why wouldn't he? If our story lives on, his *work* lives on, thus making the scribbler likewise symbolically immortal. But however important living on may be, it's not the only thing the writer-in-residence cares about as you and he saunter through the latter stages of the elbow. The state of your memories is the scribbler's principal and overriding preoccupation. *Will they hold up?* If so, which ones? British psychotherapist Philippa Perry has a generativity-friendly theory about that. "As we get older it is our short-term memory that fades rather than our long-term memory," she says. "Perhaps we have evolved like this so that we are able to tell the younger generation about the stories and experiences that have formed us which may be important to subsequent generations if they are to thrive."

14   *Snowbirds at Sunset*

Birth, marriage, death," historian Will Durant said. "Everything else is ornament." If only we'd left it at that. Instead, we've convinced ourselves that life's one hell of an obstacle course. There's the treacherous elbow to navigate. Eight psychosocial phases to struggle through, each with its own conflict or task. One damn passage after another—the Urge to Merge, the Trying Thirties, the Deadline Decade.

I think back to when Linda and I escaped to Florida for a brief respite. I was far enough into this project that I needed some distance from it. So we took off for a small island just off the mainland. We needed to clear the decks, put our electronic devices to sleep. The place had nothing going for it, just what the doctor ordered. Not a single fast food joint. No condominium towers. Not even a CVS or Walgreens on every corner, not even on one corner. God help you if you needed a Lipitor refill. No Starbucks. No movie theater. Nightlife? Nonexistent. Everyone flosses and tucks in early. The only celebrity was a middle-aged novelist who goes there to fish, a pastime he's always found meaningful to the point of transcendental, much the way Hemingway did until he took what he thought was the honorable path and blew his brains out.

The day before we left, news came that the actor/

screenwriter Harold Ramis—everyone knew him from *Ghostbusters* and *Stripes*—had died at age sixty-nine. His longtime friend Dan Aykroyd issued a statement: "May he now get the answers he was always seeking." The obit carried no hint as to what the questions may have been.

On the island, it took about ten seconds before I was back in the fray, gathering field evidence on how the region's three principal species—birds, fish, and snowbirds—were wrestling with the demands of their existence. At first I kept my eagle's eye on the birds. There's a wide assortment on the island: herons, egrets, cormorants, American coot, and, most prominently for us, ospreys.

A pair of those fearsome hawks happened to be tending a nest on a platform you could see from our window. The female osprey was straight out of a Thurber cartoon (or R. Crumb, if you like). She was much larger and more vocal than her mate, whose natural role—which he performed without argument or apparent resentment—was to commute back and forth from the nest, each time bringing back a doomed fish in his talons. The female ripped the fish apart with her formidable beak and dropped bits into the mouths of her two chicks. Those ospreys seemed to know exactly what their life story at that moment called for: *generativity*. Nurture the next generation and resist the impulse to eat it, which ospreys have also been known to do. Thanks to some sort of instinctive osprey prenup, and when not consuming their own offspring, male and female work in partnership for eight or so weeks until their chicks are able to launch themselves from the nest. The island is perfectly suited to supporting this ageless scenario. The bay outside our window teemed with pinfish that even the clumsiest of henpecked ospreys could pluck from the water at will. Not that there's such a thing as a klutzy osprey. An osprey can dive-bomb into the water at forty miles an hour from a height of fifty feet and almost always get its pinfish. Ospreys have opposable thumbs, just like us, which is where any similarity ends, except that we, too, want to launch our kids safely from the nest.

As for the fish, I spent some time along the bay shore, caught a few sea trout and unsavory hardhead catfish, releasing them back to continue their voyages through whatever psychosocial stages a fish must swim through. Around the time we left the island, an impressive armada of silvery tarpon moved in. They come here to spawn. Thus will the species replenish itself, though some number of ill-fated procreators will be hooked and gaffed, then mounted to be displayed in seafood restaurants or in man caves. No life cycle for you—sorry, Charlie. These casualties aside, procreation and generativity, birth and marriage, play out according to plan on the island, one season to the next.

As for the snowbirds, it wasn't clear to me how they fit into the grand scheme of things. The island is seasonal home to several thousands of them: late midlifers or golden agers who migrate here annually from colder climes. Neither procreation nor nurturing their young is the order of their day. Their procreation window had closed. Their kids were launched from the nest a long time ago. John Kotre hit the nail on the head in *Outliving the Self*: biological sterility can be a fact of life for decades, now that we're living longer.

Not surprising, then, that when you're of snowbird age, whether lying in the sun down south or freezing your buns off up north, you take stock. There are memories to preserve, and before it's too late. A friend of mine gathered old snapshots and a journal his mother kept and published a limited-edition book about her life. Linda, sensing an opportunity, has come up with a business scheme: a Digital Mausoleum, she calls it. It would be marketed to those who want to produce a polished tribute to a recently departed loved one but don't know how to go about it. So you'd go to the Digital Mausoleum site, where you would hire an experienced creative team—writer, editor, and graphic designer—to produce a multimedia life story that will live permanently in the cloud. Or as permanently as technology will allow. Should someone someday rewrite the code, or if a digital format became obsolete and unplayable on future hardware, or were the cloud itself to dissipate—then what? Personal photos, diaries, all vanish. Departed loved ones would die all over again, this time for good, which is the only catch that I can see.

More evidence: the *New York Times* reports that we're in the throes of a creative writing boomlet. Not quite Paris in the twenties, but a definite trend. The article mentions a growing number of adult education programs set up to teach "techniques to retrieve and describe compelling moments." We're living in "the age of memoirs," one instructor says. I'm totally supportive of this trend. These would-be memoirists, a good many of them of snowbird age, have something they need to nail down. They sense there's a worthwhile story banging around inside that they'd like to capture by writing it down. When I ask about this, some midlifers sheepishly confess they don't have the discipline to get off the dime. (No one seems aware of the Christopher Hitchens crack: "Everybody has a book in them, but in most cases that's where it should stay.") When I then ask *why* getting the story down is so important to them, a few bemoan how families are now scattered all over the map. When relatives are in the same room on a special occasion or a holiday—Thanksgiving, say—nobody tells family stories anymore. Everyone's glued to a screen, often two screens at a time. Even Gramps snoozes in front of the football game with an iPad on his lap. We don't tell or listen to family stories the way we used to. E-mail or Skype isn't a substitute. (Lady Gaga, from the stage at SXSW: "When you leave this earth," she said, "no one's gonna give a fuck what you tweeted.") Instant messaging isn't conducive to keeping family lore alive. A clan's Facebook page is mostly untended, and nobody looks at it anyway. Writing a personal history is a way of filling these perceived gaps.

But the most common answer I hear about why midlifers want to get their stories down is this: "For our kids' sake." Their kids or their kids' kids might be curious someday, they say. Wishful thinking? Maybe. But you must admit it's comforting to think that our kids or our kids' kids *might* wonder about us someday, and that our stories will live on as a happy consequence. Yet when I ask people whether the desire to get their stories down might have something to do with "immortality," suggesting that the "age of memoirs" is the result of baby boomers wanting to make sure that proof of their existence won't evaporate in the mists of time, most are quick to dismiss the idea. "Nah," they say with a wave of the hand. "When you're gone, you're gone." The meaning of life is that it stops.

I really don't believe they believe this.

Look, our stories, parts of them anyway, do live on. I hope I've established that much. They endure for a variety of reasons, some on an epic scale, others in bits and pieces. A story lives on in a big way if the leading character plays a role in a drama of historical significance. Gandhi's and bin Laden's life stories live on. Other life stories live on because the leading character leaves behind something of unsurpassed originality and beauty. Michelangelo's, Shakespeare's, and Billie Holiday's life stories live on for that reason. Elvis's life story not only lives on, Elvis himself deigns to make a public appearance from time to time.

Less celebrated life stories live on, too. We encounter evidence of it all the time. Minutes ago, I checked my e-mail and found an unsolicited letter from someone I never knew but who was an alum of a school I'd gone to. She said she was writing in reference to another alumna, a woman named Anca Romantan. Anca, born in Romania, had gone on to get a PhD. At the time of her death at age thirty-three, she was a professor at UMass Amherst, remembered for "her proficiency in multiple languages, her deep commitment to complex social theories, and...the care with which she advised graduate students." In Romanian Orthodox teaching, memorials are held for the deceased at intervals up to seven years following death, which was approaching in Anca's case. The letter asked for a donation to endow a fund that would offer grants to current students—a "living legacy to Anca and her passion for research." Anca's story lives on.

And your story, my story, will live on, too. At least for a while. How long can most of us reasonably expect? If you have kids, and they have kids, about seventy years, more or less, which seems to be the consensus view of those who study life stories. Your grandchildren will almost certainly remember your name and perhaps quite a bit about the beginning, middle, and end of your story. Your great-grandchildren will know little or nothing about your life story, unless you do something stupendously good or bad and wind up making history. Seventy years is seventy years. It's not forever. But it offers way more comfort than "the meaning of life is that it stops."

PART III

The End

If life passes into anything, it passes into pages.
  —James Salter, *Burning the Days:*
  Recollection

15 *Ghost Theory*

I can't honestly say that I fully succeeded in depriving death of its strangeness by hanging out in the old country grave-yard. I did make a bit of headway, however. Thanks to those books about death and dying that were piled up in the spare bedroom, I sifted through some key questions: To what extent does the end shape what comes before? And were it not for death, would we care whether the point is everywhere but we just don't see it, or is it somewhere and we just can't find it? Or is it nowhere?

I might have made more progress on these sticky questions had I not gotten hung up on what others, Freud in particular, had to say about the end. "If you want to endure life, prepare yourself for death," he advised. Easier said than done, my good Sigmeister. Who the hell wants to think about the end? Who wants to prepare? Recently on an airplane I saw a fifty-something man with a copy of Atul Gawande's *Being Mortal: Medicine and What Matters in the End*. He'd force himself to read a page or two, then put the book aside, retreating into a sudoku puzzle he kept in the seat-back pocket as a handy escape.

One of the lesser pleasures of my weeks spent on Long Island was cobbling together a conscientious list of the reasons we're so mortally afraid of dying (*thanatophobia*, Freud called it, Thanatos being the Greek personification of death). My inquiries told me that death is a riddle wrapped in a mystery inside an enigma enveloped in the heebie-jeebies and shrouded by stabs in the dark. Getting over the fear of it? Now *there's* a hill to climb. Maybe you have to get lucky. Like the woman who survived the sinking of the *Lusitania*. In *Dead Wake*, Erik Larson tells of a woman whose lifelong horror of death was cured when she almost drowned after the ship was torpedoed. "The only explanation I can give," she said, "is that when I was lying back in that sunlit water I was, and I knew it, very near to death." She wasn't at all frightened. "Rather, somehow, one had a protected feeling, as if it were a kindly thing."

It's hardly a wonder that we need to deprive death of its strangeness. The Grim Reaper is a shapeshifter. "It is the unknown we fear...nothing more," said Dumbledore to Harry as they confronted the dead bodies guarding the Horcrux. Dumbledore, sharp as he was, didn't put a dent in the multitudinous reasons we fear death. Holed up in that spare bedroom, I inventoried a profusion of death anxieties. There are, you'll excuse the expression, three main buckets: We're afraid that death will disrupt our personal goals. We're afraid that death will do damage to our close relationships. We're afraid of what happens in the hereafter. To break these down a notch further: We're afraid of pain and suffering. We're afraid of nothingness. We're afraid we'll miss out on something. ("I'm going to die, and die very much alone, and the rest of the world is going to go merrily on without me," David Foster Wallace, then thirty-one, said in an interview fifteen years before his suicide.) We're afraid we won't finish our important business, even if we're not sure we have any important business to finish. We're afraid we won't meet our Maker. Or we're afraid we *will* meet our Maker and find out that what happens after death is worse than death itself. We're afraid of losing our future *and* our past. Milan Kundera observed that memory loss is a foretaste of death, the single greatest fear the writer upstairs harbors. No more memories, nothing left for a scribbler to do. One more writer out of a job.

We're also afraid of leaving alone and unprotected those we love most. I ran across a short article by a retired grief counselor who'd been diagnosed with ALS. He said he was worried that his wife wouldn't be able to hold things together after he's gone. In the next breath, though, he let on that *she's* been the one who's held everything together throughout the decades they've been together. His concern for her, he had to admit, was really a "proxy for self-grief."

This hit home for me. Linda and I have gone around and around about who wants to go first. We sound like third graders at a slide. I want to go first! No, *I* want to go first! While on the surface wanting to go first seems selfless and noble, who are we kidding? Going first isn't doing the other one a favor. It's the survivor who gets to suffer.

How would you like to be the writer upstairs who must try to make sense of a life story with so much apprehension about death echoing through the paper-thin walls of the brain? The late surgeon Sherwin Nuland observed that doctors and nurses see death all the time but rarely write about it. On the other hand, poets, essayists, philosophers, and, of course, writers-in-residence—those who rarely come face-to-face with death—are obliged to take on the subject.

My quiet walks through the graveyard yielded some respite from all this theorizing. They also inspired a brainstorm or two, not a few of which were, thinking back, pretty weird. Take, for example, this day:

I'd spent the morning poring over G. Stanley Hall's turn-of-the-nineteenth-century journal article about how young children don't naturally cozy up to a corpse even though they have no inkling yet of what death is. Hall went on to reflect on why corpses are disturbing to the human psyche at any age. Why, for instance, from earliest history on, have we felt compelled to place the dead where the sun never shines, chop-chop, as soon as humanly possible? Hall said it's because we don't want to confront in the flesh what's going to happen to us corporally. Judging from Hall's monograph, it would appear that in the early twentieth century folks really did believe that the worms crawled in, the worms crawled out, the worms played pinochle on your snout. (A "poetic abomination" Hall called that ditty, but you have to agree it was hilarious when we first heard it in the schoolyard.) Hall went to some lengths to make sure we understood that we, in fact, don't wind up as carrion for worms, grubs, and maggots. What happens is at once more benign and more terrifying than that. We're gently and gradually consumed by our own bacteria. It made me wonder whether the patriarchs in their massive mausoleums had deluded themselves into thinking that tons of limestone might offer decay prevention, like fluoride in toothpaste.

Hall also had interesting things to say about why we're afraid of ghosts, none of whom, by the way, I'd crossed paths with in the old cemetery. There are four principal reasons why ghosts annoy us: (1) the way they look and dress; (2) the way they float through the air and pass through solid doors and walls; (3) the fact that they have nothing to lose so they're capable of highly irrational acts; and (4) how they haunt us with guilt. This last I found intriguing. After friends or loved ones die, we often admit to ourselves that we weren't nearly as nice to them as we could or should have been when they were alive. Thus, since they've got nothing to lose, the ghosts of those underserved loved ones may return to give us our deserved comeuppance. Reading that, I understood for the very first time why kids are said to feel guilty when a parent dies. And it reminded me of those bleak nights long ago when I checked under the bed before going to sleep.

Hall's lengthy paper made no mention of anything resembling a writer upstairs. Nor was I expecting it. Then, on a sweet afternoon in the graveyard, as I sat under a sign that read NO PLANTINGS, FOUNDATIONS OR MONUMENTS WITHOUT PERMISSION, a thought hit me, one of my higher-grade brainstorms, or so it seemed at the time: an absolutely never-before-imagined thesis that goes a long way toward explaining the true nature and mission of ghosts.

What if these avenging apparitions aren't the spirits of the dearly departed? What if a ghost is actually the spirit of the dearly departed's *scribbler*, who returns to deliver payback for how we may have slighted or wrecked the departed's life story? Maybe we didn't offer enough love or support. Maybe we turned our back on an aging parent, shunting off the task to a hapless sibling. Maybe we leveraged a colleague's bright idea, hogging the credit and rewards. Maybe we were a shitty husband or wife and never made amends. Whatever we did, we did something to turn someone's life story into a less meaningful tale, and this understandably offended his or her ghostwriter. Maybe we fucked up someone's *point*. Wouldn't you be pissed if *you* were that scribbler and had invested so much time and effort in getting the story right, only to have a thoughtless or selfish sibling, boss, friend, parent, or child come along to muck it up for all eternity?

16   *In Search of a Good Ending*

I don't want to leave the impression that I was starting from square one in those weeks on Long Island. I'd done a bit of spadework on the subject of death prior to arriving there. From the start, questions about death and dying were included in the interviews I'd been collecting. One woman—she'd recently turned fifty—said she accepts the idea of death "so long as it comes at the right time. In an ideal world, I'd like to live to 110." She quickly added that her children's mortality terrifies her more than her own. On the bright side, her grandmother was fortunate to have had a really terrific end, she said. She had been a cellist who'd performed with a string quartet on the day before her unexpected death. "Her mind was sharp as a tack," the woman recalled. Shortly before she expired, her grandmother watched *Jeopardy!*, which was her favorite show, and right before that had completed in full the *New York Times* crossword puzzle. Then, feeling a little tired, she lay down for a nap and that was that.

While many of us want our end to be low-key, like falling off a log, things rarely work out so conveniently. " 'Natural death,' almost by definition, means something slow, smelly and painful," wrote George Orwell in an essay called "How the Poor Die." Slow, smelly, and painful is precisely the kind of end most people say they'd prefer to avoid. Especially if it takes place in a soulless hospital where—after days or weeks of expensive, futile medical procedures, gruff manhandling by Nurse Ratched, and clumsy groping by interns no older than Doogie Howser—death is "cleansed of its organic blight [and] packaged for modern burial," as Sherwin Nuland describes the terminus that awaits eight out of ten of us.

Many people told me they'd be agreeable to a humane, responsibly assisted end, the kind of end still inexplicably outlawed in all but a handful of states and a few countries. But no one I interviewed said anything about death that I consider particularly original. It takes a really fine writer to capture death in a compelling new way. Don DeLillo is one of the few who's managed to pull it off: "a swan dive, graceful, white-winged and smooth, leaving the surface undisturbed" is how one of DeLillo's fictional characters said he wanted his end to turn out.

I'd go like that in a heartbeat, wouldn't you?

So, tell me, if I may ask now that we've been together for a while: How *are* you coping with the idea of death? Is the end driving your life story? Are you convinced that you'll burn in hell if you step out of line even a tiny bit? Do you regard every minor twitch as a warning sign of a terminal affliction? If so, life can't be much fun. "Spending your life concentrating on death is like watching a whole movie and thinking only about the credits that are going to roll at the end," says novelist Nicholson Baker.

Or, if you're not actively obsessed with death, are you sending mixed messages upstairs? That, you know, you'll actually "die happy" if this or that thing happened in your life? As I write this, the hometown Cubs are shaping up as one of baseball's most promising young teams. Sooner or later, they'll make it to their first World Series in over seventy years. Then what? Chicago meets Jonestown? Is Rahm Emanuel preparing for city-wide mass extinction? Perhaps he should. Untold numbers of Cubs fans young and old have sworn blood oaths that they'll die happy if the Cubs ever win a World Series. A perceptive writer upstairs knows—maybe Rahm does, too—that they're blowing smoke. A wise scribbler will have a hard time picturing diehard Cubs fans queuing up at the stairway to heaven as soon as the ticker tape settles in the Loop. What the scribbler *can* picture is every last one of them jammed into the Billy Goat Tavern, getting shitfaced and chanting for a repeat. Just one more, maybe two, and *then* they'll die happy.

Do you kid around about death as if it's no big deal? Clive James, the marvelous essayist, is right now battling leukemia. He's a veritable quip machine. He says that he no longer has to worry about quitting smoking. That he's in the "slightly embarrassing" position of writing poems saying that he's going to die, and then he doesn't. As for me, I freely admit to a decades-old case of AKS, Allan Konigsberg Syndrome, more commonly known as Woody Allen Personality Disorder. It's the tendency to veil one's true feelings about death and existentialist gloom in general under a blanket of wisecracks. ("Can we actually 'know' the universe? My God, it's hard enough finding your way around in Chinatown." "I'm not afraid of death; I just don't want to be there when it happens.")

No, I don't like the prospect of death one bit. Nor do I like talking about it, though I really do believe my time in the graveyard has loosened me up, deprived death of a trace of its strangeness. Before, I talked about death obliquely. I reminded Linda that I wouldn't be around forever to show her how to download a JPEG. I'd find spontaneous occasions to unburden myself, as in, "Oh, you know what I just realized? I'll never have to buy another shirt!" It happens that I really do have more shirts than I'll ever need, because until recently I traveled on business a great deal and needed a bunch of clean shirts ready to go. Apparently I'm not the only one who tiptoes around death this way. There was an op-ed by a novelist named James Collins, who's in his early fifties, I gather. Collins has gone to the trouble of figuring out that he has 4,850 staples left in a box that originally held 5,000. Estimating that he uses fifteen staples a year, he calculates it will be another 323 years before he'll need to buy another box of staples.

I, too, have more than enough staples, but that doesn't give me the night shivers. Knowing I'll never have to buy another *shirt*, however, is sobering. One's personal myth is more closely tied to one's shirts than to one's staples—at least mine is. I have enough shirts for two healthy men to get by on for at least another fifteen or twenty years, which should give me peace of mind but makes me a little melancholy.

Getting back to you, though, and if I may ask: Are you not entirely sure how you feel about dying? If so, then there's a handy exercise in the appendix (page 255) that may help you know where you stand. Answer a few questions and you'll arrive at your Death Attitude Profile-Revised. The DAP-R is a widely accepted scale that "terror management" counselors use to establish where on the death "acceptance" spectrum a person falls. Researchers also employ the DAP-R to measure attitudinal differences about death among various population sets. Who's more accepting of death? Women or men? Believers or nonbelievers? Papuan tribesmen or actors living in Greenwich Village? In other words, whatever comparative set piques a researcher's interest and warrants grant funding.

If you're curious, give the Death Attitude Profile a test drive. Once you've calculated your DAP-R score, you may discover one of the following about yourself:

You're *neutral* about death: you accept it as part of life. To be neutral about death suggests that you neither fear death (terribly) nor look forward it.

Or you *lean in* toward death: you accept it on the assumption that it's not really the end. If you lean in toward death, you're likely to believe in an afterlife. You may also approach acceptance of death if you have zero religious faith in any afterlife. In this case, you've convinced yourself that you'll live on in some symbolic way, such as through the work you've done or the people you'll leave behind.

Or your DAP-R results might point to how you view death as an *escape*: you accept it as a welcome alternative. It's not that you want to be dead, but under the circumstances—you're seriously ill, desperately alone, or profoundly unhappy—it's preferable to be dead than alive.

I see no reason to beshroud one's DAP-R findings under HIPAA privacy rules, so I'm happy—well, not happy, but willing—to share my own. Then we can compare.

First—no surprise to me—my DAP-R results point to a strong propensity to disagree with any suggestion that death takes us to a happier or better place; or that death offers the likelihood of a reunion with loved ones; or that my soul will rocket into orbit and make an eventual soft landing back on this or another planet.

Second, I take a decidedly neutral stance on acceptance of death. I view it as undeniable and unavoidable. Death is what it is. It's part of life.

Third, notwithstanding my overall neutrality, *of course* there are days when the idea of death gives me a raging case of the willies. But the uncertainty of not knowing what will happen to me after death has never once kept me up at night.

17 *Butterfly in the Cafe*

One morning, this was a few weeks before heading east for Long Island, I got up, showered, put on one of the several dozen clean shirts in my closet. I contemplated an event I'd not been looking forward to. Linda, who'd agreed to join me, was as calm and collected as always. We climbed into the car and drove up to Evanston. It happened to be one of those gorgeous spring days that make you feel happy to be alive and death be damned. But gamboling hand in hand through some fragrant arboretum wasn't on the agenda that day. We were off to attend the inaugural meeting of a local Death Cafe, one of some fifteen thousand chapters around the world. Maybe you've heard about the Death Cafe. It's a self-described "social franchise," a nonprofit—not sure what to call it—cause? movement? crusade? catharsis?

The Death Cafe phenomenon started in London a few years ago, inspired by a similar concept that had been tried in Switzerland ten years prior. Whether it takes place in Oslo, Tasmania, or suburban Chicago, a Death Cafe is an informal gathering of the living. Most attendees haven't met before. You come together at someone's home, a church, a bakery, or a pub, where you'll share a cup of coffee, munch chocolate-chip cookies, and admit, if you're so inclined, to deep-seated death anxieties. Or, if you harbor no such terror, you can muse sociably about what death and dying mean to you in the abstract. Some people are naturally reserved and say very little. Others chatter on as if at the Laundromat, waiting for the spin cycle to complete. Some talk so much they suck the air out of the room, which is enough to make you want to strangle them right there in their folding chairs.

Our session was held at a bustling social center for seniors. A large poster had been set up in the busy lobby— DEATH CAFE—with a big green arrow pointing down a long corridor. I can only surmise what unsuspecting seniors made of that placard. Funeral parlor pop-up store? If I were eighty and saw a sign pointing to a Death Cafe, I wouldn't proceed down that corridor for a million dollars. Keeping my head down, I'd hasten straight to water aerobics.

The folks who showed up for the Death Cafe ranged in age from the mid-forties to late eighties. They were overwhelmingly female. I was one of only a half-dozen men, all of us with neatly trimmed facial hair, which I'm sure has to do with wanting to project virility or is a futile attempt to fool the Reaper into thinking we're not as old as we really are.

Who were all these people? A mixed bag. There was a woman who worked in a grief-support center (you'd assume she'd have something more pleasant to do on her day off); an octogenarian who'd been a Jungian analyst; a former librarian; a Holocaust survivor; a nondenominational minister who said he has to console grieving families but is personally terrified at the thought of death. One woman said she'd come because a friend had taken her to a Cubs game, so she brought the friend to the Death Cafe as a way of returning the invitation.

The session's organizer—she was very chipper—opened

up things by reading a poem about a butterfly. Then she suggested we go around the room so we could introduce ourselves and offer a personal tidbit about how we felt about death or what we were looking to accomplish at the Death Cafe. When Linda's turn came, she smiled, nodded at me, and announced straightaway that ours was "an interfaith marriage"—as if no one could tell by looking. She then explained how she'd been raised Catholic and that over the years she and I had had several "contentious discussions" about whether or not there's an afterlife. In fact, I can remember exactly *one* such contentious discussion, and it lasted all of two seconds. We were walking along the lakeshore when, for reasons I honestly don't recall, we got onto the subject of what happens after we move on (from life on earth, not Chicago). Linda said how "comforting" it was to think that there might be something that comes after this life, and that keeping one's mind open to the possibility elevates the spirit. I truly forget what I said in reply, but it was snarky enough to end the discussion before it grew any more contentious. Looking back on it now, yes, I was a pill. Why do I, why do so many of us, keep ourselves incurious or intolerant of others' spiritual beliefs, not least those belonging to the people we love? So, yes, I'm apologizing here and now in case I get hit by a bus later on.

When my turn came, I naturally took the high road. I said nothing contentious about the afterlife, nor did I get into what we really bicker about: that Linda's always leaving lights on in unoccupied rooms, and that my eating toast while standing up in the kitchen gets a lot of crumbs on the floor and annoys the hell out of her. I confined my brief remarks to how the two of us generally approach the subject of death— legalistically, you might say, keeping our emotions at a safe distance. Are our estate documents up-to-date? Should we revisit our wills now that we've moved to Illinois from Wisconsin? The guardians and powers of attorney we assigned decades ago, do you remember who they are, and are they still alive, and if not, whom do we know who isn't ancient and can be counted on in a pinch?

The next two hours went by quickly. The conversation ranged widely. The Holocaust survivor said that she hasn't the slightest fear of dying; she'd come close to it "nine times before." There was much back-and-forth about the difference between a "good death" and a "bad death," a distinction I personally have trouble making. Someone talked about how much she'd benefited from *Tuesdays with Morrie*. Another person recommended *The Four Things That Matter Most: A Book About Living*. Curious to know what those four things were, I looked them up when I got home. Before you die, the book advises, you should (1) ask for forgiveness; (2) extend forgiveness; (3) thank the people who've loved you; and (4) say you love them as well. (This presupposes that you really mean it.) The nondenominational minister said a "good death" is when a dying person can say, "I'm at peace with my loved ones," which earned the most sustained, collective head nod of the entire session.

Finally, there was a fascinating exchange between Linda and the retired Jungian analyst. Synchronicity? Linda mentioned that the opening butterfly poem had brought back the memory of the afternoon her mother died. She'd spent three weeks at her mother's bedside, keeping vigil at a hospice. When the end finally came, Linda went out into the garden and sat down on a bench to collect her thoughts. A large white butterfly suddenly appeared. It hovered just inches away, and for a remarkably long time, as if to attract and hold Linda's attention. The analyst listened, then told of how the butterfly (*psyche* in Greek, which also means "soul") is an archetype that commonly appears in dreams involving death. Jung associated butterflies with transformation, resurrection, and the immortality of the soul. Some Jungians also associate the creature with observation. A butterfly can be seen as watching us. It alights and closes its wings, then gently opens them, as if uncovering its eyes to stare.

Then it was back to the emotional security of our homey apartment, where, as I say, death isn't routinely discussed. All in all, Linda and I agreed, the Death Cafe was a worthwhile experience. For those few hours, death had lost some of its strangeness. Listening to people talk about death is of special benefit to the writer upstairs. A scribbler will realize that there are other scribblers facing the same challenges: those mixed messages of ours, our denials, the laundry list of fears. It also helps a scribbler understand that death can sometimes be, as we say, a blessing. By dragging your scribbler to a Death Cafe and opening up a little, you're signaling that you're not afraid to try to make some sense of death. It affirms that death's not driving the story—it's *you*, steadfast writer-in-residence, who's driving it. This should give the scribbler a bit of a confidence boost. And what writer, real or metaphorical, couldn't use a little more of that?

Attending a Death Cafe, I now realize, is one way among many to deprive death of its strangeness. Making a party, a spectacle, or a fool out of death also works. Folks in New Orleans are unusually adept at this: mourners, for example, marching to Dixieland jazz strikes the right chord. Some in the Big Easy go even further. In 2014, the body of a fifty-three-year-old New Orleans woman wasn't laid out in a coffin, it was propped up at a kitchen table with an ashtray, a can of Busch beer, and a couple of mini–New Orleans Saints helmets. The corpse wore sunglasses and held a cigarette in her hand—a so-called sitting pose. (If you're into yoga, by the way, consider a final, heroic Warrior III.)

There are people for whom, as Sylvia Plath said, dying is an art. A New York City woman suffering from uterine cancer threw herself a month-long farewell party, hosting a procession of family and friends in her apartment. A local newscaster in Illinois announced matter-of-factly on the air that he had only four to six months to live: "I believe that I'm in God's hands, I'm at peace. I know that he's going to take care of the days ahead, and that the goal here is to have the best ones possible." A fifty-six-year-old father in Cleveland, dying of cancer, fulfilled his pledge to give his daughter away at her wedding. He was driven to the church in an ambulance, wheeled in on a gurney, and walked his daughter down the aisle with the aid of a team of volunteer medics. When his twenty-four-year-old daughter burst into tears, he cautioned her not to streak her makeup. He died three weeks later.

These are the sort of human-interest stories a writer upstairs should take to heart. They will further help deprive death of its strangeness. Some stories will have the opposite effect. I'm thinking of the millennial in Los Angeles who asked a funeral director to text him a photo of his mother's corpse, saying that it was less upsetting than having to view it in person.

18   *A Place in the Shade*

One day I returned from a stroll through the graveyard and made a beeline for the kitchen. Linda was about to bite into a mozzarella-and-sun-dried-tomato panini.

"I've had a great idea!" I said. "I'm thinking we should be buried right over there in that old cemetery." It sounded no more solemn than if I'd told her I'd thought of a nice place for dinner that night. "I'm not talking about anything over the top," I said. "No hulking mausoleum or soaring obelisk, just a double-wide plot with a tastefully designed stone that's big enough for both our names, dates, and brief, carefully chosen sentiments. I'll write yours, you write mine. Trust me, this is the way to go."

She was taken aback. Not because I'd suddenly hurled death into the room the very second that she was about to bite into something warm and savory. Nor was she stunned at the prospect of yet another relocation. By now, she's perfectly open to trying out new places. We've moved around a lot these past few decades, albeit in connection with work, not death—New York City; London; Knoxville; the New York suburbs; Madison, Wisconsin; Chicago; plus short-term stints in southwest Florida, where a company I worked for was based. Linda's terrific when it comes to settling in and making new friends, gets right in the thick of a new situation.

Not that such skills would be necessary were we to put down final roots across the street.

No, what stunned her was how *concrete* the proposal was. Over the years we'd spoken only vaguely about our disposition preferences. We danced around them. Back when we visited Esalen, while hiking through a redwood forest magnificent beyond words, we chatted cheerfully about where we wanted our ashes dumped. The issue was whether we'd rather be dumped at sea or in the woods, those Big Sur woods being as good as woody dumping grounds get. Linda, who grew up on a small island off the coast of the Bronx, said she'd prefer the water. I opted for a woodland scatter, having never loved sailing, let alone the prospect of being cast adrift. But now, out of the blue, just as she was about to take a bite of the panini, came the all-too-specific prospect that she'll wind up buried in an actual cemetery, under an actual stone marker, in a specific, actual town where we have a few actual friends but no actual kinfolk and where we've spent a grand total of less than two weeks in our entire lives. It all begged for a bit of processing, so we agreed to take a few days to think it over. We sat in silence for a minute. Then she looked up and asked: "Tell me, which part of this is so appealing to you? Is it the burial-in-a-cemetery part? Or is it the having-a-marker part?"

A really, *really* good question.

I said I'd like to think about that, too, and would get back to her. Meanwhile, I asked if she could please keep an open mind about what I absolutely, positively believed was a truly inspired idea. I was dead certain of it.

Leaving Linda to enjoy her by now cold lunch, I bounded up the stairs and sought refuge in my books about the dead and dying. To be honest, my weeks-long journey into the jowls of death had begun to lose some of its charm. I was getting sick to death of death. Nobody wants to be dead, okay? What's so hard to understand? Everybody *will be* dead. Got it? Why do we have to make it so bloody complicated? Which, I'm afraid, brings me back to Freud.

In the early years of his practice (later on he'd soften a bit), Freud ventured that the bony hard grip we feel closing around our neck, the reason we erupt in a cold sweat over what Shakespeare euphemistically called the "untimely frost," isn't really the fear of death. How can we fear what we haven't experienced? (Don't all answer at once.) What we're really afraid of is any number of things: fear of castration, a tussle between our ego and superego, etc. We thus look on our own demise as a distant observer might. Here I am at my own funeral, my mind a total blank, powered down in an overpriced box, tucked in with my beloved 5-wood, per the best-ever Larry David episode. Or, see that tombstone over there, with LEE B. EISENBERG carved into it? With the quote from Kahlil Gibran's *The Prophet*: ONLY WHEN YOU DRINK FROM THE RIVER OF SILENCE SHALL YOU INDEED SING? That would be me. And you know the worst part? My superego doesn't write, never calls.

In trying to explain Freud's apparent blind spot—it isn't death we fear, it's something buried in our childhood— critics argue that Freud himself was so leery of dying he opted to evade it in his formulations. Freud had a history of predicting that he would die at a young age. (He made it to eighty-three.) I ruminated about all of that and more, devoting a good many precious summertime hours to how Freud might have weighed in on many of the issues I was dealing with. I mused on how he would have been sympathetic to the notion that there's an immortalizing writer-type person inside each of us. Freud, as we all know, was big on the persuasive power of narratives. He was a story man through and though.

But a tiny ghostwriter in denim shirt and mom jeans with unfettered access to our memories? Freud would have ground the theory into *frankfurter würstel*. Scribbler, shmibbler, it's our unconscious needs, our sexual drives, that steer our life story. Freud would point out, as every *furshlugginer* college sophomore knows, that our psyches are "layered." We have a conscious mind, a preconscious mind, and an unconscious mind. Patronizingly, he'd argue that for the scribbler hypothesis to be valid, there'd have to be a second, possibly even a third, penman hidden in the brain.

Frankly, I find multiple storywriters a fascinating possibility. If Freud were around, I'd shoot him an e-mail to say I'd be open to working with him on a multiple-scribbler theory. I'd suggest that maybe there *are* two or three writers-in-residence, sort of like a writing team on a TV series. They wear their baseball caps backward and kibitz in a room with pizza boxes, candy wrappers, and Dr Pepper bottles scattered everywhere. The place smells like a stall at Aqueduct. I could sign on to that scenario right now. Would it be a peaceful collaboration? Not a chance. Would the writers inevitably lock horns? Absolutely. Authors are notoriously fratricidal, even when they're not in their cups. Look at Vidal and Capote. Vidal and Buckley. Vidal and anybody. Or even look at Jane Austen—generally perceived as gentle, polite Jane Austen—who wrote in a letter to her niece: "Walter Scott has no business to write novels, especially good ones.—It is not fair.—He has fame and profit enough as a poet, and should not be taking the bread out of other people's mouths."

If the multiple-scribbler compromise managed to put Freud in a more receptive mood (which I doubt it would), he might run with it farther, suggesting that Oedipus himself had somehow broken into the writers' room, not unlike a Watergate plumber. After all, what does a team of run-of-the-mill ghostwriters who've never been out of the writers' room know from incest, penis envy, suppressed libidinous drives? It would be way out of their depth.

By this point, I'd give up trying to reach any accommodation with Freud. Why did I even care what Freud would have made of the scribbler hypothesis? His life and work have by now been picked clean. Dissenters have asked whether all that talk about the unconscious reflected the "unconscious ideas of patients [or] the conscious theories of the therapist," as one critic sniped. Freud's major insights were the result of a determined study of a single, endlessly fascinating life story: his own. Cognitive scientist Steven Pinker and others have speculated that Freud's boyhood stirrings for his mother, and thus his analytic leap to how mother-lust/father-hate shape our life stories, could have stemmed from a ridiculous case of mistaken identity. We know for a fact that Freud misremembered *when* he'd spied his mother in the nude, the event that started it all. He wasn't two years old, he was four. There was also a nurse in the Freud household. It was common for middle-class families in Austria-Hungary to choose comely help in the hope that it would encourage their sons to get off to a healthy, heterosexual start. What if it was the nurse, not his mother, for whom young Freud lusted? In his early work, he consistently pointed to maids, governesses, and other domestics as being associated with the neuroses his patients developed. This all being the case, he had no bloody business dragging your mother and mine into his theories about the so-called night side of the soul. Yes, to be sure, mothers can and sometimes do cast a blanket of guilt across the chapters of a child's life story. The fact that I'm not a doctor or a lawyer (I'm sitting here in my underwear typing words into a computer) is something that my mother—who loved me and I loved her—never let me forget. Yes, absolutely, how our life stories come to be written is vastly complicated, but not complicated in the way Freud tried to get us to believe. The notion of a traditional nuclear unit—mother, father, and child, all tussling over who wears the penis in the family—feels hopelessly out of sync in an era when babies are now routinely reproduced by third parties or raised from the get-go by same-sex parents, among any number of other modern-family permutations.

Freud's "tortuous formulations" about death can now be consigned to "the dust bin of history," Ernest Becker says in *The Denial of Death*. Becker's book won a Pulitzer Prize in 1974, the year he died of cancer at age forty-nine. The work has had a major influence on social scientists, psychotherapists, and unlikely others, such as Bill Clinton, who includes it among his all-time favorite titles, along with Marcus Aurelius's *Meditations* and that masterwork of historical philosophy, Hillary Clinton's *Living History*. *The Denial of Death* even makes a cameo in *Annie Hall*. Remember the bookstore scene? Right after Woody and Diane Keaton start dating? Woody picks up a copy of *The Denial of Death* while Keaton leafs through a big picture book about cats. Keaton (glancing over): "Hmm, that's pretty serious stuff there." Woody: "I'm,

I'm obsessed with death.... A big subject with me. I have a very pessimistic view of life. I think you should know that about me if we're going to go out."

I've owned a paperback copy of Becker's signature work—it's thoroughly defaced with underlining and marginal notes—for I don't know how many years. I was about to add "and bought it for reasons I don't remember," but of course I remember. I bought it because I thought it might be of some use to me now that I was more than halfway between wherever I was and the last chapter of my life story. Even then, I suppose I was looking to deprive death of some of its strangeness.

The Denial of Death lays out the case that our death anxieties stem from a concern more profound than our conflicted ego running off with the UPS driver. Death "is the final destiny of man," Becker declares. "The idea of death, the fear of it, haunts the human animal like nothing else; it is a mainspring of human activity—activity designed largely to avoid the fatality of death...." Thus we do our best to deny it.

In his poignant foreword to the book, Sam Keen tells of visiting Becker a few days before Becker succumbed to cancer. This was no chatty Death Cafe encounter about butterflies and interfaith marriage. In the hospital room the two "talked about death in the face of death," after which they said a quiet good-bye over a paper cup of sherry. In Keen's view—difficult to top, so I won't try—Becker weaves his death-denial argument out of multiple strands. The first is that our exalted status in the evolutionary hierarchy notwithstanding, we're creatures like all the rest, bugs on the windshield of life, varmints skittering across the desert. Like forest-dwelling stoats, we, too, shit in the woods, not often, but if and when necessary. As babies, before the scribbler takes up residence, we root around in our most unsavory cavities. We learn firsthand that we emit foul-smelling substances, no better smelling than your average wild boar's. Our task as humans "becomes the denial of what the anus represents." Nature's values are bodily. Human values are mental. Dimensional conflict!

Becker's second strand is, yes, we exist as creatures but there's an asterisk attached. Alone among animals, we're conscious of *self*. As the stones in the old country graveyard attest, that self is driven to build strong whaling ships, dance graceful *Coppélias*, write powerful novels, raise children who are virtuous. We want to express ourselves for as long as possible, thereby inviting in the terror that one day whatever we've built, danced, written, or otherwise brought into this world will be no more. A terrifying prospect we need to defuse.

The third strand is how, looking to defuse the terror, we search for ways to demonstrate how much we actually do count. Becker, though unaware of any scribbler upstairs, put his finger on the scribe's dilemma, especially in midlife: "the heroic seems too big for us, or we too small for it." How do we convince ourselves we count? By signing on to a variety of "systems" that promise to make us feel bigger, stronger, smarter than death itself—religion being the ultimate such system. We flatter ourselves to death. We tell ourselves we're created in God's image and have divined a path to eternal life. The hero system offers, says Becker, "a feeling of primary value, of cosmic specialness, of ultimate usefulness to creation, of unshakable meaning."

The final strand of his argument is the way our quest for

the heroic lures us into all kinds of holy messes. Competing systems clash to disastrous effect. My God's more powerful and righteous than yours.

In a nutshell, there you have it. We must convince ourselves that we're not simply here to emit foul-smelling substances, only to wind up the same organic matter as every dead squirrel in the graveyard around the corner. Becker said that for us to concede that that's all there is, that that's the point, would represent "a devastating release of truth."

True to my word, I spent several days reflecting on Linda's question: Was it the buried-in-a-cemetery part, or the I-want-a-marker part, that had gotten me so hopped up about our coming to rest in the old country graveyard? Truth is, in all these years, aside from that walk through the coastal redwoods, I'd never given a thought to whether I wanted to wind up in a casket, urn, cigar box, or Mason jar. Still, I did draw the line at cryonics. Not only is the procedure expensive and of dubious utility, but I live in Chicago, so believe me, I know what cold feels like. Nor had I ever really thought about a marker or no marker. Had all this obsessing over death and the writer upstairs gotten to me? All I can say is that if *I* were the writer upstairs, I'd certainly want me to wind up in a place that fit the narrative drift of the story. Ending in the right place makes an overall life story more consistent and well rounded. If, for example, yours is a life story of extreme derring-do, then doesn't it follow that your remains ought to be finely pulverized, mixed with an explosive powder, packed into an aerial shell, then fired into the sky such that your ashes would burst forth in a giant chrysanthemum over

Soldier Field? Wouldn't that be far more fitting than winding up in a cheap canister from Bed Bath & Beyond, then left to gather mold in your third cousin's dingy apartment? Some people, in fact, do a nice job of matching their final resting places with the things that mattered in their lives. I'm thinking of the sax player who paid $25,000 for burial plot No. 10836 GR2-5 at the Woodlawn Cemetery in Queens, New York. One day he'll be just fifty yards away from Duke Ellington, whom he idolized. *Sir* Miles Davis (by the royal order of his tombstone) and Illinois Jacquet will also be close by.

So, yes, I'm inclined to think that our final resting place *ought* to matter to us, which is what I said to Linda when we finally sat down to try to resolve the issue of the graveyard. I ticked off the many reasons I liked the place. It's peaceful and quiet. It's steeped in history. It boasts a wonderfully diverse population—Christians and Jews, gays and straights, sea captains and ballerinas, war heroes and manufacturing moguls, honest working folk and a handful of VIPs who were always assured of a good table at Elaine's (may she rest in peace).

The graveyard was light-years more appealing, I told Linda, than where my parents are now: a sprawling, soulless "memorial park" in the northeastern suburbs of Philadelphia, hard by a roaring interstate. I can remember—this was back when I was ten or so—when my parents purchased four plots there: for themselves, my sister, Barbara, and me. I'm assuming they got a nice deal, as the plots were located in a newly opened and as yet entirely barren section of the cemetery. One Sunday we got into our two-tone green Buick Roadmaster and drove up there to take a look. The already decrepit Langhorne Speedway was practically next door, home to the notorious stretch of asphalt that race drivers referred to as "Puke Hollow." "The most dangerous, treacherous, murderous track there ever was," Indy champion Bobby Unser called it.

Bury me at Puke Hollow? It was not an appealing prospect, even to a ten-year-old. I remember how bitingly cold it was that day. But I also remember being warm in the glow of how nice it'd be that we'd all be together no matter what happened between then and whenever. It wasn't to be. In time, my sister and I had our own families and our reserved plots were resold. But for decades my mother talked about how one day she'd be reunited with my father, not in heaven but side by side in the memorial park that, as memorial parks will, filled up nicely over the years. If my mother had a purpose in life, it was to join my father there, to be reunited with the myth she'd created of him. And in the end she was. Hers was a long life but a love story all too brief, I thought as I stood shivering on still another frigid day in late December 2007.

Cormac McCarthy, in *All the Pretty Horses*: "They'd put an awning up over the gravesite but the weather was all sideways and it did no good."

Robert Penn Warren, in an exquisite passage near the end of *A Place to Come To*: "As long as you have a parent alive, you are a child; and mystically, the child is protected, the parent is the umbrella against the rain of fate. But when the umbrella is folded and laid away, all is different, you watch the weather with a different and more cunning eye, your bones ache when the wind shifts, all joy acquires a tinge of irony (even the joy of love for a child, for you feel yourself as the umbrella or lightning rod, if you will, and know the frailty of such devices). Furthermore, with the death of your parent you begin to see in each death the weight of a 'tale told'...and you begin to feel the fleeting impulse to verbally sum it up for yourself, or for some common acquaintance."

19   *Is There Ever a Right Time?*

Like most writers' day-to-day lives, the scribbler's day is stressful. There's the constant fear of making a mistake, such as twisting memories the wrong way, or forgetting or misinterpreting a particularly important memory. Imagine spending days, months, years putting up with *your* adolescent mood swings, then your midlife travails, then your anxieties about the end, while trying to remain reasonably upbeat through it all. The harried storywriter wants to write you a story that builds to a meaningful conclusion but doesn't know how many pages she's been given to complete the job. One day a stranger in a cowl, holding a scythe (see Monty Python's *The Meaning of Life*), pounds on the door of your scribbler's writing cottage: "Time's up. Hand it over," the phantasm snarls. But it's not finished yet! the scribbler retorts. My leading character's unresolved! Supporting characters will be left in the lurch! They both want to go first! If it ends here, there'll be loose ends all over the place!

Indeed. Too few pages presents a problem for a writer-in-residence. But so does too *many*. Thanks to new drugs and procedures, life stories run longer than they used to. Is that good or bad? It's *good*! A surfeit of pages can be a boon—many more pages in which to paint, enjoy nature, follow our bliss, be generative, seek symbolic immortality. And it's also *bad*! More pages can mean more pages in which little or nothing happens, or horrible things happen. Real writers will tell you that the more pages they try to fill, the more likely meaningless fluff will creep in, self-indulgent detours, blind alleys leading nowhere. A leading character can wear out her welcome in a story that's too long for what little happens in it. Characters with time on their hands grow tedious and self-pitying. While friends and family can tune out a leading character's complaints, the writer upstairs needs to hang in there and listen to the whining. There's no escape.

Writers, artists, composers, they all wrestle with the dilemma: How *do* you decide when something's finished? When is it good *enough*? A writer can tinker with a story forever, sometimes making it better, oftentimes worse. When is a *life story* good enough to be over? Is there a right time to die?

One evening in the graveyard—it had been an unusually long day of trying and failing to decipher a word of Martin Heidegger—I found myself thinking about a chilly afternoon in March a few years ago. Along with former colleagues at *Esquire*, I attended a memorial service in Manhattan to celebrate the life and work of Richard Ben Cramer, an uncommonly talented, chain-smoking reporter who died at sixty-two. Complications of lung cancer. An outsized character, Cramer won a Pulitzer Prize for his reporting from the Middle East and later wrote what many regard as the finest piece of sports journalism of the past fifty years, a monumental profile of Ted Williams. He was also the author of a 1,072-page book, *What It Takes*, that chronicled the 1988 presidential election, when George H. W. Bush defeated Michael Dukakis. Cramer sweated over the reporting and writing with such fanatic detail that the book didn't make it out until five years after the polls closed on a race that was forgettable to begin with. Joe Biden, who got to know Cramer on the campaign trail, came to New York to speak at the service.

"It is a powerful thing," the vice president said, "to read a book someone has written about you, and to find both the observations and criticisms so sharp and insightful that you learn something new and meaningful about yourself." In other words, Cramer's take influenced how Biden "read" his own life story. A meaningful experience for Biden, a meaningful accomplishment for Cramer.

At the reception, a few of us traded memories about how singularly eccentric and skilled Cramer was. There wasn't a soul present who didn't lament that Richard had died way too soon. By most reckonings, he had. Robert Nozick, the Harvard philosopher who gave us the halfway-between-this-and-that trick, observed that "Deaths are called 'untimely' when they end lives where much still was possible that went unfulfilled."

But why were we so sure that Cramer had died too soon? A lifetime of unfiltered cigarettes would have caught up with him anyway; he could well have suffered even longer and more painfully than he did. It's also fair to assume that he'd have been intensely crabby had he lived longer. Cramer could be very crabby under the best of circumstances. Imagine him having to operate in today's beleaguered newspaper and book businesses. It's also hard to imagine Richard ever topping the extraordinary work he'd already accomplished. He'd induced Joe Biden to look deeply into the meaning of his own life. Given his pace and the level of care Richard invested in his projects, another book could well have taken him into his eighties, if it ever got finished. So, did he die too soon? It's not the length of life that matters, it's the depth, Ralph Waldo Emerson said. On one of her albums Laurie Anderson says we can think about time as being long or wide. Cramer's time on earth was gloriously wide. So given what Emerson and Anderson are saying, *did* Cramer die too soon? In any event, it's not an appropriate issue to debate over drinks following a memorial service. For now, let's just leave it that Cramer was deeply admired and will be very much missed, which would have been the case had he died at ninety-five.

When word reaches us that a scribbler has dotted the final "i" on the life story of someone like Richard Ben Cramer, we reflexively ask about two things: "How?" and "How old?" Then we silently conduct a rapid three-step exercise. We swiftly scroll through the departed's mental and physical condition. We assess the departed's accomplishments or lack of same. We consider the prospects of his or her survivors. Then we render a verdict. We conclude whether the life story was difficult, or tragic, or charmed, or dull, or exciting, or happy, or sad, or a waste, or one of a kind, and so forth, and we render judgment on whether the end came "too early," "too late," or more or less "at the right time."

Again, what *is* the right time?

For some, there's no time like the present. They throw open the door and invite the Reaper in. Why put it off? Albert Camus wasn't advocating that we kill ourselves when he said suicide was the fundamental philosophical question. He was saying that if you believe that life is absurd, then suicide is a perfectly rational option. Some are remarkably cool-headed about reaching that decision. George Eastman, founder of Kodak, left an unambiguous note: "My work is done, why wait?"

In *Notes from Underground*, Dostoevsky's narrator declares that age forty is precisely the right time to die. To live longer than forty, he says, is bad manners and vulgar. The character obviously isn't in high spirits. He's bitter, aggressive, insufferable. It just so happens he's forty years old.

Jump cut to Ezekiel Emanuel, bioethicist and law professor, older brother of the mayor of Chicago (Rahm) and a powerful Hollywood agent (Ari), who generated a little buzz with a 2014 *Atlantic* magazine article titled "Why I Hope to Die at 75." Emanuel's reasoning went as follows: Even though he was a hale fifty-seven, Emanuel assumed that by seventy-five his faculties would have deteriorated, his ability to be "creative" would be significantly diminished, and he'd be an emotional and financial burden to his loved ones. So he was resolved to do everyone a favor by checking out. Nietzsche would applaud Emanuel's decision. The right time to die, Nietzsche's Zarathustra declared, is when you know you've taken care of your important business, at which point you can "die free." What counts as important? Valiant performance in battle, spake Zarathustra—which means that most of us will need to define for ourselves what our important-enough business is.

At the very end of his piece, Emanuel backtracks. "My daughters and dear friends will continue to try to convince me that I am wrong and can live a valuable life much longer. And I retain the right to change my mind and offer a vigorous and reasoned defense of living as long as possible."

The takeaway here is that there's no magic number of years in a life story, any more than there's a magic number of pages in a written story. Some lives are brief—they're short stories. Some are longer—they're novels. (Some are too long, William Vollmann's and Donna Tartt's, for sure.) That we tend to value a longer life over a shorter one is understandable. "Long books...are usually overpraised, because the reader wishes to convince others and himself that he has not wasted his time," said E. M. Forster.

But it's not how long it is, it's what you do with it. As Don DeLillo said in one of his rare interviews, "It's my contention that each book creates its own structure and its own length." The main thing is that a story, long or short, and a life story, long or short, be well resolved by the end. Does the story deliver? And does it satisfy?

That we don't like looking death in the eye, and kick around theories about the right time to die, *none* of this would be necessary had we only listened to Epicurus. His soothing proposition is so succinct it can fit on a Post-it: "When death is come, we are not." Translation: When you're dead, you're dead. It's nothing to lose sleep over. Epicurus believed that life's purpose was pleasure. We'll experience no pleasure after we're dead, but neither will we suffer. This reasoning is so self-evident it's hard to fathom how the fear of death still ranks high among our most common anxieties, right up there with flying, public speaking, heights, spiders, and intimacy. Had we listened to Epicurus, we wouldn't despair that "never again will our dear children race for the prize of our kisses and touch our heart with pleasure too profound for words," as Lucretius wrote so long ago. Had we listened to Epicurus, religion, if we even needed a religion, would be vastly different from the religions we cling to. The promise of an afterlife—a surefire customer-acquisition tool for faiths ancient or newly minted—would be irrelevant. Had we listened to Epicurus, the early Christian church, had it existed at all, would never have floated the idea that earthly riches can be offloaded to allay anxieties about the hereafter, which was "arguably the most successful development campaign for any institution in the Western world," says historian G. W. Bowersock. Had we listened to Epicurus, we wouldn't be so befuddled about how resurrection works. The questions surrounding it would be less pressing: What's the timetable between when we bid adieu to the living and return? Is there a storywriter upstairs the second time around? If so, is it the same writer-in-residence as before? And what about our memories? Are we tricked out with the very same ones? Or does the storywriter, whether she's the same scribbler or a successor, collect and arrange brand-new memories as she goes about producing *The Life and Times of My Enduring Self II*?

Had we listened to Epicurus, well, everything would be different. In *Immortality: The Quest to Live Forever and How It Drives Civilization*, philosopher Stephen Cave says our quest for immortality is no less than "the foundation of human achievement...the muse of philosophy...the architect of our cities and the impulse behind the arts." He outlines four principal immortality narratives that are as old as the hills. The ancient Egyptians are notable because they managed to twist all four into "a single beguiling thread":

1. *The "Staying Alive" narrative.* Think Ponce de León, not Bee Gees. The narrative is not to grow old but to stay young. We all but run ourselves into the ground trying to maintain a youthful and healthy glow, remaining firm and fit. We drag our bones off to Swiss sanitaria to be shot through with sheep-placenta extract. We linger at the vitamin and cosmetic shelves at Rite-Aid. Dabbing on anti-aging, under-eye concealing balm

won't make us immortal, but it holds out the promise of keeping us in the game until such time as science rides to the ultimate rescue. Now that we have genetically modified corn down to a science, Craig Venter, among the first to sequence the human genome, is working on genetically extending the human expiration date.

2. *The "Resurrection" narrative.* Cave calls this humankind's "best backup plan." The mummies at the Met are by now old news. The new news, Cave says, is computational resurrection. To be computationally resurrected is to have your brain's current assembly of neurons and associated molecules digitally scanned, burned or ripped, or otherwise preserved in an electronic medium to be announced, then uploaded into bodies real or robotic, therein to live on forever.

3. *The "Soul" narrative.* Cave cites statistics indicating that seven out of ten Americans believe they have something called a soul; that nearly everyone in Africa believes they have a soul; billions upon billions worldwide are certain of it. Not long ago, a comment by Pope Francis set off a round of feverish discussion over whether he was making a veiled declaration that even dogs have souls. The news story prompted thousands of reader comments, including several that wondered whether mosquitoes go to heaven. On the very same day there was a confrontation at an ashram in India. Facing off were government forces and followers of "the frozen baba," a religious leader who'd been kept on ice for nearly twelve months after dying of cardiac arrest. "His soul is very clean," said a follower. "He is in Samadhi, and he will come out of it."

4. *The "Legacy" narrative.* Simply stated, this is the urge to extend ourselves somehow into the future. The poster boy has always been Achilles, who, rather than settle pragmatically for a humdrum retirement, opted for a prize of greater value: eternal glory, his good name remembered. "No one," philosopher Blaise Pascal said, "dies so poor that he does not leave something behind." Nor, one might add, dies so rich that he does not leave his name (or those of his parents) on a building at NYU. I happen to be sitting in one right now.

•

It's difficult, isn't it, accepting the idea that *nothing whatsoever* comes after this? That our brief time on earth is, per Alan Watts in *The Wisdom of Insecurity*, but a flicker of light between one eternal darkness and another? That after our life story rattles to a close, taps sound, piper plays, fat lady sings, curtain drops, screen goes to black, *nothing else* happens save for whatever our designated "legacy contact" on Facebook posts in our memory, assuming she doesn't delete our account altogether? It rankles us, said Jorge Luis Borges, that we're the only creatures on earth who know they aren't immortal. The others—mammals, reptiles, fish, mollusks—don't know that they're going to die. It's unfair, isn't it? So rather than be outfoxed by ferrets and jellyfish, we try to convince ourselves that we might live on. *Might* is our life raft. My beloved Linda clings to the might. François Rabelais, Renaissance man, doctor/scholar/monk, and composer of bawdy tales, also clung to the might, famously declaring on his deathbed: "I go to seek a Great Perhaps."

But *had* we listened to Epicurus? For one thing, we'd be indifferent to how long we lived. With nothing to worry about, why even wait around to be dead? Bring it on. Why bother to accomplish anything? The conundrum prompted a philosopher named Steven Luper to propose a "*neo*-Epicurean" view of things: set meaningful, short-term goals that we can achieve within our lifetime.

Since we didn't listen to Epicurus, it's all academic. We're as afraid of death as we ever were. Some say it's actually a good thing, that death makes us all the more appreciative of life. Knowing that there's an end keeps poets and philosophers gainfully employed. Emily Dickinson wrote: "That it will never come again is what makes life so sweet." Death gives us something to measure everything else *against*. My friend Becky Okrent reminded me of a line in Junot Díaz's novel *The Brief Wondrous Life of Oscar Wao*: "Dude, you don't want to be dead. Take it from me. No-pussy is bad. But dead is like no-pussy times ten."

20 Chiseled and Engraved

Linda was spot-on about the marker part, I finally decided on one of my last visits to the old country graveyard. Thanks to all the time I'd spent there, the idea of leaving behind some tangible evidence of my existence had grown on me. A simple stone, unveiled at a brief good-bye ceremony. Call me a schmo, but it's never occurred to me to leave behind production notes for my own memorial service, as Nora Ephron did prior to her death in 2012. Having worked with Nora for years at *Esquire*, I was fully expecting the Lincoln Center affair to be classy, witty, and moving. It was all of that and more, owing to Nora's attention to detail. The playlist was impeccable (Ella Fitzgerald, Louis Armstrong, Jimmy Durante's "As Time Goes By"). Nora had cast the eulogizers. Meryl Streep gave a bravura impersonation of how Nora moved her hands when she spoke. Brilliant. Tom Hanks and Rita Wilson were stellar in their reenactment of how Nora and husband Nick Pileggi kibitzed at their East Hampton barbecues. "I believe that when people pass, they zoom into the people that love them the most," said Martin Short, who was first in order of appearance. "So, if that's the case," he went on, "then all of us here have a piece of Nora. If she's a part of us, we must be more like her: read everything, savor everything, talk to the person on your left, embrace laughter like it's a drug, drink more pink champagne, and yes, brush up your style."

Personally, I'd always thought it a touch vainglorious that someone would have the *chutzpah* to sit down with a pencil and scratch out their own tombstone copy before it was too late, tucking the paper into a sealed envelope, then placing it in a desk drawer with explicit instructions that those *exact words* be carved into a granite slab to keep the record straight for all eternity. Risky business, that. You're going to have to live with those words for a very long time. Holden Caulfield, in *The Catcher in the Rye*: "If I ever die...and I have a tombstone and all, it'll say 'Holden Caulfield' on it, and then what year I was born and what year I died, and then right under that it'll say 'Fuck you.'" (Tell me, how would you like to be his surviving kinfolk?)

If you're going to do it, then you need to do it right. Rule one: Wait until you're at least a grown-up and have some vague idea of who you really are. Rule two: Even then, don't be hasty. Just as a master carpenter measures twice and cuts once, you need to be super careful before deciding what becomes a tombstone most. John Updike said he was inclined to go with this: "Here lies a small-town boy who tried to make the most out of what he had, who made up with diligence what he might have lacked in brilliance." Thankfully, Updike never followed through, and he wound up with something much niftier, thanks to a bright idea that one of his kids had. Inscribed on the back of Updike's black slate marker is the first piece of writing he ever submitted to the *New Yorker*, a poem he wrote when he was sixteen. (It was rejected.)

Some do get it right. Screenwriter and director Billy Wilder led an irrepressible life, escaping the Nazis when he was in his late twenties. He arrived in Hollywood speaking little English, with only eleven dollars to his name. Wilder persevered, leaving behind a treasury of classic American movies (including *Some Like It Hot* and *Sunset Boulevard*). Wilder lies in a cemetery on the west side of L.A., along with a good many movie stars and a portion of Truman Capote's ashes, the rest of the tiny terror having been scattered on a Long Island pond.

BILLY WILDER
I'M A WRITER BUT THEN NOBODY'S PERFECT

(The "nobody's perfect," of course, echoes the immortal last line of *Some Like It Hot*.)

Robert Frost, flinty and nomadic, moved from farmhouse to farmhouse throughout his long life, looking for a place where he felt truly settled. It wasn't easy. After his wife, Elinor, died, Frost revisited Derry, New Hampshire, to select a burial site. Decades before, the couple had lived on a farm in the town, and Elinor had always expressed a desire to be buried there. Over the years, however, much had changed ("a house that is no more a house / Upon a farm that is no more a farm," is how Frost dismissed the place in a later poem). For a couple of years, he kept Elinor's ashes on a cupboard shelf, eventually deciding on a country graveyard in Bennington, Vermont. Locals say he chose it because of its mountain view and the old white church that overlooks it. Two decades later, he would be lying there as well, his epitaph the final line from a well-known poem about death he'd written decades before:

ROBERT LEE FROST
MAR. 26, 1874–JAN. 29, 1963
I HAD A LOVER'S QUARREL WITH THE WORLD

Of all the last words I collected for possible use in this book, none rival the courage and eloquence of the two words

Irish poet Seamus Heaney sent to his wife, Marie, shortly before he died in 2013. The words weren't engraved in metal or inscribed in stone. They were transmitted in a text message, of all things. And they were in Latin: *Nolle Timere*—"Don't be afraid." How much better than Holden Caulfield's "Fuck you" is that?

Getting the words right, I decided as I walked through the graveyard, was too important to be left to a whim or dictated by whatever foul mood you happened to be in on a given day. Which was why, I told Linda, I want her to write mine and I'll write hers—to keep us from going overboard. And yet we kept putting off making the larger decision. Our burial plans still under advisement, I paid daily visits to the cemetery right up to the day we left for home. I nevertheless kept an eye out for the perfect plot, wide enough for two, with just the right drainage and mix of sun and shade, as if scouting for a good spot to build a dream house.

Returning to Chicago, I felt a little out of sorts now that I was no longer a hop, skip, and jump from an arcadian cemetery. I did what I could under the circumstances. I began taking long walks in nearby Lincoln Park, where there's a zoo, conservatory, playing fields, the usual recreational diversions. It occurs to me now that I was drawn there out of some ineffable need to commune with the city cousins of the country ghosts I'd left behind back east. Stretches of Lincoln Park were once Chicago's municipal burial grounds (pop. 15,000). There was a vast potter's field for the poor. The remains of 4,000 Confederate soldiers were also buried here; they'd died as prisoners of war at Camp Davis, a few miles to the south. Adjacent to the main city cemetery were members-only graveyards for Catholics and Jews, the latter area having given way to a baseball diamond. Grave robbing was a significant enough scourge that Pinkerton guards were hired to protect the dead of all persuasions, the thefts perpetrated by cadaver-seeking med students heedless of Shakespeare's warning "Curst be he that moves my bones." The bygone city cemetery was no bucolic country graveyard. It was rank. An 1867 newspaper story reported a "putrid and sickening smell" after wastewater from a nearby distillery seeped into the ground. Two recently interred children had to be exhumed; thankfully, their buds had already bloomed in heaven.

Then, in 1871, the Great Fire swept through and laid waste to many grave markers, which led to the mass relocation of the thousands of mortal remains otherwise unperturbed by the inferno. Now, every so often, when new pathways are paved or the underground infrastructure calls for repair, a shard or two of some left-behind Jew, Catholic, Reb, or pauper turns up for a quiet look-around before it's gently relocated elsewhere in Chicagoland.

Without headstones to muse over, the scribbler and I made do with the many memorial plaques found on benches throughout the park: In fact, we'd started keeping notes on these things when we were still on Long Island, gradually honing our aesthetic preferences. Some plaques we thought could use a little something extra:

GOOD WITH KIDS AND DOGS

Others we liked, not knowing whether to question the copyediting or loosen up and accept it as a koan:

HUSBAND, FATHER,
DOG LOVER
AIR TRAFFIC CONTROLLER,
TRI ATHLETE
COME. SIT BESIDE ME

Some we outright didn't approve of, such as the salute we ran across not far from the graveyard: "IN MEMORY OF _____" stamped on a street sign mounted on a stake, directly below another sign that reads "ADOPT A ROAD. KEEP OUR TOWN CLEAN."

Really, if you truly loved and now miss someone who's no longer, fight the urge to memorialize her on a rusted metal stake. A park bench is all it takes, or the base of a tree. Keep in mind, though, nothing's forever. Benches rot, trees fall victim to storms, bugs, and blight. Even granite stones are subject to recall. In 2013, nearly two thousand inscribed stones that had been cemented into a bankrupt megachurch's Walk of Faith were ripped out when the property was taken over by the Roman Catholic diocese, which commenced a major renovation.

Ideally, in my opinion, a memorial plaque or stone belongs in a place that figured meaningfully in the departed's narrative. Someone walked her dog there, or was good to kids, or read good books, or watched the tide roll in, or fell in love there. As for production values, keep the commemoration brief, graceful, and sincere, never mawkish. Choose a traditional, tasteful typeface. Avoid abbreviations wherever possible. Check spelling and punctuation with the ruthless eye of a *New Yorker* copyeditor. The more minimal, the better. I saw a nice example of this at a beach near Naples, Florida, a simple recognition of the bond between man and place:

WILLIAM NORTH

SEPT. 6, 1927–OCT. 13, 2011

"A PAINTER'S PARADISE"

Now and then you come across a head-scratcher. One afternoon, in Washington Square Park in New York City, I plopped down on a bench with a brass plate screwed into the backrest. There were no dates engraved on the plate but the brass was spiffy and shiny, so it couldn't have been there for more than a few years. Or maybe someone regularly takes the Brasso to it, a heartwarming, effortful commitment to the departed. The plate was affixed with four screws, neither slotted nor Phillips. Some sort of special two-pronged tool is called for. A security measure. Why anyone would want to pilfer a memorial plaque—symbolic grave robbery—is a mystery. Where would a lowlife in Manhattan even go to fence a memorial plaque? Would a smelter, even a Big Apple smelter, stoop so low?

There were three lines of copy on the plaque in question, nicely designed. Uppermost, engraved in the largest font, is the name of the woman whose family, friends, or neighbors thought to remember her on this bench in a shady corner of a downtown park. Beneath her name and in smaller type: SHE WAS MOST HAPPY WHEN HELPING OTHERS. Underneath that, in midsized type: IT WAS, FOR HIM, AS THOUGH THE ROCK WERE A GIANT HARD DOOR INTO ANOTHER WORLD. The line was unfamiliar. There was no source citation. The words lacked the elegiac elegance one expects on a memorial plaque—a carefully chosen snippet from a sonnet by Shakespeare or Wordsworth, a poem by Whitman or Frost, an essay by Thoreau or Emerson, or even a calming thought culled from an Alan Watts guided-meditation tape. There was a self-published quality to the words. Curious, I Googled the sentence on my phone and the answer popped up instantly. "It was, for him, as though the rock were a giant hard door..." is a line lifted from Richard Bach's *Jonathan Livingston Seagull*. Remember that book? The bestselling parable published in the early seventies, later made into a truly terrible movie? ("This has got to be the biggest pseudocultural, would-be metaphysical ripoff of the year," said Roger Ebert, who walked out after forty-five minutes.)

I Googled the book's jacket copy: "This is a story for people who follow their hearts and make their own rules... people who get special pleasure out of doing something well, even if only for themselves... people who know there's more to this living than meets the eye: they'll be right there with Jonathan, flying higher and faster than ever they dreamed."

There it is, the meaning of life, the point, for one woman, anyway, in the estimation of someone who knew her. She followed her heart, drew special pleasure from doing things well, believed there was more to life than meets the eye. That was her story. Or maybe she *tried* to be that kind of person but wasn't quite able to take wing. Either way, the story lives on in the memories of those who survive her. And who've so testified to it on a brass plaque screwed into a park bench so that countless others, the scribbler and I that day, and now you, would be kept in the loop.

One morning when the weather was too foul to hunt for brass plaques or do anything else outdoors, I walked over to the Newberry Library, just a few blocks from our apartment. The Newberry is a hulking Italian Renaissance pile that opened in 1887. It was endowed by the estate of Walter L. Newberry, a taciturn railway baron and banker who in 1868 died at sea while on a European journey. According to a curious account in the *New York Times*, a fellow passenger had recognized Newberry and prevailed on the ship's captain not to dispose of Newberry's corpse the easy way. The man reportedly assured the captain that the deceased's family would spare no expense in getting the patriarch's body safely back to America. The captain obliged, ordering that the corpse be preserved in a cask of rum until the vessel landed in New York. Newberry's marinated remains were then sent via freight train to Chicago, where, at least according to the *Times*, the cask was interred in a North Side cemetery. While that makes for a fabulous story, it's not altogether true. Newberry was only *temporarily* preserved in the barrel. He was subsequently properly embalmed and conventionally casketed before burial. His grave, by the way—I know this because I treated Linda to a Sunday afternoon pilgrimage there—is marked by a so-called fancy obelisk, a gigantic one at that, a design highly favored by the upper crust in the mid-nineteenth century. Its inscription reads IN THE HOPE OF A BLESSED IMMORTALITY.

I very much hope Walter Newberry found a blessed immortality, as I now feel deeply indebted to him. A good portion of this book was written at the Newberry Library. Not only was the rummy urban legend morbidly appropriate to the project, the library is almost always deserted—a clean, well-lighted, cavernous place, a perfect setting in which to think and write. On the day in question, I settled down in my usual spot at a table on the third floor and laid out my index cards and fired up my laptop. The only other regular was already at his usual spot, a gray-haired gent who toiled diligently, surrounded by what appeared to be rare books, some of them illustrated, a few in Latin. We never spoke, nor could I make out from a distance what he was working on. A treatise on some aspect of Roman art was my best guess. Something abstruse, anyway. His monkish demeanor—expressionless, intensely focused on his work—suggested a scholarly calling.

A calling, be it academic, divine, patriotic, creative, or nefarious—Pol Pot believed he had a calling—is a mission that chooses you as much as you choose it. Callings are central to mythology. Joseph Campbell made it his calling to explain how classic callings play out. The hero goes forth on a dream-like adventure. It's unrefusable. Decline the call and you're consigned to a life of tedium and powerlessness—as may have tragically befallen me had not I panicked and entered the *Esquire* contest. Answer the call, however, and you set off on a journey that leads deep into a forest, or high onto a mountaintop, or marooned on a distant island, or, for that matter, cloistered in a library working on a book about ancient art.

Depending on the circumstances, nonhumans often lie in wait to torment, delight, or enlighten he who is called, though I never encountered any of those at the Newberry. (On the other hand, I never went above the third floor.) But callings needn't be otherworldly. A strong commitment to a church, social program, ethical cause, neighborhood, school, or Planet Earth, for example, offers the opportunity for a calling, full time or on weekends. Viktor Frankl talked a good deal about how invaluable a calling is. A calling fills the existential void. A calling "endows one's life with a sense of meaning, responsibility and dignity," says psychologist Paul T. P. Wong.

While callings are deeply gratifying, they're not always fun. Joan of Arc, Nathan Hale, and Amelia Earhart all perished in pursuit of their respective callings. Nelson Mandela spent twenty-seven years in prison before his calling liberated a nation. Callings can also be unfair or cruel to those who are dependent on the callee. In early midlife, Gauguin famously abandoned his wife and five children because, he said, his calling was to paint—*adieu, ma chérie!* Off he went to Tahiti, leaving the family to fend for itself. A sympathetic psychologist will tell you that Gauguin should be admired for not allowing social conventions to blunt his drive to self-actualize, which is the apogee of a meaningful existence. Others see Gauguin as a self-indulgent bully and, worse yet, a rumored wife batterer, a gifted painter who had his values up his ass.

In any event, there I was at the Newberry that morning, working on the chapter about Richard Ben Cramer's memorial service, if I remember correctly. Needing to stretch, I got up and walked over to a window that looked out on Bughouse

Square across the street, so nicknamed because it was once Chicago's answer to London's Hyde Park Corner. In the thirties and forties, characters on soap boxes railed against the evils of capitalism, the most fervent of them in the grip of a calling deemed subversive by the powers that be.

While I stood at that window, a memory materialized out of the blue. It could have been sparked by a spot of decay in one of my reverberating neural circuits. Or maybe the writer upstairs was refiling a few moldy memories when one of them happened to go live. Accidents happen. Whatever caused it, the bolt from the blue turned out to be exceedingly helpful to how I came to think about the point: I remembered that once and only once in my life did I keep a journal. No one's ever read it. I don't believe I even mentioned it to anyone until now.

When I returned home that afternoon, I discovered that the Word document ("Diary.doc," created August 29, 1989) was intact, tucked away in an ancient folder on my current hard drive. The file had traveled through time and space, nesting unbeknown to me in seven or eight successive computers, transferred from desktop to laptop to desktop to laptop, surviving at least a dozen Apple operating system upgrades. It survived Steve Jobs himself.

The journal dates from the day after Ned was born and runs until shortly after Katherine's arrival on the scene. Why I stopped writing it I don't remember, nor am I entirely sure why I started. Nobody ever said, Hey, having kids is a life-changing event, a turning point, and if you're smart you'll keep a journal. I just started typing entries into the Word document, usually in the evening, not daily but frequently. "Some moments are nice, some are nicer, some are even worth writing about," Charles Bukowski wrote in a poem. That's precisely what I was doing: writing down moments that seemed worth writing about at the time. The first entry is a basic who, what, where, and when account of the morning Ned was born:

Arrived at New York Hospital around 10 p.m., spent a few hours in the labor room, walked the halls, got used to the fetal monitor, etc. Linda transferred upstairs, where we hung out for ten hours or more. Dr. S., just back from vacation, prowled impatiently, finally joined by longtime partner Dr. M. Everyone finally had enough. Docs wanted to go home. Linda was ready. I was ready. Dr. S. stood at the foot of the table, Dr. M. leaned over Linda's abdomen and pushed down with his *forearm*. Nada. Pushed down again. Nothing. Jumping out of my skin by now. S. reached for the forceps (gleaming, oversized salad tongs, terrifying), gave a strong pull or two and out comes slowly a red, squirming, slippery little human. A boy!! A nurse weighed him and wiped him down, asked if I wanted to cut the cord, holding out a surgical scissor. Unprepared, I shook my head. First fatherly test and I wimp out. Not knowing what else to do, I did the manly thing and took some Polaroids.

From there on, the document's mostly a fanatically detailed series of notes on one infant's entirely unnewsworthy developmental progress as observed in gaping wonderment by someone who apparently never before laid eyes on a nascent human life form. No emergent facial or vocal expression, no subtle change in hair or eye color, went undetected, unappreciated, or unremarked upon. Now and then, there's a fleeting confession or a flash of introspection. Three months in, for instance, I note how it's difficult to remember what life was like in the four-plus decades before Ned came along. A few pages later, I whine about the prospect of an upcoming business trip, fearful I'll miss out on some extraordinary feat of developmental progress. What if he lifts his head while I'm away? Turns over on his stomach? Some pages after that, I again cogitate on how conscious of time you become when you have a child late in life. (I was forty-three, taking my first steps through the elbow.) And there's an entry about what happened the day I was on an unavoidable business trip to Milan. Back at *Esquire* I was obliged to attend the men's fashion shows in Europe—fly the magazine's flag, schmooze the advertisers, etc. If you think that attending men's runway shows is enviable and glam, don't, not unless you enjoy sitting in a non-air-conditioned tent in extreme heat and humidity as bare-chested Zoolanders in fake-fur vests and tailored shorts pound the catwalk in sockless Timberland boots to an ear-shattering loop of Depeche Mode's "Enjoy the Silence." It's enough to make you feel shorter, chubbier, and more adrift in a world gone purposeless than you already do.

Anyway, there I was in Milan the day before the shows were to start. Ned was by now approaching his first birthday. I had a day to kill, so I wandered alone through the city, fighting off existential dread:

> Lonely guy afternoon. Sat under a tree on a bench in a big park near the hotel. Watch a husband/wife organ-grinder act. The woman pumps a foot pedal that activates a mechanical accordion player sitting on a metal folding chair. Her husband is wearing an ascot

and fedora, he's the vocalist, sings Italian folk songs. Something out of a goofy old Italian cartoon. A man comes up on a bike. In a seat on the crossbar is his son. Around 2 yrs, built like Ned. The father sets him on the ground and the boy just stands there, completely transfixed by the music, stares in amazement at the mechanical accordion player. The father hands him a bill, urges the boy to take a couple of steps and drop the money into the pail which is right next to the clanking accordion thing. Boy freezes. Won't dare move an inch closer. Father gently urges him again. The boy takes a tiny step or two, then *flings* the bill into the air in the direction of the pail. It seems to hang forever in midair then flutters directly into the little bucket. Fucking incredible. Boy scuttles back into his father's arms. I tear up. Can't put into words how much I miss Ned at that moment.

Just as I'd never force you to sit through our home movies, I won't foist much more of the long-lost journal on you. As I said, it winds on for a couple more years, the entries getting sparser over time. There's a flurry of activity when Katherine's born (July 27, 1991, 2:23 a.m., for the record). By now we were living in London, where I'd been sent to help launch a British edition of *Esquire*. The account of Katherine's birth serves as a nice bookend to Ned's. Whereas Ned arrived to a fanfare of blaring trumpets weeks after his due date, Katherine arrives weeks ahead of schedule, no muss, no fuss, her entrance accompanied by soft guitar chords. She's delivered effortlessly. No tag team of highly ranked New York City obstetricians. No forearm pushing her out of Linda's belly. No giant salad tongs. All it takes is a midwife from Singapore named Lily Fernandez. Lily's calm, gentle proficiency that morning, her name and presence that day, had gone entirely missing from my memory until she turned up again in the pages of the journal the afternoon I returned from the Newberry Library.

22 *Diaries Dearest*

Rediscovering the long-lost diary got me thinking about diaries and their relationship to life stories. Why do some people keep a journal in the first place? Do you? Did you ever? If not, or if so, why? I added those questions to my interview list.

Some people who've never kept a diary can be pigheaded about it. Who do they think they are, Rudyard Kipling, who boasted that if something wasn't worth remembering, it wasn't worth writing down? Others told me that they'd like to keep a diary but don't have the time. I'm sure that's true; it's tough enough dealing with the demands of work and family. Still others said they had nothing much to say to a diary; their day-to-day life was ordinary, and besides, there were plenty of other places—Facebook, Instagram, Twitter—where they could dump mundane, half-baked thoughts at the drop of a hat. Keeping a journal and posting on social media, however, are two different things, I tried to point out. With a journal, your comments don't scroll out of existence. They're linked one to the next, resulting in an open-ended, running account uninterrupted by commercial messages or the quotidian bleats of others. There's also plenty of stuff that occurs to us that we'd rather *not* share with others—not on Facebook or Twitter, not anywhere—but they're worth keeping a record of. And there's stuff we don't fully understand and can't easily put into words. A diary doesn't care how you say something. A diary's not judgmental. Nothing's not important enough. Everything's not unimportant until time proves it fatuous or incomprehensible.

One person said she never kept a journal because writing doesn't come easily for her. As if that matters. Virginia Woolf, whose lifelong diary stretches across thirty-eight handwritten volumes, said that how a diary's written "doesn't count." Reading through one of her own journals, she confided that she was "much struck by the rapid haphazard gallop at which it swings along, sometimes indeed jerking almost intolerably over the cobbles." My modest seventy-page diary jerks intolerably over the cobbles as if yanked along in a little red Radio Flyer. Literary quality? I'd say it falls somewhere between prosaic and cringe-worthy, no big deal since I never imagined the writing would ever see the light of day.

There are many out there who think diaries are only for people who've led an epic life such as Anne Frank's. Or a train wreck of a life like Bridget Jones's. Balderdash! There's no correlation between how singular a life is and how interesting the diary. A boring life can make for a fascinating diary, and a fascinating life can make for a boring diary. George Orwell, whose writing I admire tremendously, kept one of the most mundane diaries imaginable: shopping lists, daily weather summaries, vegetable-growing reports, speculation on what may have caused his goat's loose bowels.

And then there are people who think that only the lonely keep diaries. Joan Didion predicted that her daughter would never need to keep one because the little girl was "delighted with life exactly as life presents itself to her, unafraid to go to sleep and unafraid to wake up." Those who maintain private

notebooks, Didion said, "are a different breed altogether…
anxious malcontents, children afflicted apparently at birth
with some presentiment of loss." Didion was reaching for
effect. She herself kept a journal because she couldn't bear
the thought of wasting so much as "a single observation." A
"thrifty virtue," she called it. "See enough and write it down,
I tell myself, and then some morning when the world seems
drained of wonder, some day when I am only going through
the motions of doing what I am supposed to do, which is
write—on that bankrupt morning I will simply open my
notebook and there it will all be, a forgotten account with
accumulated interest, paid passage back to the world out
there: dialogue overheard in hotels and elevators and at the
hat-check counter in Pavillon (one middle-aged man shows
his hat check to another and says, 'That's my old football
number')."

Here, though, is the best reason to keep a diary: it is a
way to create who you are. So remarked Susan Sontag, whose
posthumously published diaries recount in intimate detail
her life as a public intellectual. "In the journal I do not just
express myself more openly than I could do to any person; I
create myself," Sontag wrote in her diary.

That's exactly it, I now realize. I started the short-lived
journal to create myself. *Create myself as a father.* Or *re-
create* whatever self I'd been into a substantially revised
self, this one having one, and then another, young soul who
depended on me.

I now realize something else. When I said that the sudden
remembrance of the long-lost journal might not have been
an accident, here's what I was thinking: What if, as I stood at

the window looking out at Bughouse Square, the writer-in-residence was trying to tell me something by setting loose that memory? Such as? Such as we would be doing our scribblers one hell of a favor if, instead of letting them do all the work of figuring out which events and relationships are worth keeping, *we* did some of the heavy lifting. What if the writer-in-residence wanted me to understand that a journal that is routinely updated, no matter whether it's maintained in a moleskin notebook or a crummy spiral-bound Office Max notebook, is of immense value to *him*?

Here's what I mean. Let's say you're jogging through an old country graveyard. Something catches your eye. No, it's not the ghost of George Balanchine hoisting the ghost of Alexandra Danilova in a macabre new production of *Don Quixote*. You simply spy a mighty oak tree. Big deal. A tree's a tree. Except that this time, for some inexplicable reason, you see a tree and you think to yourself, A tree is strong. A tree is stalwart. You're hit with the blinding insight that a tree speaks to the meaning of life—whereupon you're filled with rapturous joy that you are alive at that very moment.

Granted, it's the kind of borderline-deranged insight a poet might have. In fact, Hermann Hesse had that exact borderline-deranged insight, and even went to the trouble of writing it down: "A tree says: My strength is trust. I know nothing about my fathers, I know nothing about the thousand children that every year spring out of me. I live out the secret of my seed to the very end, and I care for nothing else. I trust that God is in me. I trust that my labor is holy. Out of this trust I live."

But let's say that you'd had that insight. You can do one of two things with it. You can write a note about how strong and stalwart trees are, or you can make a mental note of it, betting that the mental note will be stored in your memory archive, to be retrieved one day by the writer upstairs—for what reason you have no bloody idea. Why, then, go to all the trouble of hauling down your journal from inside the dropped ceiling tile or typing the tree thought into your iPad? *Because the journal serves as a backup vault.* Much as we assume we'll remember things that strike us as interesting or inspiring, we don't. We're busy and easily distracted. Most things that strike us as interesting or inspiring go in one ear and out the other, never making it into our memory archive and therefore irretrievable by the writer-in-residence at a later date. But when jotted down in a journal, the insight about the tree is locked and loaded for future use. In time it may connect to another insight about, I don't know, gnats. Not how annoying gnats can be, but how joyfully gnats seem to take to the air on a gentle summer night. Now you've got a theme going, don't you see? How meaningful the world is on a quiet evening when there's nothing going on, except everything is going on. The whole damn world's swarming under the watchful security of stalwart trees. (Or something like that, I'm not a poet.) The point is, you're seeing things in nature you hadn't before, keeping tabs on them. Upon reflection, you may come to discern a pattern. You start connecting dots. The dots may add up to how there's <u>mean-</u>ing, purpose, and beauty in nature, which is not only comforting, it may even add up to the reason you're here in the first place.

The bottom line: were it not for your diary notes, your thoughts about trees and gnats would have dissipated. Noting them in a journal is like marking an important e-mail with a star or circling a date on a calendar. The real-time notation serves as a heads-up, a flag. It says to the storywriter upstairs, *this* memory's worth hanging onto.

Finally—and this is important—studies show that we routinely and predictably underappreciate certain events when they happen. And that events, when recalled in a different mood or another context, mean something entirely unexpected. Such as the evening you had this weird thought about how a tree is trustworthy. The studies show that the more ordinary an event seems at the time, the greater the likelihood that we'll make an error in judgment about how meaningful it can turn out to be.

To bring this all back home: my coming upon the mechanical accordion player who mesmerized the little boy in Milan was, at the time, ludicrous if touching. I was absolutely captivated by the event—at the time. But I probably would have forgotten about it. Thanks to the long-lost journal, however, the event's not only been preserved, it's understood in a way that holds great meaning for me. It reminds me of how captivating and magical the world is to a young child. As our kids grow up, as we ourselves get old, it's easy to forget what that magic feels like. The journal entry also brings back the ache I felt being away from my own young son; how intensely I experienced those early years of fatherhood; and how committed I was to re-creating myself *as* a father.

The same goes for Lily Fernandez, the midwife. She was a stranger who one night materialized and then disappeared just as quickly. I'd completely forgotten about her. But now, thanks to diary dearest, Lily lives on in my life story. She personifies the hundreds of characters who play seemingly minor roles in our stories, yet bear witness to events of special importance. Characters who, because we're distracted by whatever's happening on center stage at the time, we wind up overlooking on our acknowledgments page.

23   *Writing a Beautiful Sentence*

Finally, we come to a subject I swore to myself I wouldn't mention at all in this book: Sisyphus, founder and king of Corinth. I swore I wouldn't mention Sisyphus because his name pops up in nearly every book about the meaning of life. You can't avoid him. Enough already, I said to myself. Then, after thinking about it some more, I swore to myself I wouldn't *end* the book with Sisyphus. And I won't. I'll almost end it with him.

The reason everyone invokes Sisyphus when they're writing about the point is because Sisyphus rules as the undisputed rock star of pointlessness. Were philosophers ever to stage a gala black-tie awards ceremony up in the stacks, the Lifetime Achievement Owlie for tireless efforts in promoting awareness of life's meaninglessness would go hands-down to Sisyphus. He'd retire the prize.

It must have been in the sixth grade that I first learned of Sisyphus. The view was shallow: here was an unlucky loser who received the cruelest, most unusual punishment imaginable. No takeaway beyond "See, kids, crime doesn't pay." I hope, but seriously doubt, that we're now encouraging a sharper reading of the Sisyphus myth. There are few better ways to get a tender mind focused on the meaning of life in general, and in particular on the hours, years, and decades they'll spend bemoaning their jobs and significant others.

I'd gotten a much deeper appreciation of Sisyphus when I was up in the stacks. He was far from a junior offender. "The craftiest of men," Homer called him, though this was before Bernie Madoff came along. Sisyphus's rap sheet, I discovered, was more troubling than I'd known. It extended far beyond keeping the god of the underworld in chains, thus effecting a temporary hold on all earthly deaths, a breakthrough that today would earn him simultaneous Nobel Prizes in physiology, chemistry, and medicine. Sisyphus, I learned, wantonly executed innocent tourists traveling through Corinth. His incorrigible scheming led him to marry the daughter of a rival, who bore him two sons, both of whom she slew when she discovered that Sisyphus was about to exploit them as part of a scheme to overthrow her father. The Julian Assange of his day, Sisyphus notoriously revealed celestial secrets.

Over these many centuries, Sisyphus's name has been thrown around with wild abandon by those who make it their business to decide what's tedious and meaningless in everyday life. Dusting and ironing? In *The Second Sex*, Simone de Beauvoir equates housekeeping with pushing a block of stone uphill. Mowing the lawn? In *Second Nature: A Gardener's Education*, Michael Pollan decries the "hot monotonous hours" we spend cutting the grass, then dumping on fertilizer and lime to induce the same grass to grow back as quickly as possible, thereby restarting "the whole doomed process."

This is not the place to argue with de Beauvoir or Pollan, other than to say that neither housework nor tending a lawn strikes me as inherently meaningless—not that I find deep personal satisfaction in doing either. But some people do, and good for them. There are women who believe that the meticulous maintenance of a home rises to a religious calling. Martha Stewart's net worth attests to it. While I'm not aware of any research studies that probe the fulfillment inherent in mowing a lawn, I can appreciate how, for some people, a manicured lawn is aesthetically pleasing and adds to a feeling of self-worth. If repeated buffing and pruning yield satisfaction, provide a sense of order in a world of chaos, who are we to deny them?

Moreover, repetition unto itself is no sin. Consider poet Philip Larkin's daily grind: "My life is as simple as I can make it. Work all day, cook, eat, wash up, telephone, hack writing, drink, television in the evenings. I almost never go out. I suppose everyone tries to ignore the passage of time: some people by doing a lot, being in California one year and Japan the next; or there's my way—making every day and every year exactly the same."

Live and let live, I say. Boring is in the eye of the beholder.

What I certainly didn't know back in the sixth grade is how many ways there are to interpret the myth of Sisyphus. Camus, in his classic essay "The Myth of Sisyphus," argued that if you don't try to make life into something more than it is, you can wind up a reasonably satisfied human being. "The struggle itself toward the heights is enough to fill a man's heart," he wrote.

Sixty years after Camus, philosopher Richard Taylor took the mythical boulder and dragged it a bit farther. Author of a widely assigned book on metaphysics, Taylor was something of a renegade in his field. He considered modern philosophy vapid and self-absorbed, citing one philosophy department's practice of not allowing the public to sit in on events, even barring philosophers from other universities. "Academic philosophers cook up what seem to me to be artificial problems and then just kick them around among themselves," Taylor said. One of his former students recalled that Taylor marveled over how his colleagues would debate "whether earthworms have souls but scoffed at an examination of love and marriage."

Best of all, Taylor was clearly one of those rare teachers who, through force of spirit and intellect, was himself a source of meaningfulness for those fortunate enough to take one of his classes. We're lucky to have a teacher like that in our school careers. Novelist Rick Riordan had Mrs. Pabst. When Riordan was a struggling thirteen-year-old, Mrs. Pabst introduced him to Norse and Greek myths, which ignited Riordan's interest in mythology, which eventually led to the writing of the phenomenally successful *Percy Jackson & The Olympians* series and other books that have sold in the millions. Mrs. Pabst was, Riordan says, "my Chiron," the centaur the gods called on to mentor their offspring.

I didn't have a centaur, never had the pleasure of knowing a teacher with the body of any animal, though I'm tempted to say I came close. But I did have Mr. Quinn, who back in the fifth grade suggested that I think about becoming a writer when I grew up. In the eighth grade there was Miss Lippard, who, some fifteen years after we last laid eyes on each other, sent me a charming note after I'd gotten a bit of recognition from the high school I went to. A handful of others have stayed with me, too. Sometimes, when I catch a whiff of cigarette smoke, I'm transported back to an electrifying college course in political theory. It was taught by C. J. (Smiley) Burnett, an alternately obstreperous and kindly gravel-voiced character who lit up one Chesterfield after another as he managed to bring alive the bone-dry social theories of Max Weber and Émile Durkheim. I practically inhaled that class.

Richard Taylor died three years after publishing what is today regarded as a seminal essay on Sisyphus. Memorials written by his former students describe a humorous and stimulating classroom presence dressed in khakis, flannel shirt, and work boots, perched on a desk, cigar in hand. He and his dog, slumbering beneath the desk, wore matching red bandanas. He was a renowned keeper of honeybees. Taylor was indomitable. Two months after he learned he'd been diagnosed with incurable cancer and had only a year to live, he told an interviewer: "Strangely, this does not disturb me.... My life has been blessed at every turn, with a beautiful late-life marriage and wonderful children, two of which—Aristotle and Xeno—were born in my late sixties, after I had retired. I'm deep into writing a book, on marriage and divorce, and this keeps me too busy to give much thought to my mortality."

In his widely cited paper on Sisyphus, Taylor observes that the myth enchants us in part because there are so many different ways to read it. It underscores man's determined tenacity (celebrated as "perseverance," "grit," "spunk," "heart," "starch," "resolve," "stick-to-itiveness"). But however you choose to hear the story of Sisyphus, Taylor writes, it's hard to avoid the conclusion that his labors amount to nothing.

Pointless? On the face of things, yes. But Taylor asks us to consider a *what if*. What if the sentencing authorities— they were gods, after all, and could do any damn thing they wanted—had secretly injected Sisyphus with a magical, mind-altering substance? A mythological roofie. What if that potion induced in Sisyphus a compulsive *desire* or *need* to push a rock uphill? Or at least reconciled him to the seemingly pointless task? What if every time the rock crashed back down, Sisyphus couldn't wait to push it back up again? The circumstances of the story haven't changed a whit, Taylor points out. The only difference is how Sisyphus *himself* views what he's been tasked to do. He accepts it. He doesn't feel punished by it. He might even see some value in it. Indeed—stop me if I go too far—what if his otherwise purposeless toil frees up Sisyphus's mind for more valuable pursuits? What if, instead of getting mired in how tedious the work is, he's able to reflect on how unspeakably beautiful the mountain is, exulting in how its colors and shadows dance in the sun and moonlight? Not so far-fetched, I don't think. I just read a profile of a current writer who worked for a time as a bricklayer. She says the experience was more valuable than going to college because it taught her to focus. What if pushing the rock up the hill sharpens Sisyphus's concentration and perceptions? What if it frees up enough mental bandwidth that he's now able to compose gorgeous sonnets and bewitching melodies, if only in his head?

The point? Just as Sisyphus was sentenced to pushing a rock uphill, *we* are sentenced to write a life story—moment to moment, day after day, from the beginning to the end, even as we struggle through inevitable stretches of tedium and suffering.

The point? *The story's the point*, don't you see? *What you recorded in the journal's the point.* The point is to keep pounding away at a satisfying story even when conditions on the surface seem as dreary, futile, and exhausting as pushing a rock uphill.

The point is to write the best story we can. The point is to keep the story from obsessing over what's lacking, inferior, or ugly in life, and instead cast our attention on the good, the true, and the beautiful, never overlooking the pain or injustice but confronting them. As Viktor Frankl said, it isn't what you expect from life that matters—I'm looking at you, millennials—it's what life expects from you. Life expects that we give back to *it*. Frankl was shipped to the death camps and promptly stripped of everything that was important to him. His wife had been imprisoned elsewhere and was probably dead, he could only assume.* His nearly complete manuscript on the importance of meaning, his life's work, was discovered in the lining of his coat, confiscated, and destroyed. His determined attachment to the meaningfulness of both—memories of being at home with his wife in their Vienna apartment, reconstructing his manuscript using a pencil stub to scribble on scraps of discarded leather—gave him the courage and hope to endure the fearfulness and indignity of his unspeakable condition.

"Everything can be taken from a man but one thing," Frankl wrote, "the last of the human freedoms—to choose one's attitude in any given set of circumstances, to choose one's own way."

Our own day-to-day life stories are not remotely as horrifying as Frankl's, thankfully. The same lessons, however, apply. Despair, disappointment, boredom, conformity, pain, and hate are no match for passion, conviction, courage, curiosity, and love. Each of us is sentenced to write a life story. Writing it *as*

---

* Frankl's wife, Tilly, who was twenty-four, as well as his mother and brother, were all killed in the camps, though he didn't find out until after his release.

well and as creatively as you can is the point. A story with a beginning, middle, and end that, despite the ups and downs on a Vonnegut graph, moves persistently in the right direction. That's the point.

So that's it, then? Well, not entirely. I owe you a little more.

Back at the start, I said I wouldn't try to undermine your faith in a supreme being—as if I could. I promised not to pass judgment on any spiritual quests *du jour*. And I assured you I wouldn't make light of your material values even if I don't share them. We all have more than enough self-appointed oracles and arbiters of morality telling us whom to worship, where life's true purpose lies, and what will happen to us if we don't play by their rules. But I didn't say that I wouldn't pass along a few writing tips. Here, then, are some questions and answers that I hope tie up a few loose ends.

Does the beginning of the story matter?

Yes. The beginning sets everything in motion, sometimes in the right direction, sometimes not. This is the part E. M. Forster said you don't remember, which is no big deal since the beginning mostly depends on the hand you're dealt. After that, what happens depends on you. And on fate, of course, which a leading character cannot control.

Does the middle of the story matter?

Yes, the middle's crucially important. There comes a moment in every story, Kafka said, when there's no turning back. What matters in the middle is that there are more pages filled than pages to go. It's here that the story must find its focus if it hasn't already.

As for the end, does it matter?

The tail end of the story counts for a great deal. Nobody

likes a letdown, not least the writer upstairs. If memories start to slip in the final chapter or two, the scribbler faces a crisis of the greatest magnitude. I'm not referring to a senior moment now and again. Those happen to the best of us. In fact, recently there's been speculation that a senior moment is little more than a sign that by now we've collected so many memories over so many years that our storage capacity is getting tight. We therefore slide a few memories to the side—senior moments—just to clear a little space for new memories.

Serious memory impairment is something else altogether. "Our memory is our coherence, our reason, our feeling.... Without it, we are nothing," filmmaker Luis Buñuel wrote in *My Last Sigh*, his autobiography. Among its other tragic consequences, loss of memory late in the game robs the scribbler of an invaluable storywriting opportunity. Social scientists call it a "life review." "Probably at no other time in life is there as potent a force toward self-awareness as in old age," gerontologist Robert Butler said. By mining distant memories and retelling the past, the writer upstairs will often discover fresh insights into bygone events and relationships. It's when "hidden themes of great vintage may emerge," Butler explained. In a life review the scribbler will frequently rewrite certain memories into more mythic ones. He does so to clarify our story. At life-review time, the scribbler takes liberties. For example, research indicates that when we reach our seventies and beyond, we often make our parents into far better human beings than we once believed they were. At this stage, the writer-in-residence figures, coherence is more important than truth, though that's not to say that our parents *weren't* better than we once thought.

Finally, what's a great life story about?

I hope it's clear by now that a great life story can be about a lot of things—but not chiefly about sex, money, power, or fame, though these all have an appropriate place in a great life story. A great life story also isn't a story about gazing at your navel. And it's certainly not about how life did you wrong and owes you. Stories like that are dead on arrival.

A great life story is a story that adds up—that's what it's about, adding up. A story that adds up bulges with meaningful memories. Not to harp on the value of keeping notes as you go, but a journal's a surefire way to keep the scribbler from overlooking meaningful memories. The idea is to tag events and relationships as meaningful *at the time*; to recognize the good, the true, and the beautiful *when they occur*, as Viktor Frankl told us. These moments needn't rise to the heroic experiences or accomplishments that will whoosh you out of your living room into a hall of fame or a history book. Meaningful memories can seem pretty ordinary. You did right by your kids. You achieved a hoped-for goal. You worked your ass off and got your foot in the door. You found something to care deeply about in your off hours. You took an opera appreciation course that opened up a lifetime passion.

To wind up with a sufficient number of meaningful memories, two things have to happen. The first is that you need to pay attention, be a sharp-eyed observer. You need to recognize beauty or truth when you see it. You need to notice how the colors and shadows dance on the mountain, or what a tree might stand for. These are the kinds of moments that will define you and how others will come to see you. They might even earn you a little plaque on a park bench or at the base of a maple tree.

You also have to believe in your writer-in-residence. He or she starts out as gifted as any other scribbler, but many of us doubt our ability to "write" a great life story. "A man should learn to detect and watch that gleam of light which flashes across his mind from within," said Emerson. And yet, he continued, he "dismisses without notice his thought, because it is his. In every work of genius we recognize our own rejected thoughts: they come back to us with a certain alienated majesty."

A year or so after I first jogged through the iron gates of the country graveyard, Linda and I returned to the village and I went back over to the cemetery. For old time's sake. By then I'd done more than enough thinking about the end and was working on the diary chapters. Having rediscovered my long-lost journal, I'd brought east with me a tote bag full of other people's journals. Anaïs Nin's started with a letter she wrote in 1914, when she was eleven. She would eventually fill up two hundred notebooks over the course of the next sixty-three years. In one of her diaries—by now she was in her thirties—Nin responds to the age-old question of why some people are compelled to write:

> We…write to heighten our own awareness of life, we write to lure and enchant and console others, we write to serenade our lovers. We write to taste life twice, in the moment, and in retrospection. We write, like Proust, to render all of it eternal, and to persuade ourselves that it is eternal. We write to be able to transcend our life, to reach beyond it. We write to teach ourselves to speak with others, to record the journey into the labyrinth, we write to expand our world, when we feel strangled, constricted, lonely. We write as the birds sing. As the primitive dance their rituals.

If you do not breathe through writing, if you do not cry out in writing, or sing in writing, then don't write.

Now, please read that one more time. But this time, substitute the word "live" for the word "write" and there you have it—the point that's always been right there in front of our nose.

Afterword

That's all we have, finally, the words, and they had better be the right ones.

> —Raymond Carver, "A Storyteller's Shoptalk"

A few months into this project, I was briefly tempted to go all in on the notion that however our life stories come to be, each is fundamentally and unavoidably a *mystery* story. A life story, like a mystery story, is built on a complex plot, full of novel twists and unexpected turns. Why we're here in the first place is murky. Shady characters turn out to be good guys. It's the ones who are too good to be true we need to watch out for.

For a while I played around with pushing this high concept as far as I could. I looked into whether those who'd mastered the mystery genre might offer lessons to us on how we might go about "writing" the mystery called you or me. P. D. James—there've been few more accomplished practitioners—extended a promising checklist. Her first and most adamant piece of advice was that we make certain we know how, where, and when the mystery ends before we start. That's when I knew I was barking up the wrong tree. The end? The only thing we know for sure is that a life story will.

There were, though, a few tips on James's checklist that struck me as useful in thinking about our life stories. A good mystery writer, she said, keeps her senses open to experiences good and bad, an admonition right out of Viktor Frankl's playbook. Noticing and appreciating small, everyday details—being "mindful"—makes for a more surprising and enriched story, be it a good mystery or a satisfying life story. To live in the moment, to allow free-flowing thoughts, feelings, and sensations to be experienced while keeping a lid on snap judgments, is to invite a deeper appreciation of the day-to-day.

James also reminded us that characters in a mystery story must rise to the level of "real human beings"—not "pasteboard characters to be knocked down in the final chapter." Frankl basically said that as well. The meaningfulness of human existence, he wrote, lies in "the uniqueness of the human person." It's up to us to go looking for those qualities in the characters we meet.

When writing her mystery stories, James spent a lot of time hanging out with police and forensics teams. Granted, these may not be the best sources for unraveling clues to the meaning of life, but there are other experts out there to be consulted, among them philosophers, poets, inspired teachers, spiritual guides, and yes, even kids (see below).

Finally, James said she never suffered from writer's block, though sometimes she had to wait out a long dry spell before nailing down the idea for a new novel. While biding her time, she made it her habit to do some writing no matter what—little stuff, anything, if only to keep the gears greased. Even better for our purposes, she explained how she started keeping a diary—her one and only—when she was well into her seventies. Eventually published in book form, *Time to Be in Earnest: A Fragment of Autobiography* came out a few years before James died in 2004. In the prologue she wrote: "My motive now is to record just one year that otherwise might be lost, not only to children and grandchildren who might have an interest but, with the advance of age and perhaps the onset of the dreaded Alzheimer's, lost also to me." Then, a couple of pages later: "There is much that I remember but which is painful to dwell upon. I see no need to write about these things. They are over and must be accepted, made sense of and forgiven, afforded no more than their proper place in a long life in which I have always known that happiness is a gift, not a right."

There were a few times during this project when I was tempted to let a thousand metaphors bloom. Reading writers on how they write will do that to you. Metaphors have a way of running amok, however, so I drew the line and resolved to stick with one abiding metaphor, the you-know-what upstairs. But now that we're finished, I thought I'd mention a couple more metaphorical writer types in the hope that they might present other ways to think about how your life story's composed.

Game of Thrones author George R. R. Martin says that there are two kinds of writers: "Architects" and "Gardeners." They lay out their plots in completely different ways. Architects create "blueprints before they drive the first nail," Martin explained in a newspaper interview. "They design the entire house, where the pipes are running, and how many rooms there are going to be, how high the roof will be."

Gardeners, on the other hand, "just dig a hole and plant the seed and see what comes up."

Which better describes how *your* life story is getting drafted? Do you make your decisions and choices with forethought and care, according to some overall life plan? Do you do your level best to anticipate challenges and avoid unpleasant surprises? Or do you just let the chips fall where they may? Do *you* drive the plot or does the plot drive you?

Julian Barnes had the same idea, though he gussied it up a bit in a piece he wrote in the *London Review of Books*. Barnes maintained that some of us are in control of how the plot unfolds, while for others it's a case of *que sera sera*. If you think you're driving the action, then you've got what Barnes calls a "narrativist" up there banging out your life story. You see constant connectivity in whatever befalls you. You take responsibility for your actions and feel guilty about your failures. You are what moves the story from point A to point B.

If, on the other hand, you're someone who's buffeted by external events, Barnes would say there's an "episodicist" toiling in the rafters. You perceive little connection between the various parts of your life—work, family, play. They are what they are. You don't try to sync everything up. You think of your life story as a stream of events that flow seamlessly one to the next, carrying you along for the ride.

Which is it better to be—a narrativist or an episodicist? Neither is better than the other, Barnes says. Narrativists think episodicists are irresponsible; episodicists think narrativists are boring and bourgeois. We all harbor elements of both. I'm a narrativist with episodicist rising; Linda, the reverse. Yet we still manage to coexist, and even complete each other's sentences now and then.

One day when I needed some editorial counsel, I had a long phone conversation with a friend of mine, also a writer. Right after she hung up, her fifteen-year-old son walked into the room. Without any lead-in, she asked him what the meaning of life was. She then sent me this account:

> He didn't blink. He said he had been asking himself lately what made being alive special. It couldn't be just its beauty, he said, because there are so many things you can look at that are beautiful but not alive. A rock can be stunning in its striations and shape. But it doesn't have meaning in the same way. He said the reason anything living has meaning is that it can, is supposed to, replicate itself, to go on creating life, even on the level of a cell. He put his hand on his chest and reminded me that the Romans thought there was actually a little candle in every person, and that death snuffed it out. He said: "The reason things that are alive are more meaningful is that they have something to lose."
>
> After I'd gotten over the "that's-my-boy" moment, I said, Yes, but what's the point?
>
> "Really pretty close to the same thing," he said. "It's to make connections to other living things."

Maybe it *is* that simple?

When I was interviewing various folks about what they wanted out of life, I heard time and again how important it was to figure out some way to "do what I love." Midlifers and millennials alike invoked the phrase repeatedly. Millennials, however, were relentless on the topic. Most of them were well educated and were holding jobs, which is more than you could say for millions of their less fortunate peers.

A woman two years out of college, living in the Mid-Atlantic region, started out proofreading food labels. That didn't last long. She then took a job as a researcher in a marketing operation. It's better but isn't great, she says. Her day consists of interviewing customers over the phone, getting those who'll talk to her to provide product feedback. The work's stressful, she says, because she's naturally shy and hates the rejection that comes with the territory.

A medical student, twenty-seven, is feeling highly disillusioned. He says he had dreamed of becoming a doctor since childhood. Now that he understands "the business aspects" of medicine, he regrets the decision. He's bothered by how little time doctors get to spend with patients; he's overwhelmed by the debt he's taken on; he says he's physically exhausted. The demands of school are so overwhelming, he says, that he feels guilty devoting what little spare time he has to anything recreational. He's neither happy nor fulfilled, he reports.

When asked what they *would* do if they could do what they loved, most people replied that whatever it was, it would be more "creative" and "fulfilling" than what they're doing now. But few could tell me what "whatever it was" *was*. Many or most of us simply don't know, or can't decide. It's a case of, We'll know it and love it when it falls into our lap. That's one reason more people aren't doing what they love. Another reason is that getting to do what you love, assuming you know what that is, takes effort. It's usually a royal pain in the ass to get to do what you love.

The best example of someone I know who both knew what he'd love and worked like a possessed millennial to get there, is the son of a good friend—Oscar's son, in fact. He's just completed his third year of residency at a New York City hospital. In a few months he'll become, in his father's words, "the worst-paid physician in America." Oscar couldn't be prouder. His son couldn't be more excited. Come this fall, he'll be working in a mobile clinic that calls on homeless shelters around the city, providing health services to the uninsured and dispossessed.

The kid has a big heart. And plenty of guts. That he made it into and through medical school, and now on to a career that'll be a truly meaningful life experience by anyone's standards, is testament to his flat-out perseverance. A decade ago it was inconceivable that he'd wind up a doctor. He went to St. John's College, where the curriculum consists of the Great Books, heavy on the Greeks and Romans. None of his courses met the requirements of a med-school application. Even his undergraduate lab work was based on experiments conducted at the time of Galileo. After graduation, he banged around, harvesting berries in the Pacific Northwest, working at a day care center. Aspiring to be the kind of family physician who's lucky enough to be the worst-paid doctor in America, he enrolled in a post-bac program to take the necessary chemistry, physics, and biology classes, none of which came easily.

In short, he pushed himself, with absolutely no spiritual guidance or encouragement from his godfather—for the record, that would be me. I, too, am deeply proud of him. Everyone is. So, too, would Aristotle be, in light of the kid's tenacious drive to acquire the scientific knowledge needed to fulfill his ambition. He's now earned every right to kick back and enjoy the ride, doing what he loves on the most disadvantaged streets of the city.

* * *

Finally, I'm sure it's apparent by now that face-to-face contact with the writer-in-residence isn't physiologically possible. Even if it were, it would be perceived as a sign of grave emotional distress if you were observed sitting on a park bench having a heart-to-heart with someone you introduce as the little ghost who lives in your crawl space. However, if you *could* have a sit-down with the writer-in-residence, what would you ask? Talk about an opportunity: Here is someone who knows you inside out, who has instant recall of every single event or relationship stored in your memory. Wouldn't it be fascinating to compare notes?

So if you *could* ask just one question of the writer-in-residence, what would it be?

I'd ask mine what was going through his head in those days, weeks, and months after my father died. I'd be curious to know how much pressure he was under, whether he worried that if he were to miswrite that chapter he'd be putting the longer life story at risk. But he didn't screw things up, not for the long haul, anyway. The scribbler did a nice job rewriting that chapter over time. The pain of the event endures, but the meaning of it has changed. Now there's consolation in knowing that if Buddha had miraculously shown up at my bedside, he'd have pointed out that inherent in my suffering was a pathway out of suffering. If Jung had been called in to consult, he'd have foreseen a possible silver lining. A parent's death can be forever damaging to a child, but Jung would have said that my father's sudden death triggered a step in the direction of individuation, the process of how we wind up distinct from all other humans present or past, a hundred billion strong since the dawn of human history. Suffering, I learned from Viktor Frankl, who learned it from philosopher Baruch Spinoza, "ceases to be suffering as soon as we form a clear and precise picture of it."

All things considered, I'm feeling pretty good these days about my life story. Memories are flowing smoothly and new chapters are being added. This book is but the latest. What's to complain? Of the 161 boys in my high school graduating class, twenty-six are known to be dead, eight can't be located. If some of the disappeared are also dead (though I hope not), it means that close to 20 percent of my classmates are, sadly, no longer works in progress.

There's also some reason to think that if I play my lousy genetic hand right, I'll live for another twenty-plus years. Why so cocky (sort of)? Because not long ago I went online and laboriously filled out a questionnaire that asked after my medical history, family's medical history, marital status, the degree to which I travel in a car, whether I floss regularly, plus a few pages of other details. With a click of the mouse, I learned that I'll likely live nearly twice as long as my father and about the same number of years as my mother, who, despite a half century of mourning, survived to a ripe old age. The bad news is—happiness is transitory, don't forget—nobody might hear of my demise, not right away. Or if they heard about it, they wouldn't be able to make it to the country graveyard for the burial, assuming that Linda and I ever get around to making a decision about that.

The online calculation, you see, has me checking out in 2038. Just my rotten luck. 2038 is projected to be the Year of the Unix Millennium Bug, a technical programming issue like Y2K. It has something to do with how Unix-based operating systems handle time. Unless addressed, on January 19, 2038, at 3:14:07 (Coordinated Universal Time), we'll reach the highest number representable by Unix's "signed 32-bit integer" time format. Unix will think we're back in the year 1901. Systems that rely on UNIX-based programming with embedded time values will be at risk of crashing. The bug, according to doomsayers, might take down cell phones, routers, air and automotive transportation systems, and a whole lot more, perhaps even my own smart kitchen appliances. So I can see it now, an obit headline I never could have imagined in a hundred lifetimes:

LEE EISENBERG DEAD AT 92,
WORLD STANDS STILL

Appendix

Throughout this book I've mentioned many studies that social scientists have conducted over the past fifty years. Such research is typically not undertaken in the hope that it will lead to therapeutic cures for loneliness, boredom, or passivity. (For those we have a generous assortment of compounds with bizarre names: Cymbalta, Pristiq, Viibrid. They add up to a mighty mountain of pills, a twelve-billion-dollar business.) No, the studies I've mentioned here have nothing to do with chemicals. Nor are findings generated by testing on animals or via molecular analysis. The lab monkeys are us. We fill out survey sheets or share our personal histories with graduate students assigned to harvest them for further study. The objective is to draw a bead on the most subjective of all questions: What makes for a meaningful life?

While the question itself is an ancient one, research into the answer is ever young. One of the very first meaning-in-life surveys—the Frankl Questionnaire—was developed in the late 1950s. The intent was to provide some quantitative underpinning to Viktor Frankl's philosophy and therapeutic approach to patients suffering from emotional distress. There was but one key question: "Do you feel your life is without purpose?" The results solidly confirmed what Frankl knew going in:

20 percent of those seeking psychological counseling admitted to a severe lack of purpose in their lives. Over half the general public was found to be unmoored to some degree.

In the five decades since, there have been scores and scores of surveys that attempt to nibble away at what "meaning" means to us and the relationship of meaningfulness to our happiness. Examples include the Life Attitude Profile, the Life Engagement Test, the Psychological Well-Being Scale, and the Sense of Coherence Survey. Now and then I ran off a hard copy of this or that survey and sharpened a pencil, if only to take my existential pulse. Curiosity about who we really are is yet one more variable that makes us human. Besides, self-referential quizzes are fun and diverting, which is why there are so many online. Who can resist knowing what percentage of us is male and female? How our behavioral pattern matches up with our pet's?

To give you a sense of what these surveys are like, I've included three of the more prominent ones on the pages that follow. The first will take a quick, three-minute reading of whether or not you think you've found meaning and value in your life. The second, a bit more extensive, gets at the same question in a different way. The third is the classic Death Attitude Profile-Revised, which I discussed in Chapter 16. Dig in, as it were.

The fourth exercise is something else altogether. It reflects the other methodology deployed in meaning-in-life research—downloading one's life story to a trained listener. Chances are slim that you'll cross paths with a research assistant who's armed with Dan McAdams's life-story protocol, so I've come up with an alternate occasion.

THE MEANING IN LIFE
QUESTIONNAIRE

The MLQ is brief: just ten questions whittled down from an original set of eighty-four. It is not designed to indicate whether you're happy or depressed. Nor does it discriminate between kinds of meaning: e.g., is attaching yourself to a larger idea more meaningful than attaching yourself to your own success? The survey is chiefly used to determine the degree to which one is experiencing meaning or searching for it. And how that correlates with whatever variable a researcher happens to be looking into: physical health; frequency of prayer; charitable involvement; and so on. A 2010 study, for example, found that same-sex couples who were in a legally recognized relationship (marriage or civil union) reported a higher "presence of meaning" than lesbian, gay, and bisexual couples who were single, dating, or merely in a "committed" relationship.

———

Instructions

Please take a moment to think about what makes your life feel important to you. On the following page, respond to the ten statements as truthfully and accurately as you can, keeping in mind that these are very subjective questions and that there are no right or wrong answers. Please answer according to the seven-point scale listed at the top.

Absolutely Untrue	Mostly Untrue	Somewhat Untrue	Can't Say True or False	Somewhat True	Mostly True	Absolutely True
1	2	3	4	5	6	7

1. ____ I understand my life's meaning.
2. ____ I am looking for something that makes my life feel meaningful.
3. ____ I am always looking to find my life's purpose.
4. ____ My life has a clear sense of purpose.
5. ____ I have a good sense of what makes my life meaningful.
6. ____ I have discovered a satisfying life purpose.
7. ____ I am always searching for something that makes my life feel significant.
8. ____ I am seeking a purpose or mission for my life.
9. ____ My life has no clear purpose.
10. ____ I am searching for meaning in my life.

Scoring

Presence [of meaning] score = subtract the rating for item 9 from 8, then add the ratings for items 1, 4, 5, and 6. Scores range between 5 and 35.

Searching [for meaning] score = add together the ratings for items 2, 3, 7, 8, and 10. Scores range between 5 and 35.

———

Scoring Interpretations

Those who employ this questionnaire offer these informed "guesses" about what your results may indicate:

If you scored above 24 on Presence and above 24 on Searching, you evidently think your life does have meaning and purpose. Yet you're looking for more. You're someone who's drawn to the *question* of "What can my life mean?" more than you're looking for a single specific *answer*. People who know you probably see you as conscientious, emotionally stable, and open to new experiences.

If you scored above 24 on Presence and below 24 on Searching, you're likely satisfied that you grasp what makes life meaningful, have an understanding of why you're here, and have a good idea of what you want to be doing with your life. People who know you probably see you as organized, friendly, and socially outgoing.

If you scored below 24 on Presence and above 24 on Searching, you probably don't feel your life has much meaning/purpose but you're actively searching for something or someone who'll provide it. You may occasionally (or often) feel anxious, nervous, or sad. People who know you would likely describe you as someone who plays things by ear; goes with the flow whenever it comes to making plans; worries a lot; and may not be particularly active socially.

If you scored below 24 on Presence and below 24 on Searching, you evidently don't feel your life has very much meaning or purpose; you're not actively seeking to discover them; nor do you believe it's much worth thinking about. People who know you would likely describe you as disorganized; at times nervous or tense; and not to be counted on as the life of a party.

THE PURPOSE IN LIFE TEST

The development of the PIL Test (1964) is regarded as a milestone in the development of so-called existential psychology. The authors, James C. Crumbaugh and Leonard T. Maholick, set out specifically to give researchers a reliable tool with which to assess Viktor Frankl's central tenet that the essence of human motivation is "the will to meaning," and that failure to find meaning leads to "existential frustration" and a variety of emotional and behavioral stresses. The PIL has been used in many hundreds of studies dealing with a wide assortment of questions. For example, is a high Purpose in Life score associated with a lower risk of stroke, heart attack, or other physical afflictions? (It seems to be.) Does it correlate with emotional well-being and happiness? (Directionally, sort of.) Some studies show that women have higher PIL scores than men, some indicate the opposite. It's inconclusive. One study, now forty years old, found that African Americans scored significantly higher than whites, while other studies have contradicted that. A solid Purpose in Life score depends heavily on the individual, not on his or her demographic set.

———

Instructions

On the following page, write the number (1 to 5) next to each statement that is *most true* for you right now.

1. I am usually:

               1   2   3   4   5
           bored   enthusiastic

2. Life to me seems:

               1   2   3   4   5
   completely routine   always exciting

3. In life, I have:

               1   2   3   4   5
    no goals or aims   clear goals and aims

4. My personal existence is:

               1   2   3   4   5
   utterly meaningless   purposeful and meaningful

5. Every day is:

               1   2   3   4   5
   exactly the same   constantly new and different

6. If I could choose, I would:

               1   2   3   4   5
 prefer never to have been born   want 9 more lives just like this one

7. After retiring, I would:

               1   2   3   4   5
 loaf completely the rest of my life   do some of the exciting things I've
                                 always wanted to do

8. In achieving life goals, I've:

               1   2   3   4   5
  made no progress whatever   progressed to complete fulfillment

9. My life is:

               1   2   3   4   5
 empty, filled with despair   running over with exciting things

10. If I should die today, I'd feel that my life has been:

               1   2   3   4   5
  completely worthless   very worthwhile

11. In thinking of my life, I:

               1   2   3   4   5
 often wonder why I exist   always see reasons for being here

12. As I view the world in relation to my life, the world:

               1   2   3   4   5
 completely confuses me   fits meaningfully with my life

(continued)

13. I am a:

	1	2	3	4	5	
very irresponsible person						very responsible person

14. Concerning freedom to choose, I believe humans are:

	1	2	3	4	5	
completely bound by limitations						totally free to make all life choices of heredity and environment

15. With regard to death, I am:

	1	2	3	4	5	
unprepared and frightened						prepared and unafraid

16. Regarding suicide, I have:

	1	2	3	4	5	
thought of it seriously as a way out						never given it a second thought

17. I regard my ability to find a purpose or mission in life as:

	1	2	3	4	5	
practically none						very great

18. My life is:

	1	2	3	4	5	
out of my hands and controlled by external factors						in my hands and I'm in control of it

19. Facing my daily tasks is:

	1	2	3	4	5	
a painful and boring experience						a source of pleasure and satisfaction

20. I have discovered:

	1	2	3	4	5	
no mission or purpose in life						a satisfying life purpose

Scoring

Just add up the items. The higher the score, the more purpose and value you see in your life. Setting a numeric threshold for what's high, medium, or low is dicey. The higher, the better, one would think. I did come across one source that said that a score of less than 50 may be taken as evidence that one is drifting perilously close to the dreaded "existential void." It might also be taken with a grain of salt.

THE DEATH ATTITUDE
PROFILE-REVISED

The DAP-R, as I described earlier, offers a reading on how accepting you are of an idea that not all of us wish to accept. Although a counselor specializing in "terror management" may use the DAP-R to gain insight into an individual's feelings about death, it's widely used to compare attitudes within or between specified sets of individuals: for example, how healthy people's attitudes toward death differ from those with a serious illness; how a given ethnic or racial group views death; how teenagers in general feel about death, or how their attitudes compare to those of another age group.

Instructions

The questionnaire on the following pages contains a number of statements related to different attitudes toward death. Read each statement carefully, and then decide the extent to which you agree or disagree. For example, an item might read: "Death is a friend." Indicate how well you agree or disagree by circling one of the following: SA = strongly agree; A = agree; MA = moderately agree; U = undecided; MD = moderately disagree; D = disagree; SD = strongly disagree. Note that the scales run both from strongly agree to strongly disagree and from strongly disagree to strongly agree.

If you strongly agreed with the statement, you would circle SA. If you strongly disagreed, you would circle SD. If you are undecided, circle U. However, try to use the undecided category sparingly.

It is important that you work through the statements and answer each one. Many of the statements will seem alike, but all are necessary to show slight differences in attitudes.

1. Death is no doubt a grim experience.	SD	D	MD	U	MA	A	SA
2. The prospect of my own death arouses anxiety in me.	SA	A	MA	U	MD	D	SD
3. I avoid death thoughts at all costs.	SA	A	MA	U	MD	D	SD
4. I believe that I will be in heaven after I die.	SD	D	MD	U	MA	A	SA
5. Death will bring an end to all my troubles.	SD	D	MD	U	MA	A	SA
6. Death should be viewed as a natural, undeniable, and unavoidable event.	SA	A	MA	U	MD	D	SD
7. I am disturbed by the finality of death.	SA	A	MA	U	MD	D	SD
8. Death is an entrance to a place of ultimate satisfaction.	SD	D	MD	U	MA	A	SA
9. Death provides an escape from a terrible world.	SA	A	MA	U	MD	D	SD
10. Whenever the thought of death enters my mind, I try to push it away.	SD	D	MD	U	MA	A	SA
11. Death is deliverance from pain and suffering.	SD	D	MD	U	MA	A	SA
12. I always try not to think about death.	SA	A	MA	U	MD	D	SD
13. I believe that heaven will be a much better place than this world.	SA	A	MA	U	MD	D	SD
14. Death is a natural aspect of life.	SA	A	MA	U	MD	D	SD
15. Death is a union with God and eternal bliss.	SD	D	MD	U	MA	A	SA

16. Death brings a promise of a new and glorious life.   SA   A   MA   U   MD   D   SD

17. I would neither fear death nor welcome it.   SA   A   MA   U   MD   D   SD

18. I have an intense fear of death.   SD   D   MD   U   MA   A   SA

19. I avoid thinking about death altogether.   SD   D   MD   U   MA   A   SA

20. The subject of life after death troubles me greatly.   SA   A   MA   U   MD   D   SD

21. The fact that death will mean the end of everything as I know it frightens me.   SA   A   MA   U   MD   D   SD

22. I look forward to a reunion with my loved ones after I die.   SD   D   MD   U   MA   A   SA

23. I view death as a relief from earthly suffering.   SA   A   MA   U   MD   D   SD

24. Death is simply a part of the process of life.   SA   A   MA   U   MD   D   SD

25. I see death as a passage to an eternal and blessed place.   SA   A   MA   U   MD   D   SD

26. I try to have nothing to do with the subject of death.   SD   D   MD   U   MA   A   SA

27. Death offers a wonderful release of the soul.   SD   D   MD   U   MA   A   SA

28. One thing that gives me comfort in facing death is my belief in the afterlife.   SD   D   MD   U   MA   A   SA

29. I see death as a relief from the burden of this life.   SD   D   MD   U   MA   A   SA

30. Death is neither good nor bad.   SA   A   MA   U   MD   D   SD

31. I look forward to life after death.   SA   A   MA   U   MD   D   SD

32. The uncertainty of not knowing what happens after death worries me.   SD   D   MD   U   MA   A   SA

(continued)

Scoring Key

Dimension	Items
Fear of Death (7 items)	1, 2, 7, 18, 20, 21, 32
Death Avoidance (5 items)	3, 10, 12, 19, 26
Neutral Acceptance (5 items)	6, 14, 17, 24, 30
Approach Acceptance (10 items)	4, 8, 13, 15, 16, 22, 25, 27, 28, 31
Escape Acceptance (5 items)	5, 9, 11, 23, 29

Scores for all items are from 1 to 7 in the direction of *strongly disagree (1)* to *strongly agree (7)*. For each dimension, a mean scale score can be computed by dividing the total scale score by the number of items forming each scale.

———

What Your Scores May Be Trying to Tell You

Once you've calculated your scores, you'll see where you fall across the five "dimensions" listed above. Two of them reflect negative attitudes toward death:

Fear of Death: You fear death and you admit to it. If you fear it a great deal, your high anxiety can lead to depression.

Death Avoidance: You fear death and avoid thinking or talking about it. Failure to admit to it can cause "psychological discomfort."

And there are three types of "death acceptance":

Neutral Acceptance: You accept death as an integral part of life; you neither fear nor welcome it. Neutral acceptance is positively related to psychological and physical well-being.

Approach Acceptance: Your death anxiety is mitigated by a certain belief—typically, you believe that there's an afterlife. As a side note, to believe in an afterlife is more positively associated with a feeling of well-being in older adults than in younger adults who believe in an afterlife.

Escape Acceptance: You view death as a welcome alternative to pain and misery.

AN EXERCISE FOR BOOK GROUPS

How cool would it be if you and the other members of your group, instead of deconstructing some stranger's published work, exchanged enlightened judgment on each other's life stories? Here's one way to go about it: Everyone gets twenty minutes to tell the story of her or his life. At minimum, each account must include the eight "nuclear episodes" a narrative psychologist would like to hear about: a positive and a negative childhood memory; a "wisdom event"; a vivid adult memory; a high point and a low point; a spiritual experience; and a turning point.

Feel free to agree beforehand on a set of questions around which to build discussion. Here are a few to get you started:

How do you think this life story as a whole comes across?

Borrowing from Christopher Booker's The Seven Basic Plots, *which genre does it belong to? Comedy? Tragedy? Rebirth? Voyage and Return? Quest? Rags to Riches? Overcoming the Monster?*

Is there a book (or movie) this story brings to mind?

Does the leading character remind you in any way of another character in a book or movie? Who is that, and why?

What's the takeaway, the moral of this story?

Finally, what words would you carve onto a granite slab (or engrave on a brass plaque) that provide an appropriate coda to the story just told? (These can be original or lifted from any movie, book, play, television series, or ancient sacred text—so long as the words are sincere.)

Acknowledgments

Accepting his Emmy Award for Lifetime Achievement, Fred Rogers reduced Radio City Music Hall to tears when he asked everyone in the audience to take ten seconds to acknowledge *silently* those who cared enough to help them along the way. Then he looked at his watch and timed it. As the seconds ticked off, cameras zoomed in on celebrities who indeed took this brief meditative opportunity to conjure up parents, teachers, friends, spiritual guides, talent agents, producers, and, for all I know, strangers they'd met once at the upstairs piano bar on a flight from New York to L.A. While I can't quite do it in just ten seconds, I'd like to acknowledge here a few characters—some were flat, some were round, I won't say who was which—who helped me through this particular chapter of my life story.

The first tranche of silent acknowledgment goes to a passel of characters who had no idea that the simple fact of their company came as blessed relief after a long hard day at the cemetery. With an eye on Mr. Rogers's wristwatch, I'll just mention four representative supporting players in Chicago, Judy and David Fardon and Anna and Steven Soltes; and four back east, Betsy Carter and Gary Hoenig, and Becky and Dan Okrent. The latter four indulged me even as I hijacked an important birthday dinner (not mine) by going on and on about the travails I was muddling through at the time.

Silent acknowledgment and deep gratitude also go out to two fine people at the University of Pennsylvania who helped me unlock doors that enabled me to move the plot along: Mingo Reynolds at the Center for Programs in Contemporary Writing, and Al Filreis, Kelly Professor of English. Thanks to their interventions, I was granted the run of the Van Pelt-Dietrich Library at Penn and the Elmer Holmes Bobst Library at NYU. I also enjoyed many hours of blessed sanctuary in a cubicle in the quiet-as-a-tomb Frederick Lewis Allen Room at the New York Public Library. Odd, isn't it, how the suffocating confines of a tiny Dilbert cube, typically derided by writer types as soulless and oppressive, the very space they've been running away from their entire lives, suddenly becomes a lifesaving refuge in a noisy, crazy city? As I mentioned earlier, I also found peaceful asylum in the third-floor reading room at the Walter L. Newberry Library in Chicago. I'd silently like to thank the staffs at all of these irreplaceable institutions for their assistance and courtesies.

I am grateful to Dan P. McAdams at Northwestern for helping me get started; and to John Kotre, an early exponent of narrative psychology, for spending some quality time with me. I'd like to thank psychology researchers Paul T. P. Wong and Gary T. Reker for granting permission to reprint the DAP-R scale; and Michael F. Steger for allowing me to share the Meaning in Life questionnaire.

The interviews that appear throughout the book were conducted with the determined help of Kathleen Brady and Amaris Cuchanski. Drawing on an equal measure of grace and determination, these persevering researchers had no qualms about striking up intimate conversations with dozens of complete strangers; asking them whether their day-to-day lives really mattered; and, oh, by the way, just how terrified are you that when you're dead, you're dead, and your story won't live on? I'd also like to thank the estimable Rochelle Udell, who, with an able assist from Jonathan Caplan, conceived the idea for the cover.

Even though my acknowledgments are itching to go vocal, I'll stick to the rules and give silent praise to those without whom this book wouldn't so much as exist: Deb Futter, my editor at Twelve, who was from day one staunch in her support and enthusiasm; her able and multitalented assistant, Elizabeth Kulhanek; and my agent, Esther Newberg, who was, as she always is, indomitable and a great friend to boot.

By now, my silent acknowledgments are straining not only to go vocal, they're begging to be set to music. Chris Jerome and Lisa Grunwald offered hours of invaluable suggestions on matters ranging from the structure and shape of the narrative to whether anyone really wants to know that Martin Heidegger believed that "the less we just stare at the hammer-thing, and the more we seize hold of it and use it, the more primordial does our relationship to it become." Make this book as personable as you can, Grunwald and Jerome told me time and again; this isn't a textbook, buster. That said, if I haven't been personable enough, or if you really *did* want to know what Heidegger meant by the hammer-thing, you should absolutely blame me and not Lisa or Chris.

As for Linda, I'm already on record as saying that I want to share a tombstone with her. What else *is* there to say? Only that this intelligent, funny, patient, and highly spiritual human being provided warmth, wisdom, and encouragement throughout. Her editorial insights unraveled knots in the story from the beginning to the end. I simply wouldn't have made it through the cursed elbow without her astute reading. And another thing: one day as I was cruising the shelves in the stacks, I happened to pick up a volume of Bertrand Russell's autobiography. I spent the rest of the day with it, jotting down this and that, only a little of which found its way into this book. Before I returned the book to the shelf, I opened it to the front and noticed that Russell had dedicated the story of his long and remarkable life to his wife Edith. The publisher had chosen (wisely) to reproduce the dedication exactly as Russell had scribbled it in his own hand:

To Edith

Through the long years
I sought peace.
I found ecstasy, I found anguish,
I found madness,
I found loneliness.
I found the solitary pain
that gnaws the heart,
But peace I did not find.

Now, old & near my end,
I have known you,
And, knowing you,
I have found both ecstasy & peace,
I know rest,
After so many lonely years.
I know what life & love may be.
Now, if I sleep,
I shall sleep fulfilled.

I'd like to close by silently acknowledging that one day, when I'm really, *really* old, I'll feel exactly the same way about Linda.

Further Reading

The following titles, some general, some academic, provide additional information and insight into the main themes of this book.

Aging and Memory

Aging and Biography: Explorations in Adult Development, James E. Birren, Gary M. Kenyon, Jan-Erik Ruth, Johannes J. F. Schroots, Torbjorn Svensson, eds. (New York: Springer, 1996)

Being Mortal: Medicine and What Matters in the End, Atul Gawande (New York: Metropolitan, 2014)

The Feeling of What Happens: Body and Emotion in the Making of Consciousness, Antonio Damasio (New York: Mariner, 1999)

How We Die: Reflections on Life's Final Chapter, Sherwin Nuland (New York: Vintage, 1995)

In Search of Memory: The Emergence of a New Science of Mind, Eric R. Kandel (New York: W. W. Norton, 2006)

White Gloves: How We Change Ourselves Through Memory, John Kotre (New York: Free Press, 1996)

Why Survive?: Being Old in America, Robert N. Butler (New York: Harper Torchbooks, 1985)

Biographies and Memoirs

Erik Erikson and the American Psyche: Ego, Ethics, and Evolution, Daniel Burston (Lanham, MD: Rowman and Littlefield, 2007)

Freud: A Life for Our Time, Peter Gay (New York: W. W. Norton, 2006)

Identity's Architect: A Biography of Erik H. Erikson, Lawrence J. Friedman (New York: Scribner, 1999)

In the Shadow of Fame: A Memoir by the Daughter of Erik H. Erikson, Sue Erikson Bloland (New York: Viking, 2005)

Mirages: The Unexpurgated Diaries of Anaïs Nin, Paul Herrin, ed. (Athens, OH: Swallow Press/University of Ohio Press, 2013)

Nothing to Be Frightened Of, Julian Barnes (New York: Alfred A. Knopf, 2008)

Reborn: Journals and Notebooks, 1947–1963, Susan Sontag; David Rieff, ed. (New York: Picador, 2009)

The Year of Magical Thinking, Joan Didion (New York: Alfred A. Knopf, 2005)

Meaningfulness

The Doctor and the Soul, Viktor E. Frankl (New York: Alfred A. Knopf, 1968)

The Examined Life: Philosophical Meditations, Robert Nozick (New York: Simon & Schuster, 1990)

Immortality: The Quest to Live Forever and How It Drives Civilization, Stephen Cave (New York: Crown, 2012)

Man's Search for Meaning, Viktor E. Frankl (Boston: Beacon, 2006)

Meaning in Positive and Existential Psychology, Alexander Batthyany and Pninit Russo-Netzer, eds. (New York: Springer, 2014)

The Meaning of Life, E. D. Klemke (New York: Oxford University Press, 2000)

The Meaning of Life: A Very Short Introduction, Terry Eagleton (Oxford: Oxford University Press, 2007)

The Meaning of Life: Religious, Philosophical, Transhumanist, and Scientific Perspectives, John G. Messerly (Durant and Russell, 2012)

Triumphs of Experience: The Men of the Harvard Grant Study, George E. Vaillant (Cambridge, MA: The Belknap Press of Harvard University Press, 2012)

What Does It All Mean?: A Very Short Introduction to Philosophy, Thomas Nagel (Oxford: Oxford University Press, 1987)

What's It All About?: Philosophy & the Meaning of Life, Julian Baggini (Oxford: Oxford University Press, 2004)

Philosophy/Mythology/Religion

The American Soul Rush: Esalen and the Rise of Spiritual Privilege, Marion Goldman (New York: New York University Press, 2012)

Buddhism: A Brief Insight, Damien Keown (New York: Sterling,1996)

The Cry for Myth, Rollo May (New York: W. W. Norton, 1992)

The Denial of Death, Ernest Becker (New York: Free Press, 1973)

Esalen: America and the Religion of No Religion, Jeffrey J. Kripal (Chicago: University of Chicago Press, 2007)

Escape from Evil, Ernest Becker (New York: Free Press, 1975)

Examined Life: Philosophical Meditations, Robert Nozick (New York: Simon & Schuster, 1989)

Existential America, George Cotkin (Baltimore: Johns Hopkins University Press, 2003)

Existentialism: From Dostoevsky to Sartre, Walter Kaufmann (New York: Penguin, 1956)

From Counterculture to Cyberculture: Stewart Brand, the Whole Earth Network, and the Rise of Digital Utopianism, Fred Turner (Chicago: University of Chicago Press, 2008)

The Hero with a Thousand Faces, Joseph Campbell (Novato, CA: New World Library, 2008)

The Oxford Handbook of Philosophy of Religion, William J. Wainwright, ed. (Oxford, MS: Oxford University Press, 2005)

Pathways to Bliss: Mythology and Personal Transformation, Joseph Campbell (Novato, CA: New World Library, 2004)

The Swerve: How the World Became Modern, Stephen Greenblatt (New York: W. W. Norton, 2011)

The Tao of Te Ching, Brian Browne Walker, trans. (New York: St. Martin's, 1992)

The Wisdom of Insecurity, Alan Watts (New York: Vintage, 2011)

Psychology/Narrative Psychology

Acts of Meaning: Four Lectures on the Mind, Jerome Bruner (Cambridge, MA: Harvard University Press, 1990)

The Essential Jung: Selected Writings, C. G. Jung (Princeton, NJ: Princeton University Press, 1983)

Learned Optimism: How to Change Your Mind and Your Life, Martin E. P. Seligman (New York: Vintage, 2006)

Meanings of Life, Roy F. Baumeister (New York: Guilford, 1991)

Narrative Knowing and the Human Sciences, Donald E. Polkinghorne (Albany, NY: SUNY Press, 1988)

Outliving the Self: Generativity and the Interpretation of Lives, John Kotre (Baltimore: Johns Hopkins University Press, 1984)

The Redemptive Self: Stories Americans Live By, Dan P. McAdams (New York: Oxford University Press, 2013)

Stories We Live By: Personal Myths and the Making of the Self, Dan P. McAdams (New York: William Morrow, 1993)

The Undiscovered Self, C. G. Jung (Princeton, NJ: Princeton University Press, 1990)

The Uses of Enchantment: The Meanings and Importance of Fairy Tales, Bruno Bettelheim (New York: Vintage, 2010)

Writing and Writers

The Creative Process, Brewster Ghiselin (Berkeley: University of California Press, 1952)

On Writing: A Memoir of the Craft, Stephen King (New York: Scribner, 2010)

The Sense of Style: The Thinking Person's Guide to Writing in the 21st Century, Steven Pinker (New York: Viking, 2014)

The Seven Basic Plots: Why We Tell Stories, Christopher Booker (London: Bloomsbury, 2005)

The Trip to Echo Spring, Olivia Laing (New York: Picador, 2013)

Why I Write, George Orwell (New York: Penguin, 2005)

The Writing Life, Annie Dillard (New York: Harper Perennial, 1989)

The Writing Life: Writers on How They Think and Write, Maria Arana, ed. (New York: PublicAffairs, 2003)

Writers on Writing: Collected Essays from The New York Times, Introduction by John Darnton (New York: Times Books, 2002)

Writing the Self: Diaries, Memoirs, and the History of the Self, Peter Heehs (New York: Bloomsbury, 2013)

Index

About the Author

LEE EISENBERG is the bestselling author of *The Number* and other books. He's a former editor in chief of *Esquire* and has been a visiting scholar at the University of Pennsylvania, among other stops in a wide-ranging career. His work has appeared in numerous publications, including *Fortune*, *Businessweek*, *Time*, *Newsweek*, and *New York* magazine. He divides his time between Chicago and New York City. For news and updates, please visit LeeEisenberg.com.

ABOUT TWELVE

TWELVE

TWELVE was established in August 2005 with the objective of publishing no more than twelve books each year. We strive to publish the singular book, by authors who have a unique perspective and compelling authority. Works that explain our culture; that illuminate, inspire, provoke, and entertain. We seek to establish communities of conversation surrounding our books. Talented authors deserve attention not only from publishers, but from readers as well. To sell the book is only the beginning of our mission. To build avid audiences of readers who are enriched by these works—that is our ultimate purpose.

For more information about forthcoming TWELVE books, please go to www.twelvebooks.com.

Storytelling for Young Adults

Storytelling for Young Adults
Techniques and Treasury

Gail de Vos

1991
LIBRARIES UNLIMITED, INC.
Englewood, Colorado

LIBRARIES UNLIMITED, INC.
P.O. Box 3988
Englewood, CO 80155-3988

_____

Library of Congress Cataloging-in-Publication Data

De Vos, Gail, 1949-
  Storytelling for young adults : techniques and treasury / Gail de
Vos.
  x, 169 p. 17x25 cm.
  Includes bibliographical references and index.
  ISBN 0-87287-832-5
  1. Libraries, Young people's--Activity programs.   2. Young adults-
-Books and reading.   3. Storytelling.   I. Title.
Z718.5.D4   1991
027.62'51--dc20   91-6856
                                                                        CIP

With love and appreciation for
Anna Altmann,
Peter,
Esther, and Taryn de Vos

Contents

Introduction

Storytelling is identified in the literature as a very ancient art used to entertain and educate *children* through the sharing of tales passed on orally (Wilkens 1980, 190).

While the literature of librarianship contains considerable information on the values of storytelling for children, there is very little information on the values of storytelling for young adults. As early as 1913, Andrus listed in *Library Journal* the following reasons for telling stories to children (in libraries):

1) to give familiarity with good English
2) to cultivate the power of sustained attention
3) to establish a friendly relationship between child and storyteller
4) to cultivate a literary standard by which a child may judge other stories
5) to develop a right sense of humor
6) to cultivate the imagination
7) to develop sympathy—an outcome of imagination
8) to give a clear impression of moral truth
9) to lead to books.

(Andrus 1913, 169)

Research on the values of telling stories continues to focus on children. On very rare occasions is storytelling, in the literature, associated with any other age group.

Historically, storytelling was the accepted mode of entertaining, educating, and informing a populace. Stories were told to adults, and the children reaped benefits by listening along with their elders. In the eighteenth and nineteenth centuries, in Europe, the intelligentsia regarded listening to folk literature as a childish and plebeian pastime. This attitude influenced society, and listening to stories, as an activity, became the prerogative of younger children only (L'Engle 1978, 448). Today, many people still consider oral folk literature, as well as storytelling, something for young children only, and for that reason disdain it.

Today, there is a resurgence of interest in storytelling for all ages. This revival results not merely from a nostalgia for the values of the past or a concern for preserving the enduring stories of other cultures. We no longer have definitive examples or rituals that prepare us for puberty, adulthood, old age, and death. Stories, oral and written, have evolved and been created to provide guidelines to help people cope with milestones in their lives. The remarkable history of human experience, imagination, moral strength, and wisdom that is available in story continues to aid people in finding their place in the world (Simms 1983, 349). Storytelling, like film, bypasses the barriers of illiteracy and reluctance of nonreaders to take the messages of story to the people. Many appropriate stories, although widely available, are not actively searched for, or even stumbled upon, by readers. It is the storyteller who makes these stories available and makes them come alive.

Because storytelling continues to be regarded as an activity for young children, young adults do not regard listening to stories as a suitable activity for themselves. Convincing them that listening to stories should be an integral part of their lives is very difficult because they are very aware of their position in the transition from childhood to adulthood and do not want to be reminded of picturebook hour. Young adults resent approaches that reduce them to the status of children (Sutton 1983, 44).

This book is designed to demonstrate to storytellers, librarians, and educators the importance of telling stories to young adults. It is divided into two major sections. The first section discusses the values of listening to stories for the young adult audience, basic storytelling techniques to use with this audience, and how to integrate storytelling and storytelling activities into the regular classroom or public library program.

The second section provides a guide to appropriate tales for young adults that encompasses the world of literature from folk tales to modern urban belief tales. It is composed of approximately two hundred story summaries. They are included because storytellers today are dependent on printed sources for their tales. "Selecting the right story out of the vast body of literature available today is one of the most important aspects of storytelling" (Baker and Greene 1987, xiii). The stories are summarized, timed, and arranged in broad categories, which include folk and fairy tales, myths and legends, ghost stories, urban belief legends, love and romance stories, twists and tall tales, and literary stories and novel excerpts.

The story summaries are followed by twenty-one complete stories that have been tried and tested with young adult audiences. These stories can be used as they appear or may easily be modified for your specific audience.

The author, title, theme, and collections indexes will aid in locating appropriate tales.

REFERENCES

Andrus, Gertrude E. 1913. "Why to Tell Stories." *Library Journal* 38, no. 3: 169.

Baker, Augusta, and Ellin Greene. 1987. *Storytelling: Art and Technique*. 2d ed. New York: R. R. Bowker.

L'Engle, Madeleine. 1978. "What Is Real?" *Language Arts* 55, no. 4: 447-51.

Simms, Laura. 1983. " 'Words in Our Hearts': The Experience of the Story." *The Horn Book* 59, no. 3: 344-49.

Sutton, Roger. 1983. "Telling Tales for YAs." *School Library Journal* 30, no. 3: 44.

Wilkens, Lea-Ruth C. 1980. "Love Gifts to Texas Children through Storytelling." *Texas Library Journal* 56, no. 4: 190-91.

Telling Stories to Young Adults – The Values

1

Eaglen defines young adults as "that age group who no longer consider themselves children but are not yet considered adults by the adult world" (Eaglen 1983, 420). Pedak defines a young adult as "a member of the public who is in transition from childhood to adulthood; usually between the ages of thirteen to eighteen" (Pedak 1978, 45). In Canada and the United States, this encompasses people who are usually in junior high school and high school.

Adolescence is the term psychologists and educators use to identify the developmental stage marked by the onset of puberty and the end of structural physical growth. The term *young adult* is synonymous with *adolescent* and *teenager* but is preferred by librarians throughout the professional literature and so will be used in this book.

For the purpose of this book, the term *young adults* refers to people between the ages of thirteen and eighteen.

Young adults have special needs: the need for entertainment and information, the need to belong, the need to learn in a social context, the need to experience responsibility, the need to establish a self-concept, and the need to communicate with adults who have an interest in them and their concerns (Amey 1985, 26). Storytelling, like reading books and watching films, is an activity that addresses these special needs by engaging the attention and the emotions of an audience. If the storyline works, the recipient enters into the story and identifies with a character or situation portrayed. It is by entering into the story and "living" it that young adults are open to the benefits of the experience.

Many of the reasons listed by Andrus for telling stories apply equally to the reasons for experiencing print and visual media. Storytelling, therefore, performs a function similar to that of literature and the motion arts, but it also imparts several elements to its audience that are distinctive to its unique art form.

Listening to stories, like reading books or watching films, can serve as an outlet and testing ground for the strong emotions that young adults are experiencing and, in many instances, trying to camouflage. Conflicting values and roles can be explored through stories, as storytelling is a problem-solving activity.

Characters in the stories are faced either with crisis situations or with common, everyday concerns. Carefully selected stories define both process and problem themselves and specify the nature of the solution (Livo and Rietz 1986, 11). Not only do members of the audience become aware of how others deal with problems similar to their own, but the stories can be used to discuss alternate solutions to the problems. Young adults can examine themselves within their environment through stories in which events and solutions are manipulated and evaluated (Yoder 1978, 24). They are able to try out their own dreams, fantasies, fears, and concerns without experiencing real-life consequences. Storytelling keeps the young adult safe from consequences while strong, even extreme, emotions and roles are tried out in the stories. For this reason, storytelling has long been utilized as a tool for psychotherapy to mold a mentally stable individual (Yolen 1981, 18).

> In one British secondary school for educationally subnormal children, weekly story hours are given ... to selected second- and third-year pupils, aged thirteen-fifteen, who respond spectacularly to the fairy stories they never had in their disadvantaged childhood and to the stories and the excerpts which relate to their adolescent needs and interests in their contemporary surroundings. (Marshall 1975, 66)

Story hours should not be offered only to disadvantaged and learning-disabled young adults. All young adults can benefit from the therapeutic aspects of listening to stories. Konopka states, in her key concepts of adolescence, that young adults have a need to experiment with their own strengths and value systems and must have an element of risk (Konopka 1973, 299). Listening to stories offers the opportunity for experimentation in combination with safe risk-taking.

HOW YOUNG ADULTS BENEFIT
FROM STORYTELLING

There are thirteen key reasons for young adults to listen to stories.

As an aid in the search for identity. A major task confronting the young adult is to develop a sense of individual identity. The search for personal identity involves deciding what is important or worth doing and formulating standards of conduct for evaluating one's own behavior as well as the behavior of others. Young adults' sense of identity develops gradually out of the various identifications of childhood.

> Every adolescent has to deal with the realization that, so far, his or her identity has been imposed by adults. Breaking free from those impositions is one of those struggles of that time of life. In order to achieve freedom they begin by trying to shrug off the identities given them as children. (Chambers 1986, 409)

The expectations of peers and authority figures concerning the behavior and attitudes of young adults are a major concern for young adults. Stories about people their own age, who are facing predicaments with which they can identify, help young adults in clarifying these expectations.

Because the search for identity becomes conscious and highly emotional during adolescence, young adults need a chance to reflect on the self in relation to others (some use their peers as mirrors) and to test the self in a variety of settings (Konopka 1973, 302). As mentioned previously, stories provide vicarious experiences for young adults: the chance to probe various situations, roles, and values without suffering any consequences. Storytelling offers the opportunity for experimentation. The needs of young adults to meet various kinds of people and cultures and to experiment with their own strengths and value systems can be answered in part by listening to appropriately selected stories that involve the listeners in contemplating themselves as individuals.

Many experts believe that adolescence should be a period of role experimentation in which the young adult can explore different ideologies and interests. For example, experimentation is especially important for young adults in the definition of gender roles (Mitchell 1986, 18). Mitchell states that gender roles, the concepts of appropriate sex behavior, are absorbed from the outside culture through various media, and that one of the elemental tasks for young adults is the sorting of cultural stereotypes to find those that are appropriate for them as individuals (Mitchell 1986, 18).

Cultural stereotypes abound particularly in the body of folk and fairy tales that are, in themselves, stories of the search for identity. Many opponents of traditional literature feel that several of the stories perpetuate the very stereotypes that educators, parents, and social workers are attempting to modify (Moran 1987, 22). This issue will be reviewed more fully in the discussion of folk and fairy tales.

As an aid in developing value systems. Adolescence is a time for reevaluation of values. Young adults examine the values, beliefs, attitudes, and ideas they have uncritically accepted and absorbed from their adult role models and accept, discard, and remold these values until they have established a value system that reflects the person they are becoming. The challenge for young adults is to accumulate, organize, and evaluate enough values, beliefs, attitudes, and ideas to build their own value systems. If their value systems are incompatible with the accepted standards and values of their society, the problem is one of reassurance (Grams 1968, 127).

Besides opening a door to a world of values and beliefs, storytelling offers the insight that the search is universal. This is especially critical today, for not only are young adults in a state of flux, but the society that they are trying to come to terms with is also in a state of constant change. The search for a personal value system is related to the significant mental growth that is a factor in middle adolescence. This mental growth fosters an awareness of political and social systems previously unnoticed (Mitchell 1986, 138). Young adults become conscious of the inconsistencies in society as they perceive the clash between the values exhibited by institutions and the general intent of the ideological system. Value confrontations are inevitable (Konopka 1973, 299).

> Because of the conflicting values adolescents encounter in a rapidly changing world, they should have the opportunity to thrash out their reactions, consider the pluses and minuses, and try to determine where they themselves stand so that they will be better able to deal with ideas of all shades—including demagoguery. (Konopka 1973, 302)

Scharf, in his review of Kohlberg's conventional level of moral judgement, stated that young adults during early adolescence have fixed definitions of social duty, concern with firm social rules, and a respect for formal authority (Scharf 1978, 18). There is a shift in middle adolescence to a questioning of the moral order of society. Rejection is a critical step for young adults in the process of defining for themselves an autonomous value base (Scharf 1978, 20). Storytelling offers, along with recognition of the universality of the search, insight into the motives and patterns of human behavior.

As an aid in establishing a sense of belonging. Young adults prefer to learn and to seek information within a social context. Storytelling brings young adults together for a shared purpose and reaffirms their sense of belonging to a group. Besides being included in a group, each member of the storytelling audience is included in the story as his or her needs for attention, security, belonging, or aesthetic satisfaction are met (Seaberg 1968, 247).

Konopka, in her study of the conditions necessary for healthy development of youth, states that young adults need to have a sense of belonging both to their own age group and among adults (Konopka 1973, 301). Storytelling can help fulfill this need because it can create a bond between the adult storyteller and the young adult audience.

As an aid for individual contemplation. Listening to a story takes place in a group context, but every listener hears a different story and responds to it on the basis of his or her own beliefs, perceptions, ideas, and experience. Eye contact between the storyteller and the audience helps to maintain the immediacy and intimacy of the sharing experience. Each member of the storytelling audience is sure that the story is just for him or her and that it pertains to the situation the individual is personally facing at that moment. Storytelling, as well as being a group activity, is intimate and respectfully private: Listeners do not have to reveal to anyone their personal thoughts as they listen.

As an aid to encourage emotional release. Storytelling, along with reading and viewing films, encourages audience participation by offering an emotional release. By becoming involved in the storyline and the characters, young adults safely experience the emotions of the characters. The fear, anger, sorrow, lust, and laughter experienced by the characters are experienced vicariously by members of the audience. Listening to the story engages the mind, supplants the everyday concerns of the listener, and frees members of the audience to experience, unselfconsciously, a rich and subtle range of emotions.

Young adults, who are constantly dealing with a multitude of emotional responses, struggle to maintain a "cool" facade. They wish to appear in total control over their emotions at all times. In many instances, this attempt at emotional control results in avoiding any display of emotional response. Young adults, listening intently to a story, unconsciously mirror their emotional responses on their faces as they interact with the characters, the storyline, or with a particular word choice they find appealing. The storytelling experience allows them a chance to relax their tight control.

As an aid in developing imagination. One of the chief attractions of story-telling is that it is a participatory, rather than a passive, activity. In television programs and movies, the concrete characters, the setting, and the action are all products of someone else's vision. While listening to a story, however, the audience has to imagine every scene, action, and character, all while listening intently to what the teller is saying and how it is being said. Television is a one-way means of communication, but in storytelling there is interaction between the teller and the audience. Listeners are active, working with the teller to conjure up images. One of the aims of storytellers today is to restore what television is destroying: the ability to visualize and to use one's imagination (Stewart 1981, 20). The basis of creative imagination is the ability to visualize and fantasize. Storytelling informs, stimulates, and keeps alive the capacity to absorb and use information.

As an aid in entertaining. For any audience, listening to stories is relaxing and enjoyable. It is a time-honored form of entertainment and intimate sharing.

> Since the stories are mirrors that reflect our passions and inclinations
> through the employment of archetypes and humor, we are entertained
> by laughing and crying over our own circumstances. (Livo and Rietz
> 1986, 11)

Because young adults, at the outset, react negatively to the connotation of storytelling as being an activity for "babies," they can present quite a challenge to the storyteller. Some have never heard a story told aloud and are reluctant to show any sign of interest or responsiveness (Barton 1986, 23). It is not unusual for young adults to hover on the fringe of open-air storytelling sessions, at first to mock but eventually to listen. It is the enjoyment of the story—a story that is properly selected for the developmental stage of the audience—that converts the mockery of young adults to attentiveness and enjoyment.

As an aid in the creation of bonds. An intrinsic part of storytelling is the direct and ever-deepening relationship between the teller and the listener (Simms 1983, 345). The storyteller transmits not only the content of the story but something of him- or herself, and individual members of the audience often reciprocate by sharing something of themselves with the teller. This bond between teller and young adult carries over into other activities that involve both of them—in the library, the classroom, or the home.

For example, the benefits of storytelling for young adults in libraries include the opportunity for the librarian-storyteller to communicate and interact with library users on a more personal, one-to-one level (Harrington 1985, 57). Young adults have been found to be more willing to approach a "familiar face" when they have information and reading needs (Harrington 1985, 59). If librarians can create a climate of openness for the exploring young adult, they can play a vital role in the process of moral development (Scharf 1978, 22). This ultimately leads to a satisfied clientele and to a developing adult community strongly supportive of public libraries.

As an aid in developing listening skills. People in Western society are accustomed to a noisy existence and have conditioned themselves to ignore much of the noise around them, so much so that they no longer know how to listen. Less than one-half of the main ideas heard by an audience are retained by the average listener (Briggs and Wagner 1979, 133).

Listening habits are primarily conditioned by the adult community. "A child now observes his adult models talking to each other as they watch their [television] programs and leaving him alone in the room during his program" (Briggs and Wagner 1979, 134). Briggs and Wagner feel that children no longer have adequate role models to aid in the development of listening skills.

Egocentric young adults, as well as others, tend to ponder their own thoughts and possible responses when listening to a conversation or lesson and do not fully attend to what is being said. Communication skills are enhanced by listening to a variety of stories and tellers: Young adults, their attention caught by the story, may develop the habit of listening courteously and critically. Well-developed listening skills are crucial to the education of young adults. Listening demands more of the audience than any other form of communication. In reading, it is possible to adapt one's rate to the difficulty or nature of the materials; difficult materials can be reread, unfamiliar words looked up, and there is time for reflection on one idea before proceeding to the next. These luxuries are not available to the listener, who must follow the speaker's rate regardless of the nature or content of what is being said. A listening audience must be able to recognize the meaning, intensity, color, and inflection of the words the speaker uses to manipulate the audience.

Listening to stories is an extremely painless way to develop listening skills. Young adults should have the opportunity to hear many stories and many storytellers to develop the keen perception and alertness that is necessary to fully utilize potential listening skills. Young children have very short attention spans, and it is not until they are older that their listening skills can be honed; unfortunately, when they are older, listening to stories is an activity that is put on the shelf.

As an aid in preserving traditions. Storytelling preserves traditional materials as well as the traditional methods of imparting information and knowledge.

> With the breakdown of family, ethnic, social and religious codes, the advantage of tradition in learning to deal with goods and evils now appears to be lost to the adolescent. (Flanagan 1984, 65)

Not only does storytelling connect the present with the past by telling ancient tales in much the same way that they have been told for generations, but storytelling offers young adults a world of traditions to aid them in their search for stability in an unstable time. The preservation and presentation of folk and oral traditions is a legitimate and valued service in and of itself.

As an aid in remembering cultural stories. In many cultures, storytelling has remained a powerful vehicle for the transmission of values, beliefs, and ideas. The stories of these cultures, because they provide essential channels for the communication of ideas, moral values, and observations on the behavior of the human species, have remained alive, meaningful, and relatively unweakened (Wolkstein 1974, 22). Such stories are not commonly told in our society, even though they are available in print. The print sources in which these stories appear usually are not actively sought out or even stumbled upon by young readers. It is only as a storyteller finds them and brings them alive that the stories will be remembered by an audience (de Wit 1979, 5).

As an aid to exposing young adults to oral language. Through the magic quality of the spoken word, storytelling reveals the charm and subtle connotations of word sounds, word combinations, and the flow of rhythmic prose. By being exposed to different tellers and different storytelling styles, young adults can observe that language is personal. Exposure to oral language helps young adults develop a descriptive style that they can use in expressing to others and to themselves the changes and emotions that they are experiencing.

When listening to stories, young adults learn to appreciate and enjoy the sound of language. Increasingly today, visual communication is used, and there is a fear among educators that the scope of language is lessened (Johnson et al. 1977, 719). Storytellers share this fear. Jane Yolen, storyteller and young adult author, concluded that people today face a serious deprivation: "the loss of the word, of words" (Yolen 1981, 19).

Storytelling can help combat this danger, but it must be remembered that to work well and to hold the attention of young adults accustomed to being visually stimulated by films, television, and music videos, the stories have to be very strong.

As an aid in developing discrimination. Storytelling can lead young adults to books, but this goal, according to Sutton, must be secondary (Sutton 1983, 44). Sutton states that the primary reason for telling stories to young adults is to help them in their search for identity, values, and vicarious experiences (Sutton 1983, 44). Briggs and Wagner, on the other hand, feel that exposing young adults to literature that they may wish to read for themselves should be challenge enough for any storyteller (Briggs and Wagner 1979, 32). All storytellers agree, however, that listening to stories improves listeners' discrimination in choice of books and stories for reading. Literary tales, told by a teller, introduce specific authors to an audience, and members of the audience frequently seek out either the same stories or additional material by the same authors because they enjoyed the telling.

This rationale, that storytelling leads to books, has kept storytelling alive in public libraries. The first library story hours were established for children over the age of nine because the children were expected to have mastered reading by that age (Greene and Shannon 1986, xx). With the advent of widely published, good-quality picturebooks, librarians were quick to discover that using picturebooks in story hours was much more time- and cost-efficient than learning all the tales for the story hour. Consequently, "the more the story hour came to be associated with picture books, the more the older children stayed away, believing such things were for 'babies' " (Pellowski 1977, 146). Today, storytelling in libraries is directed almost exclusively at preschool and early elementary school-children. Telling stories to a group of young adults is rarely considered a library activity.

REFERENCES

Amey, Larry. 1985. "The Special Case for YA Programming." *Emergency Librarian* 12, no. 3: 25-26.

Barton, Bob. 1986. *Tell Me Another*. Markham, Ont.: Pembroke Publishers.

Briggs, Nancy E., and Joseph A. Wagner. 1979. *Children's Literature through Storytelling and Drama*. 2d ed. Dubuque, Iowa: William C. Brown Co. Publishers.

Chambers, Aidan. 1986. "All of a Tremble to See His Danger." *Top of the News* 42, no. 4: 405-22.

de Wit, Dorothy. 1979. *Children's Faces Looking Up: Program Building for the Storyteller*. Chicago: American Library Association.

Eaglen, Audrey B. 1983. "Services to Young Adults in Public Libraries." *Illinois Libraries* 65, no. 7: 420-24.

Flanagan, Leo. 1984. "Nothing Personal Intended." In *Kids and Libraries: Selections from Emergency Librarian*, edited by Ken Haycock and Carol-Ann Haycock, 65-68. Vancouver B.C.: Dyad Services.

Grams, Armin. 1968. "Understanding the Adolescent Reader." *Library Trends* 17, no. 2: 121-31.

Greene, Ellin, and George Shannon. 1986. *Storytelling: A Selected Annotated Bibliography*. New York: Garland Publishing.

Harrington, Janice N. 1985. "The Risks of Storytelling." *Illinois Libraries* 67, no. 1: 57-60.

Johnson, Edna, et al. 1977. *Anthology of Children's Literature*. 5th ed. Boston, Mass.: Houghton Mifflin. pp. 718-25.

Konopka, Gisela. 1973. "Requirements for Healthy Development of Adolescent Youth." *Adolescence* 8, no. 31: 291-315.

Livo, Norma J., and Sandra A. Rietz. 1986. *Storytelling: Process and Practice*. Littleton, Colo.: Libraries Unlimited.

Marshall, Margaret R. 1975. *Libraries and Literature for Teenagers*. London: Andre Deutsch.

Mitchell, John J. 1986. *The Nature of Adolescence*. Calgary, Alta.: Detselig Enterprises.

Moran, Barbara. 1987. "The Passive Princess Theme in Traditional Stories." *National Storytelling Journal* 4, no. 3: 21-23.

Pedak, Maria. 1978. "Public Library Programming for Young Adults: Frill or Necessity?" *Drexel Library Quarterly* 14, no. 1: 45-52.

Pellowski, Anne. 1977. *The World of Storytelling*. New York: R. R. Bowker.

Scharf, Peter. 1978. "Moral Development and Literature for Adolescents." In *Young Adult Literature in the Seventies: A Selection of Readings*, edited by Jean Varlejs, 17-23. Metuchen, N.J.: Scarecrow Press.

Seaberg, Dorothy I. 1968. "Can the Ancient Art of Storytelling Be Revived?" *The Speech Teacher* 17, no. 3: 246-49.

Simms, Laura. 1983. " 'Words in Our Hearts': The Experience of the Story." *The Horn Book* 59, no. 3: 344-49.

Stewart, Barbara Home. 1981. "The Folktellers: Scheherazades in Denim." In *Storytelling for Teachers and Media Specialists*, edited by Carol Lawrence, Jenabeth Hutcherson, and James Thomas, 18-22. Minneapolis, Minn.: T. S. Denison and Co.

Sutton, Roger. 1983. "Telling Tales for YAs." *School Library Journal* 30, no. 3: 44.

Wolkstein, Diane. 1974. "An Interview with Harold Courlander." *School Library Journal* 20, no. 9: 19-22.

Yoder, Jan Miller. 1978. "The Rites of Passage: A Study of the Adolescent Girl." In *Young Adult Literature in the Seventies: A Selection of Readings*, edited by Jean Varlejs, 24-31. Metuchen, N.J.: Scarecrow Press.

Yolen, Jane, 1981. *Touch Magic: Fantasy, Faerie and Folklore in the Literature of Childhood*. New York: Philomel.

Storytelling Techniques

2

The term *storytelling* carries a negative connotation for the average young adult. While a story can be easily introduced into a regular classroom activity by the teacher or librarian without any label, any storytelling activity that is based on voluntary attendance must be named with care if it is to attract an audience of young adults. A program entitled "Horrible and True: Happenings in the Neighborhood" will appeal more strongly than a program entitled "Urban Belief Legends." The term *storytelling* need not appear in either the title of the program or the description that accompanies it.

INTRODUCING THE CONCEPT OF STORYTELLING

Before telling stories to a group of young adults for the first time, in either a school setting or a public library, introduce the concept and practice of telling stories. Depending on the situation, this may be done very briefly or in a comprehensive manner. When I am a guest teller in the schools, I start the session by asking the audience how many tell stories. A few hands tentatively rise. Then I ask how many have ever manufactured an excuse for a teacher or a parent. Hands shoot up, the audience giggles, and I start the session by briefly discussing the function of storytelling in history.

I begin with the role of bards in Europe and comment on the price of ransom for the king's bard (four hundred head of cattle) and the number of colors a bard was entitled to wear (five, only one fewer than royalty, while more common folk could wear only two or three). Depending on the time available and the purpose of my visit, I may discuss one of the most famous bards of today, Cacofonix, a man of extremely limited talent created by Goscinny and Uderzo (1967) in their *Asterix* series, which is reprinted in more than fifteen languages and read by young adults throughout the world.

A valuable source for background on the history of storytelling is Harrell's *Origins and Early Traditions of Storytelling* (1983). Harrell discusses the formal development of storytelling which, according to him, began with the gift of fire of Prometheus.

I also like to introduce the concept of storytelling as a medicinal resource, as discussed by Olson.

> Most of the medieval regimens argue that a moderate cheerfullness is the best mental disposition to have in order to maintain well-being.... Conversation and storytelling in this view have medical relevance to people's health. (Olson 1987, 19)

After presenting the medieval view of the benefits of laughter and listening to stories, not very different from medical theories today, I introduce Boccaccio's *Decameron*. Boccaccio retold legends, tall tales, and contemporary gossip in his collection of one hundred tales supposedly told by ten young men and women to keep healthy in the face of the Black Plague in Florence (Boccaccio 1930).

Young adults should be aware of the importance and function of stories and storytelling in various cultures today. Storytelling is still a high priority for many Africans, as well as Native Americans.

CHOOSING THE RIGHT STORY

After you have attracted the interest of the young adult audience with a brief discussion of the function of storytelling or with evocative titles and subject matters in library programs, it is essential to keep that interest. The first story that you tell to young adults is of the utmost importance: It is the hook that captures your audience. It is imperative that the teller know the story very well; the teller also must be comfortable with both the story and the audience. I recommend starting with a ghost story or urban legend, but if you have problems telling these tales, as some people do, begin with a strong, evocative myth. The images of "the killing of Pelops, Demeter chomping at the shoulder bone, and Tantalus's final punishment" capture and hold students' attention and imagination when they are told the Greek myth (Rosen 1988, 79). A full-text version of this myth is included in Rosen's *And None of It Was Nonsense* (1988).

I cannot emphasize enough the importance of selecting a story that is appropriate for both the audience and the teller. This book contains more than two hundred suggested stories that are appropriate for young adult audiences, but not all of the stories are appropriate for every storyteller. The teller must enjoy the story to tell it successfully. If you are unsure of or unhappy about any aspect of the story you tell, the audience also will be unsure and unhappy without knowing why.

Get to Know the Story

Before you learn a story, you should research it. To do the story justice, the teller must know something of the origin of the story, the background and motives of the author if it is a literary tale, and the culture and characters that are introduced in the story. Read as many different versions or adaptations of the story as you can find. This will help you formulate your own perception of the characters, action, and resolution. It is this perception that you will transmit to the audience in your version of the story. One responsibility of storytellers is to adapt stories to make them more relevant to today's audiences, but storytellers also have a responsibility to the story itself.

> Modifications and modern adaptations are generally acceptable if, warns Laura Simms, the changes 'protect the intrinsic value of the story.' But most storytellers agree that some stories should *never* be changed: sacred, ritual stories in reverence for the culture and its tradition, and literary tales out of respect for the author's literary process, labor and love. (Smith 1988, 322)

TELLING THE STORY

Telling stories to young adults is not so different from telling stories to other age groups. In all situations, tell the story in a sincere, straightforward manner, in your natural voice. Young adults appreciate being spoken to as if they were your peers and will definitely tune you out if they feel you are condescending in any way. Sound effects may be added to your telling, but only if you do them effectively and use them sparingly. Nothing distracts an audience as much as a poorly executed bark or the constant repetition of the same sounds. This technique in storytelling may be effective with preschoolers but will quickly lose a young adult audience. Do not be afraid of silence and pauses within your story. They are effective tools in the telling of stories and are necessary to enable the audience to see and experience the action, setting, and characters of the story while it is being told. Gestures should be used sparingly, as they easily distract an audience that has been raised on visual images. Instead of focusing on and listening to the words of your story, the audience will follow your gestures. Remember to make eye contact with members of the audience. This may prove to be the most daunting aspect of telling stories to young adults. Members of this audience, unless they have been exposed to the pleasures of listening to stories recently, adopt a bored, glazed look that retains a trace of cynicism. At the beginning of the session, they are conscious of the reactions of other members of the audience and do not want to react any differently from their neighbors. Proceed with enthusiasm and confidence and tell your story well. The listeners will quickly realize that you enjoy the story and are telling it so they can enjoy it as well.

Expect Little Response

The most important thing to remember when telling stories to young adults is not to expect any overt response. A young adult audience may not demonstrate any appreciation or evidence of listening to a story. Do not assume, however, that the story has not had an effect. Young adults are hesitant to display their feelings, particularly in a large group. Time must be allowed for individual members of the audience to absorb the story and to relate it to their own experiences and background.

Pause between Stories

Listening is hard work! Allow breathing space between the telling of one story and the next or a follow-up activity. The breathing space can take the form of a brief introduction to the next story or information about the tale just told. During this pause you may explain why you are telling the story or give some background on the culture that produced the story or on the author that created it.

Prevent Distractions

A brief introduction to each tale should point out any aspects of the story that may distract the audience. Do not assume that high school students understand seldom-used words or allusions to specific cultures. A colleague of mine told an Inuit myth to a Canadian eleventh-grade class, assuming that the students were familiar with both the vocabulary and Inuit culture. In the opening minutes of the story, she used a term not clearly understood by several audience members. In horror, I watched the ripple created as audience members nudged their neighbors to ask if they knew what the word meant. By the time the story ended, the concentration of more than half of the listeners had been disturbed, leaving the teller shaken and the tale virtually unheard.

Horner also advises storytellers to prevent distractions.

> Before some myths I point out that some parts of a story (such as falling in love with the moon) may seem "stupid" and "unrealistic". I suggest that if they simply accept these "unrealistic" elements as part of the story and not let them be distracting, they will enjoy the story more. (Horner 1983, 461)

This eliminates the need for members of the audience to react negatively at that point in the story to demonstrate to their peers that they are too mature to be taken in by such nonsense. If everyone already knows it is nonsense, there is no need for such demonstration. The audience will, instead, listen and experience the story as it is told.

CONCLUSION

Storytelling to young adults involves eradicating the barrier of program labels that carry negative connotations, choosing stories that appeal to both the audience and teller, telling the story well, and having little expectaton of audience response. It is challenging to face this age group and tell a story. It is extremely rewarding when members of this group tell you, usually weeks later, that they enjoyed the story and ask you to please tell them another.

There is a tendency in the school environment to follow each enterprise with a meaningful activity. The following chapter discusses many follow-up activities to integrate storytelling into the curriculum, but it is imperative to remember it is not necessary to analyze a story after telling it and, in fact, most storytellers highly discourage it. Analysis can be insulting to the teen listener and can kill interest in the story. (Horner 1983, 462)

REFERENCES

Boccaccio, Giovanni. 1930. *The Decameron of Giovanni Boccaccio*. Translated by Richard Aldington. New York: Dell Publishing.

Goscinny, René, and A. Uderzo. 1967. *Asterix and the Normans*. Montreal, Quebec: Dargaud Canada.

Harrell, John. 1983. *Origins and Early Traditions of Storytelling*. Kensington, Calif.: York House.

Horner, Beth. 1983. "To Tell or Not to Tell: Storytelling for Young Adults." *Illinois Libraries* 65, no. 7: 458-64.

Olson, Glending. 1987. "Confabulatio: A Medieval Medical View of Story-telling." *National Storytelling Journal* 4, no. 2: 19-21.

Rosen, Betty. 1988. *And None of It Was Nonsense: The Power of Storytelling in School*. Richmond Hill, Ont.: Scholastic.

Smith, Jimmy Neil, ed. 1988. *Homespun: Tales from America's Favorite Story-tellers*. New York: Crown Publishers.

Extensions for the Classroom

3

This chapter addresses the most common question I hear from teachers at workshops on storytelling for young adults. The teachers are concerned about how storytelling can be integrated into the classroom.

I highly recommend reading Rosen's *And None of It Was Nonsense: The Power of Storytelling in School* (1988) before attempting any storytelling to young adults, especially in a classroom setting. In her book, Rosen discusses her use of storytelling to develop communication skills, both oral and written, in male adolescent students. Not only does she work miracles with her students but she motivates readers of her text to do the same.

Rosen suggests setting aside a special time each week for storytelling, with the only demands made on the students being that they sit, listen, and tell. She found that

> the special sense of anticipation created quite simply by a gathering together for the "Once upon a time" experience was enough to sink all antagonisms and create an essential—albeit short-lived—harmony. (Rosen 1988, 43)

She further discovered that "the effect of listening to the story was such that the ensuing individual work by the pupils was of a much higher standard than they generally achieved" (Rosen 1988, 43).

A spontaneous discussion usually followed Rosen's storytelling sessions. This frequently led to the assignment of written exercises that involved retelling the tales just heard. The assignments were of three basic types: retelling the story as told, retelling the story from a different point of view, and retelling the story with as many changes as the students wished to make. The last type of assignment ultimately created a totally different story. "My experience tells me that a told story gives rise to a wider scope of responses than any other language stimuli in the repertoire of an English teacher" (Rosen 1988, 91). Harold Rosen, in the postscript to Rosen's book, explains that the reteller is freed from certain basic burdens of invention by listening to the story and therefore is able to use the imagination to play inventively with what is available (Rosen 1988, 171).

Other classroom teachers have proclaimed the benefits of retelling stories, both orally and in written form. Warawa uses retelling techniques with her high school students with both poetry and Shakespeare.

> As they worked on their versions, the students returned to the original, studying it both for ideas and imagery. I realized that they were learning more from Browning's poem than any other classes had. (Warawa 1989, 49)

A secondary benefit of retelling stories is the students' discovery of "how stories are picked up and transmitted from one teller to another" (Rosen 1988). This discovery can lead to discussions about the transmission, reliability, and purpose of gossip, rumors, newspaper and television reporting, and the evidence of judicial witnesses.

FOLKTALES AND FOLKTALE MOTIFS

Many traditional tales and folktale motifs are used as the basis for literary tales and modern fantasy. To readily recognize the motifs, however, students must have sufficient grounding in folktales. This can be accomplished by telling the students a wide variety of folktales and then discussing and examining the motifs exhibited in the tales. An excellent aid is MacDonald's *The Storyteller's Sourcebook: A Subject, Title and Motif Index to Folklore Collections for Children* (1982). *The Storyteller's Sourcebook* is usually available in public libraries.

Flanagan and Hudson illustrate the use of folktales and motifs in literary tales in their book, *Folklore in American Literature* (1958). This volume discusses Irving, Melville, Hawthorne, Twain, Benet, Steinbeck, and other authors, together with a number of their stories that contain folklore motifs or are elaborations of known folktales. For example, "The Devil and Tom Walker," by Washington Irving, with its wide variety of folk beliefs delivered in a "half-ironic tone," is compared with Stephen Vincent Benet's "The Devil and Daniel Webster." Not only do both stories deal with the motif of the Devil making bargains, but both authors are known for appropriating European folklore and for their skill in adapting it to the American setting.

Students can compare assigned literary tales based on the same folk motif, as Flanagan and Hudson demonstrate, by identifying the motif, discussing the tone utilized by the author (mild disbelief or total conviction), and discussing what purpose the folk motif has within the body of the literary tale (basis for tale, versimilitude, or characterization). Students also can discuss how successful each author is in the literary adaptation: Is the motif easily recognizable, does it enhance the storyline (if it is not the storyline), or is it cumbersome?

As an alternative to having the students examine two or more literary tales for evidence of similar folktale motifs, the teacher may tell a specific folktale and introduce the novels, short stories, and poetry that have evolved from the tale. The students can then examine how various authors have manipulated, changed, or illuminated the original storyline in their own tales. One example of a story that has appeared frequently in the body of young adult literature is the ballad, "Tam Lin." Tell the story and then introduce Ipcar's *Queen of Spells* (1983), Jones's *Fire and Hemlock* (1985), and Vinge's short story, "Tam Lin" (1986). Tell the folktale "Kate Crackernuts" and examine the novel of the same name by Briggs (1979). Relate Andersen's "The Wild Swans" (1983) and let the students follow the fate of the eleventh prince in Synge's *The Swan's Wing* (1981).

A third way to explore folktales and motifs is to introduce literary ballads and discuss how the literary form is derived from the folk ballads of both Europe and North America. Henry Wadsworth Longfellow, for example, drew his subjects from the myths and legends of many countries, and the popularity of "Paul Revere's Ride" has made a folk hero out of Paul Revere (Flanagan and Hudson 1958, 492). Robert Frost introduced a romantic history for Paul Bunyan in "Paul's Wife" (1968), and in "Telling the Bees" (1984). John Greenleaf Whittier used an old folk belief that it is necessary to inform the bees of a death in the family to prevent them from swarming and disappearing (Flanagan and Hudson 1958, 315).

Advertisements utilize both folktale motifs and folktale storylines to influence consumer behavior. In *The Black Cat Made Me Buy It!*, Muncaster and Sawyer discuss folk beliefs relating to black cats and how these beliefs were utilized to promote various products.

> Because of the legends and superstitions that surrounded black cats many years ago, black cats naturally drew considerable attention to themselves wherever they appeared. That meant they could also draw attention to any product they posed with or were intended to represent. (Muncaster and Sawyer 1988, 18)

Young adults can pore over modern magazine advertisements, watch television commercials, and listen to radio commercials to find examples of folklore in modern advertising. After collecting various samples, they can identify the motif or tale, the reason why it is used to attract the consumer's attention, and the relationship, if any, between the folklore and the product.

This is not difficult to accomplish. In just two weeks, I collected several advertisements depicting familiar tales ("Rapunzel" and "The Three Little Pigs") to sell house insurance, several puns and allusions to the Grimm brothers to advertise movies, and several headlines that assume newspaper readers know nursery rhymes and mythology. And all of this in only one local newspaper!

Folktales and motifs are also very prominent in cartoons. Hardly an issue of *The New Yorker* is published without a cartoon alluding to or satirizing a folktale, myth, or folk belief. Popular cartoonists, such as Gahan Wilson, Dan Piraro (Bizarro), Gary Larson (The Far Side), Berke Breathed (Bloom County), and Bill Waterson (Calvin and Hobbes) refer to folklore for much of the humor and bite in their work. Young adults digest collections of these cartoons as a steady diet. It is hoped they can fully appreciate the message the creator is attempting to put across. Have the students bring in examples of these cartoons and explain the humor. If they recognize but do not fully understand the folklore references, have them search out the original tales and discuss how the illustrator utilized the storylines, stereotypes, or characters in his or her own creations. Then have the students create their own cartoon from a folktale or myth of their choice.

MYTHS AND LEGENDS

Young adults need to have a grounding in both myths and legends to fully comprehend the allusions that are so prevalent in today's society. However, because myths cannot be easily removed from their cultural contexts, they are usually more difficult to introduce to children than other forms of traditional folklore, and for this reason they are sometimes neglected. "When introducing myths and mythologies to elementary and junior high school children, it is useful to develop a systematic, step-by-step method of presentation" (Moss and Stott 1986, 257). Moss and Stott recommend that myths and legends be told as stories to students in grades one to three to increase students' familiarity with a large number and wide variety of myths. In the upper elementary grades, these students can begin to examine the various genres, recognizing myths, folktales, legends, and fables. Then, with a firm grounding in mythology, junior high students may begin extensive examinations of the myths.

The following activities can be used after telling myths and legends to young adults to familiarize them further with world mythology or to serve as an introduction if the students were not acquainted with myths in elementary school.

Have students "investigate myths as the encyclopedias of scientific information or preliterate societies." The students can classify and organize the myths into topics: creation, technology, morals, and explanations of natural phenomena (Livo and Rietz 1986, 353). After the encyclopedia is organized, the students can offer descriptions of the society as seen through its mythology.

Or, a specific type of myth can be examined. Every culture has creation myths. Not only are these myths readily available in collections of myths, but several collections of creation myths have been published recently. Look specifically to the myths about the creation of human beings in different cultures, and have the students compare the myths about how the first woman was created (Lipson and Bolkosky 1982, 68). Students can identify music that captures the mood and reflects the culture of a creation myth. After the music has been found, they can perform a reading of the myth with musical background.

Pourquoi myths, which explain why and how the natural phenomena of the world came into being, also appear in every culture. Moss and Stott state that "two of the most common of these explain the acquisition of fire and the cycle of the seasons" (1986, 254). Pourquoi myths can be compared, and new ones can be created by students. *Storytelling: Process and Practice* (Livo and Rietz 1986) contains a substantial unit on the biblical account of Noah and the Ark and the rainbow. The unit includes an introduction to Noah and the various mythological explanations of the rainbow from different cultures. The authors describe numerous activities based on the theme of rainbows, many of which can be easily adapted for both junior high and senior high school students. An annotated bibliography is also included (Livo and Rietz 1986, 404-416). In addition to the activities Livo and Rietz describe, students can compare the various flood myths around the world: Noah, Gilgamesh, the Greek myth of Deucalion and Pyrrha, Manu in India, and kindred stories from China, Burma, and both American continents.

American myths can be examined against the backdrop of today's environmental movement. After introducing young adults to Native North American legends, discuss why Native Americans might make excellent advisers for policies on environmental issues, conservation, and natural resources. Have the students research native myths to reinforce their arguments. Bring in a Native American storyteller, if possible, to explain the importance of myths and storytelling to the native culture today.

Greek and Roman myths have provided the English language with innumerable words and expressions. Have students compete to identify words that have been derived from the classical myths. Public libraries contain many etymological dictionaries that can aid in this endeavor. Another helpful source is *Brewer's Dictionary of Phrase and Fable* (Evans 1981). Have students locate the myths that are the source of the terms *Herculean task, Olympic games, Trojan horse, Sisyphean toil, tantalize*, and *narcissistic*, for example. Have the students tell the myth and explain how the term is used today and how it relates to the original myth. Venture further and explore the Norse myths that have yielded (along with Greek and Roman myths) the names of the planets, the days of week, and the months of the year. "If you understand the roots of your language, you are less likely to abuse it and more likely to delight in its liveliness and variety" (Freeman 1985, ix).

When the Romans conquered the Greeks, they borrowed the Greek gods and gave them new names. The Romans occasionally changed an individual's character to fit their own customs and ideas. The Greek god of war, Ares, for example, was a complete villain, but his Roman counterpart, Mars, glorified war. Have the students compare the paired Greek and Roman gods for characteristics that typify the society that gave birth to their myths.

After the students have this grounding in mythology, they can scan advertisements and product names for references to mythological characters or produce their own advertising and marketing campaigns. Have the students assume the role of a person in the communications business who must produce an advertisement with pictures and slogans to attract paying customers to the weaving contest between Athena and Arachne or to other confrontations common in classical mythology (Lipson and Bolkosky 1982, 37).

Students can turn to popular fiction, particularly fantasy, to uncover mythological references in the names of characters and worlds. For example, in the adult fantasy *Dragon Wing*, Weis and Hickman (1990) introduce the character, Iridal, whose name means "of the rainbow." This name is a direct adaptation of the name of the Greek goddess of the rainbow, Iris.

Author Joan Aiken advises writers,

> If you wish to write myth-based fantasies, there is an enormous wealth of material to choose from ... beyond the better known classic Greek and Roman and Egyptian canons. Of course you have an advantage if you first came to your legends as a child and are deeply familiar with them; if not, you will need to immerse yourself in them "thoroughly": read as deeply and as widely as you can, finding as many different versions of the same story as possible, acclimatising yourself, until you feel free to play with them and manipulate them in your own way. (Aiken 1982, 77)

Young adults are notorious for devouring fantasy and may enjoy adapting a myth or character from a particular myth or legend to produce their own creative work. Have them follow Aiken's advice and immerse themselves in different versions of a myth before attempting to write their own version.

Utilizing sources such as *The Arthurian Encyclopedia* (Lacy 1986) and *The Return from Avalon: A Study of the Arthurian Legend in Modern Fiction* (Thompson 1985), a class can delve into the characters of the Arthurian cycle and follow them through modern adaptations of the legends, including picturebooks, fantasy and film, and the decorative arts. "Like other figures from legend, Arthurian characters have been adapted for role-playing games, such as *Dungeons and Dragons*" (Lacy 1986, 204). Have the students identify one of the Arthurian characters and follow him or her through legends, comparing the legendary character with the parallel character in a role-playing game.

Once familiar with mythological and legendary heroes, the students can identify modern heroes and discuss their appeal, comparing the modern with classical heroes.

URBAN BELIEF LEGENDS

Urban belief legends are "stories that most people have heard as true accounts of real-life experiences" (Brunvand 1981, xi). Developed from incidents and rumors that reflect the fears and anxieties that people have about certain aspects of their lives, urban belief legends often contain elements of suspense and horror. People from all walks of life believe the tales, and publications including *Time, Reader's Digest*, and local newspapers reprint them frequently as true incidents (Brunvand 1978, 110).

Urban belief legends are an immediate hook for the young adult audience. Tell the students an urban belief legend and explore both the legends and the society that encourages and fosters the transmission of the legends.

One method of exploration is to have the students collect stories that they have been *told* by friends — stories that they have not read in a book. Have the students tell the stories to the class. Teacher Kathryn Johnson assigns the collection of transcripts of the stories heard, not read, and the telling of these stories to her ninth-grade English classes.

> However introverted this age group may seem to be during class discussion requiring academic preparation, all one has to do is mention the above situations [slumber parties, camping trips and hall-talk] in relationship to storytelling, and the extrovert in all of them appears. (Bronner 1988, 261)

Numerous versions of urban belief legends, all using the same motifs, can be collected and analyzed. Brunvand provides different versions grouped by motif in his four volumes of urban belief legends and his syndicated newspaper column (1981, 1984, 1986, 1989). Other collections of urban belief legends are included in the references at the end of this chapter.

Many urban belief legends have been printed as actual news items. Collect examples of the tales printed in daily newspapers and magazines, and have the students discuss possible explanations why the item was printed as news and how they can tell that it is an urban legend. If you do not have the time to build a collection of these items, which appear fairly frequently as fillers or letters to Ann Landers and "Dear Abby," use Brunvand's collections. He reprints news items and articles verbatim in the texts. An interesting task is tracing the urban belief cycle: When was the motif last circulated and how has it been changed? Brunvand, among others, does this and can be used as either reference or example. In addition, students can update some of the older articles. They also may be able to follow up the item to find a possible disclaimer in the publication that recently published it.

Listeners will be quick to point out that they have seen the urban belief legend motif in a movie or on the television screen. They recognize the story of the babysitter and telephone caller from late-night viewing, as well as the "Runaway Grandmother" in the movie *National Lampoon's Vacation* and "Cat Food Contamination" in the movie *Her Alibi*. Have the students compile a list of tales that have been used in movies and on television and obtain some videos of these programs for class viewing. Compare the tales on film with the oral tales, discussing the impact of the tales, their credibility, and the purpose for putting them on film. An older movie that the students may not recognize is *With Six You Get Egg Roll*. The movie utilizes an urban legend that still circulates today.

Urban belief legends can be used as an introductory unit to the study of ballads and epics. Teacher Mary B. Nicolini believes that her high school students will better understand and appreciate the folklore of the past with a foundation in the folklore of the present. She distributes copies of twelve different accounts of the same local legend for her students to examine, discuss, and analyze (Nicolini 1989, 82). Then she has her students chart the variants of the seven versions of "The Choking Doberman" (Brunvand 1984, 41-49) before proceeding to a wider examination of other legends that Brunvand has examined.

Tell the students one version of an urban legend that enjoys a wide distribution, and have them follow that particular urban belief tale through time and space (with the help of Brunvand and others) to discover the social and technological changes that mirror society. Several legends that reappear faithfully are "The Vanishing Hitchhiker," "The Secondhand Evening Gown," and "The Dare," which involves people frightening themselves to death in a graveyard.

Poetry is a fertile field for both storytelling and writing exercises. Numerous collections of narrative poems for a young adult audience have been recently published. Within these collections are poems that have been told as urban belief legends or are certainly candidates for future urban belief tales. Introduce a poem and have the students retell the story as an urban belief legend, localized to their area and time. Tell or read Bayly's "The Mistletoe Bough" to your class (Wilson 1988, 86-87) and then read Cohen's "The Missing Bride" (Cohen 1983, 65-71). The students cannot help but notice that it is indeed the same story brought forward in time. I have also heard this story from junior high students about hiding in a school locker during a game of hide-and-seek with the same macabre results.

Several poems in Wilson's *Every Poem Tells a Story* (1988) provide an imaginative starting point for the exercise, as do "The Stone," by Gibson (Jones 1966, 67-72) and "Outhouse Blues," by Nelms (Janeczko 1988, 10).

TALL TALES

"Like almost everyone, children respond to hyperbole in humor. Two intriguing forms are the tall tale, which is essentially a joke in slow motion, and the lie, a related mode" (Schwartz 1977, 286). Junior high school audiences particularly enjoy the blatant humor of the tall tale juxtaposed with the deadpan delivery that is part and parcel of the form.

> The tall tale is a comic fiction disguised as fact, deliberately exaggerated to the limits of credibility or beyond in order to reveal emotional truths, to awaken his audience, to exercise fears, to define and bind a social group. (Brown 1987, 1)

Turn the students into tellers. Speaking formally before one's peers is extremely daunting for most young adults, but through various exercises and frequent practice, young adults (as well as any first-time teller) become more confident about public speaking and peer-group activities. Telling tall tales, being allowed to lie creatively before their peers, helps build self-confidence and self-esteem. A tall tale, like an urban belief legend, can be very short and therefore is not as daunting as a longer tale.

Printed versions of tall tales lack the impact, and often the humor, that is evident in oral transmission because the human element must be present to make the humor work. As Brunvand points out, "the art is primarily a verbal one, deriving from the skill of the teller rather than from the originality of his material" (Brunvand 1968, 116). This art depends upon the pace of delivery ("never hurried, never dragged"), skillful timing, the dramatic use of the pause for emphasis, and drawing out the ending to deliver a more emphatic punch (Botkin 1975, 497).

The success of tall tales also depends on a willingness to lie and be lied to while keeping a straight face (Brunvand 1968, 116). The straight face and practiced nonreaction to external stimulus is a mechanism that young adults strive to maintain all the time! Encourage your students to tell tall tales, to research them, or to develop their own. Young adults appreciate permission to lie creatively.

Tell tall tales regularly. The tales can be very short and usually can be slipped into any topic that is being discussed. Make no demands on the students other than that they enjoy the tales.

Have the young adults read through various collections of tall tales and anecdotes and tell their favorites to their peers. The tellers should begin with a basic situation common to the listeners, one with which they all can identify. Then, the core tale should be embellished with supporting details from everyday life and local landmarks. The tales work best if they appear to be a spontaneous, factual reminiscence. "I've made improvements of my own all along the way—fixed up fact after fact to make it truer than it ever was before" (Blair 1944, 257). Remind the students that the art of tall tales demands wit and a real knowledge of what one is lying about (Battle 1986, 540).

In *Storytelling Activities*, Livo and Rietz (1987) encourage the stringing together of tall tales to produce a single tale. This activity is simplified by the fact that tall tales tend to cluster by topic. The authors suggest giving each student or group of students a collection of six to ten short tales and lies about specific items or topics and having them construct a monologue by combining some or all of the items (Livo and Rietz 1987, 80).

Tall tales can also be developed from songs, especially ballads that originated on the North American frontier. Sanders retells traditional folk songs in prose in *Hear the Wind Blow: American Folk Songs Retold* (1985). Two of these retellings, "The Blue-Tail Fly" and "Yankee Doodle," are summarized in this volume. The stories can be read or told to the students, and then each student can find a ballad, folk song, or poem to retell as a tall tale.

The history of the tall tale can be studied. The tall tale developed on the North American frontier because the land, weather, and geographic isolation were frightening to many of the pioneers. Exaggeration made the experience more bearable. Young adults also live in frightening territory. The humor and hyperbole of the tall tale can help make their experience more bearable, too.

Tall tales can be formulated from local history and early regional newspapers. The first newspapers were not always known for their factual content. Many articles were created when there was a lack of legitimate news, and small tidbits that were printed often beg to be developed into a larger tall tale. The story of "The Snoring Pigs," found in full text in the last section of this volume, was developed from a true incident. Finally, tall tales can be formulated to explain certain aspects of local history and geography. The topic should be adequately researched before the tales are developed.

Neider researched the nonfiction writings of Mark Twain. "I was piqued by his habit of inserting yarns of pure fiction in a nonfictional work, yarns tossed in just because they were good ones which he had in his head at the time" (Neider 1957, xiii). Neider goes on to say that Twain is the American writer closest to folklore (that is, who draws most from folklore and whose stories are like folktales) and that both Twain and the tall tale, of which he was a great proponent, are related to the frontier.

> The sentimentality of the frontier, which ranged all the way from an exaggerated regard for females to the most deadly sort of sadism; the lack of form in social behavior, together with certain codes of behavior which smack of juvenile delinquents; the relative contempt for the written as against the spoken word; the racy language; the attitudes towards dudes and the East, the two being almost synonymous; the impatience with the ways and principles of law—all these characteristics of the American frontier are to be found in Twain's best work. (Neider 1957, xxi)

Other authors employ tall tales in their work. Have students search for the tall tales, as well as references to the characteristics of the American frontier, in Wister's classic, *The Virginian* (1929), Berger's *Little Big Man* (1964), or Keillor's three volumes of Lake Wobegon tales (1985, 1986, 1989). Or, have students compare the characteristics of frontier life described by Neider to the North American youth culture of today.

Start a "Liar's Club" or "Tall Tale Swap." This can involve a school, a neighborhood, or an entire community. It could be a contest with levels of competition or a noncompetitive gathering of tall tale enthusiasts. Schwartz remarked that a lie-telling contest run at the New York Public Library was not very successful. "Few children of school age are told enough tales any more to know how to create them or tell them" (Schwartz 1977, 287). This is even more true for the older child, the young adult. However, once young adults have been introduced to tall tales and have a chance to create them, this problem disappears.

STORYTELLING AND THE VISUAL ARTS

Storytelling can be combined with drama, theater, mime, dance, or the visual arts in the presentation of a story. Sets can be built, costumes designed, and productions written and performed as interpretations of a tale that has been told. Young adults can produce picturebook editions of stories that can be donated to a hospital or an elementary school library.

After discussing the elements of setting, tell a story and have the students design several miniature backdrops to demonstrate the changes in setting. Sutherland, Monson, and Arbuthnot define setting as the geographic location and the time. "Other aspects of setting may be an occupational pattern or a general milieu or atmosphere, social or emotional" (Sutherland, Monson, and Arbuthnot 1981, 41). Discuss how color affects and alters the mood of a scene, and have the students use color in the backdrop to create the mood after listening to the tone of the story.

The backdrop exercise can be used to emphasize that stories develop in scenes and episodes. It can be extended for use in a puppet theater. Students enjoy staging familiar folktales for a younger audience.

Compare the art work, the medium used, the mood created, and the purpose in three or more picturebook editions of the same folktale. Discuss with the students the similarities and differences, not only in the art work but in the text. Students should identify phrases in the text that triggered certain visual images and how the images were interpreted. Let the students find phrases that trigger images that are not pictured in the book and decide why they were not illustrated. Tell your version of the same folktale and have the class illustrate the whole tale or individual significant scenes.

REFERENCES

Aiken, Joan. 1982. *The Way to Write for Children*. New York: St. Martin's Press.

Battle, Kemp P. 1986. *Great American Folklore: Legends, Tales, Ballads, and Superstitions from All across America*. Garden City, N.Y.: Doubleday.

Blair, Walter. 1944. *Tall Tale America: A Legendary History of Our Humorous Heroes*. New York: Coward-McCann.

Botkin, B. A. 1975. *A Treasury of Western Folklore*. rev. ed. New York: Crown Publishers.

Bronner, Simon J. 1988. *American Children's Folklore: A Book of Rhymes, Games, Jokes, Stories, Secret Languages, Beliefs and Camp Legends*. Little Rock, Ark.: August House.

Brown, Carolyn S. 1987. *The Tall Tale in American Folklore and Literature*. Knoxville, Tenn.: Univ. of Tennessee Press.

Brunvand, Jan Harold. 1978. *The Study of American Folklore: An Introduction*. New York: W. W. Norton.

_____. 1981. *The Vanishing Hitchhiker: American Urban Legends and Their Meanings*. New York: W. W. Norton.

_____. 1984. *The Choking Doberman and Other "New" Urban Legends*. New York: W. W. Norton.

_____. 1986. *The Mexican Pet: More "New" Urban Legends and Some Old Favorites*. New York: W. W. Norton.

_____. 1989. *Curses! Broiled Again! The Hottest Urban Legends Going*. New York: W. W. Norton.

Cohen, Daniel. 1983. *Southern Fried Rat & Other Gruesome Tales*. New York: M. Evans.

Evans, Ivor H., ed. 1981. *Brewer's Dictionary of Phrase and Fable*. New York: Harper & Row.

Flanagan, John T., and Arthur Palmer Hudson, eds. 1958. *Folklore in American Literature*. Evanston, Ill.: Row, Peterson & Co.

Freeman, Morton S. 1985. *The Story behind the Word*. Philadelphia: iSi Press.

Jacobs, Joseph. 1968. *English Fairy Tales*. London: The Bodley Head.

Janeczko, Paul B., ed. 1988. *The Music of What Happens: Poems That Tell Stories*. New York: Orchard Books.

Jones, Theodoric, comp. 1966. *Great Story-Poems*. New York: Hart Publishing.

Lacy, Norris J., ed. 1986. *The Arthurian Encyclopedia*. New York: Garland Publishing.

Lipson, Greta Barclay, and Sidney M. Bolkosky. 1982. *Mighty Myth: A Modern Interpretation of Greek Myths for the Classroom*. Carthage, Ill.: Good Apple.

Livo, Norma J., and Sandra A. Rietz. 1986. *Storytelling: Process and Practice*. Littleton, Colo.: Libraries Unlimited.

_____. 1987. *Storytelling Activities*. Littleton, Colo.: Libraries Unlimited.

Macdonald, Margaret Read. 1982. *The Storyteller's Sourcebook: A Subject, Title and Motif Index to Folklore Collections for Children*. Detroit: Neal-Schuman/Gale Research.

Moss, Anita, and Jon C. Stott. 1986. *The Family of Stories: An Anthology of Children's Literature*. New York: Holt, Rinehart and Winston.

Muncaster, Alice L., and Ellen Sawyer. 1988. *The Black Cat Made Me Buy It!* New York: Crown Publishers.

Neider, Charles, ed. 1957. *The Complete Short Stories of Mark Twain*. Garden City, N.Y.: Doubleday.

Nicolini, Mary B. 1989. "Is There a FOAF in Your Future? Urban Folk Legends in Room 112." *English Journal* 78, no. 8: 81-84.

Rosen, Betty. 1988. *And None of It Was Nonsense: The Power of Storytelling in School*. Richmond Hill, Ont.: Scholastic.

Sanders, Scott. 1985. *Hear the Wind Blow: American Folk Songs Retold*. New York: Bradbury Press.

Schwartz, Alvin. 1977. "Children, Humor and Folklore." *The Horn Book* 53, no. 3: 281-87.

Sutherland, Zena, Dianne L. Monson, and May Hill Arbuthnot. 1981. *Children and Books*. 6th ed. Glenview, Ill.: Scott, Foresman and Co.

Thompson, Raymond H. 1985. *The Return from Avalon: A Study of the Arthurian Legend in Modern Fiction*. Westport, Conn.: Greenwood.

Warawa, Bonnie. 1989. "Write Me the Story: Responding to Literature through Storytelling." *English Journal* 78, no. 2: 48-50.

Weis, Margaret, and Tracy Hickman. 1990. *Dragon Wing: The Death Gate Cycle, volume 1*. New York: Bantam.

Wilson, Raymond. 1988. *Every Poem Tells a Story: A Collection of Stories in Verse*. London: Viking Kestrel.

ADDITIONAL READINGS

Folktales, Myths, and Legends

Andersen, Hans Christian. 1983. *The Complete Illustrated Stories of Hans Christian Andersen*. London: Chancellor Press.

Briggs, K. M. 1979. *Kate Crackernuts*. New York: Greenwillow.

Frost, Robert. 1968. *The Poetry of Robert Frost*, edited by Edward Connery Lathem. New York: Holt, Rinehart and Winston.

Hamilton, Edith. 1942. *Mythology*. Boston, Mass.: Little, Brown and Co.

Ipcar, Dahlov. 1983. *The Queen of Spells*. New York: Viking.

Jones, Diana Wynne. 1985. *Fire and Hemlock*. London: Methuen.

Longfellow, Henry Wadsworth. 1985. *Paul Revere's Ride*. New York: Greenwillow.

Synge, Ursula. 1981. *Swan's Wing*. London: The Bodley Head.

Vinge, Joan. 1986. "Tam Lin." In *Imaginary Lands*, edited by Robin McKinley. New York: Greenwillow.

Whittier, J. G. 1894. *The Complete Poetical Works of Whittier*. Boston, Mass.: Houghton Mifflin.

Tall Tales

The asterisk preceding entries indicates sources of anecdotes and core tales that students can incorporate easily into tales of their own.

*Battle, Kemp P. 1986. *Great American Folklore: Legends, Tales, Ballads and Superstitions from All across America*. Garden City, N.Y.: Doubleday.

Bedore, Bernie. 1979a. *Scotty the Pike: More Tall Tales of Joe Mufferaw*. Toronto: Consolidated Amethyst Communications.
Based on Joseph Montferrand, the giant of the Ottawa Valley.

_____. 1979b. *Tall Tales of Joe Mufferaw: Whimsical Humour from Canada's Ottawa Valley*. Toronto: Consolidated Amethyst Communications.
Based on Joseph Montferrand, the giant of the Ottawa Valley.

Berger, Thomas. 1964. *Little Big Man*. New York: Dial Press.

Bird, E. J. 1984. *Ten Tall Tales*. Minneapolis: Carolrhoda Books.
  A collection of ten Western tall tales.

Blair, Walter. 1944. *Tall Tale America: A Legendary History of Our Humorous Heroes*. New York: Coward-McCann.

*Botkin, B. A. 1944. *A Treasury of American Folklore: Stories, Ballads, and Traditions of the People*. New York: Crown Publishers.
  A treasure trove of stories and anecdotes.

_____. 1975. *A Treasury of Western Folklore*. rev. ed. New York: Crown Publishers.

*Finnigan, Joan. 1985. *Legacies, Legends & Lies*. Toronto: Deneau Publishers.

_____. 1983. *Look! The Land Is Growing Giants: A Very Canadian Legend*. Montreal: Tundra Books.
  Based on Joseph Montferrand, the giant of the Ottawa Valley. Picturebook format for all ages.

*Fowke, Edith. 1976. *Folklore of Canada*. Toronto: McClelland and Stewart.

Keillor, Garrison. 1985. *Lake Wobegon Days*. New York: Penguin.

_____. 1986. *Happy to Be Here: Even More Stories and Comic Pieces*. New York: Penguin.

_____. 1989. *Leaving Home: A Collection of Lake Wobegon Stories*. New York: Penguin.

*Schwartz, Alvin. 1979. *Chin Music: Tall Talk and Other Talk Collected from American Folklore*. New York: J. B. Lippincott.

_____. 1990. *Whoppers: Tall Tales and Other Lies Collected from American Folklore*. New York: Harper & Row.
  First published in 1975.

Stone, Ted. 1984. *Hailstorms and Hoop Snakes*. Saskatoon, Saskatchewan: Western Producer Prairie Books.
  Surprising and witty whoppers about small town and rural life on the prairies.

_____. 1986. *It's Hardly Worth Talking if You're Goin' to Tell the Truth*. Saskatoon, Saskatchewan: Western Producer Prairie Books.
  Second volume of tales and whoppers about small town and rural life on the prairies.

*Stoutenburg, Adrien. 1968. *American Tall-tale Animals*. New York: Viking.
Fantastic creatures that populate tall tales, includes squonks, rattlers, gigantic bears, and other amazing wildlife.

Wister, Owen. 1929. *The Virginian: A Horseman of the Plains*. New York: Macmillan.

Urban Belief Legends

Baker, Ronald L. 1976. "The Influence of Mass Culture on Modern Legends." *Southern Folklore Quarterly* 40, 3 & 4: 367-76.

Baughman, Ernest. 1945. "The Cadaver's Arm." *Hoosier Folklore Bulletin* 4: 30-32.

Beardsley, Richard K., and Rosalie Hankey. 1942. "The Vanishing Hitchhiker." *California Folklore Quarterly* 1, 4: 303-35.

_____. 1943. "A History of the Vanishing Hitchhiker." *California Folklore Quarterly* 2, 1: 13-25.

Degh, Linda. 1968a. "The Boyfriend's Death." *Indiana Folklore* 1, 1: 101-106.

_____. 1968b. "The Hook." *Indiana Folklore* 1, 1: 92-100.

_____. 1969. "The Roommate's Death and Related Dormitory Stories in Formation." *Indiana Folklore* 2, 2: 55-74.

Degh, Linda, ed. 1980. *Indiana Folklore: A Reader*. Bloomington, Ind.: Indiana Univ. Press.

Grider, Sylvia. 1980. "From the Tale to the Telling: AT 366." In *Folklore on Two Continents: Essays in Honor of Linda Degh*, edited by Nikolai Burlakoff and Carl Lindahl, 49-56. Bloomington, Ind.: Trickster Press.

Samuelson, Sue. 1984. "The Man Upstairs: An Analysis of a Babysitting Legend." *Mid-America Folklore* 12: 2-10.

Smith, Susan. 1976. "Urban Tales." In *Folklore of Canada*, edited by Edith Fowke, 262-68. Toronto: McClelland and Stewart.

An Annotated Bibliography of Good Stories

4

Storytellers "need to know where to find good stories before they begin the difficult task of preparation. They need more than a list of anthologies. They should know where to find stories for the interest level of the children." (Briggs and Wagner 1979, 47)

This chapter will help you find good stories. Included are about 250 stories appropriate for young adults, arranged by genre: folktales and fairy tales; myths and legends; ghost, horror, and suspense tales; urban belief legends; love, romance, and sexuality; twists, satire, and exaggeration; and literary stories. Within each genre, stories are categorized by type; for example, in the section on folktales and fairy tales you will find the categories magic, romances, humor, trickster tales, American hero folktales, and so forth.

After a brief introduction to the genre, the stories are listed by title. Also included are the approximate time to tell the story, a brief summary of the story, and the source, usually a collection of similar stories. Because the number of stories included in this list is limited, they are only representative of the stories that appear in the collections referenced. The collections should be searched for other good stories.

CRITERIA FOR SELECTION

The stories included here were carefully chosen according to several criteria, as described in the following paragraphs. If more than one version of a story was located, the version that best met the criteria was chosen.

Suitability. The story must be suitable for telling. Baker and Greene (1987) discuss seven characteristics of a good story. Stories selected for inclusion here encompass these characteristics. According to Baker and Greene, a good story has:

1. A single theme, clearly defined.

2. A well-developed plot. A brief opening introduces the main characters, sets the scene, arouses pleasurable anticipation, and then, almost immediately, the story plunges into action. Action unfolds through word pictures, maintains suspense, and quickly builds to a climax. Each incident must be related in such a way that it makes a vivid and clear-cut image in the listener's mind. The ending resolves the conflict, releases the tension, and leaves the listener feeling satisfied.

3. Vivid word pictures, pleasing sounds, and rhythm.

4. Characterization. The characters are believable, or, in the case of traditional folktales, they represent qualities, such as goodness, evil, or beauty.

5. Faithfulness to the source material. Emaciated adaptation and vocabulary-controlled tales are not suitable.

6. Dramatic appeal.

7. Appropriateness for the listener.
   (Baker and Greene 1987, 29-30)

In addition, the stories included in this list must be in English and must not be too difficult for the beginning storyteller to tell.

Availability. The source material must be widely available. In order to be useful to storytellers, this bibliography includes only stories that have been published and can be easily located.

Recommendations. Stories were selected from collections recommended by the literature or from stories familiar to the author through storytelling experience. Many titles were contributed by practicing storytellers.

Appeal. The stories must appeal to a young adult audience. The stories must touch young adults, either by frightening them or by enlightening them about themselves or about their own or other cultures. The stories must, above all, entertain them.

Appropriateness for the Teller. A word of caution! Although these stories are appropriate for young adult audiences, they may not be appropriate for every teller. Each story must have meaning for the one who is telling it. If it does not, the lack will be immediately apparent to the audience, which may already view the procedure with skepticism. It is only through the constant reading and experimenting with stories that tellers gradually learn to recognize what is suitable for them to tell (de Wit 1979, 7).

FOLKTALES AND FAIRY TALES

"Most storytellers rely on the traditional narrative material found in folklore, because of its timelessness, antiquity and capacity to elicit laughter, tears, or bravos" (de Wit 1979, ix). Because these tales can be understood on a number of levels at once, they appeal to a broad spectrum of the population.

Historically, fairy tales and folktales gave vent to the frustrations of the common folk and united the members of a community. The tales revealed, in an entertaining and enlightening way, the foibles and strengths of mankind.

The two terms, folktales and fairy tales, are used interchangeably today. Both are traditional types of stories that have formulaic language and structure, supernatural motifs, and sympathy for the underdog or commoner. The differentiating factor is that fairy tales are stories that involve the "little people," such as fairies, dwarfs, and leprechauns. Folktales are stories in which quite ordinary people have extraordinary adventures involving magical objects and transformations (Baker and Greene 1987, 169). Fairy tales were originally cultivated by upper-class Europeans to assure that their young people would be properly groomed for their social functions (Zipes 1983, 14). Folktales, on the other hand, were transmitted to the children of upper-class parents through the servants employed within the homes. The tales passed on the mores and standards of the common people and their challenges against people in authority.

Storr defines folktales and fairy tales as "myths of the struggle to become human, to attain a unique identity, and to attain the stature of an individual" (Storr 1986, 66). The majority of the tales are not overly concerned with the older generation, as "it is the business of these young [characters] to discover who they are; to get away from their parents, to shake off the cloak of family identity and to find their own" (Storr 1986, 66). Because a basic task of young adults is the search for identity, these tales are specially suitable for telling to young adults.

Problems in the tales test the character of the protaganists and illuminate possibilities for attaining personal autonomy and social freedom. The tales are a comment on personal and social questions that still concern the young adult today: how couples conduct their relationships and how young people set about solving dilemmas perplexing to themselves or the community (Phelps 1978, viii). The stories stress the need and the right to grow beyond parental decisions and consent. They depict the young adult's necessary growth from a "yes-man" to parents and other authority figures to a sense of self-trust and self-knowledge (Shannon 1981, 34).

Folktales and fairy tales are bearers of cultural archetypes. Archetypes are "subconscious images, ideas, or patterns of thought universally present in memory in all individuals within a race" (Livo and Rietz 1986, 16). They are tools that can be used, through storytelling, to expand and extend human knowledge and awareness. Archetypes aid young adults in, first, recognizing, in themselves and in others, the capacities for such universal behavior and, second, identifying such behavior when they meet it (Livo and Rietz 1986, 17).

The reception of folktales and fairy tales in the Western world today (and to a great extent throughout the entire world) has been heavily influenced by the animated film versions of these tales produced by the Walt Disney studios and by the mass market books that derive from them. Young adults have preconceived notions of what a tale should be; it is one of the responsibilities of the storyteller to alter these preconceptions.

> The mass-mediated fairy tales have a technologically produced universal voice and image which impose themselves on the imagination of passive audiences.... The original tale was cultivated by a narrator and the audience to clarify and interpret phenomena in a way that would strengthen meaningful social bonds.... The [mass-media] narrative is no longer responsive to an active audience but manipulates it according to the vested interests of the state and private industry. (Zipes 1979, 17)

Many contemporary educators disapprove of fairy tales and folktales and discourage the practice of exposing students to them. The cruel stepmother, the passive princess, and the "happily ever after" endings are recurring themes that have received negative attention. Storytellers have a responsibility to not portray stepmothers, as a group, as totally negative; if a "cruel stepmother" story must be told, then the program should be balanced with a story involving a positive stepmother character.

Young women are sometimes depicted in the tales in "a dormant or passive state in order to indicate that between the onset of puberty and the time of marriage and motherhood there needed to be a quiet period of growth" (Moran 1987, 21). Moran feels that young adults should be told how passive princess stories served the crucial function of preparing young girls to endure whatever came their way as they were not to take an active part in molding their own destinies (Moran 1987, 22). Stories today can help to form a young person's consciousness of herself as a strong, vital person ready to undertake the challenges that will come. Phelps feels that there was no lack of active heroines in the folktales, but that these tales were not common among the folktales that survived by finding their way into print, and it is the printed survivors that are the main sources of the tales we know today (Phelps 1978, xv). Phelps published two volumes of traditional tales that have positive, active female (and male) characters. There is no need to present young adults only the antiquated stereotypes.

The dream of living "happily ever after" has always been a fantasy. Storytellers have a responsibility for helping young adults look for a more realistic vision of the future. They can do this by either leaving off the "happily ever after" or slightly altering the ending. "Young people of today, both boys and girls, need to be convinced that they must take their own lives seriously; that there will be helpers along the way, but no rescuers" (Moran 1987, 21).

Well-known fairy tales should not be told to young adults because the tales will be too familiar as childhood relics (Sutton 1983, 44). It is advisable to avoid beginning a story with "once upon a time" for the same reason.

Magic

Childe Rowland
In a mixture of prose and ballad, the story tells of Childe Rowland's adventure in Elfland and the rescue of his sister and two elder brothers.

Jacobs, Joseph. 1968. *English Fairy Tales*. London: The Bodley Head. pp. 74-78. 11 min.

The Costly Ring
When a father leaves a costly ring to his children as an inheritance, he has no idea what trouble will result. The beautiful daughter is taken by a giant, and the mother offers the ring to any of her three sons who rescues the daughter. On their journey, each son acquires ancient wives and mothers-in-law, who aid them in their quest. However, it is all for naught because, while they argue over who should receive the ring, it is stolen, never to be seen again.

Told by the husband of the woman who is rescued in a humorous and cynical manner.

Ransome, Arthur. 1984. *The War of the Birds and the Beasts and Other Russian Tales*. London: Jonathan Cape. pp. 40-50. 14 min.

The Cow-Tail Switch
A young boy, born after the disappearance of his father, is the catalyst for a search that results in the finding of the father's bones. His brothers have magical powers that bring their father back to life. The father acquires a cow-switch that is desired by everyone. He will give the switch to the son who was the most responsible for the father's return. Which son will it be?

Courlander, Harold, and George Herzog. 1947. *The Cow-Tail Switch and Other West African Stories*. New York: Holt, Rinehart and Winston. pp. 5-12. 8 min.

The Fairy Bird
After being turned out of the house by their angry mother, two children grow to maturity with aid from the fairy bird. When they reach maturity, they have several adventures with monsters before the fairy bird turns the children into splendid birds themselves. The transformed birds are captured by royalty, regain their original shape, and marry well. A Swazi story that gives an authentic taste of the culture. Terms are defined in the glossary of the book.

Berger, Terry. 1975. *Black Fairy Tales*. New York: Atheneum. pp. 106-23. 20 min.

The Hungry Old Witch

In order to stop the annual plunder of the village's harvest by the old witch, Stout Heart goes off to do battle with her. Her magic is too strong, and he is captured as a replacement for her slave, a beautiful young girl. There is high excitement as the two, using the witch's magic objects, barely escape the witch. An Uruguayan Indian story that is a good choice for Halloween.

Finger, Charles J. 1958. *Witches, Witches, Witches*, edited by Helen Hoke. New York: Franklin Watts. pp. 90-100. 19 min.

Kate Crackernuts

Kate and her stepsister leave their home and take refuge in a nearby castle. While there, Kate cures the son of the house of his enchanted illness and then marries him.

Jacobs, Joseph. 1968. *English Fairy Tales*. London: The Bodley Head. pp. 124-26. 7 min.

The Lion Makers

A tale from the *Panchatantra*, in which four friends, three scholars and a man of common sense, bring a lion back to life. The man of common sense is the only survivor.

Rugoff, Milton. 1949. *A Harvest of World Folktales*. New York: Viking. pp. 447-48. 3 min.

The Magic Tree

An unloved twin leaves his home and, with the help of magic, finds himself a wife, home, and people. Although he is cautioned not to reveal the source of these changes, he forgets the warning when visiting his mother, and he loses everything. The ending of the story in this version is supplied only by the illustrations.

McDermott, Gerald. 1973. *The Magic Tree: A Tale from the Congo*. New York: Holt, Rinehart and Winston. 5 min.

The Proud Princess

The boast of a proud father after the birth of his daughter on the eve of a great victory has serious repercussions. The princess grows up believing that her father will provide an enormous feast to mark her coming of age, and when she demands her due, the father feels that he must fulfill her expectations. When his warriors raid the cattle of the Lord of the Cattle, the princess is abducted and humbled.

Hayes, Barbara. 1987. *Folk Tales and Fables of the World*. Buderim, Australia: David Bateman. pp. 129-33. 10 min.

The Son of the Ogress

The human son of the ogress escapes with his human father from the mother's control, and ventures to a nearby kingdom. There he uses the magic given to him by his mother to protect the treasures of the king. The king decides to test the young man's abilities and steals the treasure himself. Not only does the boy recover the treasure and expose the thief, but he is given the throne.

Hayes, Barbara. 1987. *Folk Tales and Fables of the World*. Buderim, Australia: David Bateman. pp. 157-60. 9 min.

The Story Spirits

Every evening a young boy is told stories, but he does not share them, and the spirits of the stories, good and evil, are kept in an old leather bag with no chance of release. Throughout the years the spirits, becoming more and more crowded and discontented, await their chance for revenge. On the eve of the boy's wedding they plot their vengeance. Luckily for the boy, their plans are overheard.

Williams-Ellis, Amabel. 1981. *The Story Spirits and Other Tales from around the World*. London: Heineman. pp. 9-16. 13 min.

Tatterhood

A tale of twin sisters who are the opposites of each other in nature but are very fond of each other. The unconventional twin saves her sister from a wicked spell and in doing so discovers possible mates for the two of them.

Phelps, Ethel Johnston. 1978. *Tatterhood and Other Tales*. New York: The Feminist Press. pp. 1-6. 11 min.

White Lotus Magic

A sorcerer of the White Lotus Society in ancient China has one of his students changed into a pig and butchered because he displeased him. The sorcerer is taken to the capital, with his family, to answer for his crime. On the journey, the soldiers who are escorting the sorcerer are confronted by a giant. The sorcerer offers first the services of his wife and then his son to conquer the giant, but both are eaten alive. In despair, the sorcerer offers his own services to destroy the dangerous giant, but he, too, is eaten alive. It is not until the giant is gone that the soldiers realize that they have been tricked into allowing their prisoners to escape!

Roberts, Moss, ed. 1979. *Chinese Fairy Tales and Fantasies*. New York: Pantheon. pp. 42-44. 5 min.

Rugoff, Milton. 1949. "The Sorcerer of the White Lotus Lodge." In *A Harvest of World Folktales*. New York: Viking. pp. 191-93. 5 min.

Romances

The Beggar King's Daughter

A poor scholar arranges to marry a young woman of wealth, and while he is pleased with her beauty he is ashamed of her background: She is the daughter of the king of the beggars. Ambitious for position, the scholar throws his bride into the river and uses her money to establish himself in a new city. But his wife does not drown. Rather, she is rescued by the scholar's new employer, who then plots to teach the scholar a lesson. A twelfth-century tale from China, which includes details about the society and culture.

Manton, Jo, and Robert Gittings. 1977. *The Flying Horses: Tales from China*. London: Methuen. pp. 109-15. 13 min.

The Blue Rose

An emperor decrees that anyone who can find the blue rose can marry his daughter. Many men try, but the princess asserts that the blue rose they bring, no matter how fine, is not *the* blue rose, until a minstrel comes her way. A romantic tale from China.

Shedlock, Marie L. 1951. *The Art of the Storyteller*. 3d ed. New York: Dover Publications. pp. 204-12. 12 min.

Count Bertrand

Count Bertrand, a very arrogant and cruel master, comes face-to-face with death. He bargains with her for his life and, in the process of winning a stay of execution, learns many truths about himself. However, this does not deter him from behaving as he always has, until one day a young page shows him the power of inner worth.

Picard, Barbara Leonie. 1964. *The Faun and the Wood Cutter's Daughter*. New York: Criterion Books. pp. 209-32. 28 min.

The Crane Wife

A poor farmer marries a beautiful stranger not long after he rescues a wounded crane. Content with his new happiness, he obeys her request that he not watch her weave. Eventually, he loses his innocence by listening to bad advice and becoming greedy, and he breaks his promise to her. In this way he loses everything. A Japanese folktale.

Yagawa, Sumiko. 1981. *The Crane Wife*, translated by Katherine Paterson. New York: William Morrow. 9 min.

Duke Roland's Quest

Duke Roland is afraid of physical dangers. The lovely Lady Alison will not marry him because he is a coward, so he goes on a quest to find courage. Following a wise man's advice, Duke Roland makes four journeys, attempts and succeeds in four challenges, and returns home a wiser man.

Picard, Barbara Leonie. 1964. *The Faun and the Wood Cutter's Daughter*. New York: Criterion Books. pp. 29-43. 20 min.

The Enchanted Cow

An orphan girl, Artemisia, decides to marry the man she loves, but her employer, a witch, objects and turns her into a cow. The enchantment is detected by the lover, and he and a magician free Artemisia from the spell and rid the town of the witch. An Italian folktale.

Davis, Mary Gould. 1958. *Witches, Witches, Witches*, edited by Helen Hoke. New York: Franklin Watts. pp. 37-44. 11 min.

The Green Willow

A young nobleman forsakes his duty to his prince for the love of a young woman, who also deserts her duty to her parents. They live in total happiness for three years, until the willow tree outside her parents' home is chopped down. With the death of the tree comes the death of Green Willow.

Hearn, Lafcadio. 1958. *Japanese Fairy Tales*. Mount Vernon, N.Y.: Peter Pauper Press. pp. 13-21. 10 min.

The King in Rags

The young king of Scotland, curious about conditions outside his royal dwelling, makes numerous forays in disguise into various corners of the country. As he tries his hand as workman, beachcomber, weaver, baker, and beggar, his court becomes concerned over his unexplained absences and arranges a marriage to a princess of France. On the day that the approaching wedding is announced, a farmhand arrives at a farm in Orkney and stays the summer. The farmer has a daughter, Inga, who teaches the king the meaning of responsibility and honor.

A long tale that may be shortened or adapted or told effectively in episodes.

Brown, George Mackay. 1974. *The Two Fiddlers: Tales from Orkney*. London: Chatto & Windus. pp. 27-44. 27 min.

Owl

Owl thinks he is very ugly and goes to all lengths to avoid having his face seen by the girl he loves and who loves him. After a dance in his honor, his hat is removed, and, although the girl thinks Owl very handsome, he leaves and is never heard from again. The telling involves singing and can involve dancing. A very active story.

Wolkstein, Diane. 1978. *The Magic Orange Tree and Other Haitian Folktales*. New York: Alfred A. Knopf. pp. 30-36. 6 min (without dance).

Three Strong Women

Three generations of strong women develop a relationship of equality, mutual respect, and affection with a wrestler. The wrestler changes his former blustery ways and returns to the three women after winning a wrestling match in the capital. This Japanese folktale clearly affirms equality in relationships between people of different ages and sexes.

Phelps, Ethel Johnston. 1978. *Tatterhood and Other Tales*. New York: The Feminist Press. pp. 39-48. 17 min.

The Tiger's Whisker

When her husband comes home from the wars greatly changed, a young woman seeks a potion from the wise hermit. An essential ingredient for the potion is a whisker from a living tiger. The young woman obtains the whisker by taming the tiger. She takes the whisker back to the wise hermit only to have him throw it into the fire. It is not a potion she needs, but patience and love for her husband! A demonstration that experience is the best teacher.

Courlander, Harold. 1959. *The Tiger's Whisker and Other Tales from Asia and the Pacific*. New York: Harcourt, Brace & Co. pp. 16-19. 6 min.

The Two Donkeys

The love story of two donkeys who turn into humans in order to make it through the bad times. The female donkey, as a human, marries and is quite content until the male donkey comes to find her.

Wolkstein, Diane. 1978. *The Magic Orange Tree and Other Haitian Folktales*. New York: Alfred A. Knopf. pp. 24-28. 4 min.

White Wave

A snail shell found by a lonely Chinese farmer transforms his life, because the shell is the house of the moon goddess, White Wave. A magical story from the Taoist tradition.

Wolkstein, Diane. 1979. *White Wave: A Chinese Tale*. New York: Thomas Y. Crowell. 8 min.

Whitebear Whittington

A young woman, given to a beast to repay a promise that was made by her father, bears him three children and then returns to the house of her father for a visit. She forgets the warning that her husband has given her and spends the next seven years finding him. An American folktale that is a curious blend of "Beauty and the Beast" and "Cupid and Psyche."

Chase, Richard. 1948. *Grandfather Tales*. Cambridge, Mass.: The Riverside Press. pp. 52-64. 15 min.

The Woman of the Sea

A seal woman marries a human man and bears him three children. When she discovers her lost sealskin, she returns to her own people, leaving behind her human family. A familiar theme in folklore.

Colwell, Eileen. 1976. *The Magic Umbrella and Other Stories for Telling*. London: The Bodley Head. pp. 35-38. 10 min.

The Youngest White Goose

The gray gander allows no dissent in his farm yard: All the fowl must follow his lead. But the youngest white goose is always questioning his reasons for directing their behavior. A swan arrives in the area, and the goose disobeys the gander's orders, thereby discovering a wider world, into which she escapes.

Killip, Kathleen. 1980. *Twisting the Rope and Other Folktales from the Isle of Man*. London: Hodder & Stoughton. pp. 77-83. 13 min.

Humor

Abu Kassem's Slippers

The story reveals how a pair of shoes reflects the true character of the man who owns them. The miser Abu Kassem is so well known for the shabby slippers he refuses to part with that when he does finally try to dispose of them, everyone recognizes them. This causes the miser a lot of bother and costs him a lot of gold!

Travers, P. L. 1976. *Two Pairs of Shoes*. New York: Viking. first story. pp. 1-15. 8 min.

Foster, James R., ed. 1955. *Great Folktales of Wit and Humor*. New York: Harper & Brothers. pp. 278-81. 7 min.

The Goat's Funeral

A goat is well loved by the old couple that owns him. When he uncovers a chest filled with gold, the couple use the gold to pamper him. When the goat dies, the couple tries to give it a Christian burial but incurs the wrath of all the men they approach: the priest, deacon, bell ringer, and bishop. Each of the men rapidly changes his mind about the burial when he is told the goat left him money in his will.

Riordan, James. 1976. *Tales from Central Russia: Russian Tales, Volume One*. Harmondsworth, England: Kestrel Books. pp. 73-75. 5 min.

Good Day, Fellow! Axe Handle

A very deaf man practices a conversation that he imagines between the bailiff and himself. When the bailiff doesn't follow the man's imagined script, a very funny story results.

Asbjornsen, Peter Christen, and Jorgen Moe. 1960. *Norwegian Folk Tales*. New York: Viking. pp. 158-60. 4 min.

Gudbrand of the Hillside

Gudbrand trades his cow for a succession of smaller creatures until he is left with twelve shillings, which he spends on a meal. When he tells his adventure to his neighbor, the neighbor is sure that Gudbrand's wife will be very angry. Gudbrand is very sure that she will be pleased by any action he takes. The wife very amusingly proves Gudbrand right.

Asbjornsen, Peter Christen, and Jorgen Moe. 1960. *Norwegian Folk Tales*. New York: Viking. pp. 178-80. 8 min.

The King and the Shirt

In order to cure his father, the king, a young man searches the entire kingdom to find a happy man; it is only a shirt from a happy man that will cure the king. However, when the son finds a truly happy man, the man is much too poor to own a shirt!

Tolstoy, Leo. 1988. *The Lion and the Puppy and Other Stories for Children*, translated by James Riordan. New York: Henry Holt. p. 19. 2 min.

Spalding, Andrea. 1989. "The Shirt of a Happy Man." In *A World of Stories*. Red Deer, Alta.: Red Deer College Press. pp. 49-51. 2 min.

The Seventh Father of the House

A traveler, wishing shelter, approaches an old man and asks if he may spend the night. The old man sends him to his father, who, in turn, sends the traveler to his father, and so on until the seventh father, a man so old and tiny that he fits in a horn, grants the traveler leave to spend the night.

Asbjornsen, Peter Christen, and Jorgen Moe. 1960. *Norwegian Folk Tales*. New York: Viking. pp. 13-14. 5 min.

The Three Sillies

Upon discovering his fiancé and her parents crying in the basement over the projected fate of a future child while the beer flows over the floor, a man leaves on his travels, promising to return only if he can find three bigger sillies. After meeting a woman who forces her cow onto the roof to eat, a man who takes an hour to jump into his pants every morning, and a group of villagers attempting to rescue the shadow of the moon from a pond, the man returns to his fiancé and marries her.

Jacobs, Joseph. 1892. *English Folk and Fairy Tales*. 3d ed. New York: G. P. Putnam's Sons. pp. 10-15. 7.5 min.

The Two Fools

A humorous folktale about two fools who, while trying to eliminate blame for their actions, write their confessions on the wall for all to see.

Bonnet, Leslie. 1963. *Chinese Folk and Fairy Tales*. New York: G. P. Putnam's Sons. pp. 115-16. 3 min.

Turnabout

Dissatisfied with the amount of labor he does in the field, a man trades places with his wife for a day. Confident that her job is much easier than his, the man soon finds himself deep in cider and spilt batter, up the chimney, and in the porridge pot. The telling will be more pleasing if the "updated" ending is left off.

> Wieser, William. 1972. *Turnabout*. New York: Seabury Press. 7 min.

Trickster Tales

Aina-Kizz and the Black-Bearded Bai

A young girl outsmarts a rich man (Bai), not once but twice, and earns for herself and her father a fortune. First, the bai attempts to purchase her wood and get her mule in the bargain by buying the wood "exactly as it is" — on the mule. But she agrees to the bargain if he pays the price "exactly as it is." He does not realize that she is asking for the arm and hand that holds the money! The bai then sets a wager to see which one of them can tell the biggest lie, and again she makes a fool out of him.

> Riordan, James. 1984. *The Woman in the Moon and Other Tales of Forgotten Heroines*. London: Hutchinson. pp. 42-46. 7 min.

Anansi's Fishing Expedition

An exceptionally lazy man attempts to gain a livelihood without putting forth any effort by outwitting his neighbors. He, in turn, is tricked into doing all the labor and giving all the proceeds to his new partner. Even after a beating, Anansi does not realize that he has been outmaneuvered.

> Courlander, Harold, and George Herzog. 1947. *The Cow-Tail Switch and Other West African Stories*. New York: Holt, Rinehart and Winston. pp. 47-57. 11 min.

The Beggar in the Blanket

A dramatic tale in which the wife of Kim, an industrious and rich man in the village, sets out to prove to her husband that the love of his poor brother is more valuable than the love of his rich friends. Pretending to have killed a beggar, Kim's wife asks her husband to bury the body in the forest. When he asks his friends to help him, each finds an excuse and then reports him to the authorities.

> Graham, Gail B. 1970. *The Beggar in the Blanket and Other Vietnamese Tales*. New York: Dial Press. pp. 11-21. 10 min.

The Bitter Pill

After many years of having one lone voice among his eleven councillors give a dissenting opinion, the king decides to test them. He offers spoilt wine as a treat, first remarking on its fine flavor. Ten men agree with him, and again the eleventh councillor offers the truth. The ten men, not realizing that they have failed a test, recommend that the man who lies to the king be executed. And so they are.

Appiah, Peggy. 1967. *Tales of an Ashanti Father*. London: Andre Deutsch. pp. 84-89. 7 min.

Brer Rabbit and the Mosquitoes

Ravenous mosquitoes deter the hopeful swains of Brer Wolf's attractive daughter. All, that is, but Brer Rabbit, who uses his cunning and storytelling abilities to eradicate them. A slapping good story!

The story probably evolved from the African folktale that tells how a young man shows his cleverness by staying in a room full of mosquitoes without scratching himself.

Lester, Julius. 1987. *The Tales of Uncle Remus: The Adventures of Brer Rabbit*. New York: Dial Press. pp. 124-27. 4 min.

Appiah, Peggy. 1977. "The Spotted Cow." In *Why the Hyena Does Not Care for Fish and Other Tales from the Ashanti*. London: Andre Deutsch. pp. 21-23. 2 min.

Brer Rabbit Gets Caught One More Time

In the ongoing battle of wits with Brer Wolf, Brer Rabbit is captured, tricked by a basket of sweet-smelling sparrow grass. After unsuccessfully trying to escape Brer Wolf's clutches, Brer Rabbit finally asks that grace be said before he becomes a meal. When Brer Wolf closes his eyes and folds his hands for the prayer, the meal makes good his escape.

Lester, Julius. 1987. *The Tales of Uncle Remus: The Adventures of Brer Rabbit*. New York: Dial Press. pp. 37-40. 5 min.

The Buried Money

King Solomon's wise understanding of human nature aids a merchant in finding his stolen money.

Rugoff, Milton. 1949. *A Harvest of World Folktales*. New York: Viking. pp. 574-75. 3 min.

Buttercup

The story of the battle of an old witch with a young, plump boy named Buttercup. While the witch repeatedly captures Buttercup by appealing to his greed, Buttercup always manages to escape and get the better of her. In the end, he destroys her family and takes all her riches for himself.

Undset, Sigrid. 1958. *Witches, Witches, Witches*, edited by Helen Hoke. New York: Franklin Watts. pp. 32-36. 7 min.

Clever Manka

Manka solves several riddles for her father. Her cleverness brings her to the attention of the burgomaster, and, after he tests her wisdom, the two marry. The burgomaster sets a provision that Manka will not interfere with his decisions, but after a while, she gets involved with a judicial decision and is thrown out of the house. She is allowed to take from the house the one thing that she likes best. And she takes the burgomaster! A humorous story that has many surprises.

Fillmore, Parker. 1958. *The Shepherd's Nosegay: Stories from Finland and Czechoslovakia*. Eau Claire, Wisc.: E. M. Hale and Co. pp. 144-52. 11 min.

The Crafty Servant

This French folktale relates the havoc created by a sly peasant when he enters service under various names. When he takes his leave from his employer, taking his employer's belongings, the peasant easily makes good his escape in the anticipated confusion.

Hardendorff, Jeanne B. 1970. *Clever-Clever-Clever: Folktales from Many Lands*. London: Macdonald. pp. 74-77. 4 min.

Dinner for the Monk

A greedy monk refuses to share the bounty of a large fig tree with the inhabitants of the area. Two men decide to trick him into giving them some of the fruit. A humorous story that would be fun to enlarge and dramatize.

Courlander, Harold. 1959. *The Tiger's Whisker and Other Tales from Asia and the Pacific*. New York: Harcourt, Brace & Co. pp. 111-14. 4 min.

Duke Pishposh of Pash

A trickster, in the guise of a beggar, rewards a poor man, the gossipy neighbor of the richest man in Delft, with a gold coin for each kindness that he received in the beggar's home. The next day, the trickster goes to the home of the rich man and is welcomed because the rich man thinks he will receive gold for each of his kindnesses as well. The trickster helps himself to the man's riches and thus wins a wager with Prince William of Orange in a way that surprises both the Prince and the audience.

Williams, Jay. 1975. *The Wicked Tricks of Tyl Uilenspiegel*. New York: Four Winds Press. pp. 26-37. 10 min.

The Goat Well

While rescuing a goat from a dry well, a man is approached by a trader, who exchanges everything he owns for a well that produces goats. Later, when searching for the trickster, the trader is angered by the responses he receives in the various villages when he asks for the man by name: "Where-I-Shall-Dance." The trader finally reaches a village where his story is heard, and, through the chief's clever intervention, the trader is reunited with his belongings. An Ethiopian folktale.

Johnson, Edna et al. 1977. *Anthology of Children's Literature*. Boston: Houghton Mifflin. pp. 528-30. 8 min.

The Gypsy and the Priest

A gypsy swindles a priest of money and food, but, because of a gypsy curse, the priest does not realize he has been swindled.

Riordan, James, trans. 1986. *Russian Gypsy Tales*, collected by Yefim Druts and Alexei Gessler. Edinburgh, Scotland: Canongate Publishers. pp. 120-21. 3 min.

How Grigori Petrovitch Divided the Geese

A traditional trickster tale that demonstrates the wisdom of the peasant and the greed of the rich. In this tale, however, the aristocracy is shown to have a sense of humor. Grigori, needing some seed grain, takes a roasted goose to the "barin" as a gift. When he is asked to divide the goose fairly, Grigori manages to give everyone a section and keep the bulk of the fowl for himself. The amusement he gives to the barin is amply rewarded, so much so that the greedy rich neighbor down the road tries the same thing—with very different results. A version of the tale was retold by Tolstoy.

Wyndham, Lee. 1970. *Tales the People Tell in Russia*. New York: Julian Messner. pp. 16-21. 5 min.

Tolstoy, Leo. 1988. "How Many Geese Make Six?" In *The Lion and the Puppy and Other Stories for Children*, translated by James Riordan. New York: Henry Holt. pp. 38-39. 3 min.

How Nehemiah Got Free

Nehemiah, a clever slave, does not last long with one master, for no one enjoys being outsmarted by him. His last master, Mr. Warton, promises Nehemiah his freedom if Nehemiah can make him laugh, something that Mr. Warton has not done for a long time. Nehemiah's clever wit wins his freedom.

Hamilton, Virginia. 1985. *The People Could Fly: American Black Folktales*. New York: Alfred A. Knopf. pp. 147-50. 3 min.

The Hunter and the Tortoise

A hunter finds a tortoise singing and playing the accordian. The hunter spares the tortoise's life and brings him back to the village, where the hunter tells the chief about his find. The chief warns the hunter that if he is not telling the truth he will lose his head, but the hunter insists on a demonstration of the tortoise's talents. The hunter is executed because the tortoise refuses to cooperate, but the people all learn a lesson.

Appiah, Peggy. 1967. *Tales of an Ashanti Father*. London: Andre Deutsch. pp. 33-36. 5 min.

Appiah, Peggy. 1977. "Why the Hunter Lost His Head." In *Why the Hyena Does Not Care for Fish and Other Tales*. London: Andre Deutsch. pp. 28-31. 5 min.

The Judgement of Hailu

A slave of a wealthy merchant wins a wager by staying alone on a cold mountaintop without clothes, shelter, or fire. His friends light a fire on a nearby mountaintop to show their support, but the merchant rules that this fire, although it offered no warmth, broke the rules of the wager. In an attempt to overthrow this ruling, the slave appeals first to a judge and then to an old wise man.

A version of a folk motif that appears in many different cultures.

McNeill, James. 1984. *The Double Knights: More Tales from Round the World*. Toronto: Oxford Univ. Press. pp. 63-66. 5 min.

The King's Thief

To protect his reputation as a clever man, the thief strikes a bargain with a doubting king. He demonstrates his prowess by stealing oxen from the ploughman, the royal charger from a well-guarded stable, and the ring from the queen's finger. His reward is guaranteed to get a roar from the audience!

McNeill, James. 1984. *The Double Knights: More Tales from Round the World*. Toronto: Oxford Univ. Press. pp. 123-28. 10 min.

Mac a Rusgaich

A farmer is taught to be fair and just after hiring a young man who obeys the farmer's words literally. The young man "holds" the plough, "herds" the mountain moor, and cleans the horses "inside and out," just as his master tells him to do.

Wood, Wendy. 1980. *The Silver Chanter: Traditional Scottish Tales and Legends*. London: Chatto & Windus. pp. 77-81. 8 min.

Man Shy

It takes a mighty clever man to convince the wild young Scottish lassie of anything. The girl is terrified of men, and, in his courtship, the young man pretends to be terrified of women. He eventually shows her that he is the one exception to her notion that all young men are dangerous.

Foster, James R., ed. 1955. *Great Folktales of Wit and Humor*. New York: Harper & Brothers. pp. 123-25. 6 min.

The Man Who Climbed down a Moonbeam

A rich man hears a thief on his roof and devises a plan to capture him. He asks his wife to ask him certain questions and in this way feeds the thief a story about escaping on a moonbeam. When the thief attempts this feat, he falls and is captured.

Jablow, Alta, and Carl Withers. 1969. *The Man in the Moon: Sky Tales from Many Lands*. New York: Holt, Rinehart and Winston. pp. 53-55. 3 min.

The Marvelous Pear Seed

A young man, driven by need and hunger, eats a stolen pear. He is sent to prison but subsequently proves that all men, even the Emperor, at some point deviate from truth and honesty. Therefore, why should a poor man who steals only from hunger be cast into prison?

Wyndham, Robert. 1971. *Tales the People Tell in China*. New York: Julian Messner. pp. 20-24. 5 min.

The Miller of Abingdon

Two scholars match their wits with a miller who is bent on stealing from them. A fifteenth-century version of a French Fabliau and best known in a variant form, "The Reeve's Tale" in Chaucer's *Canterbury Tales*.

Foster, James R., ed. 1955. *Great Folktales of Wit and Humor*. New York: Harper & Brothers. pp. 61-66. 10 min.

Molly Whuppie

A robust and bold story about the courage and dauntlessness of Molly, the youngest of three children turned out from their home. Molly outwits the giant and his wife with whom they first seek shelter and secures royal husbands for her two sisters and herself. This version comes ready for the telling and will appeal to all ages.

Jacobs, Joseph. 1892. *English Folk and Fairy Tales*. 3d ed. New York: G. P. Putnam's Sons. pp. 130-35. 9 min.

The Moon in the Pond

A southern variant of the European folktale about fools who try to rescue the moon only to discover that it is the reflection that they have been attempting to capture in their nets. In this story, Brer Rabbit and Brer Turtle not only prove their companions fools but they end up with their girlfriends!

Lester, Julius. 1987. *The Tales of Uncle Remus: The Adventures of Brer Rabbit*. New York: Dial Press. pp. 96-99. 6 min.

The Monk of Leicester

A popular story about the untidy end of an amorous monk. "The Story of the Hunchback" in the *Arabian Nights* is a well-known variant. Dan Hugh is accidently killed by a tailor, who, in fear for his own life, moves the body to the abbey. There Dan Hugh is accidently killed a second time and his body again moved to prevent discovery. This happens four times until the body is buried.

The story is written in old-fashioned English and may be reworked to be more relevant to the audience.

Foster, James R., ed. 1955. *Great Folktales of Wit and Humor*. New York: Harper & Brothers. pp. 273-77. 9 min.

The Most Useful Slave

John has a reputation as a prophet at the plantation, and his master is so impressed by this that he stages a demonstration of John's powers for other plantation owners. A lot of money rides on the results. John manages to impress everyone and in the process makes his master quite a bit richer, making John the most useful slave.

Hamilton, Virginia. 1985. *The People Could Fly: American Black Folktales*. New York: Alfred A. Knopf. pp. 160-65. 4 min.

Once There Was and Once There Was Not

Kasim, a great and proud storyteller of tall tales, meets his match in a young girl. A story that demonstrates the art of fast thinking.

Wyndham, Lee. 1970. *Tales the People Tell in Russia*. New York: Julian Messner. pp. 16-21. 5 min.

Patches

When Patches, a young actor, meets a dangerous serpent spirit on the mountain, he dons a disguise and tricks the serpent into revealing his weaknesses. This information saves the village from the serpent, and the serpent decides to get revenge! An amusing tale from Japan.

Bang, Garrett. 1973. *Men from the Village Deep in the Mountains and Other Japanese Folk Tales*. New York: Macmillan. pp. 15-19. 5 min.

Peter the Great and the Stonemason

Several trickster motifs are blended in this tale of the "peasant czar" and the senators of his court. A stonemason poses a riddle that delights Peter the Great, who, in turn, poses the riddle to his senators. When the senators cannot answer the riddle, they bribe the stonemason, with unexpected results.

Dorson, Richard M. 1975. *Folktales Told around the World*. Chicago: Univ. of Chicago Press. pp. 127-29. 5 min.

Weinreich, Beatrice Silverman, and Leonard Wolf, eds. 1988. *Yiddish Folktales*. New York: Pantheon. pp. 240-42. The same story appears here as "Why the Head Turns Gray before the Beard," involving a king and a poor Jewish farmer.

The Princess Who Always Had to Have the Last Word

A king offers his daughter to any many who can prevent his daughter from having the last word in a conversation. Three brothers try their luck, but it is the younger brother, with a collection of objects that he finds along the way to the castle, who wins the bride.

Asbjornsen, Peter Christen, and Jorgen Moe. 1960. *Norwegian Folk Tales*. New York: Viking. pp. 77-80. 7 min.

The Rabbi and the Inquisitor

A Rabbi outwits a Spanish Inquisitor by twisting the inquisitor's own cunning and is released from a trumped-up charge related to the "Blood Libel" of Passover.

Yolen, Jane, ed. 1986. *Favorite Folktales from around the World*. New York: Pantheon. pp. 157-58. 3 min.

The Rich Man and the Tailor

A sharp, humorous tale in which a mean, rich man is distrustful of his tailor. The rich man has given the tailor a piece of cloth to make into a cap. The rich man continually returns to the tailor's shop, each time increasing the number of caps ordered for fear the tailor will cheat him out of his cloth. The tailor makes the required number of caps, but they will never grace anyone's head.

Spellman, John W. 1967. *The Beautiful Blue Jay and Other Tales of India*. Boston: Little, Brown and Co. pp. 69-70. 2 min.

Solomon's Way of Getting to the Truth

One of three merchants traveling together steals the money of the other two and hides it. When the merchants cannot get to the bottom of the matter themselves, they take the matter to King Solomon. He listens attentively and then asks their advice on a matter, telling them a story. With the conclusion of the story comes the unmasking of the thief, betrayed by his greed.

Schram, Peninnah. 1987. *Jewish Stories One Generation Tells Another*. Northvale, N.J.: Jason Aronson. pp. 46-49. 8 min.

The Song of Gimmile

King Konondjong does not like the composition of a bard and punishes him with fifty lashes. In retaliation, an old man, Gimmile, composes a song that is sung by everyone. When the king tries to stop people singing the song, he learns that deeds can not be undone and a song can not be unsung. Contains a song that can be sung by audience.

Courlander, Harold. 1962. *The King's Drum and Other African Stories*. New York: Harcourt, Brace & World. pp. 9-12. 5 min.

The Squire's Bride

A squire and the father of the young girl that the squire wishes to marry hatch a plot to force the girl to marry him. The clever girl misdirects a young man that is sent to fetch her, and the fun begins. The squire's new bride, forced into the house, up the staircase, and into a wedding dress is a mare!

Asbjornsen, Peter Christen, and Jorgen Moe. 1960. *Norwegian Folk Tales*. New York: Viking. pp. 56-60. 6 min.

Three Questions

There are more than 600 known versions of this story. In each, a humble man, shepherd, or miller, disguises himself as a particular abbot or person of influence and saves the latter's life, or position, by answering three questions put to him by the king or another dignitary. See the section of story examples for an Orkney version, "The King and the Miller."

Foster, James R., ed. 1955. *Great Folktales of Wit and Humor*. New York: Harper & Brothers. pp. 59-61. 5 min.

Tom Otter

When Tom appears before the king accused of killing the king's advisor, Tom presents his case eloquently. The king challenges Tom to create a riddle the court cannot answer within three days. If he does so, Tom will be set free. The king is quite sure that he has set Tom an impossible task, but Tom earns his freedom.

Price, Susan. 1984. *Ghosts at Large*. London: Faber and Faber. pp. 46-50. 5 min.

The Trial of the Stone

A young boy's money is stolen during the night from beneath a stone. The chief of the town arrests the stone and brings it to trial. When the audience can no longer restrain their merriment at the ridiculous spectacle of the trial, they are each fined one penny. The fines are collected and presented to the boy as compensation for his loss.

Courlander, Harold. 1959. *The Tiger's Whisker and Other Tales from Asia and the Pacific*. New York: Harcourt, Brace & Co. pp. 24-28. 5 min.

The Ugly Son

An extremely ugly young man is married to the daughter of the richest man in the village. He hides his face from the girl and her family until the wedding night when, with the help of his friends, he convinces his in-laws that his ugliness has been acquired before their very eyes.

Yolen, Jane, ed. 1986. *Favorite Folktales from around the World*. New York: Pantheon. pp. 158-60. 5 min.

The Wise Priest

When the people of the community ask the priest to pray for rain to end the drought, the priest agrees, but only if he can get the entire community to agree on the day the rain should fall. Of course, everyone is concerned with his own agenda and no agreement can be reached.

Hardendorff, Jeanne B. 1970. *Clever-Clever-Clever: Folktales from Many Lands*. London: Macdonald. pp. 83-85. 3 min.

Would You Like to Be Rich?

A gypsy tricks a greedy peasant into planting all his money in the ground in the hope of a bumper harvest.

Riordan, James, trans. 1986. *Russian Gypsy Tales*, collected by Yefim Druts and Alexei Gessler. Edinburg, Scotland: Canongate Publishers. pp. 122-23. 3 min.

The Young Head of the Cheung Family

A variant of the riddle story. A young girl proves to be so clever that the father of the Cheung family arranges her marriage to his youngest son and appoints his new daughter-in-law as head of the household. In this position, she increases the fortune of the family by common sense and clever dealings with both a merchant and a mandarin.

Wyndham, Robert. 1971. *Tales the People Tell in China*. New York: Julian Messner. pp. 25-33. 9 min.

American Hero Folktales

Emily's Famous Meal

The story of sixteen-year-old Emily Greiger's courage. She is captured by the British while carrying American dispatches to General Sumter. Her famous meal? The dispatches that she is carrying.

Jagendorf, M. A. 1972. *Folk Stories of the South*. New York: Vanguard Press. pp. 210-13. 6 min.

Fearless Ema
During the American Civil War, fourteen-year-old Ema refuses to give her horse to Northern soldiers. The soldiers are chased away by the arrival of an enemy battalion. Ema shows the Southern army a place to ford a river, as the bridge is held by the would-be horse thieves.

Jagendorf, M. A. 1972. *Folk Stories of the South*. New York: Vanguard Press. pp. 4-9. 7 min.

The Proud Tale of David Dodd
David Dodd is caught by the Yankees in Little Rock, Arkansas. Rather than betraying the Confederate operative in the Yankee contingent, young David accepts the death sentence. This true tale has become a folktale in the Southern states.

Jagendorf, M. A. 1972. *Folk Stories of the South*. New York: Vanguard Press. pp. 35-41. 8 min.

The Witch Who Spoke in Many Tongues
Witches were easily discovered in the early years of the settlement of the New World. Ann Jones must be a witch—not only does she speak several languages but she bewitches the young men in the village to be attracted to her and she is seen on several occasions conversing with the Devil. When the villagers trap Ann and the Devil in a neighbor's home, both disappear without a trace. Several years later, the truth is discovered.
A good story to demonstrate the effects of prejudice and ignorance as well as the courage of individuals who fight back.

Raskin, Joseph, and Edith Raskin. 1973. *Ghosts and Witches APlenty: More Tales Our Settlers Told*. New York: Lothrop, Lee & Shepard. pp. 60-68. 12 min.

MYTHS AND LEGENDS

In most parts of the world mythologies have been analyzed and separated out into various branches: myth proper (gods and heroes), folktale (stories about ordinary people whose lives are touched by magic...), and historical legend (Arthur, Roland). (Egoff 1975, 17)

Myths and legends, like folk and fairy tales, spring from the oral tradition and are best presented orally rather than visually. While they represent the collective imagination of a people, they have always changed with time and circumstances and the mood of the teller. A frequently cited rationale for telling myths and legends is Plato's suggestion that the future citizens of his ideal republic begin their education with the telling of myths rather than with mere facts or rational teachings (Schwab 1946, 15).

Myths are attempts to explain cosmic phenomena, natural history, the origins of human civilization, and the origins of religious and social customs (Sutherland 1981, 197). Myths, particularly Greco-Roman myths, are the source of innumerable allusions the listener will encounter again and again in literary, artistic, and even commercial endeavors. "The myths of Psyche and Eros or Oedipus are so fundamental that their very names have become symbols larger than themselves" (Egoff 1981, 210).

Legends tell the stories of the heroes of old, whereas myths deal chiefly with the gods and forces of nature in the remote past or an earlier world. Legends often contain mythical elements but are based upon some historical truth. They frequently are stories of the tests that a hero must pass in growing from a powerless child to a position of leadership in society. They appeal to young adults because young adults continually imagine themselves as heroes. They like the excitement, admire the virtues of the heroes, and understand the heroes' human weaknesses.

Heroes are vital to every society because they provide people with examples of realistic men and women who, almost incidently, have magical powers or extraordinary qualities. Joseph Campbell, as quoted by Jane Yolen, identified a hero as someone who

> ventures forth from the world of common day into a region of supernatural wonder: fabulous forces are there encountered and a decisive victory is won: the hero comes back from this mysterious adventure with the power to bestow boons on his fellow man. (Yolen 1986, 201)

Native North American legends often resemble the myths of other lands. "Prometheus stole fire for the Greeks; Raven stole it for the West Coast Indians; Nanabozho for the Ojibway or Chippewas; and Glooscap for the East Coast Indians" (Egoff 1975, 20). The native people of North America do not make the distinction between god and hero that is found in other cultures, and for that reason many of their myths are referred to, improperly, as legends (Egoff 1975, 21).

Myths and legends are a necessary part of a reader's education. Northrop Frye claims that education brings true freedom when it teaches the child to imagine and transform the existing social order. "Such education begins, says Frye, where literature begins, that is in the teaching of mythology, legends and folktales" (Stohler 1987, 31). Stohler emphasizes that myths and legends are not just entertaining but essential to the emotional growth and to the development of the imagination of young adults. Young adults, as they mature, begin to take the stories and images as patterns and metaphors that enrich their imaginations and allow them to consider the world in deeper terms (Stohler 1987, 31). What was real or quasi-real for a young child becomes an idea whose truth is symbolic, rather than literal, for the young adult.

Literature becomes more meaningful and enjoyable when young adults can understand the allusions in the literature by understanding the myths and legends behind them. Aylwin states that a vital ingredient in the progression toward becoming a mature reader is traditional mythical stories. They keep alive "an awareness of the primitive associations and worlds that lie behind complex novels" (Aylwin 1981, 83).

Young adults, as a group, have begun to realize that people are not simply either entirely good or entirely bad (Armstrong 1949, 10). Myths and legends, although far removed from modern society, deal with universal emotions and dilemmas that are being explored by young adults. They are tales of initiation. The initiatory ordeals include battles with monsters, insurmountable obstacles, riddles to be solved, and impossible tasks. The protagonists pass, "by way of a symbolic death and resurrection, from ignorance and immaturity to the spiritual age of an adult" (Eliade 1963, 201).

As discussed earlier, storytelling offers the opportunity for young adults to experience their dreams, fears, and fantasies with "safe" consequences. Listening to myths and legends helps young adults contemplate powerful but alarming feelings they may already find in themselves (Aylwin 1981, 88). The imaginative quality of the tales and the exposure of the audience to various cultural backgrounds make myths and legends appropriate material for storytelling, especially for young adult audiences (Briggs and Wagner 1979, 17).

The Adventures of Gilgamesh

Gilgamesh and his friend, Enkidu, go to the sacred Cedar Mountains and have numerous adventures: a fight with the guard of the Cedar, the giant Khumbaba; the resistance of the temptation of the goddess Ishtar; and the fight with the bull. Ishtar, in retaliation against Gilgamesh, takes the life of Enkidu. Gilgamesh cannot accept death and searches for immortality. The gods deny him immortality, but he is given a plant of eternal youth, which he loses to a serpent. Gilgamesh comes to terms with the fact of his own death. A tellable rendition of the epic of the Mesopotamian king.

Green, Roger Lancelyn. 1965. *A Book of Myths*. London: J. M. Dent & Sons. pp. 45-52. 17 min.

The Ages of Man

A creation story from Poland. Several animals disagree with their ruler, the lion. The resulting punishment is the death of these animals. Their bodies are devoured, but their heads are buried in a communal grave. The mud used to create man came from this exact spot, thus giving man distinct animal qualities — but only men, for women were created later!

Dorson, Richard M. 1975. *Folktales Told around the World*. Chicago: Univ. of Chicago Press. pp. 106-7. 3 min.

The Apple of Discord

An apple inscribed "To the Fairest" is thrown among the immortals on Olympus. Zeus arranges for a mortal judge, Paris, who had already proved his impartiality, to settle the ensuing quarrel between Hera, Athene, and Aphrodite. The goddesses attempt to bribe Paris with power, wisdom, and the most beautiful woman in the world for his wife. Paris selects the latter and gives the goddess Aphrodite the apple. This decision starts Paris, unknowingly, on the path that results in the destruction of the city of Troy.

Lines, Kathleen, ed. 1973. *The Faber Book of Greek Legends*. London: Faber and Faber. pp. 146-50. 9 min.

The Apples of Iduna
Loki, the trickster, delivers the goddess Iduna and her apples to the giant Thiazi in order to save his own life. The gods must get her and the apples back, as it is the apples that keep the gods young. Loki volunteers to rescue her, and in the process the giant is killed.

Hosford, Dorothy. 1977. *The Faber Book of Northern Legends*, edited by Kevin Crossley-Holland. London: Faber and Faber. pp. 57-61. 9 min.

Baucis and Philemon
When Zeus and Hermes descend in disguise to explore the selfishness, greed, and inhumanity of mortal man, they are appalled to find that not one household in an entire town will aid a stranger. They are finally welcomed in a small cottage that is separated from the rest of the town. The gods reward the old couple that are their hosts by granting one wish. They ask to die at the same time, and when that time comes, Zeus changes Baucis into a lime tree and Philemon into an oak and gives them a new life together.

Lewis, Naomi. 1973. *The Faber Book of Greek Legends*, edited by Kathleen Lines. London: Faber and Faber. pp. 122-28. 14 min.

The Boy Israel and the Witch
A youth, after drinking from a magic spring, can understand the language of the birds. By listening to them and acting promptly on their words of wisdom, Israel clears up a drought and brings on a battle between himself and the witch that caused the drought. A tale told of a famous eighteenth-century Rabbi. For an audience that is not familiar with some of the Judaic terms and holidays mentioned in this story, the teller can interject brief explanations or define them before proceeding with the story.

Schwartz, Howard. 1983. *Elijah's Violin and Other Jewish Fairy Tales*. New York: Harper & Row. pp. 203-9. 14 min.

The Boy Pu-Nia and the King of the Sharks
Fish could not be taken from the sea because the sharks are very fierce. Pu-Nia tricks the sharks one by one until he battles with the king of the sharks. Enjoyable legend for all ages.

Colum, Padraic. 1937. *Legends of Hawaii*. New Haven, Conn.: Yale Univ. Press. pp. 92-96. 9 min.

Cupid and Psyche

Psyche, the youngest daughter of a king, marries a mysterious creature. Urged by her jealous sisters, Psyche displays distrust and causes her husband, the god Cupid, to leave her. After many trials and encounters with several goddesses, she is reunited with him and becomes immortal. A romantic Greek myth that contains many familiar elements of folktale and fairy tales. This version uses Roman names for the deities.

Arbuthnot, May Hill. 1961. *Time for Fairy Tales: Old and New.* revised ed. New York: Scott, Foresman and Co. pp. 243-47. 16 min.

The Death of Balder

Through the trickery of Loki, Balder is killed by his blind brother, Hodur. The underworld is petitioned to restore Balder, but the condition demanded cannot be met, and Balder and his wife remain with Hel. An adaptation of the Norse myth, which is a story of strong contrasts and foreboding.

Colwell, Eileen. 1976. *The Magic Umbrella and Other Stories for Telling.* London: The Bodley Head. pp. 26-30. 12 min.

Demeter and Persephone

This version of the original Greek myth of the creation of winter does not embody the rape of Persephone by Hades. Persephone descends into the Underworld to aid the lost souls of the newly dead to their final resting place. This is part of her mother's responsibility, but it has been ignored by Demeter. Demeter mourns the time of separation and does not allow any growth of the crops until her daughter returns.

Spretnak, Charlene. 1984. *Lost Goddesses of Early Greece: A Collection of Pre-Hellenic Myths.* Boston: Beacon Press. pp. 109-18. 9 min.

Erigone and Her Dog

Dionysus gives the gift of the grape and of wine to a farmer named Icarius. Icarius shares the new drink with his neighbors, but when they become intoxicated they fear that Icarius has poisoned them and they slay him. Remorseful the next morning, they bury him under an oak tree. His daughter, Erigone, anxious about his prolonged absence, dreams that he needs to have proper burial rites. She sends her dog to find Icarius, and together they perform the burial rites. Erigone hangs herself from the oak tree, and her dog refuses to leave the site until he, too, is dead. The gods punish the townspeople, but the festival in honor of Erigone and Icarius becomes a happy one, complete with the invention of the swing.

Green, Roger Lancelyn. 1973. *The Faber Book of Greek Legends*, edited by Kathleen Lines. London: Faber and Faber. pp. 101-6. 11 min.

Gawain and the Lady Ragnell

Gawain promises to marry an extremely repulsive woman who has aided King Arthur in defeating a foe. On their wedding night, Gawain discovers that a spell has been cast on Ragnell, and his regard for her ability to make her own decisions breaks it completely. A romantic tale about one of the heroes of Arthur's court.

Phelps, Ethel Johnston. 1981. *The Maid of the North: Feminist Folk Tales from around the World*. New York: Holt, Rinehart and Winston. pp. 35-44. 20 min.

The Golem

Rabbi Lev shapes a sacred piece of clay into a protector, the Golem, for the inhabitants of the Jewish ghetto in Prague just before Passover. When an uprising occurs, the Golem becomes a power unto himself and creates more havoc than the evil he had been summoned to avert. There are many versions of this legend. With additional background information edited into the story, this is an extremely powerful and dramatic rendition.

McDermott, Beverly Brodsky. 1976. *The Golem: A Jewish Legend*. Philadelphia: J. B. Lippincott. 10 min.

How Finn Found Bran

The story explains the origin of the magical properties of the hound Bran, who belonged to Finn (or Fingal, the great Gaelic legendary hero). Finn and a band of seven special warriors recover three children for their royal parents from the land of Faerie. A puppy that is taken at the same time is the only reward that Finn wants for his courageous deeds; Bran becomes Finn's constant companion and protector.

Hayes, Barbara. 1987. *Folk Tales and Fables of the World*. Buderim, Australia: David Bateman. pp. 50-54. 11 min.

How Krishna Killed the Wicked King Kans

A wicked king devises a foolproof method of legally murdering his nephew, Krishna, in a wrestling match but instead perishes himself.

Jaffrey, Madhur. 1985. *Seasons of Splendour: Tales, Myths & Legends of India*. New York: Atheneum. pp. 32-36. 9 min.

How Thor Found His Hammer

When Thor's hammer is stolen, Asgard, the home of the gods, is in danger. The ransom asked for the hammer is the marriage of Freyja to the thief, the giant Thrym, but Freyja refuses the honor. The gods then decide that Thor should travel to Thrym disguised as the bride. Thrym receives his strange bride, one that does not speak or show her face but consumes vast amounts of food and ale. The hammer is placed on the bride's lap to fulfill Thrym's part of the bargain. At this, Thor throws back his veil, takes up the hammer, and wields it mightily to destroy the wedding party before returning with Loki to Asgard.

Arbuthnot, May Hill, and Mark Taylor, comps. 1970. *Time for Old Magic*. Glenview, Ill.: Scott, Foresman and Co. pp. 311-13. 10 min.

A Legend of Multnomah Falls

At the wedding party of the daughter of the Multnomah chief, a plague descends, killing many of the people. The oldest medicine man tells the people that only a willing sacrifice of a chief's daughter will appease the anger of the spirits and halt the plague. The chief refuses to follow the advice, but when her new husband becomes afflicted, the chief's daughter throws herself off a high cliff. All of the sick immediately recover, and a new waterfall forms on the cliff.

Erdoes, Richard, and Alphonso Ortiz. 1984. *American Indian Myths and Legends*. New York: Pantheon. pp. 306-8. 8 min.

The Man Who Was Made a Magician

Widjek, a very willing but awkward and clumsy Indian brave, is not highly respected by his tribe. After several disastrous adventures, Widjek meets Glooscap. Armed with the knowledge learned from his disasters and with the faith that Glooscap has in him, Widjek returns to the village a magician and is highly respected.

Hill, Kay. 1963. *Glooscap and His Magic: Legends of the Wabanaki Indians*. Toronto: McClelland and Stewart. pp. 118-25. 11 min.

Meleager and the Boar

The most famous heroes of Greece are invited to hunt the boar that Artemis set upon the countryside. Atalanta, the warlike daughter of Iasus, is included in the hunt. When Meleager rewards Atalanta with the spoils because of her participation in the killing, Meleager's uncles are angered. In his anger, Meleager kills his uncles. Meleager's mother is torn between her desire for revenge for her brothers and love for her son. She decides to revenge the murders, causes the death of Meleager, and hangs herself.

Schwab, Gustav. 1946. *Gods and Heroes: Myths and Epics of Ancient Greece*. New York: Pantheon. pp. 143-46. 10 min.

The Old Woman and the Storm

A new myth about the origin of the rainbow. The old woman, who is the storm, is very distraught about the worship the sun receives from the people. Her anger manifests itself in a powerful hail storm that traps a young man with her. He tells her stories, and the last one pleases the woman so much that she smiles — the rainbow. The use of imagery is superb.

McKillip, Patricia. 1986. *Imaginary Lands*, edited by Robin McKinley. New York: Greenwillow. pp. 27-35. 20 min.

Perseus and the Medusa

The oracle at Delphi warns King Acrisius of his death at the hand of his grandson, yet unborn. To prevent this occurrence, the king has his daughter Danae imprisoned in a tower. Zeus appears in a golden shower, and nine months later Danae has a son, Perseus. The gods follow the fate of mother and child and eventually help Perseus defeat Medusa, destroy a sea monster, and become king. And yes, he kills his grandfather!

Switzer, Ellen, and Costas Switzer. 1988. *Greek Myths: Gods, Heroes and Monsters: Their Sources and Their Meanings*. New York: Atheneum. pp. 81-90. 18 min.

The Red Lion

Because of his fear of confronting the red lion, a young prince runs away on the eve of his coronation. He tries to escape his destiny, only to find lions waiting for him wherever he goes. Finally, the prince returns home to face his lion and finds it not a difficult task. Based on a Sufi "teaching tale." Wolkstein includes notes for the storyteller that emphasize the need to produce very loud roars — to wake up both the prince and the audience.

Wolkstein, Diane. 1977. *The Red Lion: A Tale of Ancient Persia*. New York: Thomas Y. Crowell. 10 min.

Rom

Rom unwittingly commits incest with his mother and punishes himself with immolation. He is reborn magically many years later with the help of an old woman and because of this is proclaimed king.

Knappert, Jan. 1971. *Myths & Legends of the Congo*. Nairobi, Kenya: Heinemann. pp. 26-28. 5 min.

Sohrab and Rustem

A tragic story of war, in which a father and son, their identities masked from each other by pride, fight until the son is killed. From a Persian epic of the eleventh century adapted by the author.

Colwell, Eileen. 1978. *Humblepuppy and Other Stories for the Telling*. London: The Bodley Head. pp. 76-81. 20 min.

Tam Lin

A prose version of an old English ballad that tells the story of an enchanted young man and his rescue from the Faerie Queen by his mortal lover, Janet. This version, one of many available for telling, is quite chilling and appropriate for Halloween.

Fairies and Elves. 1984. Enchanted World series. Alexandria, Va.: Time-Life Books. pp. 100-107. 10 min.

The Theft of Light

A sun-stealing legend that features Raven the Giant, a favorite hero of many Northwest Coast tribes. Raven becomes the newborn infant of the daughter of the chief of heaven. He cries for the box in which daylight is kept, and to hush his cries his "grandfather" gives him the box to play with. Gradually lulling the chief with his innocent handling of the box, Raven manages to steal it away and return to earth, where he shares it with his people.

Erdoes, Richard, and Alphonso Ortiz. 1984. *American Indian Myths and Legends*. New York: Pantheon. pp. 169-70. 5 min.

The Wedding of the Hawk

A gold ring made for the hawk on his wedding day is lost or stolen. The wedding is canceled and hawk and his friends are changed permanently by the search for the ring. A pourquoi myth that explains several animal characteristics.

Courlander, Harold. 1962. *The King's Drum and Other African Stories*. New York: Harcourt, Brace & World. pp. 41-44. 5 min.

The Werewolf

The Baron is a great friend of the king and much loved by all who know him, with the exception of his own wife. Believing her to be true, he succumbs to her pleas to explain his regular absences from his estates. Upon learning that he is a werewolf, she and the knight of her heart steal the Baron's garments, leaving him in his feral state for all time. The wolf is befriended by his king and proves to be gentle and tame to all but his false lady and her knight. The king trusts the wolf and obtains a confession from the lady. The Baron gets his clothing and his human shape back, and the lady and her knight are driven from the country.

Picard, Barbara Leonie. 1955. *French Legends and Fairy Stories*. New York: Henry Z. Walck. pp. 93-98. 8 min.

Otten, Charlotte F., ed. 1986. *A Lycanthropy Reader: Werewolves in Western Culture*. Syracuse, N.Y.: Syracuse Univ. Press. pp. 256-61. 10 min.

Hope-Simpson, Jacynth. 1964. *The Hamish Hamilton Book of Myths and Legends*. London: Hamish Hamilton. pp. 177-80. 7 min. A somewhat simplified version, the language is not as poetic as the others.

GHOST, HORROR, AND SUSPENSE TALES

Stories of the supernatural continue to be popular, because people are fascinated by the unknown and the unexplained. Young adults are drawn to stories that shock, frighten, and amaze them while they are safely in their homes, theaters, classrooms, and at their firesides. There are three basic types of supernatural tales that are told to young adults.

1. Ghost stories that reflect great extremes in human experience and are usually told as true happenings. These tales are told either in a way that illustrates just how terrified the storyteller was or nonchalantly to emphasize the courage of the storyteller in frightening circumstances.

2. "Jump tales," which are the most popular of all the ghost stories, told to frighten the audience. "Jump tales" are usually very short and precise. When the tale is well told, the audience is pulled into the story by the teller and released screaming, frightened by the teller's explosive "You've got it!" at the end of the tale.

3. Urban belief tales, many of which have the same basic features as classic ghost stories: apparitions, hidden menaces, assaults and murders, and the presence of the dead. Urban belief tales are discussed in the next section of this chapter.

Most storytellers agree that telling sessions for young adults should begin with a ghost story because it will hook the most unwilling listeners and make them receptive to the stories that follow (Horner 1983, 460). Names, places, and dates may be changed to give the story more intimacy and verisimilitude.

The Bed by the Window
The patient that has been at the hospital the longest occupies the bed by the window. This patient relates to the other two bedridden patients in the room the wonders that can be seen from the window. Finally, not able to stand it any longer, the man in the middle bed causes the death of the other and moves to the bed by the window. He sees ... a brick wall. A concisely constructed horror story.

Cerf, Bennett A. 1945. *Try and Stop Me: A Collection of Anecdotes and Stories, Mostly Humorous*. New York: Simon and Schuster. pp. 288-89. 3 min.

The Blood-Drawing Ghost
Kate, drawn into helping an old ghost leave his coffin, his tomb, and the graveyard, carries him to the village in search of a home that has not been cleansed with "holy" water. There she cooks the ghost a meal made with the blood of the sons of the house. On the return journey to the tomb, the ghost tells her of hidden gold. Kate later revives the sons and collects the gold.

Hardendorff, Jeanne B. 1971. *Witches, Wit, and a Werewolf*. Philadelphia: J. B. Lippincott. pp. 107-17. 15 min.

Bang, Molly. 1973. "Mary Culhane and the Dead Man." In *The Goblins Giggle and Other Stories*. New York: Charles Scribner's Sons. pp. 29-40. 10 min.

The Boarded Window

When Murlock's wife dies in the wilderness, Murlock prepares her body for burial. During the night, the sleeping Murlock and the body of his wife are disturbed by a panther, which Murlock frightens away. Murlock regains consciousness after the shock of the panther attack only to find something even more ghastly! A great ghost story.

Bierce, Ambrose. "The Boarded Window." Retold by Barbara Walker. 1975. In *The Scared Ghost and Other Stories*. New York: McGraw-Hill. pp. 51-54. 7 min.

The Boy Who Had No Story

A boy, who is unwelcome because he has no stories to share, has a queer encounter with three men and a coffin. Not only do the men pull him from his bed, they make him help them carry a coffin to the graveyard. There they force him to lift it over the wall, dig the grave, open the coffin, and get in it himself! An Irish ghost story on the value of storytelling.

Danaher, Kevin. 1970. *Folktales of the Irish Countryside*. New York: David White. pp. 1-8. 6 min.

The Calico Coffin

A young girl dies and is buried in the coffin that was being saved for her mother, a coffin with calico lining. That night the mother is inconsolable, screaming in terror that her daughter is still alive. To put her fears to rest, the family digs up the coffin and finds the calico lining ripped to shreds by the girl's frantic attempt to escape the airless coffin. A horror story.

Pennington, Lee. 1988. "The Calico Coffin." In *Homespun: Tales from America's Favorite Storytellers*, edited by Jimmy Neil Smith. New York: Crown Publishers. pp. 165-67. 5 min. This volume is a treasure trove of stories that are suitable for a young adult audience. *Homespun* also includes a chapter on learning stories.

Come Again in the Spring

Death arrives, ledger in hand, in the midst of winter to collect Old Hark. Old Hark does not want to go until spring arrives when the birds that rely on him for food can fend for themselves. Death gives Old Hark three chances to get a stay of execution by answering questions about his very early life. The birds help him with the first two but do not know the answer to the third. While preparing to die "quietly, gently and peacefully," Old Hark accidently answers the third question, leaving death to adjust his ledger for the fourth time.

Kennedy, Richard. 1976. *Come Again in the Spring*. New York: Harper & Row. 14 min.

The Dark Legend
The actual events of the death of Captain Meriwether Lewis still remain a mystery, but visitors to his grave feel a restless presence and hear the whispers of a man. Was Lewis murdered or did he take his own life? The shooting in 1809 of the famous explorer created a legend that is still being told today.

Windham, Kathryn Tucker. 1977. *Thirteen Tennessee Ghosts and Jeffrey*. Huntsville, Ala.: The Strode Publishers. pp. 61-69. 14 min.

Deadline
A horror story about a man who ages two years every week, thus living his life span in exactly one year. His name is "1959"! The horror of the story is not realized until the last sentence. The year (name) in the story should be changed to correspond with the year of the telling. Told from a male point of view, it would have to be altered slightly for a female teller.

Matheson, Richard. 1977. *Spectres, Spooks and Shuddery Shades*, edited by Helen Hoke. London: Franklin Watts. pp. 171-77. 11 min.

Did the Tailor Have a Nightmare?
A contented Russian tailor has an encounter with Napoleon. To thank the tailor for his help in saving his life, Napoleon grants him three wishes, two of which are granted easily. The granting of the third is the material of which nightmares are made.

Serwer, Blanche Luria. 1970. *Let's Steal the Moon: Jewish Tales, Ancient and Recent*. Boston: Little, Brown and Co. pp. 59-67. 9 min.

The Dog and the Ghost
When his master is set upon by a ghost, the dog attacks the ghost. The master quickly runs home and retires safely to his bed. Much later the dog returns, unharmed, but he does not forgive his master for his desertion, and the master has to find another home for the dog.

Price, Susan. 1984. *Ghosts at Large*. London: Faber and Faber. pp. 76-78. 4 min.

Fearless Mary
Mary is not afraid of anything, alive or dead, and she proves it to the farmer's friend by getting a skull at midnight from the church. Her fame spreads and another farmer hires her: There is a ghost at his farm and everyone is frightened of it. Mary charms the ghost, and, after showing Mary two bags of gold, the ghost disappears forever. Mary claims the larger bag and lives out her life in comfort.

Price, Susan. 1984. *Ghosts at Large*. London: Faber and Faber. pp. 9-17. 11 min.

Fiddler, Play Fast, Play Faster

Billy Nell Kewley accepts the offer of "the Enemy of the Soul" to play his fiddle on Christmas Eve for a dance. He is repeatedly told to play faster and does so, mesmerized by the beauty and color of the dancers, until he is reminded of the Abbott's advice to play a hymn. When he does this, the beauty and color are unmasked. A fairly shivery Christmas story from the Isle of Man.

Sawyer, Ruth. 1949. *The Long Christmas*. New York: Viking. pp. 35-43. 15 min.

The Fog Horn

A story of loneliness that revolves around a primeval creature that arises out of the depths of the ocean to respond to the cry of the fog horn. The story must be modified for telling, but editor Colwell explains these changes in her notes on page 171.

Bradbury, Ray. 1978. *Humblepuppy and Other Stories for the Telling*, edited by Eileen Colwell. London: The Bodley Head. pp. 112-20. 25 min.

The Ghost in the Shed

After a new family moves into the house where a peddlar had been murdered, the peddler's ghost tries to draw their attention to his unmarked grave. His method of communication is the shed door, which he opens and closes at will. At first, the door is an inconvenience, then a problem to solve, and finally something to be feared by the entire family. When the ghost destroys the shed, the family finally finds the body and lays it, and the ghost, to rest.

Roach, Marilynne K. 1977. *Encounters with the Visible World: Being Ten Tales of Ghosts, Witches and the Devil Himself in New England*. New York: Thomas Y. Crowell. pp. 1-8. 9 min.

The Ghost's Bride

A young girl sits on a stone beside a stream and dangles her feet in the water. Her feet become very numb. Soon, the girl is barely able to walk, and eventually she cannot move at all. This has been brought about by a ghost, living under the stone, who has chosen her as a bride. Her mother, with the aid of a wise old woman, arranges a wedding for the ghost with a different bride, one that is no longer living, and the daughter is saved.

Yep, Laurence. 1989. *The Rainbow People*. New York: Harper & Row. pp. 55-59. 7 min.

The Golden Arm

After his wife's death, a man removes her golden arm from her coffin and takes it to his room. During the night, his wife comes for it. The ancestor of countless "jump tales."

Jacobs, Joseph. 1968. *English Fairy Tales*. London: The Bodley Head. p. 86. 3 min.

Huw

A story about a helpful Welsh ghost, a teenager named Huw. It is not a scary ghost story, but it does evoke a feeling of wonder as the narrator shares with the audience his discovery that the young hitchhiker, who warns the teller and syphons his petrol, has been dead for three years.

Palmer, Geoffrey, and Noel Lloyd. 1973. *Haunting Tales*, edited by Barbara Ireson. London: Faber and Faber. pp. 11-24. 24 min.

I'm Coming Up the Stairs

A "jump tale" about a girl who is afraid to go to bed. Fun to tell and fun for the audience.

Leach, Maria. 1974. *Whistle in the Graveyard: Folktales to Chill Your Bones*. New York: Viking. pp. 57-58. 2-3 min.

Kismet

When Mary becomes ill, her doctor takes very good care of her. One hot and muggy night, Mary leaves her hospital bed and goes for a walk. Her doctor finds her and convinces her to return to her bed—and her body. After returning home fully recovered, Mary finally finds out why her doctor has not been to see her since that evening: He had been killed in a car accident before he could arrive at the hospital!

Polberg, Johann. 1988. *13 Canadian Ghost Stories*, edited by Ted Stone. Saskatoon, Saskatchewan: Western Producer Prairie Books. pp. 109-15. 15 min.

The Knife in the Hay

A young farmer throws his knife at a whirlwind in an attempt to stop it. (There is a folk belief that whirlwinds are either witches in disguise or caused by witches and can be stopped by iron objects.) He does not find the knife then but locates it later at an inn where it caused the death of a young girl, his sweetheart.

Dorson, Richard M. 1975. *Folktales Told around the World*. Chicago: Univ. of Chicago Press. pp. 85-86. 3 min.

The Lady or the Tiger

The fate of the accused is decided by the opening of a door. There is a choice between two identical doors; behind one is a tiger and behind the other is a very eligible lady. Depending on which door the accused opens, he is either punished (eaten by the tiger) or rewarded (married to the lady). But what happens when the ruler's daughter has an interest in the case?

Stockton, Frank R. 1968. *The Storyteller's Pack*. New York: Charles Scribner's Sons. pp. 165-75. 17 min.

The Lambton Worm

The young and feckless heir of Lambton catches a worm on his fishing line and in anger tosses it into a well. The young man rides off to the Crusades and the worm grows to an immense girth and length and terrorizes the kingdom. Upon his return, the heir, tempered by his experiences of war, consults a wise woman and, with her advice, defeats the worm. To complete the victory, the young man is to kill the first living thing that he meets after the battle with the worm, but love for his father stays his hand. Nine generations of violent deaths is the price paid.

Hayes, Barbara. 1987. *Folk Tales and Fables of the World*. Buderim, Australia: David Bateman. pp. 35-39. 10 min.

Levitation

In the midst of levitating an unwilling hypnotic subject, the hypnotist has a fatal heart attack. As there is no one available to counter the hypnotist's command, the subject slowly levitates out of sight.

Brennan, Joseph Payne. 1977. *Eerie, Weird, and Wicked*, edited by Helen Hoke. Nashville, Tenn.: Thomas Nelson. pp. 37-41. 10 min.

May Colvin

May Colvin, a very spoiled young lady, rides off with an undesirable man and two horses and two bags of gold from her father's treasury. When her false love tries to drown her, May Colvin pushes him into the water and refuses to help him. The story was developed from a ballad and aptly demonstrates the wisdom of prudence before adventure.

Manning-Sanders, Ruth. 1968. *Stories from the English and Scottish Ballads*. London: Heinemann. pp. 24-29. 10 min.

A Meeting on the Road Home

Gabriel Fisher, on his way home from the local pub, meets a young woman carrying a basket. He offers to carry the basket for her, and when he does so, he is horrified to find that the woman's very vocal head is inside the basket. The head and the headless woman chase him down the road until they reach a stream of water flowing over the road that ghosts cannot cross.

Ghosts. 1984. The Enchanted World series. Alexandria, Va.: Time-Life Books. pp. 63-69. 10 min.

Mr. Fox

A chilling tale of a girl who explores her fiance's home and finds that he captures young ladies and kills them. She denounces him very cleverly the next day, and he is immediately dealt with by her brothers and her friends. This story shows how storytelling had its place, even on such occasions as betrothal parties. The English "Blue-Beard."

Jacobs, Joseph. 1968. *English Fairy Tales*. London: The Bodley Head. pp. 92-94. 7 min.

Mujina

A traveler encounters a faceless woman on a haunted hillside. He runs away in fright and reaches a safe haven, but his savior also seems to be faceless! A Japanese ghost story retold.

Hearn, Lafcadio. 1962. *Tales to Be Told in the Dark: A Selection of Stories from the Great Authors, Arranged for Reading and Telling Aloud*, edited by Basil Davenport. New York: Dodd, Mead & Co. pp. 236-38. 6 min.

Nightstalker of Croglin Grange

A vampire disturbs the new inhabitants of Croglin Grange. After recovering from the attack, the three siblings prepare a trap and remove the threat of the vampire forever.

Night Creatures. 1985. The Enchanted World series. Alexandria, Va.: Time-Life Books. pp. 98-107. 9 min.

On the Brighton Road

A tramp wakes up from a sleep in a snowdrift and continues walking down the road, where he meets a fellow traveler, a fifteen-year-old boy. The boy informs the tramp that both of them are dead, but the tramp refuses to believe him until the boy proves it to him without a doubt.

Middleton, Richard. 1975. *The Scared Ghost and Other Stories*, edited by Barbara Walker. New York: McGraw-Hill. pp. 1-5. 6 min.

Room for One More

A young woman is disturbed by a coachman who appears several times in her dreams. He beckons to her and tells her that there is room for one more. Several days later, the woman attempts to get on a full elevator but recoils and refuses to get on the elevator when the operator turns out to be the coachman of her dreams. She is saved from certain death when the elevator cable breaks. This story has appeared in several different anthologies.

Cerf, Bennett. 1945. *Try and Stop Me: A Collection of Anecdotes and Stories, Mostly Humorous*. New York: Simon and Schuster. pp. 277-79. 3 min.

The Signalman

The signalman unknowingly prophesies his own death in this haunting tale that has been abridged for telling. "It is well worth spending time on the preparation of this story as an antidote to the many trivial ghost tales found in anthologies today" (Colwell 1976).

Dickens, Charles. 1976. *The Magic Umbrella and Other Stories for Telling*, edited by Eileen Colwell. London: The Bodley Head. pp. 112-17. 12 min.

The Smuggler

Just after World War II, Peter passes through "Checkpoint Charlie" every day on the way to work. The American guard, Eric, suspects that Peter is smuggling but does not know what is being smuggled. The answer to Eric's suspicions will delight audiences of all ages.

Bauer, Caroline Feller. 1977. *Handbook for Storytellers*. Chicago: American Library Association. pp. 311-12. 3 min.

The Stolen Liver

When the wife absentmindedly eats the liver meant for her husband's meal, she is frightened. Her husband, an abusive man, purchased the liver for himself. In her panic, she steals the liver from an old woman's body that is lying in state in the church next door, cooks it, and serves it to her husband. The ghost of the woman demands her liver back, but since it has been devoured, the husband brings her a substitute—the liver of his wife.

This story is one of the best loved by junior high students. Localize it, give the characters names, and tell it in the most gory manner possible!

Cohen, Daniel. 1984. *The Restless Dead: Ghostly Tales from around the World*. New York: Dodd, Mead and Co. pp. 113-19. 6 min.

The Stone Avenger

A ghost story that explores the disappearance and death of Don Juan. Don Juan sees the statue of a man he has murdered. Out of bravado, the Don invites the statue to dinner. The statue actually comes and repays his host with an invitation of his own, from which Don Juan never returns.

The Lore of Love. 1987. The Enchanted World series. Alexandria, Va.: Time-Life Books. pp. 61-63. 5 min.

The Totem Pole

A story within a story. One Friday night, a man at a bar is told a story about a newly acquired totem pole at the museum. The totem pole is haunting one of the curators. The story is told by a very frightened museum attendant. Both men are now distraught. Together with a policeman, they go to the museum to find six happy, bloody grins on the faces on the totem pole.

Bloch, Robert. 1986. *Midnight Pleasures*. Garden City, N.Y.: Doubleday. pp. 165-77. 25 min.

Two Anecdotes

Two short pseudo-ghost tales, hardly more than jokes, that are perfect for ending a storytelling session. The first one involves a pun on the phrase "to strike a happy medium" and the second is a deliberate build-up of horror that is humorously diffused.

Davenport, Basil. 1962. *Tales to Be Told in the Dark: A Selection of Stories from the Great Authors, Arranged for Reading and Telling Aloud*. New York: Dodd, Mead and Co. pp. 244-47. 2.5 min. each.

Unreasonable Doubt

A man in desperate need of relaxation goes by train for a vacation. Before he has traveled very long he overhears a story about two brothers who have attempted to get away with murder. The two brothers had almost succeeded except for one thing — and that thing is not revealed because the storyteller and his listener disembark from the train at that time. So much for the relaxed vacation of the eavesdropper! A story within a story.

Ellin, Stanley. 1979. *Terrors, Terrors, Terrors*, edited by Helen Hoke. New York: Franklin Watts. pp. 180-91. 20 min.

The Voyage of the Deborah Pratt

Jemmy and the African boy he befriends are the only two members of a crowded slave ship that return unscathed. All of the other Africans commit group suicide after being blinded by a highly contagious eye disease. All crew members, except Jemmy, become blind after ten spirits of the Africans climb on board and infect the crew. A horror story, both in the literal sense and in the descriptions offered about the slave trade voyages. The story is written as if it is being told; no adaptation for storytelling is necessary.

DeFord, Miriam Allen. 1978. *Terrors, Torments and Traumas*, edited by Helen Hoke. Nashville, Tenn.: Thomas Nelson. pp. 40-48. 20 min.

The Waiting Men

A picture of a hanging tree and two men, purchased by John, horrifies everyone with its evilness but quite fascinates John. Eventually it consumes him; he suffers from stress and then disappears from his lodgings only to be found within the picture, hanged in the previously empty noose on the hanging tree.

Wallace, Penelope. 1977. *Eerie, Weird, and Wicked*, edited by Helen Hoke. Nashville, Tenn.: Thomas Nelson. pp. 97-104. 17 min.

The Weeping Lass at the Dancing Place

The bitter tears of a young girl draw her drowned lover from the grave. When the handsome stranger wishes to dance with the weeping girl, she tries to refuse, but he is forceful. While dancing with him she realizes that he is her lover, presumed to be dead and buried far from home. When she says once again that she wishes to be with him always, the young man takes her at her word and rides with her across the country to a graveyard. He tries to pull her into his grave to keep her with him always.

Leodhas, Sorche Nic. 1971. *Twelve Great Black Cats and Other Eerie Scottish Tales*. New York: E. P. Dutton. pp. 41-49. 11 min.

Which Was Witch?

A scholar, confronted with two identical wives, realizes that one must be a witch—but which one? The scholar, in order to protect his wife and drive the witch away, acts quickly, grabbing the arm of each wife and holding it tightly until dawn. At this, the witch-wife struggles to get free, loses her false shape, and eventually escapes. Or does she?

Arbuthnot, May Hill, and Mark Taylor, comps. 1970. *Time for Old Magic*. Glenview, Ill.: Scott, Foresman and Co. pp. 220-21. 7 min.

The Whole Town's Sleeping

"The Lonely One" preys upon women and terrifies the entire town. Lavinia Nebbs refuses to be frightened, even after discovering the latest victim. As she returns home alone through the ravine, she becomes very frightened but manages to get home and lock herself safely in her house ... or so she thinks. A chapter of the novel.

Bradbury, Ray. 1946. *Dandelion Wine*. New York: Alfred A. Knopf. pp. 181-99. 31 min.

Witch and Warlock

A powerful and jealous warlock casts a spell on a local witch who refuses to admit his sovereignty. His spell is written above her door and causes all who enter to throw off their clothes and dance with wild abandon. The witch cannot stop dancing and dies. The story is stark and extremely powerful.

Aitken, Hannah. 1973. *A Forgotten Heritage: Original Folktales of Lowland Scotland*. Edinburg, Scotland: Scottish Academic Press. pp. 52-53. 4 min.

URBAN BELIEF LEGENDS

The predominant tellers of and audience for these modern folktales are young adults. They are intrigued because the urban legends relate events that are possible (Horner 1983, 460). The popularity of urban belief legends among young adults substantiates the premise that storytelling is a viable activity for this age group.

Horner suggests that urban belief legends serve as an excellent vehicle for opening a discussion about stories and storytelling in a group of young adults (Horner 1983, 460). Frequently, the young adults have heard different variations and are interested in sharing their versions with the teller. The legends, according to Brunvand, reflect how American society expects young people and authority figures to behave in times of crisis (Brunvand 1981, 12). Young adults are constantly seeking pertinent information on "proper" behavior and "correct" attitudes that can be explored in safety. Brunvand found that young adults, in their early teens, reject the overdramatic and unbelievable supernatural tales that delighted them in younger years and embrace a new lore of more realistic tales that deal with "people like themselves who are subjected to gruelling ordeals and horrible threats" (Brunvand 1981, 47).

Urban belief legends are concerned with violence, horror, threats posed by technology, impurity of food, personal embarrassment, relationships with friends and family, death, the supernatural, and other sources of anxiety (Schwartz 1981, 97). A constant theme of these tales is the young adult leaving home. The tales deliver a warning, "Watch out! This could happen to you!" (Brunvand 1981, 47). The tales also contain thinly-disguised sexual themes that serve as both entertainment and cautionary notices. "Thus from the teenager's own major fears, concerns and experiences, spring their own favorite 'true' oral stories" (Brunvand 1981, 48).

Printed urban belief legends vary in length, depending on the amount of embellishment that the author has added to the basic story. Folklorists like Brunvand and Fowke provide the basic outline of many of these tales. Schwartz and Cohen have fleshed out the basic outlines and published their collections of urban belief tales for young adult reading audiences.

Storytellers should localize all details in the tales to ensure the fullest impact on the audience. Storytellers adapt the basic story to suit the storytelling occasion, and, for this reason, several different versions of each tale are recommended.

The Babysitter

A telephone call that is repeated every half hour frightens a babysitter and the children she is looking after. The caller warns her that something will happen soon but does not elucidate any further. The telephone operator traces the calls and finds that they are made from an upstairs phone. The babysitter and children flee the house just as the police arrive. In some versions the children and the sitter are slain before the police can arrive.

Brunvand, Jan Harold. 1981. *The Vanishing Hitchhiker: American Urban Legends and Their Meanings*. New York: W. W. Norton. pp. 53-57. 2 versions. 1 min. each.

Schwartz, Alvin. 1981. *Scary Stories to Tell in the Dark*. New York: J. B. Lippincott. pp. 69-71. 4 min.

Smith, Susan. 1976. "Urban Tales." In *Folklore of Canada*, edited by Edith Fowke. Toronto: McClelland and Stewart. p. 263. 1 min.

The Babysitter Mistakes Child for Turkey

A hallucinating babysitter cooks the baby under the misapprehension that it is a turkey.

Brunvand, Jan Harold. 1981. *The Vanishing Hitchhiker: American Urban Legends and Their Meanings*. New York: W. W. Norton. pp. 65-69. 5 versions. 1 min. each.

Smith, Susan. 1976. "Urban Tales." In *Folklore of Canada*, edited by Edith Fowke. Toronto: McClelland and Stewart. p. 265. 1 min.

The Five-Pound Note

An elderly woman goes by train to do some shopping. After a short nap, she checks her purse and finds her money gone. The only other person in the car is asleep. The old woman quietly checks the sleeping woman's bag and finds the money. Because she does not want to make a scene, she just takes her money back without alerting anyone and does her shopping. When she returns home, she finds that she left her money behind!

A story that is begging to be localized and embroidered.

Dorson, Richard M. 1975. *Folktales Told around the World*. Chicago: Univ. of Chicago Press. p. 56. 1 min.

Briggs, Katherine M., and Ruth L. Tongue. 1965. *Folktales of England*. Chicago: Univ. of Chicago Press. pp. 101-2. 2 min.

Brunvand, Jan Harold. 1984. *The Choking Doberman and Other "New" Urban Legends*. New York: W. W. Norton. p. 188. 1 min. A modern version.

High Beams

Driving home from a basketball game, a young girl is followed closely by a truck. The driver of the truck periodically aims his high beams into her car. When she reaches home, the girl tells her father to call the police because she is frightened by the truck driver. The police find a man with a knife crouched in the rear of the car. The driver of the truck saw him and continually tried to warn the girl on the journey to her home.

Brunvand, Jan Harold. 1981. *The Vanishing Hitchhiker: American Urban Legends and Their Meanings*. New York: W. W. Norton. pp. 52-53. 3 versions. 1 min. each.

Schwartz, Alvin. 1981. *Scary Stories to Tell in the Dark*. New York: J. B. Lippincott. pp. 66-68. 3 min.

The Hook

A young couple, parked in a secluded spot, hear a radio report about an escaped prisoner in the locality. The prisoner is easily identified by a hook on his right hand. The couple has a disagreement about the danger, and, in frustration and anger, the boy drives off in hurry. When they reach the girl's home, they find a bloody hook hanging on the handle of the passenger door.

> Brunvand, Jan Harold. 1981. *The Vanishing Hitchhiker: American Urban Legends and Their Meanings*. New York: W. W. Norton. pp. 48-52. 4 versions. 1 min. each.

> Smith, Susan. 1976. "Urban Tales." In *Folklore of Canada*, edited by Edith Fowke. Toronto: McClelland and Stewart. p. 263. 1 min.

Laura

A modern version of the classic urban belief legend, "The Vanishing Hitchhiker." The young motorcyclist gives a ride to a beddraggled young woman at the side of the road. He also lends her his new leather jacket. After dropping her off at her home, he realizes that he has forgotten his jacket. He returns for it the next day but is told by the girl's mother that her daughter has been dead several years. The young man argues with the woman, and, in an attempt to convince him of the truth, she takes him to the graveyard. There he finds his jacket on the corner of the girl's grave. He is never able to wear the jacket again and finally, in frustration, throws it onto the fire. The sweet smell of freshly cut flowers escaping from the burning leather frightens him badly.

> Roberts, Nancy. 1978. *Appalachian Ghosts*. Garden City, N.Y.: Doubleday. pp. 7-11. 7 min.

Mall Rat

Adapted from an urban legend. Rita never locks her car doors, although her parents always remind her to do so. One cold evening, after working late at the mall, Rita finds an old woman sitting in the passenger seat. Rita has the presence of mind to get help, and the police arrive to drive the old woman home. Rita later notices a newspaper on the floor of the car and finds a cache of weapons hidden underneath.

> Gorog, Judith. 1988. *Three Dreams and a Nightmare and Other Tales of the Dark*. New York: Philomel Books. pp. 15-20. 9 min.

A Ride for a Corpse

A version of "The Vanishing Hitchhiker" from Turkey. A young man gives a ride to a young woman on his horse. By the time he reaches the town that she wished to go, his passenger is no longer alive. Afraid that he will be blamed for her death, he explains the circumstances to the villagers only to find that the corpse's trek is a yearly event.

> Cohen, Daniel. 1984. *The Restless Dead: Ghostly Tales from around the World*. New York: Dodd, Mead and Co. pp. 34-40. 4 min.

The Vanishing Hitchhiker

A hitchhiker picked up along a lonely road disappears from the car. When the driver goes to the house given by the hitchhiker as her destination, the driver finds out that the hitchhiker is the ghost of the daughter of the house. The most famous ghost story today! In many versions, the hitchhiker borrows a jacket from the driver that is later found hanging on her gravestone.

Battle, Kemp P., comp. *Great American Folklore: Legends, Tales, Ballads and Superstitions from All across America*. New York: Doubleday. pp. 336-37. 4 min.

Brunvand, Jan Harold. 1981. *The Vanishing Hitchhiker: American Urban Legends and Their Meanings*. New York: W. W. Norton. pp. 24-32. 9 versions. 1 min. each.

Fowke, Edith. 1986. *Tales Told in Canada*. Toronto: Doubleday Canada Ltd. p. 122. 1.5 min.

Smith, Susan. 1976. "Urban Tales." In *Folklore of Canada*, edited by Edith Fowke. Toronto: McClelland and Stewart. p. 265. 1 min.

LOVE, ROMANCE, AND SEXUALITY

One of the key concepts of adolescence discussed by Konopka is the experience of sexual maturity (Konopka 1973, 299). She claims that sexual maturity generates in young adults "a great wonderment about themselves and the feeling of having something in common with all human beings" (Konopka 1973, 299). It also stimulates young adults to newly assess the world.

Young adults are intensely interested in romantic relationships and the achievement of sexual experience. They enjoy hearing stories that explore the questions and problems that they are exploring themselves. Nilsen and Donelson, in *Literature for Today's Young Adults*, claim that one of the first types of stories told were romances, because people liked to hear happy endings and enjoyed the exaggeration of the storytellers that made the stories more interesting than real life (Nilsen and Donelson 1985, 112). In the text, they briefly explore the reasons that romance appeals to young adults. Romance literature, usually concerned with love and adventure, expresses in several ways the preoccupations of young adults:

1. Symbols used in the romance stories often relate to youthfulness and hope, with many of the protaganists being young adults themselves.

2. Young adults, in the middle and late stages of adolescence, are at a point in their lives when they are either leaving home or contemplating leaving. They are embarking on a romantic quest.

3. A great proportion of young adults expend a great deal of time and energy "seeking and securing a 'true love' " and respond to stories that explore romantic relationships.

4. The intensity of emotions honestly felt by young adults is mirrored by the exaggeration that is part of the romantic mode.

(Nilsen and Donelson 1985, 113)

Folklore, ancient and modern, is full of references to romance and sexual activity. The love stories in ancient folklore tend to be very stark; only the simplest and most artless reasons are offered for love or passion (Yolen 1986, 67). Urban belief legends, the folklore of modern youth, are thinly cloaked sexual cautionary tales. In the literary tales, however, the reasons for love and passion and their consequences are usually explored in detail.

Because folklore, both ancient and modern, has been explored in previous sections, the stories offered in this section are limited to literary tales of romance and sexuality. When telling stories to young adults, remember that young adults are uncomfortable with risque humor from a storyteller (if not from their peers) but do appreciate romantic stories that allude to sexuality in a subtle manner.

The Blue-Tail Fly

One of Jimmy's jobs as a personal slave is to brush away any insects that bother the master. Jimmy's sweetheart, Caroline, looks after the master's wife and looks even harder after her own tongue, which has a tendency to be sharp. Caroline loses control one evening and insults her mistress. She is beaten and sent from the house to the fields. The master discusses with Jimmy how ungrateful she is and how he is going to put her on the auction block. Jimmy has a lot to think about and somehow does not react fast enough when the dreaded blue-tail fly lands on the master's horse.

Sanders, Scott R. 1985. *Hear the Wind Blow: American Folk Songs Retold.* New York: Bradbury Press. pp. 71-81. 15 min.

Crazy in Love

A very lonely woman, Diana, is granted her wish of a loving husband by a beautiful woman who was chained to a millstone. Diana repays the woman by spending an hour each day brushing the woman's hair and talking with her. When her husband, Dan, follows Diana and sees her conversing with and brushing a donkey, he thinks she is crazy. Dan meets an old man who grants him the wish that Diana's craziness will be cured. To repay the man, Dan spends an hour a day smoking and conversing with him. When she follows Dan, Diana perceives the old man as a beaver and fears for her husband's sanity. Their love and concern for each other conquer the fears they each have.

Kennedy, Richard. 1987. *Richard Kennedy: Collected Stories*. New York: Harper & Row. pp. 163-89. 40 min.

The Dark Princess

A princess is so beautiful that no one can look at her directly without becoming blind. The princess is blind herself, but the people are not told that; consequently, they cannot understand her behavior. Before contemplating marriage she sets a test for each prospective lover: to look at her directly. No one loves her enough to lose their eyesight, except for the court fool. A powerful story about the nature of love.

Kennedy, Richard. 1978. *The Dark Princess*. New York: Holiday House. 22 min.

Kennedy, Richard. 1987. *Richard Kennedy: Collected Stories*. New York: Harper & Row. pp. 141-53. 22 min.

The Faery Flag

The son of the laird falls in love with a young fairy girl, and because his parents are anxious for an heir, they agree to the marriage. She can stay in the land of humans only a year or until she produces an heir, and after the birth of a son, she leaves. Her husband is distraught, and the rest of the clan is celebrating so lustily that no one hears the baby cry out. No one, that is, but the mother, who returns to comfort the child and leaves her shawl with him. The shawl is now referred to as the Faery Flag and still hangs on the wall, a symbol of the MacLeod clan.

Yolen, Jane. 1989. *The Faery Flag: Stories and Poems of Fantasy and the Supernatural*. New York: Orchard Books. pp. 3-11. 12 min.

The Faithful Ghost

Johnson the ghost does not haunt the household as much as he depresses it: He weeps and wails because he cannot find his long lost love, Emily. The family can no longer tolerate the absolute misery and so finds the "lost" grave in a convenient corner of the estate. A romantic story that is very humorously told.

Jerome, Jerome K. 1975. *The Scared Ghost and Other Stories*, edited by Barbara Walker. New York: McGraw-Hill. pp. 45-49. 8 min.

The Gift of the Magi

Della and Jim each sacrifice their most prized possessions (she, her hair and he, his watch) to buy a Christmas gift for the other. Unbeknownst to each other, the gifts they purchase are for the hair and watch they sacrificed. A Christmas love story.

Henry, O. 1906. *The Four Million*. New York: Doubleday. pp. 15-23. 12 min.

The Girl Who Cried Flowers

Instead of crying tears, a beautiful young woman cries blossoms of all hues and fragrances. Her new husband forbids her to cry any more, as he wants her only to be happy. Eventually, she gives in to the continuing demands of the community for fresh flowers. His anger on discovering her crying drives her out of the house, and she is transformed into an olive tree. The husbands spends the rest of his life at the base of the tree.

Yolen, Jane. 1974. *The Girl Who Cried Flowers and Other Tales*. New York: Schocken Books. pp. 1-10. 10 min.

The Hundredth Dove

Hugh, the king's fowler, is bidden to provide one hundred doves for the wedding feast of the king in honor of his bride, Lady Columba. Her name means dove. Each night he captures twenty gray doves, and each night a white dove manages to escape his net. On the last night, Hugh captures only nineteen gray doves, but he does net the white one as well. He follows not his heart but his loyalty to the king and breaks the neck of the white dove. There is no wedding and Hugh never hunts again.

Yolen, Jane. 1977. *The Hundredth Dove and Other Tales*. New York: Thomas Y. Crowell. pp. 1-9. 12 min.

I Hate You, Wallace B. Pokras

A monologue by an angry girl who sees her boyfriend out with another girl. Her soliloquy revolves around the sadistic and nasty reprisals that she would set in motion if she was a vindictive, spiteful person. A very funny and touching story that explores the pain and joys of relationships from the perspective of a young adult girl. Other stories in the collection also would be suitable, with slight alterations, for oral presentation.

Conford, Ellen. 1983. *If This Is Love, I'll Take Spaghetti*. New York: Four Winds Press. pp. 89-100. 15 min.

Molly McCullough and Tom the Rogue

Tom is a con man. He travels to the richest farms in each area and buys up a portion of the land. During the transaction, he pretends to lose a piece of paper, a map of the farm marked with an *X*. The farmers never let on that they have found the paper; rather, they buy back their land with interest. As soon as Tom leaves, they rush out to dig up the nonexistent treasure. Tom's ploy is successful until he meets up with Molly!

Stevens, Kathleen. 1982. *Molly McCullough and Tom the Rogue*. New York: Thomas Y. Crowell. 10 min.

Muldoon in Love

A retrospective and very funny look at life and love in the third grade. Crazy Eddie is totally and passionately in love with the new teacher, so much so that he even gives up recess to pound blackboard erasers. When Miss Deets seems to be dividing her attention, Eddie is determined to win her back. Show and Tell was never the same! Told from a male perspective.

McManus, Patrick F. 1987. *Rubber Legs and White Tail-Hairs*. New York: Henry Holt. pp. 1-8. 13 min.

Oliver Hyde's Dishcloth Concert

Oliver Hyde has closed himself off from the world since the death, many years before, of his young bride. When approached to play the fiddle at a wedding as a favor for an old friend, he promises to come out of seclusion if everyone will wear a dishcloth over his or her face. His concert, filled with sad and melancholy tunes, helps him to realize that living can be fun. Oliver accidently plays his concert to an empty old barn, but, armed with his new lease on life, he goes to the right barn and plays for the wedding dance.

Kennedy, Richard. 1977. *Oliver Hyde's Dishcloth Concert*. Boston: Little, Brown and Co. 15 min.

Kennedy, Richard. 1987. "Oliver Hyde's Dishcloth Concert." In *Richard Kennedy: Collected Stories*. New York: Harper & Row. pp. 201-11. 15 min.

The Very Pretty Lady

The very pretty lady has no end of suitors, but she wishes to marry someone who loves her, not her beauty. When the Devil comes to court her, she turns him down and he, in his anger, takes her beauty away with him. After a few years, the Devil becomes curious about the lady and returns to earth to find that she is very happy with her ugly husband and very ugly baby.

Babbit, Natalie. 1974. *The Devil's Storybook*. New York: Farrar. pp. 13-20. 10 min.

TWISTS, SATIRE, AND EXAGGERATION

Young adults relish stories that offer twists on traditional tales and conventional endings. Comprehension of a traditional story presented from a different point of view requires an intellectual skill that is not reached until approximately age twelve (Horner 1983, 461). Young adults particularly enjoy stories in which their predictions of outcome are led in one direction by the action and then foiled by the surprise ending or twist in the plot.

Young adults, particularly between the ages of twelve and thirteen, are intensely interested in practical jokes and enjoy the trickster stories that are found in every folklore tradition. Traditional trickster tales play an important role. They represent chaos in the ordered life and poke fun at the illusions of people (Yolen 1986, 125). Trickster characters and plot twists found in literary tales today perform the same functions. On the other hand, older young adults have developed a more subtle humor and appreciate satire, parody, and witticism (Nilsen and Donelson 1985, 336).

Young adults love the exaggeration of tall tales and enjoy making up their own tales of exaggeration. Cuddy states that the permission to lie creatively charms the imaginations of young adults (Cuddy 1984, 13). Nilsen and Donelson state that word play is popular with young adults and recommend several volumes of American tall tales for their reading pleasure (Nilsen and Donelson 1985, 339). Tall tales are distinguished from other humorous stories by their blatant exaggeration. "They are such flagrant lies that the lyingest yarn of all is the best one, provided it is *told* with a straight face and every appearance of truth" (Sutherland, Monson, and Arbuthnot 1981, 183).

Twists and Satire

Ashes

Upon Mr. Bezzle's demise, he goes to hell, where he is very content. Unfortunately for him, the ashes of his earthly remains become mixed with the ashes of a pig. Mr. Bezzle, in order to rid himself of the pig that has become his constant companion, spends several years separating his and the pig's ashes into separate piles. The task is almost complete when his wife's fastidious housekeeper descends to hell and sweeps up the piles.

Babbit, Natalie. 1974. *The Devil's Storybook*. New York: Farrar. pp. 63-71. 7 min.

A Barrel of Laughs

Alison and Nicholas, the lodger, decide to play a trick on Alison's elderly husband. Telling the story of Noah from the Bible, Nicholas has the husband hide away in a barrel hanging from the rafters, awaiting the coming of another flood. Meanwhile, Alison and Nicholas have the house clear for other activities. However, another man, imagining Alison in love with him, comes to collect a kiss through the window. To send him away Nicholas kisses him instead. Realizing he has been tricked, the man returns with a branding iron: Nicholas has his seat scorched, he calls for water, the barrel is released and all is discovered! A funny, slapstick story.

McCaughrean, Geraldine. 1964. *The Canterbury Tales*. Oxford: Oxford Univ. Press. pp. 19-25. 8 min. Usually known as "The Miller's Tale."

The Borrower

A funny tale about a silversmith outwitting a miserly rich man by appealing to his greed. The silver items that the silversmith borrows seem to reproduce themselves, much to the rich man's delight, but the gold watch is not returned because of its untimely death.

Serwer, Blanche Luria. 1970. *Let's Steal the Moon: Jewish Tales, Ancient and Recent*. Boston: Little, Brown and Co. pp. 55-58. 4 min.

Cinderella
The traditional story retold with a twist, in poetic form.

Sexton, Anne. 1971. *Transformations*. Boston: Houghton Mifflin. pp. 53-57. 6 min.

Count Sergei's Pistol
Count Sergei is bored and decides to bring excitement into his life; he puts one round of ammunition into a gun chamber, spins the cylinder and puts the gun to his head. He pulls the trigger. Eventually the odds of his firing the live ammunition are computed, and he loses interest in the activity, only to be killed by a wolf!

Dickinson, Peter. 1976. *Chance, Luck and Destiny*. Boston: Little, Brown and Co. pp. 27-30. 5 min.

Death's Murderers
Three slow-witted thieves decide to murder Death in retaliation for the Black Death. Instead of finding Death, they find an old man who directs them to a pot of gold. The youngest thief is sent to the village for some wine, and the other two decide to murder him on his return, but he has also considered how much further the gold will go if it need not be shared! After returning with two bottles of poisoned wine, the young man is slain by his companions. To celebrate, the other two drink the wine. When Death returns the next morning for his gold, he leaves the three corpses where they have fallen.

McCaughrean, Geraldine. 1964. *The Canterbury Tales*. Oxford: Oxford Univ. Press. pp. 68-75. 11 min. Usually known as "The Pardoner's Tale."

The Doko
When the problems of caring for an aged father become too tiresome, a man and his wife decide to purchase a doko (large basket) to carry away the father and leave him to his fate. The child of the household, in his innocence, requests that the doko be brought back so that he will have it handy when the time comes to discard his father!

Asian Cultural Centre for UNESCO. 1976. *Folk Tales from Asia for Children Everywhere, Book Four*. New York: Weatherhill. pp. 42-46. 5 min.

The 500 Hats of Bartholomew Cubbins
Bartholomew tries to take his hat off for the king, but the hats just keep appearing on his head. The king's advisers and the executioner cannot solve the mystery. After the 450th hat, the hats start to change and become fancier and richer. The king purchases the 500th hat and ends the succession on Bartholomew's head.

Seuss, Dr. 1938. *The 500 Hats of Bartholomew Cubbins*. New York: Vanguard Press. 14 min.

Goldilocks and the Three Bears

A satirical poem rendition of the traditional folktale. Goldilocks, an intruder and vandal, reaps her just reward.

Dahl, Roald. 1982. *Roald Dahl's Revolting Rhymes*. London: Jonathan Cape. pp. 17-21. 6 min.

He Fooled the Gestapo

Elfreid develops a scheme involving a series of letters to and from the German military machine and military honors for himself, bestowed by Adolf Hitler. For several years, his reputation and honors, planted and fueled by rumors of his own making, allow him to help his relatives and friends escape the Gestapo. When he is finally unmasked, the military machine is too embarrassed by its gullibility to punish him severely.

A true trickster story of a young Austrian prior to World War II.

Haines, Max. 1985. *The Collected Works of Max Haines. Vol. 1*. Toronto: Toronto Sun Publishing. pp. 65-68. 10 min.

How the Devil Played Hell with a Gypsy

After a successful day at the market, a gypsy drinks himself into a stupor. When the man awakens, he is confronted with the Devil demanding an explanation of his behavior. Knowing that he is not answerable to the Devil, the man beats the Devil soundly. However, when the mist of the alcohol clears, it is not the Devil but the man's wife that stands there.

Riordan, James, trans. 1986. *Russian Gypsy Tales*, collected by Yefim Druts and Alexei Gessler. Edinburg, Scotland: Canongate Publishers. pp. 118-19. 2 min.

It Floats

Timothy murders his wife by drowning her and thinks that he has gotten away with it, but his wife comes to haunt him. She taunts him with the phrase, "it floats." A twist on the traditional ghost story.

Cohen, Daniel. 1980. *The Headless Roommate and Other Tales of Terror*. New York: M. Evans. pp. 70-72. 4 min.

The Left-Handed King

King Kwadwo travels to a nearby kingdom to investigate the stories of happiness and prosperity that are told about it. When he sees that the only difference between the happy kingdom and his own is that their king eats with his left hand, Kwadwo orders everyone in his kingdom to eat with the left hand. An old man points out that King Kwadwo did not investigate why the king ate left-handed (he had no right hand), and the people topple him from the throne for making unwise decisions.

Appiah, Peggy. 1967. *Tales of an Ashanti Father*. London: Andre Deutsch. pp. 37-41. 8 min.

The Little Girl and the Wolf
A modern fable version of "Little Red Riding Hood."

Thurber, James. 1940. *Fables for Our Time*. New York: Harper & Row. p. 5. 1 min.

Many Moons
An ailing princess asks for the moon. Her father confers with the wise men of the kingdom, but they cannot see any possibility of obtaining it for her. The court jester asks the princess how she perceives the moon and then easily obtains "the moon" for her. The story has humor and youthful wisdom and clearly illustrates differences in perception.

Thurber, James. 1943. *Many Moons*. New York: Harcourt Brace Jovanovich. 23 min.

The Mirror
After the death of his beloved father, a man is distraught. When he sees a mirror (for the first time) and sees the face of his father within the frame, he brings the mirror home and sets it on the altar. However, his wife, who is also looking into a mirror for the first time, is very angry at the framed image of the young woman she perceives him worshipping at the altar.

Bang, Garrett. 1973. *Men from the Village Deep in the Mountains and Other Japanese Folk Tales*. New York: Macmillan. pp. 67-69. 3 min.

Ginsburg, Mirra. 1988. *The Chinese Mirror: Adapted from a Korean Folktale*. San Diego, Calif.: Harcourt Brace Jovanovich. A picturebook version that is more lighthearted than the Japanese version.

The Mouse
A fastidious and extremely shy gentleman traveling by rail discovers a mouse in his trousers. Observing that the woman traveling in the same carriage is asleep, the gentleman removes his clothing and the mouse, but before he can dress the woman awakes. The gentleman covers himself with a traveling rug and spends the rest of the journey trying to explain his behavior without alluding to it directly. As the train pulls into the station, he frantically pulls on his clothes, avoiding the woman's eyes. Totally humiliated by the venture, he then discovers that the woman is blind!

Saki. 1946. *A Treasury of Laughter*, edited by Louis Untermeyer. New York: Simon and Schuster. pp. 548-51. 9 min.

The Musician of Tagaung

A father decides that his son will become a famous musician, regardless of the fact that he has no talent in that direction. He buys him harp after harp and pays for lesson after lesson. The father dies, and his son continues the lessons until the day he dies. His harps are stored and forgotten, until a century later they are discovered by members of his family. They decide that their ancestor must have been a famous harpist, and thus the son finally fulfills his father's hopes.

The story comments on the vanity of success and reputations that may be built out of thin air.

Courlander, Harold. 1959. *The Tiger's Whisker and Other Tales from Asia and the Pacific*. New York: Harcourt, Brace & Co. pp. 35-37. 4 min.

Once a Good Man

A good man is rewarded by the Lord and is taken to visit both heaven and hell. The man is astonished to find that both situations are exactly the same, but in heaven people help one another.

Yolen, Jane. 1977. *The Hundredth Dove and Other Tales*. New York: Thomas Y. Crowell. pp. 53-57. 6 min.

Petronella

A youngest daughter, searching for a prince to rescue and marry, is set three tasks, gathers three rewards, and rescues the prince, who unfortunately, while very handsome, is a big bore. Instead, she marries the wicked enchanter. A very clever twist on the fairy tale theme.

Williams, Jay. 1973. *Petronella*. New York: Parents' Magazine Press. 16 min.

The Pointing Finger

When an immortal comes down to earth to try and find an unselfish man, he is extremely disappointed. Each time he points his finger at a pebble, turning it into gold, the person being tested desires more from him, until he meets a man who does not seem to want the gold. And what does this man desire? The finger!

Kendall, Carol, and Yao-wen Li. 1978. *Sweet & Sour: Tales from China*. New York: Houghton Mifflin. pp. 60-62. 4 min.

Princess Steppie

King Boruba has three principles: that everyone play the game Jack, Where are You? at four o'clock, that there be a fifteen-minute royal procession at five o'clock, and that everyone eat pea soup. King Boruba also has a beautiful daughter. When looking for a husband for his daughter, King Boruba dismisses all hopefuls that do not have the same principles as himself. Consequently, he can not find the right man, and the princess goes into a decline and dies. The king follows his daughter a year later, and the kingdom falls to ruin. Humorously told by a disgruntled storyteller!

Bomans, Godfried. 1977. *The Wily Witch and All the Other Fairy Tales and Fables*. Owing Mills, Md.: Stemmer House. pp. 20-27. 14 min.

Rumpelstiltskin
The traditional folktale retold with allusions to modern landscapes, idioms, and thought.

Sexton, Anne. 1971. *Transformations*. Boston: Houghton Mifflin. pp. 17-22. 7 min.

The Scotty Who Knew Too Much
Scotty goes to the country for a visit and assumes, because he is a city dog, that he does not need any advice from the country dogs. Because of this attitude, he is on the losing end of fights with a skunk, a porcupine, and a country dog.

Thurber, James. 1940. *Fables for Our Time*. New York: Harper & Row. pp. 29-30. 2 min.

A Scrap of Paper
The judge at a witchcraft trial in London examines the evidence, a scrap of paper on which an incantation has been written, and recognizes the hand-writing—his own. Realizing how flimsy the evidence is that has been used to convict people of witchcraft, he begins to acquit all witches that stand before him.

Dickinson, Peter. 1976. *Chance, Luck and Destiny*. Boston: Little, Brown and Co. pp. 161-62. 3 min.

The String of Trout
A boy, angry at having to take a string of fish to the parish priest, throws the fish inside the door. The priest attempts to turn the action into a lesson but learns a truth as well. A surprise ending that will appeal to young adults.

Dorson, Richard M. 1975. *Folktales Told around the World*. Chicago: Univ. of Chicago Press. pp. 448-50. 4 min.

Those Three Wishes
When she is granted three wishes by a snail, Melinda Alice immediately asks for her next thousand wishes to come true. Alternating between selfish and altruistic wishes (she is not a very nice person), Melinda Alice forgets about the big math test ... with dire results. A simple horror story!

Gorog, Judith. 1982. *A Taste for Quiet and Other Disquieting Tales*. New York: Philomel. pp. 19-20. 4 min.

Three Fridays
The Hodja gives the sermon at the mosque each Friday, but sometimes he just cannot think of anything to talk about. On three consecutive weeks, he solves his problem by asking the same simple question and using the answers to his advantage. A humorous story that gives a glimpse into the mosque and the traditional Moslem way of life.

Kelsey, Alice Geer. 1981. *Turkish Jokes: Once the Hodja, Nasr-ed-Din.* Taipei: Tung Fang Wen Hua ShuChu, Supplement of Asian Folklore and Social Life Monographs, 23. pp. 21-28. 7 min.

Three Grains of Rice: From the Bones of an Arab Folktale
When his prospective bride dies, a young man takes her body to a wise woman. He asks that she bring his bride back to life, and she agrees on the condition that he obtain three grains of rice cooked in a pot that has not been used in a time of sorrow. After asking everyone in the village, the young man comes to the realization that he is not the only person who has to face sorrow.

Gorog, Judith. 1988. *Three Dreams and a Nightmare and Other Tales of the Dark.* New York: Philomel. pp. 51-55. 5 min.

Thus I Refute Beelzy
Small Simon plays in the back garden, and no one can see his playmate Mr. Beelzy. Big Simon, Small Simon's father, is a firm believer in modern methods of raising children, and when he attempts to have his son admit that Mr. Beelzy is a fantasy, he goes too far—and gets eaten!
While the main character is a six-year-old boy, the conflicts that he deals with are easily recognized by any young adult. A lovely twist at the end!

Collier, John. 1980. *Fancies and Goodnights.* Alexandria, Va.: Time-Life Books. pp. 214-20.

Davenport, Basil. 1953. *Horror Stories from Tales to Be Told in the Dark: A Selection of Stories from the Great Authors Arranged for Reading and Telling Aloud.* N.Y.: Ballantine. pp. 96-101. 10 min.

The Wife's Story
A very powerful story in which a wife tells of her love for her husband and her horror when she discovers that he is transformed into "the hateful one" at the time of the full moon. It is not until the end of the story that the listener realizes that the wife is a wolf.

Le Guin, Ursula K. 1987. *Buffalo Gals and Other Animal Presences.* Santa Barbara, Calif.: Capra Press. pp. 67-71. 9 min.

Le Guin, Ursula K. 1982. *Compass Rose.* New York: Harper & Row. pp. 245-49. 9 min.

Tall Tales

The Celebrated Jumping Frog of Calaveras County
The famous tall tale about Jim Smiley and his betting career. The frog has been trained to jump on command, but when the stranger fills its gullet with quail shot before the contest, the celebrated jumping frog cannot move at all.

Twain, Mark. 1946. *A Treasury of Laughter*, edited by Louis Untermeyer. New York: Simon and Schuster. pp. 642-46. 12 min.

How Old Paul Invented Doughnuts
Doughpeckers, Paul Bunyan, and Sourdough Sam pull together to invent the first doughnuts, tasty but small—only "forty inches acrost."

Logan, Gloria. 1980. "How Old Paul Invented Doughnuts." In *The Princess, the Hockey Player, Magic and Ghosts*, edited by Muriel Whitaker. Edmonton, Alta.: Hurtig Publishers. pp. 37-42. 6 min.

Johnny Appleseed
A story of the early life of Jonathan Chapman and his transformation into the nomadic Johnny Appleseed.

Haviland, Virginia, ed. 1979. *The Faber Book of North American Legends*. London: Faber and Faber. pp. 196-203. 14 min.

The Norther and the Frogs
A man harvests frog legs for market by predicting precisely when the weather will freeze.

Chase, Richard. 1971. *American Folk Tales and Songs*. New York: Dover Publications. p. 97. 1.5 min.

Old One Eye
Three would-be thieves are chased away by an old woman's habit of yawning three times before cutting a slice of dried fish and retiring for the evening. An American tall tale that is fun to tell.

Chase, Richard. 1948. *Grandfather Tales*. Cambridge, Mass.: The Riverside Press. pp. 205-7. 4 min.

Pecos Bill Becomes a Coyote
Bill, lost out of his parents' covered wagon somewhere near the Pecos River when he was four years old, is adopted by the coyotes and lives with them for years until he is discovered and convinced that he is a "man-child."

Haviland, Virginia, ed. 1979. *The Faber Book of North American Legends*. London: Faber and Faber. pp. 169-74. 8 min.

The Scalded Wolf
    A woodcutter and his wife throw scalding soup at a wolf when they discover it inside their home. The wolf runs away but is met several more times by the woodcutter. Each time the woodcutter manages to escape the wolf by reminding him of the hot soup and by causing the wolf further discomfort.

    Dorson, Richard M. 1975. *Folktales Told around the World*. Chicago: Univ. of Chicago Press. pp. 60-62. 7 min.

Stormalong Fights the Kraken
    Alfred Bulltop Stormalong is a giant seaman who takes his ship, Tuscarora, on many perilous voyages. He outwits the sea monster and sails his ship through the narrow Straits of Dover by soaping down the sides. In fact, it is the scraping of the ship's soapy sides that turns the cliffs of Dover white.

    Haviland, Virginia, ed. 1979. *The Faber Book of North American Legends*. London: Faber and Faber. pp. 184-91. 15 min.

The Two Old Women's Bet
    Two women bet each other that they can get their respective husbands to believe anything, regardless how foolish. The first woman convinces her husband that not only is he ill but that he is dead, and puts him in a coffin and prepares for the funeral. The second woman convinces her husband that the wool she is carding, spinning, weaving, and eventually sewing into a suit for him cannot be seen by anyone who lies to his wife. Of course, the husband pretends that he can see it and wears his new suit to the funeral of his friend.

    Chase, Richard. 1948. *Grandfather Tales*. Cambridge, Mass.: The Riverside Press. pp. 156-60. 6 min.

When the Rain Came up from China
    A tall tale that tells of one of Paul Bunyan's camps. They are prepared for the rain in that camp—but only if it comes from the sky! A fun story that can be localized, as Paul plays a very small role in this tale.

    McCormick, Dell J. 1961. *Tall Timber Tales: More Paul Bunyan Stories*. Caldwell, Idaho: Caxton Printers. pp. 127-31. 6 min.

Yankee Doodle
    Doodle, a young stable boy, makes fools of the English army commanders when they come to the colonies to put down an insurrection. A literary adaptation of the American folk song, Yankee Doodle.

    Sanders, Scott R. 1985. *Hear the Wind Blow: American Folk Songs Retold*. New York: Bradbury Press. pp. 19-27. 12 min.

LITERARY STORIES

Literary stories begin as written rather than oral tales and are the creation of an identifiable author. "The only person with the authority to infuse the written story with its correct oral language features is the author" (Livo and Rietz 1986, 152). Livo and Rietz discuss how the written story is meant to be read and not heard, but many authors have created stories that call out to be told.

The stories included in this section are all suitable for storytelling. However, I offer a word of caution to anyone using them: The stories are all protected by copyright. They usually cannot be adapted and must be memorized. In addition, it is necessary to obtain permission to tell the stories. In many cases, if the story-teller earns a fee with the story, the author expects remuneration. A letter requesting permission to use the story should be written to the author or literary agent. Publishers will pass requests on to their authors, but they usually wait until they have a batch of requests rather than forwarding them individually. The letter must include the title of the story as well as the plans the storyteller has for the story. The author has to be informed how the story is to be used and if any adaptation of the story is being considered. The letter should tell whether the story will be told in schools and libraries or performed on stage, whether the storyteller is telling the story as part of his or her occupation (teacher, librarian, hospital aide), and whether the storyteller will be paid for the performances (Yolen 1987, 6).

Several authors whose stories are recommended throughout this book welcome the telling of their stories. Yolen and Natalie Babbit agree that story-tellers keep the authors' stories alive. "Neither of us would ask for payment or royalty on a simple telling, but we feel if the story is to go into a book, tape, or video, some arrangement for payment needs to be made" (Yolen 1987, 8). Richard Kennedy also feels that it "is a great way for the stories to remain alive for a long time, I'm complimented" (Yolen 1987, 8). He rarely requests payments for the use of his stories.

Credit the author every time the story is told. If you distribute handouts, include bibliographic information on each literary story you use in the handouts. If possible, display the books that incorporate the stories.

Excerpts from longer works are usually told to introduce the book that they are taken from or to introduce the body of work of a particular author. Often, the audience must be given background information before the story can be told. Frequently, they request additional information after the telling and will ask to read the book.

All Summer in a Day
On Venus, where it rains constantly except for a two-hour sunny period every seven years, a group of nine-year-olds eagerly await the scheduled appearance of the sun. All are too young to remember the sun, except for Margot, who came from Earth only five years before. The children lock Margot in a closet because she is different, and they remember her only when the rain returns. A chilling story.

Bradbury, Ray. 1960. *A Medicine for Melancholy*. New York: Bantam. pp. 191-97. 13 min.

The Chaser

A love potion for a dollar? Alan is delighted at the detailed description of the effects of this inexpensive potion and not a bit interested in a much more expensive "spot remover," but he will be.... A twisted marketing plan!

Collier, John. 1980. *Fancies and Goodnights*. Alexandria, Va.: Time-Life Books. pp. 325-28. 6 min.

The Corn Planting

The Hutchensons were middle-aged when they got married and had their only child, Will. When Will went to Chicago to attend the university, they lived for his weekly letters. They could never leave the farm to visit Will: the daily maintenance was too important to leave to anyone else. When Will dies in an accident, it is the farm, the planting of corn at midnight, that helps them accept his untimely death.

Anderson, Sherwood. 1962. *Sherwood Anderson: Short Stories*, edited by Maxwell Geismar. New York: Hill and Wang. pp. 199-203. 10 min.

Anderson, Sherwood. 1947. *The Sherwood Anderson Reader*. Boston: Houghton-Mifflin, 812-16.

Cranes at Dusk

In this excerpt from the book, Saya is telling her younger brother his favorite story about the cranes. A crane is caught in a trap, and a young boy rescues it and is granted his wish to fly with the cranes.

This story helps keep Saya functioning after the death of the little brother and is a pivotal point in the novel.

Matsubara, Hisako. 1985. *Cranes at Dusk*. Garden City, N.Y.: Doubleday. pp. 216-20. 7 min.

Early Earthquake Warning System

In December 1974 the people of the Chinese city of Haicheng notice the abnormal behavior of the animal life around them and report the strange occurrences to the commune committee responsible for signs of impending earthquakes. The committee reports the information to the central office, and the information is analyzed, resulting in earthquake warnings that are issued to the population. While there is widespread damage when the earth trembles violently, as predicted, the only people killed are those that ignored the warning.

Young, Louise B. 1983. *The Blue Planet: A Celebration of the Earth*. Boston: Little, Brown and Co. pp. 111-13. 3 min.

A Humbling Experience

Fresh from his first lecture on horses, James feels that he is an expert on the species. When he sees a horse on the street, he admires it in silence for a while, positive that everyone can see his expertise. When he finally decides to leave, James touches the horse in farewell. Immediately the horse grabs him by the shoulder and holds him dangling in the air until the gasping young man is rescued by the angry owner of the horse. Not only his new mac, but his pride and assurance of new knowledge are wrinkled by this humbling experience. A true story.

Herriot, James. 1972. *All Creatures Great and Small*. New York: St. Martin's Press. pp. 106-8. 6 min.

The Ink

A blob of ink sputtered from the pen as the general signed the peace treaty. It spread unfettered over the page, the room, and the building. The army was called in to stop it spreading further, but, regardless of the weapons launched against it, day by day it conquered more and more territory. Finally, a cease-fire was ordered. A blob of ink sputtered from the pen as the general signed the peace treaty. A horror story about the futility of war.

Roch, Carrier. 1974. *Stories from Quebec*, edited by Philip Stratford. Toronto: Van Nostrand Reinhold. pp. 114-15. 4 min.

Looking for a Sign

When Peter and Barbara have doubts about their relationship, they attend a church service looking for a sign from God to direct them. Peter is sure that this is the end of their relationship, but when an elderly woman in a wheelchair gives the Sunday sermon, Peter and Barbara are astounded by both her story and the sign within the story that is directed at them. A true story.

Before telling this story, some background must be offered to the audience about the conflict that Peter and Barbara are attempting to resolve. This is available in the chapter that precedes this story and in the first part of the chapter in which this story appears.

Jenkins, Peter. 1979. *A Walk across America*. New York: William Morrow. pp. 282-86. 10 min.

Louis

An escaped slave, Louis, follows the underground railroad but is not ready to go into Canada because he cannot fully comprehend the danger that he is in. He educates himself and has a good job in a grocery store, but one evening he is captured by the marshall and returned to Cincinnati for trial. The packed courthouse is listening to the judge's pronouncement. Louis notices that no one is paying any attention to him, and he starts to ease back out of the room. The sympathetic crowd protects and conceals him, and by the time the marshall realizes that he is gone, Louis is hidden safely away to make his way to Canada soon after.

The conclusion to a short story of the same name. Some explanation should be made to introduce the situation and Louis's determination to stay in the United States.

Lester, Julius. 1972. *Long Journey Home: Stories from Black History*. New York: Dial Press. pp. 28-58 (53-58). 7 min.

The Night the Bear Ate Goombaw

Nine-year-old Patrick joins Crazy Eddie and the Muldoon family on a camping trip. After frightening the family with her fears of the wildlife, Grandmother, or Goombaw, as she is called, wakes up next to a bear in the tent. Everyone panics and runs away, including Patrick, who runs so fast and hard that he has to take off the old fur coat that he uses as a sleeping bag! Slapstick that will appeal to the younger listeners, satire that will delight the older ones.

McManus, Patrick. 1989. *The Night the Bear Ate Goombaw*. New York: Henry Holt. pp. 93-101. 13 min.

The Ninth Day: First Tale

Madonna Francesca devises a test to rid herself of two unwanted admirers. One she asks to lie down in the fresh grave and shroud of an unpopular man, and the other she sends to the grave to bring her what he thinks is the corpse. She is sure that neither man will do this bidding and that she can send them away for not loving her enough. Therefore, she is very surprised to find that both men follow their bizarre instructions and is very gratified when the night watch makes an unexpected appearance.

Boccaccio, Giovanni. 1930. *The Decameron*, translated by Richard Aldington. New York: Dell Publishing. pp. 525-29. 6 min.

The Old Chief Mshlanga

A young girl remembers how meeting the old Chief Mshlanga changes her perception of the blacks around her father's homestead in South Africa. His dignity, however, is trampled by her father and the authorities, and the old chief is sent to a reservation.

The story evokes both the confusion of growing up white with European stories and values in the African environment and the inequality experienced by the blacks. The storyteller could effectively tell this story in segments, as the action is episodic.

Doris Lessing. 1988. In *Somehow Tenderness Survives: Stories of Southern Africa*, edited by Hazel Rochman. New York: Harper & Row. pp. 19-35. 25 min.

The Parable

A short excerpt from the book. Five animals quarrel over what is most important to life: eyes, ears, teeth, mind, or breath. A concrete demonstration proves that without breath there is no life!

Yolen, Jane. 1988. *Sister Light, Sister Dark*. New York: Tom Doherty Associates. pp. 74-75. 3 min.

Reed Warfare

During the invasion of ancient Greece, a large Persian fleet led by Xerxes has its anchor lines cast off by two underwater swimmers breathing through hollow reeds. The first recorded instance of an underwater breathing apparatus employed in warfare.

Young, Louise B. 1983. *The Blue Planet: A Celebration of the Earth*. Boston: Little, Brown and Co. pp. 28-29. 3 min.

Romance Lingers, Adventure Lives

A satirical look at suburban living. Two men, coming home late in the evening, go unwittingly into the wrong houses on a street of identical homes. They go to bed, but not to sleep, and do not find out their mistake until the following morning! Very well written, lyrical in its imagery.

Collier, John. 1980. *Fancies and Goodnights*. Alexandria, Va.: Time-Life Books. pp. 268-72. 8 min.

Skydiving in the Dark

Tom Sullivan describes the first time he skydives. Skydiving demands a lot of courage from Tom because he is blind.

There are several excerpts from this autobiography that are both suitable for telling and of interest for a young adult audience.

Sullivan, Tom, and Derek Gill. 1975. *If You Could See What I Hear*. New York: Harper & Row. pp. 115-18. 5 min.

The Spider's Palace

A girl who lives in a nest is invited by a spider to live in a translucent palace in the sky. Every room can be looked into except one, which has curtains on all the walls, the floor, and the ceiling. When curiosity gets the better of her, the girl discovers the secret of the room and pays a large price.

Hughes, Richard. 1977. *The Wonder Dog*. New York: Greenwillow. pp. 48-53. 10 min.

Star Mother's Youngest Child

Both a neglected, lonely woman and a young star in the heavens wish that just once they could celebrate a Christmas. And so, on Christmas Day, a grouchy old woman and a very ugly child share an unforgettable Christmas. Very memorable in its rich characterization.

Moeri, Louise. 1975. *Star Mother's Youngest Child*. Boston: Houghton Mifflin. 18 min.

The Story-Teller

A literary tale by Saki that explores the effect of "moral" and "proper" stories on small children. Great fun to tell, and young adults identify both with the bachelor storyteller and the three children of his audience.

Saki. 1982. *Storyteller: Thirteen Tales by Saki*. Boston: David R. Gooline. pp. 3-9.

Untermeyer, Louis, ed. 1946. *A Treasury of Laughter*. New York: Simon and Schuster. pp. 552-56. 10 min.

The Storytellers

Two storytellers argue over the origin of a story. The result is a contest to see who is the best storyteller. There are three finalists: one who awakens passion and the mountains, one who awakens love and the waters of the earth, and one who awakens night and dreams. A powerful story that demonstrates the awesome might of a good story.

Gorog, Judith. 1982. *A Taste for Quiet and Other Disquieting Tales*. New York: Philomel. pp. 71-73. 7 min.

The Thieves Who Couldn't Help Sneezing

Hubert, on his way home from an errand, is stopped by three thieves who take his horse and leave Hubert lying by the side of the road, hands tied behind him. Hubert manages to walk to a nearby house that, while empty at the moment, shows evidence that the occupants will be back momentarily. While waiting for the household, Hubert hears the thieves and watches as they secret themselves in a closet. When the occupants of the house return, Hubert joins them at the table, but does not tell them about the men in the closet until much later and after much good food and drink. Hubert gently blows snuff through the top of the closet door until the sneezing thieves beg for mercy. Hubert gets his horse back and goes on his journey.

The adventure takes place on Christmas Eve.

Hardy, Thomas. 1982. *Murder for Christmas*, edited by Thomas Godfrey. New York: The Mysterious Press. pp. 368-74. 14 min.

Tico and the Golden Wings

At the beginning, the bird, Tico, has no wings, but with the help of his friends Tico survives. After the visit of the wishing bird, Tico is given golden wings that enable him to soar but, unfortunately, lose him the friendship of the other birds. Tico discovers that if he gives away his golden feathers to those in need, black feathers grow in their place. Soon Tico is accepted by the rest of the birds because he looks just like them, but he knows that differences do exist in memories and dreams.

Lionni, Leo. 1964. *Tico and the Golden Wings*. New York: Pantheon. 6 min.

Unicorn

A young unicorn aids young Rhiannon in gathering truffles in the forest. The villagers use the truffles to pay the taxes. The taxman reports to his lord the existence of the unicorn. The lord's passion is for hunting, and he immediately sets off to kill the unicorn. After many failed attempts to catch the animal, the lord uses Rhiannon as bait, threatening her with the death of her parents, who are locked away in the castle. Rhiannon warns the unicorn at the last moment and is carried away on his back. The villagers later find their lord dead, but Rhiannon will not tell anyone what happened in the forest.

Dickinson, Peter. 1988. *Merlin Dreams*. London: Victor Gollancz. pp. 72-76. 10 min.

The Water Truck

The true story of the death of Peter's constant companion, his dog Cooper. Cooper is run over by a water truck on a commune. In a very moving chapter, Peter explains his immediate reactions to the accident and the burial of his special friend.

Jenkins, Peter. 1979. *A Walk across America*. New York: William Morrow. pp. 207-10. 7 min.

REFERENCES

Armstrong, Helen. 1949. "Hero Tales for Storytelling." *The Horn Book* 25, no. 1: 9-15.

Aylwin, Tony. 1981. "Using Myths and Legends in Schools." *Children's Literature in Education* 12, no. 2: 82-89.

Baker, Augusta, and Ellin Greene. 1987. *Storytelling: Art and Technique*. 2d ed. New York: R. R. Bowker.

Briggs, Nancy E., and Joseph A. Wagner. 1979. *Children's Literature through Storytelling and Drama*. 2d ed. Dubuque, Iowa: William C. Brown Co. Publishers.

Brunvand, Jan Harold. 1981. *The Vanishing Hitchhiker: American Urban Legends and Their Meanings*. New York: W. W. Norton Co.

Cohen, Daniel. 1980. *The Headless Roommate and Other Tales of Terror*. New York: M. Evans.

Cuddy, Clare. 1984. "Telling to Junior High School Students." *National Storytelling Journal* 1, no. 2: 13.

de Wit, Dorothy. 1979. *Children's Faces Looking Up: Program Building for the Storyteller*. Chicago: American Library Association.

Egoff, Sheila. 1975. *The Republic of Childhood: A Critical Guide to Canadian Children's Literature in English*. 2d ed. Toronto: Oxford Univ. Press.

_____. 1981. *Thursday's Child: Trends and Patterns in Contemporary Children's Literature*. Chicago: American Library Association.

Eliade, Mircea. 1963. *Myth and Reality*. World Perspectives, vol. 31. New York: Harper & Row.

Fowke, Edith. 1986. *Tales Told in Canada*. Toronto: Doubleday Canada.

Horner, Beth. 1983. "To Tell or Not to Tell: Storytelling for Young Adults." *Illinois Libraries* 65, no. 7: 458-64.

Konopka, Gisela. 1973. "Requirements for Healthy Development of Adolescent Youth." *Adolescence* 8, no. 31: 291-315.

Livo, Norma J., and Sandra A. Rietz. 1986. *Storytelling: Process and Practice*. Littleton, Colo.: Libraries Unlimited.

Moran, Barbara. 1987. "The Passive Princess Theme in Traditional Stories." *National Storytelling Journal* 4, no. 3: 21-23.

Nilsen, Alleen Pace, and Kenneth L. Donelson. 1985. *Literature for Today's Young Adults*. 2d ed. Glenview, Ill.: Scott, Foresman and Co.

Phelps, Ethel Johnston, ed. 1978. *Tatterhood and Other Tales*. New York: The Feminist Press.

Schwab, Gustav. 1946. *Gods and Heroes: Myths and Epics of Ancient Greece*. New York: Pantheon.

Schwartz, Alvin. 1981. *Scary Stories to Tell in the Dark*. New York: J. B. Lippincott.

Shannon, George. 1981. "The Survival of the Child." *Children's Literature in Education* 12, no. 1: 34-38.

Stohler, Sara J. 1987. "The Mythic World of Childhood." *Children's Literature Association Quarterly* 12, no. 1: 28-32.

Storr, Catherine. 1986. "Folk and Fairy Tales." *Children's Literature in Education* 17, no. 1: 63-70.

Sutherland, Zena; Dianne L. Monson; and May Hill Arbuthnot. 1981. *Children and Books*. 6th ed. Glenview, Ill.: Scott, Foresman and Co.

Sutton, Roger. 1983. "Telling Tales for YAs." *School Library Journal* 30, no. 3: 44.

Yolen, Jane. 1986. *Favorite Folktales from around the World*. New York: Pantheon.

_____. 1987. "Ethics and Storytelling." *National Storytelling Journal* 4, no. 4: 5-7.

Zipes, Jack. 1979. *Breaking the Magic Spell: Radical Theories of Folk and Fairy Tales*. London: Heinemann.

_____. 1983. *Fairytales and the Art of Subversion: The Classical Genre for Children and the Process of Civilization*. New York: Wildman Press.

Sample Stories

5

Chicho and the Ogre
Retold by Tololwa M. Mollel

There once lived a beautiful girl named Chicho, with the prettiest bangles you ever saw. Men sought to marry her, but to all of them she said no. No man was good enough for her.

One day there was a festival at her father's compound, which many suitors attended. Among them was a handsome young warrior but a total stranger. He was the most handsome man Chicho had ever seen, and when he asked her to marry him, she readily accepted and ran off with him.

After several days they arrived at an elegant-looking compound, which the warrior proudly announced was his home. However, no sooner had Chicho entered when she had the shock of her life, for the compound suddenly became overgrown with bush. When she turned to the warrior, she was shocked even more. The handsome young man had changed into an ogre!

Grabbing her, the ogre locked Chicho up in a hut, with a hunk of mutton for her meal. Chicho had a sudden idea and began to hack through the back wall with an axe. When the ogre outside asked what she was doing, she said she was chopping the meat. She continued to hack away until she had made a sizeable hole. Then she slipped out and ran.

Suddenly she stopped. Her bangles! She couldn't go home without them. She ran back. She slipped into the hut. As she searched frantically for the bangles, the door opened and the ogre stood in the doorway smiling, the bangles in his hand. "My dear child," he said, "would you live as my wife or would you prefer a fate far worse?"

"Please spare me. I'll do whatever you want," Chicho pleaded, sure she would get another chance to escape.

The next morning however, Chicho woke up to an unpleasant surprise, which dashed her hopes. An impassable wilderness had sprung up all around the compound. "Now you won't run away from me again," the ogre told her gloatingly. "Nor will your people ever come to your rescue."

Seasons came and went, and Chicho had a son. Sadly for her, instead of the human baby she had hoped for, he turned out to be an ogre like his father. The little ogre was named Konyek.

At home, no one knew what had happened to Chicho or had seen her leave with the handsome young warrior. Her people searched in vain, and as years went by they gave her up for dead. There was one person, however, who believed Chicho was not dead and was determined to find her. It was Alo, Chicho's sister, who had newly born twins.

Early one day Alo sneaked away with the twins into the wilderness. She had no idea where Chicho could be, but her hope that she was alive was so strong it lent magic to her voice as she sang:

> Path, take me to Sister.
> Carry me to Sister.
> Lead me to Sister.
> And I'll say thank you!

A path opened and took her through the wilderness, bringing her to the ogre's compound one bright morning, soon after the ogre and Konyek had left for their daily hunting.

The two sisters were overjoyed to see each other and eagerly exchanged news. Chicho told her sister about the ogre and Konyek, and heard all about home. As the ogres were away for the day, the two had plenty of time together.

In their excitement, they didn't notice the passing of time. Chicho glanced at the setting sun. "Quickly go, they will soon be back!" she gasped.

"You're coming with me!" said Alo.

Chicho shook her head. "No. If they don't find me here, they'll come after us and we will all be done for."

Alo sang:

> Path, take me home.
> Carry me home.
> Lead me home.
> And I'll say thank you!

In the wilderness, the ogres had had a plentiful day, and were in such a good mood going home that when a lame rabbit limped by, the ogre let it go. Suddenly, where the rabbit disappeared a path appeared, much to the amazement of the ogres, who happily set out on it.

Alo saw the ogres approaching on the path, and quickly thrust the sleeping twins into a little bush nearby. It was too small to hide her as well, so she climbed into the dense branches of an enormous tree riddled with creeping vines, that stood by the path. The ogre and Konyek stopped by. "I feel rather tired," groaned the ogre. "Let's rest a little under this tree."

Just then the twins awoke and began to cry. Alo looked down in horror as the ogre, bounding to the bush, picked them up and handed them to Konyek. "Ask your mother to fatten these *kidneys* for you," he laughed. "They are too small for me."

Alo came scrambling down the tree to the rescue, but in her desperation she lost her grip, banged her head and fell, and would have hurtled to her death if she hadn't got stuck in a tangle of vines midway to the ground.

On recovering, Alo quickly came down and asked the path to take her to the twins. She had little hope, however, that they were still alive, and the path didn't grant her wish. Instead, after days through the wilderness, the path miraculously returned her home, and she never found her way back to the land of the ogre.

At the ogre's compound, Chicho recognized the twins and silently grieved for Alo, whom she thought was dead. The next day, determined to save them, she hid the twins in a secret cave, and scratched two deep marks on her arm. When Konyek returned in the evening, Chicho told him that a hungry eagle had snatched his "kidneys."

"You're lying, give me those my kidneys!" bawled Konyek. "Give me back those my kidneys!"

Chicho held out her arm. "I'm not lying. You can see for yourself where the eagle scratched me as he grabbed the kidneys out of my arms."

The ogre stared at the scratches. "True, dear wife, true," he said with gruff sympathy. "A vicious eagle it must have been to have clawed you so!" And he snarled at the bawling Konyek, "Enough of your 'kidneys'! I won't have you pestering your poor wounded mother." Konyek stopped but eyed Chicho with growing suspicion.

Time passed, and every day, while the ogres were away, Chicho let the twins out, but just before sunset she took them back to the cave, then made sure to erase their footprints.

One day she forgot, and at the sight of the footprints Konyek screeched, "Someone has been here, someone has been here!"

The ogre eyed Chicho threateningly. How forgetful of me, thought Chicho; but, doing some quick thinking, she replied, "I had a long nap in the afternoon and raiders might well have been here as I slept. If so, they must still be around and I'm sure you my two brave warriors will find and catch them!"

After a long search the ogres came back empty-handed. Chicho said since they had found no one, the footprints (which she had now erased) must have been her own.

"No, someone has been here!" screamed Konyek.

The ogre, however, agreed with Chicho. "No one has been here, no one dare set foot here!" he bragged.

Konyek murmured to himself, "Mh, those my kidneys might just have something to do with this."

Soon after the incident, Chicho told the twins about the ogres. On learning about their mother's supposed death, the twins cried for vengeance, asking to do battle with the ogre.

Chicho chuckled:

> Not yet, not yet, my little ones.
> You're much too little.
> The ogre will finish you up
> With a look!

Seasons later the twins said:

> We're big and strong, dear aunt.
> May we battle the ogre
> For our dear mother
> And you, dear aunt?

Replied Chicho:

> Not yet, not yet, my little ones.
> You're still too little.
> The ogre will finish you up
> With a look!

Years passed and the twins spoke up:

> We're big and strong, dear aunt.
> May we battle the ogre
> For our dear mother
> And you, dear aunt?

Their voices were as deep as the bellow of a bull. Chicho stared at them. "So they are, big and strong!" she muttered. "I'll make them truly ready!"

That evening Chicho asked for a bull. "What for?" asked the ogre, surprised.

"I've grown ill and weak these past few days," replied Chicho, "and I need all my strength if raiders come attacking while you're away. Nothing less than a bull to feast on will make me strong again."

Konyek scowled. "Mh, it's the first time I've heard the old woman ask for a bull, all for herself. Ha, those my kidneys might just have something to do with this."

The ogre ignored him and the next evening brought back a bull. In the morning Chicho made the twins a feast of the bull. After they had feasted Chicho looked them over. Their bodies gleamed with power and the eyes glowed most fiercely.

Early next day Chicho asked for two spears. "Whatever for?" asked the ogre, amused.

Chicho flexed her shrivelled muscles. "For any enemy fool enough to attack me. The feast has made my blood boil. I'm spoiling for a fight!"

"But why two spears?" laughed the ogre.

"Two spears to throw at the enemy, one after the other!" she replied, and demonstrated by battling an imaginary enemy, with much huffing and puffing and flailing of her spindly limbs. The ogre thought this was the funniest thing he had ever seen.

Konyek wasn't amused. "Mh, it's the first time I've heard the old woman ask for two spears, all for herself. Ha, those my kidneys might just have something to do with this."

The ogre brought back the spears. Chicho armed the twins. "Now we're ready," she said. "You with the strength of youth, and I with the wisdom of age."

Before they went back to the cave, she told them of a plan and got them to strike several wooden spikes hard and deep into the ground.

As soon as the ogres returned, Chicho challenged them. "Show me how strong you are. Show me how strong and ready to do battle you are. Pull out the spikes!"

The ogre thought this another good joke. "It's too easy for me," he chuckled. "Let Konyek pull them out."

Konyek was only too pleased, and squeaked:

> I'm as strong as a lion.
> I'm as strong as ten lions.
> Who dare say I am not!

But he couldn't pull out one spike. The ogre shoved him aside. "Out of the way, weakling!"

Rumbled the ogre:

> I'm as strong as an elephant.
> I'm as strong as ten elephants.
> Who dare say I am not!

He too wasn't able to pull out the spikes, and called out to Konyek for help.

Chicho laughed. "You say you have the strength of lions and elephants and a few weak spikes defeat you!" She held her sides and laughed and laughed.

While she laughed, ever so stealthily the twins crept out of the cave.

Chicho laughed and taunted harder as the ogres pulled in vain. She rolled on the ground and laughed and laughed, allowing the twins to inch closer and closer.

Burning with humiliation, the ogres pulled and pulled, while the twins advanced, and in one swift movement sprang.

"You should have listened to me, Father," Konyek cried out as the twins despatched them. "Now I know for sure, those my kidneys had something to do with everything!"

With the twins by her side, Chicho walked out of the compound, her step light and full of hope as she sang:

> Path, take us home.
> Carry us home.
> Lead us home.
> And we'll say thank you!

Before them, a path coiled out of the compound and slithered like a long endless python through the wilderness.

Grandfather's Story of the Lost Lemon Mine
Retold by Gail de Vos and Anna Altmann

I remember spending a lot of my time, when I was much younger, being quiet up at the top of the stairwell. I tucked myself out of the way, invisible in the dimness, and spent hour after hour listening to my grandfather and his old prospecting buddies talk about the old days. They told great stories, but my mother had deemed them "unsuitable for a young girl's ears" — that's why I curled up and quiet!

They told stories about the swashbucklers they knew, and the ones that they didn't, about love, bandits, and settling the West. Naturally, a lot of their stories focused on finding the El Dorado, the big jackpot, and sometimes losing it as well. I think my favorite story — and theirs — was how the Great Spirit protected the hunting grounds of the Stoney Indians in southern Alberta. The story really wasn't all about the Great Spirit, but about how the Great Spirit played with humans and how Frank Lemon lost his big strike, and much more!

According to my grandfather, Lemon and his partner, Blackjack, had traveled with a party of prospectors from Tobacco Plains in Montana up to Alberta. The group was heading for the North Saskatchewan River, but Lemon and Blackjack, for some reason, headed off on their own, following an old lodge-pole trail up High River.

Grandfather and his friends got excited, and the volume went up when they talked about how Lemon and Blackjack followed the old trail and kept their prospecting noses to the ground. They argued about how it was that the two finally found the gold, whether it was sheer brilliance, pure luck, or the Great Spirit's sense of humor, but they all agreed on the purity of the strike. "Solid gold with a little rock shot into it!"

Well, it might not have been solid gold, but the truth was that Blackjack and Lemon had a lucky strike, or so they must have thought at the beginning.... But they had a disagreement over whether they should go to stake their claim or stay and work the diggings. They argued, fought, and finally it came to murder. Apparently not satisfied with what had been decided, Lemon stewed for a while and then chopped off the head of the sleeping Blackjack with an axe!

It was always at about this stage in the story that I got to listen to a heated argument from below — was Lemon crazy before they discovered the mine, was the gold cursed, or did Lemon just have a very bad temper? In any case, the murder weighed heavily on Lemon, and he did lose his mind. From Lemon's own accounts, he did not run away into the night as soon as he had killed Blackjack, but instead paced up and down in front of a large fire and waited for daylight.

While he paced, the dancing blaze of the bonfire blinded him to the hills and forest around him. He didn't see that he was not alone in the night. Two Stoney Indians, William and Daniel Bendow, had witnessed the entire thing — the exaltation over the discovery of the gold, the argument, and the axe murder. Not overly pleased with the behavior of these men in their hunting grounds, and in an attempt to frighten Lemon away, the two brothers whistled, shrieked, and groaned from out in the darkness during the entire long night. The strange noises in the darkness beyond the bright fire didn't make Lemon leave, but they didn't do much for his mental equilibrium, either.

At the crack of dawn Lemon left, taking only one horse with him. The Bendow brothers came in from the forest and ransacked the camp. They took the remaining two horses, then returned to Morley and told their story to Chief Bearspaw. Bearspaw listened intently and then swore the men to secrecy—he didn't want their game-filled hunting grounds invaded by any more gold-hungry miners.

Meanwhile, Lemon made his way to the mission at Tobacco Plains and confessed to the priest, who was his friend. I never knew the name of this priest because in all the stories I heard he was referred to only as "the priest." The priest sent the mountain man John McDougall to the scene. (I used to get this John McDougall confused with the missionary John McDougall in the history books because both were in the area around the same time, but this John McDougall had a lifestyle that was pretty different from that of a missionary! I never got to know too much about the mountain man, other than that he was a Metis and he liked his liquor and his women.) McDougall located the spot easily, following Lemon's directions, and buried what remained of Blackjack under a mound of stones to keep off the wolves. Then he went straight back to Tobacco Plains. Grandfather figured that McDougall didn't hear about the gold until after he got back to Tobacco Plains and therefore didn't look around the area much. He probably figured he was just cleaning up someone's mess!

Now, McDougall's actions were also watched by the Stoney Indians from the cover of the trees. And as soon as he left, they tore down the marker on the grave, scattered the stones, and destroyed all traces of the camp, the murder, and the body. They did such a good job that no one has found the location of the camp to this day!

This was not for lack of trying! Grandfather and his friends spent a lot of time talking about the people who tried to locate the rich gold mine. Lemon's bloody way of ending an argument apparently jinxed the place but good! Or perhaps it was the Great Spirit protecting the Stoney Indians from more crazy prospectors.

News of the rich strike spread quickly, but winter kept the hordes of gold seekers at bay while Lemon, with the help of the priest, tried to pull himself together. With the coming of spring, Lemon led a large prospecting party to rediscover the mine. While he had no problem finding the general area, Lemon could not find the actual site again. He searched the gullies and hillsides while the other prospectors grew angrier and angrier. They accused him of deliberately misleading them, and as the accusations flew, whatever sanity Lemon had left fled. He spent most of the rest of his life in Texas at his brother's ranch. Apparently he never fully regained his sanity.

Undaunted by this first failure, the priest arranged another expedition the following year. This one was to be led by the mountain man John McDougall, who had been to the site to bury Blackjack. Now, McDougall was as anxious as anyone to find that rich strike, and he left Fort Benton in plenty of time to meet up with the expedition at Tobacco Plains, but he never arrived. According to Grandfather, he stopped at Fort Kipp, a notorious whiskey post, and had more than one too many for the road: He drank himself to death. Once more the search was abandoned.

The next year a fierce mountain fire chased another search party out of the area. The following year the priest had Lemon brought back from Texas. I guess Lemon wasn't crazy all the time, but the closer he came to the general area of the murder, the worse he got, and finally they had to tie him up so he wouldn't harm anyone, or himself, for that matter, and take him back down to Tobacco Plains and then to Texas. After that the priest gave up his search. But then another person popped up to take on the search for the elusive mine—Lafayette French.

French had originally backed Blackjack and Lemon on their trip to Alberta, and he felt that he had a vested interest in the gold from the beginning. French had even less luck than the nameless priest—and again, Grandfather and his friends speculated on the reasons for this in loud voices and with a lot of finger jabbing.

The Stoneys had stopped using the old lodgepole trail when Chief Bearspaw had sworn them to secrecy. Nature and the effects of widespread fire had long since hidden the trail. French first looked for this trail, but he became strangely ill and had to return to Tobacco Plains to regain his strength. French had somehow found out about the Bendow brothers, who had actually seen the murder, and he bribed William Bendow. Bendow agreed to show French the trail, but on the second day out he changed his mind and refused to go any further.

French bribed him again and eventually got William Bendow to agree to a second try—but it never came about, for that night Bendow died suddenly. And at the exact moment when Bendow's body arrived back at the Stoney reserve, his son-in-law died in the same mysterious manner.

French was bound and determined that he would find the gold—after all, if it was found once, it could be found again! He kept at it, panning rivers and streams for the slightest trace of gold. And then one day French mailed a letter to a friend at Fort Benton announcing that he had found *it* and that he was coming to High River in a couple of days to tell him everything and to enlist his help. French had been staying at the old Emerson house and the same night that the letter was posted, a fire of mysterious origin gutted that house. French was burned to death and whatever he found, whatever secret he had uncovered, died with him.

This is the part of the story that really got everyone going, if you can imagine the air getting any hotter and bluer than it was already. I didn't even have to be quiet any more—they couldn't have heard me if I'd played a bugle!

Everyone had a different answer, and everyone was sure he was right. The Great Spirit had put a curse on the gold, that was the reason Lemon killed Blackjack and why French died in the fire.

No, Lemon had brought on the curse because of the murder! And French was Lemon's friend, so there was no way he would be allowed to profit from Lemon's deed.

The Great Spirit was looking out for his people. Think about how quickly the trail disappeared and how the fire chased the priest's expedition out of the hills but left the Stoney's alone. Bendow died because he broke his vow to Chief Bearspaw and French—well, French died because he was getting too close to the gold.

This argument was always followed by a heavy pause and then everyone got ready to leave.

I found out later that after French's death there were numerous other attempts to rediscover the mine and numerous stories about mysterious skeletons and lost prospectors. I never heard about them from Grandfather, though. The story of the lost Lemon mine, and Blackjack, Lemon, the priest, John McDougall, and Lafayette French lived and died again and again in the stories of my grandfather and his cronies, and in my memories.

The Graveyard Dare
Retold by Gail de Vos

At a Halloween party last year, several people, including my neighbor's niece, were talking about a nearby graveyard and the chills that they all felt when they walked past the graveyard on the way to the party. They were discussing the logical reasons for their fright when one of the boys, David, said, "Don't ever stand on a grave at midnight. The body inside will grab you and pull you under!"

One of the group, a girl dressed like Scarlett O'Hara from the movie *Gone with the Wind*, with a pale yellow skirt that fell, ruffle upon ruffle, down to the floor, laughed and laughed.

"That is one of the silliest things I ever heard you say, David," she said. "I know that graveyards are said to be haunted, but I don't believe in ghosts because I have never seen one! In fact, passing the graveyard didn't bother me at all! And as for standing on a grave, that's just pure superstitious bunk! I just cannot believe you said that. Standing on a grave is not a big deal!"

David fought to maintain his dignity, and then retorted that if she was so brave, he dared her to go into the graveyard alone and stand on a grave. "Tonight!" He looked at his watch and, realizing that it was very close to midnight, said, "Now, as a matter of fact!"

Jennifer, the girl in the yellow dress, did not hesitate at all. "No problem," said she. She put on the long gray cloak that completed her costume and off she went down the street. The entire crowd went with her, but only as far as the entrance to the graveyard, mind you, and Kevin gave her a knife. "Take this knife and stick it in the middle of one of the graves as proof that you stood on the grave."

Jennifer took the knife in her hand, pushed open the iron gates, and stepped through. Inside it was very dark. She could barely see the outline of the chapel on the far side of the cemetery.

Until this moment Jennifer had not been frightened, but the almost total darkness made her pause. She was suddenly quite sure that there was something in the shadows that reached out and grabbed at her. She noticed a flicker of movement out of the corner of her eye. A part of her wanted to cut and run, but Jennifer was strong-willed. She was determined to make good her dare. She picked out a grave and stood on it. She raised the knife to thrust it into the damp soil of the grave, then froze — she could hear a sigh and then a loud moan. It was coming from just beyond the tombstone. She could smell the freshly turned earth of an open grave, and just behind her she could hear something coming toward her. Something that moved stiffly and wetly.

Too fightened to scream, Jennifer plunged the knife into the grave. She turned to run, but she could not. Something caught her. Something held her and wouldn't let her go. The harder she struggled, the tighter it held her. Now something was tugging at her throat. In a final spasm of terror, she flung herself forward, only to feel herself dragged back toward the grave.

Jennifer's friends were waiting at the gate, and when she didn't come back after thirty minutes, they went to look for her. They found her sprawled across the grave. Her eyes were wide open in fear. She was dead.

The end of her cloak was embedded in the grave. It was held in place by the deeply planted knife. Jennifer had frightened herself to death.

The Horse Doctor
Retold by Gail de Vos

Not far from here, and not very long ago, there lived an old woman. She lived by herself in a small house in the country. Her husband had died and her children had left long before to make their own fortunes.

Her house was surrounded by fine grazing fields, and so she kept a horse, a cow, some hens, and a couple of pigs. She raised her own vegetables in a large garden and was pretty independent.

One day her horse took sick, and no matter what she did, and she did her best, it did not get any better. She called in the veterinarian, and he did what he could to help the horse, but still the horse remained ill. The old woman was afraid that she was going to lose her horse, and she didn't know what to do.

Living in the area was a young priest. It was his first appointment, and he was determined that he would help anybody with anything at any time. Everyone knew how obliging he was, so the old woman went to the priest and asked him to come and see what he could do for her sick horse.

The young priest, being born and bred in the city, was not sure what he could do to help and he told her so, but she insisted that he could surely do something to aid the horse in its pain. "I have no knowledge about horses, but I will go and see the sick animal if you think it will help you," said the priest.

The priest accompanied the old woman to the barn and put his hand on the horse's nose. He pulled out the tongue and felt it. Then he walked around the horse and looked at it from the other side. He really did not know what to do for the horse, but he did want to comfort the old woman. While he was trying to think of something constructive to do, he walked around the horse three times. Finally, the priest just shook his head and said: "You poor beast, if you live you live, if you die you die." Then he left. And believe it or not, the horse got better.

Time passed, and a few years later the priest himself became ill. There was a poisonous abscess on the inside of this throat. It had become very swollen and it threatened to choke him to death. The doctor could not do anything for him, and the priest's condition grew worse and worse.

When the old woman heard of the priest's trouble, she went to see him. She put her hand on his nose. His tongue was already protruding from his mouth, so she felt it. She walked around and looked at him from the other side for a few minutes, and then she walked around the bed three times. She stood and looked at him. "You poor beast," she said, "if you live you live, if you die you die."

Recalling that these were the very same words he had spoken to the old woman's horse, the priest started to laugh. He laughed so hard that the abscess inside his throat broke, the poison drained out and the swelling went down.

The priest recovered and lived to carry on his good works in the parish for many years to come.

The King and the Miller
Retold by Gail de Vos

Kings are not always wise or just. Sometimes their heads get turned by riches, honor or a pretty girl. In the Orkney Islands, many years ago, there lived such a king.

King Gerald was not a rich man, nor very brave, but he was passionately in love with the miller's beautiful daughter. As the king was neither young nor handsome and was but one of many suitors, he decided his approach had to be unique.

Late one autumn afternoon, King Gerald met the miller by the mill. Instead of asking the miller for his daughter's hand in marriage, as was required by custom, King Gerald demanded that the miller answer three questions. "I have three questions for you to answer, miller," said the king. "If you do not answer them I will have your head for my gate. You know that I have the power to do this!"

The miller acknowledged the king's power and said that he would try his best to answer the questions.

King Gerald then asked the miller the questions. "What is the weight of the moon? That is the first question. Secondly, I want you to tell me how many stars are there in the sky. And lastly, I want you to tell me what it is that I am thinking."

The miller looked very perplexed and bewildered, and then he replied, "It looks as if my head will grace your gate."

The king retorted that he, the king, was fair and just, and would give the miller a year and a day to supply the answers to his three questions. The place of meeting was set, 366 days hence, and the king departed with a final warning about the miller's head and the gate.

The year passed too quickly as the miller pondered the questions, but he came no closer to the answers. He became more and more morose and more and more despondent. At this time, the miller had a young shepherd working with him, and the shepherd could not help but notice the miller's growing agitation. When the shepherd asked him what was the matter, the miller told him of the three questions and the king's threat to have his head if the questions were not answered.

"If you give me your daughter as my wife I will deal with the problem," replied the shepherd. He was not blind, and was as attracted to the girl as was everyone else.

"I cannot give her," said the miller, "unless she is willing." So the miller went to his daughter. "My daughter, you know how worried I have been about answering the king's questions?"

"Yes, Father."

"The shepherd says that he has the answers to the questions and is willing to save my head if you are willing to marry him."

"Father, I would willingly marry anyone if it would save your life, and I am quite pleased to marry the shepherd. But I will do so only after he has saved your life, and not before!"

And so they reached an agreement with the shepherd. Soon it was time for the meeting between the miller and the king. The shepherd, disguised as the miller, waited at the appointed place.

"Good evening, miller," said the king.

"Good evening, King Gerald," was the reply.

Then King Gerald asked if he had the answers to the three questions, and the shepherd merely nodded his head. "The first question concerned the moon, miller. What is the weight of the moon?"

"This is a very simple question, my king. The moon is a hundred weight," was the reply. "It is common knowledge that there are four quarters in the moon and four quarters in a hundred weight."

"That is very good," said the king appreciatively. "Now, how many stars are there in the sky?"

"This is also very simple, Sire. There are seven million, four hundred and fifty seven thousand stars in the sky, and if you don't believe me, you can count them for yourself."

"I am not about to count them," countered the king. "But I am quite sure that you cannot answer my third question. Tell me, what is it that I am thinking?"

"This is the simplest question of all," was the reply. "You think that you are speaking with the miller, but you are not! You are speaking with his son-in-law."

And with these answers the shepherd saved the miller's life and won the miller's beautiful daughter.

Kit Kat
Retold by Gail de Vos

Last week a young neighbor of mine, Kathy, decided to skip school and go shopping by herself at West Edmonton Mall. Being too young to drive, she went by bus. She had a great time window shopping and trying on clothes, but after a few hours she was tired and hungry.

Kathy decided what she needed was a chocolate bar and a place to sit down for a few minutes. She bought her favorite bar, a Kit Kat, and then went looking for a place to sit. A few minutes later she found an unoccupied seat on a bench. An older woman was sitting on one end of the bench, and Kathy sat down on the other end. Both the older woman and Kathy watched the people in the mall for awhile and then Kathy opened the Kit Kat beside her and took the first section of chocolate and put it in her mouth. The woman beside her looked at her rather oddly but did not say anything.

When Kathy had finished eating three of the four sections of the bar, the woman beside her reached down and took the last section and shoved it in her own mouth!

Kathy could not believe her eyes. She was so upset and disgusted with the woman's behavior that she could not say a word. Kathy got up from the bench and left. She was so upset that she decided to go home and so went to the bus stop. When her bus arrived, Kathy opened her purse to get her fare and found her Kit Kat, unopened!

My Brother's Christmas Story
by Marie Anne McLean

Constable McLean had worked the last two Christmases and he was feeling bitter because he had been given Christmas duty again this year. Surely by now he had enough seniority to have Christmas off. After all, he had a wife and kids, and they wanted to go home to the farm and the grandparents for the holidays. It was a pretty dead shift anyway, the evening of Christmas Eve. He decided to make one last tour of town before he went home to be on call for the rest of the night.

It was cold and dark in the early evening, with the wind bringing in snow. People had finished their last rush of shopping, and the stores had closed for the holidays. The streets were nearly empty. As he drove past the lighted houses, Constable McLean could see, in the windows, groups of people home for Christmas. There were cars with out-of-province plates parked in front of some houses. That should be us, he thought, parked in Dad's yard.

Out at the edge of town by the Mohawk station, he saw a lean figure by the side of the road. It was a young man dressed in jeans and a short jacket, with his shoulders hunched against the cold and his hand held out. He was hitchhiking. When he saw the police car turn out of the alley, he turned away and began to walk purposefully down the road. The constable pulled the car up beside him and rolled down the window.

"Goin' somewhere?" he inquired.

"I'm catchin' the bus to Swan River," said the young man. "I'm going' home for Christmas."

"I'm afraid you're too late. You know the last bus left about two hours ago. Do you want me to take you to a phone or a motel? It's gonna get colder and you're not gonna get a ride tonight. I don't think I can leave you here. If you're short of cash, I can let you stay in a cell for the night and you can phone your relatives from the office." The constable eyed the young man. He looked like the type that any policeman would prefer to have leave town as soon as possible. He had long, stringy hair and looked as though he had not been on speaking terms with soap or towel recently. He did not look directly at McLean as the constable spoke to him.

"You'd better give me your name." The constable's voice became more official sounding.

The man gave his name and looked down at his feet. "I'm goin' to see my mom. I thought I'd surprise her. I think I can still get a ride if you don't stop me or somethin'." His voice held a weak hint of defiance.

Constable McLean decided that there was probably a whole story there, but he didn't think it was a happy one. "Look, I'm gonna give you some time to catch a ride. There's a phone booth at the gas station. If you don't get a ride, call the station. The switchboard will call me, and I'll come and get you. Are you short of cash?"

The man said nothing.

"I can give you a bed for the night. I'm not gonna charge you with vagrancy. Just tell me if you can afford a room or if I need to take you to the office."

The man looked away.

"Okay, it's up to you." McLean rolled up the window and drove away. As he watched the figure of the young man recede in the rearview mirror, he called the Swan River R.C.M.P. They recognized the name immediately.

"Geez, McLean. You probably did his old lady a favor, not sending him home for Christmas. He's a useless piece of crap. Wonder why he decided to come home now? Is it as quiet over there as it is here? Come to think of it, why don't you keep him? That'll be your Christmas present to us." The voice on the radio signed off, laughing.

McLean turned home for the evening.

When he got home, he changed out of his uniform and attempted to relax. He tried to tell his wife, Carol, how lucky they were compared to that boy out on the road, or his mother. The more he talked, the more Carol could see how upset he was, too upset for it just to be because he was in a temper about having to work.

"You know you did all you could. If he doesn't get a ride, he'll call. He won't freeze. Quit being such a misery about it." Carol wished he could leave the job at work.

The constable laughed. "Maybe I'm bein' tested. You know, maybe God's testin' me." His eyebrows went up and he grinned to show he was kidding. But his voice sounded almost serious. "I think I'm gonna call up the boys in Swan River. They already told me that they don't have much to do. If they meet me at the border, I could deliver him and he'd be home for Christmas. Besides that, then he won't be hangin' around here making more work for us. I know he won't have caught a ride yet. It'll only take me two or three hours and I'll be back."

He got back into his uniform and set out again. The Swan River detachment only took a little persuading to agree to the plan. They vowed that it was "only because it was so slow," so that no one could construe their motives as having anything to do with Christmas or good will.

The young man was not hard to find. He had stubbornly progressed a few hundred yards down the road. When he heard the plan, he showed his blackened teeth in a weak grin. He climbed into the warm front seat of the car. "First time I got into the front seat of one of these," he remarked.

The trip to the border passed without much speech between the uneasy occupants of the car.

Constable McLean dropped his passenger off into the care of the Swan River members and headed back home. He decided to take the road through the Provincial Park going home. It would be pretty empty at this time of the night, but it would make the trip home shorter by at least a half hour. The wind had increased and he reflected that the road might be icy, but he knew the road well and was not particularly worried.

The idea of home seemed good right now. Near the middle of the park where the trees crowded the road, the deep shadows and icy patches forced him to slow the car. He wondered at the wisdom of his choice. What he met around the next corner made him forget completely about the road, the night, and his discontent.

A family were stumbling out of the woods: a man, a woman, and a child about ten years old. The constable halted the car and stepped out into the cold darkness. They seemed nearly frozen.

They had been cross-country skiing, the man said, and they had lost their way at twilight. They had feared that no one would be on the road at this time and on this night.

They were shivering with cold and relief as they huddled in the back seat of the squad car. The constable offered them coffee from the thermos that Carol had given him as he left. In a few minutes their story came out. As he drove them back to their rented cottage, he listened and wondered at the circumstances that had brought them here.

They were Russian immigrants. They had scrimped and filled in forms and waited for years to get the necessary permits to move to Canada. They had come here to have a place to raise their family in some kind of economic security. They lived in Regina, where they had found work and a home. They had adapted well to this strange new country, but sometimes they could not bear the prairie any longer.

When Christmas came, the longing for forest became too great and they would look for a place with trees to visit for a few days. About two or three years ago they had discovered the Provincial Park, and now each year they rented a cottage for the Christmas holiday. That was how they came to be here on Christmas Eve.

As the constable took them back to their car, he listened to their story and thought about the way he had been feeling earlier in the evening. They still longed for Russia, but they were determined to make a place for themselves here. Perhaps his life wasn't as difficult as he had thought.

The man reminisced about the days of his childhood. He spoke of going to church with his grandmother on Christmas Eve. It was a custom he had outgrown many years ago.

At last the police car pulled into the cottage's yard. As they got out, they all said thank-you to Constable McLean. They seemed reluctant to break off this moment. The man smiled and shook his head.

"You know," he said, "sometimes I think of those Christmas Eves in church with my grandmother and I think I would like to go again. But I don't. Tonight I think I will go back. Tonight I think I understand why she would take me there."

He looked at his wife and child and then he turned back to the policeman. "I would like to give you something to thank you."

"No, that's okay I'm glad I was here. You guys be careful the next...." The constable began his usual public servant speech, and then he looked in the man's eyes. Something had happened that was important. This man wanted to give a gift in return.

"Well, come to think of it. You guys have this great goalie called Mishkin. If you ever happen to write to a hockey fan over there I'd love an autographed picture." He laughed because this was a strange request.

The man laughed too, but his laughter was a great shout, a shout of joy. "Oh, my cousin! He is cousin to me!" In his delight his accent thickened and his English became broken. "I get it for you. Oh yes." He slapped his leg in his excitement as he stepped away from the car to allow the constable to leave.

Constable McLean drove home silently.

As he sat at his kitchen table afterward, he tried to tell Carol what had happened. The words were not there. He needed no words. He was not thinking of the photo of Mishkin. He was thinking that he had already received the gift.

*Sisyphus**
Retold by Gail de Vos

Sisyphus built and governed the Greek city of Corinth on the narrow isthmus between two seas and two countries. But he is not remembered for his governing skills. No, Sisyphus is known as the craftiest of all mortals, remembered for his exploits of cunning and for the price he ultimately paid.

When Sisyphus was a young man, he had a battle of wits with the master thief, Autolykos. Now, Autolykos had a decided advantage over everyone because of the gifts he was given by his father, Hermes. To aid his son in his chosen profession, the god of thieves gave him the power to elude capture whenever he stole. To supplement this, Hermes gave Autolykos the power to alter the physical appearance of anything he had taken. While Autolykos roamed far and wide on his endeavors, he was not above striking close to home. His neighbor Sisyphus had a fine herd of cattle, and Autolykos decided to appropriate the cattle, a few at a time. Sisyphus quickly noticed that his herd was diminishing. He was just as quick to notice that Autolykos's herd was increasing at the same rate. Although the new cattle did not resemble his lost animals, Sisyphus was quite sure that Autolykos was responsible for the disappearance of his cows. One dark night, Sisyphus marked the underside of the hooves of his remaining cows. The marking was very distinctive but at the same time very subtle. During the following weeks he was able to track them to Autolykos's enlarged herd. In the presence of reliable witnesses, he pointed out the unusual tracks the stolen cattle had made and recovered all of the animals he had lost.

Sisyphus was not content with just recovering his cattle and besting the master thief. In further retaliation, he charmed and seduced Autolykos's daughter, Anticlea, and is said to be the actual father of her famous son, Odysseus.

His greatest exploit, however, took place when Sisyphus was no longer a young man. This was outwitting the gods themselves. Sisyphus did not set out to tangle with the gods; it happened purely by chance. One balmy summer day, as Sisyphus surveyed his kingdom, his attention was caught by the sight of a magnificent eagle. The eagle was clutching Aegina, the daughter of the river god, Asopus, and as Sisyphus watched, it flew with her to a nearby island. There the eagle resumed its normal shape and ravished the beautiful nymph. It was Zeus! Sisyphus was lost in thought, marveling at the god's deed, when he was hailed by the angry father of the nymph. Asopus had given chase when Zeus abducted his daughter but had lost the trail. Had Sisyphus seen anything? Thinking quickly, the king promised to tell what he knew in return for a spring of fresh water, something his city of Corinth lacked.

Asopus was not noted for his generosity. He guarded his water very carefully. Sisyphus watched as Asopus battled with himself, but at last his love for his daughter and his anger at Zeus overcame his stinginess, and Asopus struck the ground. From the point of impact bubbled forth a clear spring. Then Sisyphus, with relish, told the river god of the great eagle and of the scene that took place on the island. With even greater relish, he pointed out to Asopus the way Zeus had flown.

---

*A *Labor of Sisyphus* or *Sisyphean toil* is an endless, heart-breaking job.

Asopus left in a fury and soon caught up with Zeus, but was repeatedly driven away by thunderbolts thrown by the peeved god. In the end, Asopus never managed to reclaim his daughter and never saw her again. The name of the island was changed to Aegina to honor her.

The jubilant Sisyphus had his water, but Zeus was furious with him for meddling in his affairs and sent Thanatos (Death) to fetch Sisyphus to the underworld of Hades. Sisyphus pretended to be very honored when he saw Thanatos standing before him and invited the god to join him in a last glass of wine. Thanatos, who never had a problem collecting his consignments, agreed and followed Sisyphus to the wine table. There Sisyphus overcame him, bound him with chains, and left him in a locked dungeon.

The result of this action was that mortals ceased to die and the Fates got the threads of life tangled. To help the Fates, the gods sent Ares, the god of war, to release Thanatos. Once he was unbound, his first action was to collect Sisyphus once more. The wily king, who had expected this, had given his wife, Merope, careful instructions. Merope was not to give him a funeral feast, not to bury his body nor to put a coin under his tongue. By following his instructions, Merope saw to it that Sisyphus arrived in the underworld poor as a beggar.

Hades, the god of the underworld, was extremely angry. How could a wife treat her husband so? How could she neglect to give him his due? How could she not provide a coin to pay for Sisyphus's passage across the River Styx? Merope had to be punished. In a fit of anger, Hades sent Sisyphus back to earth to punish his wife and have her bury his body with the honor that it deserved. On returning to Corinth, however, Sisyphus did no such thing. Instead, he went on with his life in defiance of the gods.

Eventually, he died of old age and went to the underground realm. When he arrived, Hades was waiting for him. Sisyphus's trickery and lack of respect for the gods, as well as his tale-telling about Zeus, earned him eternal labor and frustration. He was forced to roll a great stone up a steep hill, pushing with all his might. Just as the stone reached the top, it slipped from his hands and rolled all the way down to the bottom again. This happened again and again, forevermore. The only time Sisyphus was allowed to rest was when Orpheus descended to the underworld to reclaim his bride, Eurydice. But that was only once, and for a short time only, and it is, my friends, another story.

The Snoring Pigs
Retold by Gail de Vos

The capital city of Alberta started out as a Hudson Bay fort perched on the banks of the North Saskatchewan River. The fort outlived its usefulness, and the population drifted to land holdings on both sides of the river. Reports of the rich gold discoveries in the north drew large numbers of people to the region, many of whom put down roots in the now rapidly growing frontier town of Edmonton.

Sam Barton came with his parents from the open prairies of the central United States and settled on the south bank of the North Saskatchewan river. Why he ever accompanied them to this heavily wooded wilderness will always be a mystery. Not a very adventurous sort of young man, he was positive that behind each tree stood an Indian ready to scalp him and behind each bush was a bear, ready to eat him.

Sam made friends with George Carlson who, as often happens, was very different in temperament and interest from timid Sam. George loved to hunt, fish, and explore the wild regions beyond the settlement. He was great company and a lot of fun to be with, so occasionally Sam plucked up his courage and accompanied him on his exploits.

One beautiful autumn morning, George and Sam set out for a duck shoot on McKernan's lake. The meandering trail to the lake was surrounded by clumps of willow bushes and larger trees. McKernan had not begun to work that section yet, so it was still essentially wilderness, but the neighbor's pigs and cattle felt at home there and wandered happily through the entire stretch of land.

The journey to the lake was uneventful, even pleasant, for Sam was highly entertained by George's descriptive prose. There were a great many ducks to shoot at, and Sam and George lost all track of time. Dusk fell before they realized it. Being out in the wilderness during daylight was one thing, but at night! Not even George and his stories could calm the nervous Sam. He just knew that behind each tree lurked an Indian and behind each bush a bear.

Now, I don't know how much you know about pigs, but they do tend to dig, and one of the pigs had dug a shelter for himself under a willow bush. Some pigs also snore, and this pig was a snorer! The pig snored just as Sam and George were walking past that willow bush. Sam jumped twenty feet into the air, grabbed George, and put George in front of him like a shield. George was laughing so hard he could barely stand. He finally managed to calm Sam down, explaining gently some of the habits of pigs, and they set off on the trail again. Sam, however, was still convinced in the back of his mind that they had just had a very narrow escape from a bear.

George lived on the north side of the river, and the two men parted ways when they arrived back in Edmonton. But George could not resist the temptation to have a little fun, and he circled back through the darkness and waited for Sam a little further up the path. As Sam walked by quickly, George let out a very loud Indian war-whoop. Sam started to run and did not stop until he reached the front gate of his house. He didn't stop then, either. He kept running, breaking down the gate and wrenching the latch right off the door in his hurry to get inside.

He sat up all night, terrified, and in the morning he hitched up a team of horses and drove across the river to tell George's mother that George had been scalped. He was not amused to find George loudly enjoying his breakfast! Sam became the butt of every bear and Indian story in Edmonton.

The strange thing was, however, that there had been a heavy frost that night and all the potatoes in the area froze—all, that is, except for the potatoes in Sam's yard. Apparently, Sam went through the garden so fast that he raised the temperature and kept the potatoes from freezing!

The Walking Coffin
Retold by Gail de Vos

A black night and unusual noises are a dangerous combination, especially if you start the evening already depressed. Jack had just had a very serious argument with the most beautiful girl in the world and was walking back to his home. The only good thing about the evening ahead was that everyone would be out and he would have the house to himself.

The streets were deserted and a fine mist hovered over everything. Jack really didn't notice too much of this; his thoughts were far away. As Jack walked, his head tucked into his jacket collar as much for comfort as for warmth, he heard a thumping noise some distance behind him. He soon realized that the thumping was getting much louder and much closer. Puzzled by the noise, Jack stopped and looked behind him.

What he saw made him start running for home as fast as he could run. The thumping was caused by a white coffin coming down the middle of the street!

By the time Jack made it to the front porch of his house, the coffin was at the front gate. Jack fumbled with the keys, got the right one into the lock, and made it inside with only seconds to spare. He locked the door, but to his horror, he heard the coffin thumping up the porch steps and then, with a horrible crash, it burst through the door. Jack ran up the stairs to the second floor and threw a heavy oak chair down the stairs at the coffin. The chair landed squarely on the coffin and shattered into a million pieces.

As Jack watched in horror, the coffin started up the stairs, one at a time. Slowly, but steadily, the coffin advanced toward Jack. Jack knew that if the coffin made it up to the top of the stairs, he'd had it.

Suddenly Jack had an idea. He ran into his bedroom, grabbed a small box that was on his dresser, and ran back to the top of the staircase. The coffin was halfway up the stairs when Jack reached into the box and took out a cough drop. Jack threw it at the coffin and the coffin stopped!

Boiled Eggs
Retold by Gail de Vos

In the years following his celebrated defeat of the warrior Goliath, David was involved in many escapades. But like most of us, he eventually grew older and settled down. He became the king and the father of Solomon, a man whose name became synonymous with wisdom.

David was also the commander of a massive army. One day a platoon of soldiers was served a meal of boiled eggs. One of the young soldiers, being very hungry, gobbled his eggs quickly. Still feeling ravenous, he looked around the table to see if there was any other food that he could consume. Across the table sat an older man. On his plate was a single boiled egg.

"Are you going to eat that egg?" inquired the young soldier. "If not, could you please lend it to me? I am still extremely hungry."

"Certainly," said the older man, "but you must promise me that when I recall the loan you will not only return an egg but also pay the interest that it accumulates during the period of the loan." The young soldier was so hungry that he barely listened to the other man. "Yes, yes, I promise," he mumbled while reaching for the egg. The older man asked the soldiers on either side of him if they would be witnesses to the transaction. They said they would indeed.

Several days later the platoon was disbanded. The two soldiers were sent in opposite directions and therefore did not see each other again for many years. When they did meet, the older man asked the now-not-so-young soldier to repay the loan.

The younger man was very agreeable and gave the other a boiled egg. "You lent me a boiled egg and I will repay you with another boiled egg," he said.

"You owe me much more than a boiled egg," said the older man. "You promised, before witnesses, to pay the interest as well." He then named an amount of money that was so large it left the younger man speechless. Several heated arguments did not alter the situation, and so, the old soldier took the case before King David. There he explained the situation to the king and the court. He recounted how the other man had promised, before witnesses, not only to repay the original loan but to pay the accumulated interest as well. He even produced the witnesses who testified to the original bargain.

Questioned by the king, the lender explained how he had arrived at the actual sum of money that he felt was owed to him. "Your Majesty, in the course of a year the egg would have yielded a chicken. The following year that chicken would have borne eighteen more chickens, and in the third year every one of those eighteen chickens would have given birth to another eighteen and so on. Therefore the amount of money I demand is based on the value of the hundreds of chickens that I would have sold at profit."

After listening to the soldiers, King David ruled that the borrower had to pay the lender the full amount.

The borrower of the egg left King David's court in a daze. Not fully aware of his surroundings, he collided with a young man. It was the king's son, Solomon. Upon seeing the man's obvious distress, Solomon pressed him for his story. It did not take much prompting for the soldier to relate his tale of woe.

Solomon listened intently. "Follow my advice, as strange as it may sound to you," Solomon told the soldier. "Take some beans and boil them. Then take them to that plowed field next to the road that leads to the army camp. The soldiers are constantly traveling between the town and the camp. When you see soldiers approaching, sow the boiled beans in the furrows, and if they ask what you are doing say 'I am sowing boiled beans.' They will laugh and ask, 'Who ever heard of boiled beans yielding crops?' Then you should say to them 'And who ever heard of a boiled egg producing a chicken?' "

The man did as Solomon advised. When the soldiers asked him what he was doing, he replied that he was planting boiled beans. When they laughed and said, "Who ever heard of boiled anything producing a crop?" he smiled and retorted, "And who ever heard of a boiled egg producing a chicken?" For several days every company of troops that passed asked the same question and received the same answer. It did not take any more time than that for the news of the man's bizarre behavior to reach King David. He summoned the man to appear before him.

The king studied the man very carefully. "This was not your idea, was it?" The soldier looked down at his feet and did not make a reply. "No, I thought not," continued the king. "I see the hand of my son Solomon in it." David called for his son, and when Solomon appeared before him, David asked him to pronounce judgment on the case.

Solomon stated his willingness to do so. "This soldier cannot be held responsible for something that does not exist. A boiled egg can never hatch. Therefore how can the man be expected to pay for chickens that could never be?"

King David agreed that his own judgment had been faulty. The soldier was then commanded to pay back the price of an egg and nothing more.

The Hare Dryer
Retold by Gail de Vos

About two months ago, an old friend of mine telephoned me to tell me about her new house. She was so thrilled about the house and the neighborhood that she was telephoning everyone she knew. I listened while she described, vividly and with many adjectives, the house, the garden, the park across the street, the neighbors, the neighbors' kids, and the neighbors' pets. Actually, it was about this last point that she was most excited.

Candace, my friend, has had this golden labrador retriever for many years. Midas, the dog, had long outgrown puppyhood but still had ample energy and loved to romp and run constantly. That was the beauty of the new neighborhood, Candace explained. For the first time since she acquired Midas, he was allowed to run freely and did not have to be kept in the yard. Everyone else also had pets, of all descriptions, and they were all allowed the same freedom. Why, she said, Midas had just made friends with the most adorable pet rabbit that lived next door. I was pleased for Candace, and Midas too, but did not give it much thought until I got home last night and found a frantic message from Candace on my message machine. "Please come to my house at once," she implored.

Curious about the new neighborhood and disturbed by the urgency in Candace's voice, I drove over to her house immediately. When I got there I saw that everything looked as serenely perfect as she had proclaimed. I rang the door bell and was confronted by my distraught friend almost before I lifted my finger from the bell. She greeted me with flailing hands, "Come in, come in, you are not going to believe what happened today!" So, of course, I asked the obvious, "What happened today?"

Candace said that yesterday when she came home from work, Midas was not here to greet her. This did not worry her because he was often out and about playing with the children and other dogs in the neighborhood. But when he did not return home for supper, she became rather anxious and started to walk up and down the streets calling for him. Finally, just at dusk, he came home. He was carrying something in his mouth so she bent down to see what it was. In horror, Candace realized that it was the neighbor's pet rabbit. It was covered in dirt and was obviously very dead. Candace stared at it for a few moments in shock.

She thought, "How could this be? Midas has the most gentle of souls, is not a hunter, and has never harmed another creature in his entire life. Why, he always crosses the street to avoid getting into scraps with strange dogs and cats!"

Candace very carefully took the rabbit out of Midas's mouth. All sorts of other questions tumbled through her mind. "What would the neighbors say? How could I explain this? What would happen to Midas and his freedom?"

She examined the rabbit and realized that, other than the fact that it was filthy, there was no obvious physical damage at all. There was no blood, no evidence of wounds, nothing! And at that moment she got an idea. Candace took the rabbit into the house and very carefully washed it with soap and then just as carefully she dried the rabbit's fur with her blow dryer. The fur was now soft and fluffy once again. Then, when she was sure that the neighbors were sound asleep, Candace left a confused Midas in the house and took the rabbit and quietly went into the neighbors' backyard. There she carefully placed the rabbit, in a lifelike position, back in its hutch and then went home. The neighbors would find the rabbit dead, yes, but they would not know that Midas had anything to do with it!

This morning, Midas started howling furiously and woke Candace up. She looked out the window to see if there was a reason for the barking, and there was a police car at the neighbor's house and people all around. She threw on some clothes and ran outside where she found her neighbor absolutely hysterical.

Candace tried to calm her down and when the neighbor was coherent once again, Candace asked, "What happened? Why are the police here? What is wrong?"

The neighbor answered, "I don't understand people these days! Yesterday our pet rabbit died. We buried it in the park, gave it a nice funeral, and then some weirdo dug it up and put it back in its hutch!"

And that is the story of the H-A-R-E hare dryer.

The Lynching Party
Retold by Gail de Vos

Last fall my husband and I were traveling through apple country. We were delighted with the old orchards and stately homes. We stopped for lunch in one of the small towns nestled in among the apple trees and started talking with some of the old timers who were having their coffee break. When we commented on the graciousness and wholesomeness of the area, they thanked us, but then one old man started to tell us that it was not always so. Our lunch lasted several hours, but by the time we drove off, we had a slightly different picture of the place.

Apparently, many years ago, around the turn of the century, there lived in the easternmost part of the district an old bachelor who owned and worked a fairly large orchard. The man's name was Samuel, and for some reason, the people in the district were leery of him. No one could remember exactly why, but everyone gave Samuel a wide berth. Although they gladly bought his apples, for they were the sweetest around, the people would not help Samuel at all. They would not even venture onto his land. All the work in the orchard was done by Samuel himself.

One fall, a new family moved into the area and bought the farm bordering on Samuel's orchard. One of the family, a young boy named Will, had an active imagination and plenty of energy to go with it. It did not take Will very long to discover the apple trees on the next property. He often climbed over the fence and spent his free time running and shouting and climbing in the orchard. One evening, as Will was clambering over the trees, he saw Samuel coming towards him. Being young and new to the area, Will had not heard any of the stories and gossip about old Samuel. Will did not hesitate at all. He slid down the tree and ran to talk to the old man, bubbling over with questions to ask and statements to make. Samuel seemed pleased with young Will's jabber and activity, and by spring the two had become good friends. Will spent all of his free time over at Samuel's, either following him about and helping him with his chores or climbing the trees.

One lovely evening, late in the fall when all the apples had been harvested and taken away to market to be sold, Will, as usual, was climbing one of the apple trees. Something happened and he fell. He fell in such a way that when he landed on the ground he died instantly from a broken neck. As soon as they heard of Will's death, the townspeople suspected Samuel of foul play. Under the leadership of a man named Jebediah, nine men organized a lynching party and went out to Samuel's orchard and hanged him from one of his apple trees. The orchard was sold to another farmer, and the townspeople felt that they had done their duty to Will's family and to their own families.

The next spring something very unusual happened. You see, none of the apple trees, except one, in the entire orchard produced any fruit. But that one tree, why, it produced more apples by itself than were ever produced by all the trees in the orchard in the previous years. The new owner harvested the apples and sold them at the market in town. The apples were purchased eagerly and among the people who bought and ate the apples were eight men from the lynching party. Each one of those men died suddenly and mysteriously soon after. Autopsies were performed, and it was soon confirmed that they had all died immediately after eating an apple. There were only the eight deaths, however, no one else had been affected by eating the apples.

Jebediah had been away from the area that fall, and he alone of the men that had made up the lynching party survived the winter. He felt that he had broken the curse, but he developed an aversion to apples and did not eat one the entire season.

The next spring again only one of the trees in Samuel's orchard produced any apples, but it was a different tree. This one grew very close to the road, and, in fact, one of its branches hung over the road itself. There was a lone apple on that branch. Jebediah had not forgotten the fate of his friends, and so, when he rode down the road he had no inclination to stop for an apple. But stop he did. The lone apple on that branch was so appealing, looked and smelled so delicious, was so irresistible that he felt compelled to stop. Jebediah got down from his horse, walked over to the tree and plucked the apple from the branch. Then, very methodically, he rubbed the apple on his pants leg and took a large bite from the polished apple. Jebediah died the instant his teeth pierced the skin of the apple.

Neither tree bore fruit ever again although they remained alive a long time. It appears that they had completed their task. For you see, the first tree, the tree that produced such an abundance of fruit, was the tree from which the lynching party hanged old Samuel. And the second tree? Well, that was the tree from which Will fell to his death.

The Pomegranate Seed*
Retold by Gail de Vos

There was once a poor man who, while very honest, was also very hungry. He could not obtain any work for a long time, and finally, in desperation, he stole some food from one of the market stalls. Hungry he was, a good thief he was not! And so he was caught and taken before the king to receive his sentence. He was to be hanged the next morning.

On the way to the gallows the thief naturally looked very worried. The king's guard spoke to him and tried to keep the thief calm, and finally the thief told the guard what it was that was troubling him so. He could fully accept that he was to be hanged. After all, he had committed a crime. But he was in possession of a wonderful secret and he was worried that the secret would die with him. He pleaded with the guard that he might have a chance to reveal the secret to the king. The guard took pity on the thief and instead of taking him to the gallows, he took him to the king's chamber. The king listened intently.

"Your Majesty, my father and his father before him and his father before that passed on this secret to their eldest sons. I have no son and have certainly no chance of getting one now, and so I would like to pass on the secret to you. I can put a pomegranate seed in the ground, and it will grow and bear fruit overnight," said the thief. "I am in despair that the secret will die with me."

The king thanked the thief for revealing his secret and scheduled a time the next day for the planting of the seed. The thief spent the night in relative comfort and the next morning he was taken to the appointed place. The king and all the members of his court were there. The thief dug a hole and said, "This seed can only be planted by a man who has never stolen or taken anything in his entire life that did not belong to him. Being a thief, of course, I cannot plant this seed."

The king turned to his first minister and directed him to plant the seed. The first minister looked startled. He hesitated and then said, "Your Majesty, I remember that when I was a young boy I borrowed an item that I never returned. I am sorry but I obviously cannot plant this seed."

The king turned to his treasurer. The treasurer begged the king's forgiveness. "I deal with such large sums of money—it's possible—small mistakes happen—I ... I ... may have entered too much or too little in the accounts."

The king, in his turn, recalled that he once took and kept a precious object belonging to his brother.

The thief turned to them and said, "I do not understand. First Minister, Chief Treasurer and Your Majesty, you are all powerful people. You are not in want of anything, yet none of you is able to plant this seed. Is it not ironic that I, who stole a little food to keep myself from starving, am about to be hanged?"

The king laughed, pleased with the man's clever ruse. The thief was pardoned and sent away with a purse filled with coins.

---

*Variation of *The Marvelous Pear Seed*, see page 47.

Procrustes' Bed*
Retold by Gail de Vos

An old man sat talking with a group of young men. "Heroes, you say that there are no more heroes? Well, in my time, I met a hero or two." The old man settled himself more comfortably. When the younger men pressed him to tell the tale, he smiled. "It was not that long ago," the old man started. "But the greatest hero was a young man named Theseus. At the time I met him I had no idea why he was traveling the dangerous road to Athens. I also had no idea that he would make that dangerous road safe.

"He could have easily traveled to Athens by ship, but the land journey was infamous for the robbers and cruel giants along the way. Apparently, Theseus wanted to prove himself, and prove himself he did. Before I even laid eyes on Theseus, he had dispatched most of them. He was a great wrestler and managed to wrestle an enormous club from Corynete, or 'club-bearer' as he was known. That club was one of the first things I noticed about Theseus when I met him. Corynete had been stopping travelers and clubbing them to death with that weapon. Theseus dispatched Corynete the same way and kept the club with him after that.

"Another savage robber, Sinus, stopped all travelers as well. This one they called the 'pine-bender' because he tortured his victims by tying their arms and legs on two different tall pine trees that he had bent down for that purpose. He then released the trees and the poor travelers would be torn to pieces. Theseus easily subdued Sinus and tied him between the two pines. I only wish I could have seen Sinus's face as he watched Theseus free the trees!

"There were others as well. Scion, for example, lived high on the cliff face in Megara, and he would force all travelers to stop and make them wash his feet. Well, you may laugh but it was not amusing. As the travelers stooped to do so, Scion would kick them over the cliffs. A giant tortoise lived at the bottom of the cliff, and it would eat their remains. When Theseus was challenged, he wrestled Scion down and threw him over that cliff. The tortoise put a fitting end to that heinous monster.

"Now, I met Theseus early one evening as I was struggling home with a load of driftwood. He stopped to help me with the wood, and of course we started talking. I had no idea at the time who he was but I knew that he was a kind man because no one else had stopped to help me. I was horrified when I found out that he was heading towards Athens. Not many travelers ever made their way past the most vile robber of all time, Procrustes.

"The others that I told you about, Corynete, Scion, and Pine-bender, they were cruel alright. But Procrustes had them beat, hands down. He appeared benevolent as he would smile at the travelers and invite them to spend the night in his home. His hospitality included a bed that was guaranteed to fit, perfectly, all sizes and shapes of people. Of course, he never explained how the bed could do so. He never explained that if a man was too tall for it, he would chop off the legs of his guest until he fit just right. Or how he would stretch a woman, if she was too short.

Procrustean signifies an arbitrary enforcement of conformity or the harsh enforcement of preestablished norms; any attempt to reduce men to one standard, one way of thinking, or one way of acting, is called *placing them on Procrustes' bed.*

"I told Theseus about how, just the day before, Procrustes fitted a young couple upon his bed. He cut the young man's hands and feet off and stretched the young woman by her head and feet. Yes, they fit on his bed, but they were no longer alive!

Theseus listened intently, and then he told me not to worry. That's when he told me about the adventures he had had along the road so far. 'I know what to expect now,' Theseus told me and then he left.

When Theseus met a friendly stranger further along the road, he stopped to chat. And when the man offered him the hospitality of his home, Theseus asked him if he had a special bed for him as well. Theseus told me later that when Procrustes (for that was who the stranger was) realized that this traveler would not be taken by surprise, he reached for his sword. But Theseus, for such a big man, was fast, and before Procrustes could do anything at all, Theseus leaped upon him and encircled him in his arms. Tighter and tighter he squeezed until Procrustes was unconscious. Then Theseus carried him to his house and laid him on the famous bed. Wouldn't you know it, Procrustes was about a head too tall to be a perfect fit. Theseus cut off the head!

"Before continuing his journey, Theseus searched the robber's home and found a great treasure trove, gathered from all the murdered travelers. Theseus came back and got me. He told me what had happened and then he asked me to take care of the treasury—to make sure that everyone around got a fair share. And that's what I did alright. Now I don't have to gather driftwood anymore, and I have time to talk to you young fellows.

"No heroes, you say. Well, I have heard more tales about Theseus since that time. No, I don't have the time to tell you them today, but tomorrow...."

Sixty Canyon Abandonment
Retold by Gail de Vos

Long ago, in Japan, it was thought that when people reached the age of sixty years, their time of productivity was over. To keep the economy from being burdened with old and useless people, the lord of the country commanded that when each person turned sixty, he or she would be thrown into a mountain canyon. This was known as "sixty canyon abandonment." There was no choice in the matter.

On the day that he turned sixty, a kind farmer from a small mountain village knew what was expected of him. And so, when his sorrowful son came to fetch him, the farmer climbed on his son's back and they set off towards the canyon. They traveled for some time through the trees, going further and further up the mountain, before the son noticed that his father was breaking off the tips of the tree branches as he was being carried along.

"Father, why are you marking the trail?" the son asked in confusion.

The father replied, "We are traveling through unfamiliar territory, and I worry that you may not find your way back home. I am marking the trail for you. I do not want you to lose your way."

The son stopped in his tracks. Even now, while facing death, his father had only thoughts for others. How could he possibly throw him over a cliff? The son turned around, and, with his father still on his back, returned home. There he hid his father so no one would know that he had not fulfilled his duty to the lord of the country.

The old farmer and his son lived quietly for some time, but then one day the powerful lord came to visit the district. The lord enjoyed having power; he gloried in it and in making his subjects squirm by setting them difficult and sometimes impossible tasks. It came as no surprise to the farmers in the district that they were commanded to attend a meeting with him. Once he had gathered all of the farmers he told them that they must each bring him a rope made of ashes. The farmers were all puzzled. A rope made of ashes! How would they make a rope out of ashes? The son returned home to his hidden father and told him the task the lord had set them.

"Father, how can we make a rope out of ashes?" The father thought for awhile and then said, "First you must weave a rope. You must weave it very tightly and then you must burn it carefully until it turns into ashes. Once this is done you can take the rope of ashes to the lord."

The son followed his father's advice. He wove the rope tightly and burned it carefully and then carried the rope of ashes to the lord. He was the only one who was able to do what the lord commanded and was praised highly for his effort. But the lord was not satisfied. "Everyone must bring a conch shell with a thread passed through it."

The perplexed son went to his father again and asked him what he should do. "Point the tip of the conch shell towards the light," explained the father. "Then put a piece of rice on the end of a thread and give the thread to an ant. Place the ant in the mouth of the shell. The ant will take the rice through the opening on its way out of the shell."

The son did as he was told and so was successful a second time. The lord was once again very impressed. "How is it that you, and you alone, are successful in completing the difficult tasks?"

The son hesitated, but because he was an honest man, he told the lord that he had defied the order to throw his father into the canyon. "I did not come up with the solutions to the problems, my father did."

The lord listened in amazement to the farmer's son. That a man over sixty could be so wise! In fact, the lord was so impressed by the wisdom of the old man that he reversed his orders. From that time to this, older people would be respected and be cared for by the younger generations. The "sixty canyon abandonment" was no more.

The Tamarack Tree
Retold by Gail de Vos

Everyone always talks about the weather. If it is not too cold, why then it's just too hot. Doesn't matter how much we complain though, doesn't change a bit. Now don't get me wrong, I'm not saying that the weather has not got any better lately with all the global warming and all, but we still don't have any control. All we can do is survive. And survive we do.

And survive we did. I remember one winter, boy, was there ever a lot of snow! It was awhile back when I was in my recluse phase—living up in a one-room shack in the mountains—and in training to be self-sufficient. It was late winter, and one morning, I tried to open the door, and I couldn't. I pushed and shoved for awhile before I noticed the blanket of snow on the windows. It had snowed so much that the shack was entirely covered!

I wasn't worried a bit—I was self-sufficient, was I not? I kept the stove going with the wood I had piled in the house. I didn't worry about food either: I had enough to last the winter although I was getting a little short on meat. But after about four days my wood was gone and I was still held captive by the snow. I tore out some shelves and kept the fire burning. But after burning up all of my shelves and a couple of chairs, I knew I had to get out of the house and get some firewood.

The only way out of that shack was up! Carefully I took the stovepipe down. I widened the hole in the roof with my axe and then, still holding the axe, I crawled out. I couldn't believe it. The snow went up and up like a funnel where the fire had kept it melted! Axe in hand, I chopped some toe-holds and climbed to the top of the funnel. I turned around and looked; all I could see was snow. There wasn't a treetop in sight. I looked around again, but carefully this time, and I saw, way up on a cliff of the mountain, one tree, a tamarack, that the snow hadn't drifted over and buried. I needed that wood, so I headed for the cliff. Had no problem walking, the snow crust was hard enough to hold me up. I got to the cliff finally and I cut the tree.

The exercise kept me warm so I was not in any hurry. I took my time and did the neatest job you can ever imagine. Once the tree was cut I trimmed it and stacked each limb carefully in a pile. I was being mighty self-sufficient, so I saved every twig for kindling. I was feeling mighty proud of myself too. I had only one more limb to chop off and I figured that I would have a rest before cording the log. But I guess there's truth in the old saying, "There's no rest for the wicked."

You see, when I chopped off that last limb, the log jumped and went roaring down the side of the mountain cliff. I watched my firewood gathering speed as it shot right across the bottom of the valley and right up the side of the opposite cliff. It was going so fast I was sure it would sail right over that mountain top! But it didn't. No, it slowed down just as it reached the top of the ridge and came sliding right down again. It was still traveling at a powerful speed, but this time it was heading back in my direction. I quickly cut me a few heel-holes in the snow and dug myself in, axe held in front of me. I reached out to stop that log, but it stopped coming a few inches short of where I was waiting. All I could do was watch it rush down the cliff and up the other side of the valley once again. I stood there watching the log for a few more sweeps of the valley and then I thought I had better gather up my gains. I collected the piles of limbs and kindling and headed back to the shack. I lowered the wood in through the hole in my roof, climbed inside and patched it so it was good as new. Put the stovepipe back in and sat about waiting for the thaw. I lived off the rest of my rations for about a week and had to burn up the rest of the chairs and the table to keep from freezing. I was just contemplating burning my books and eating boiled shoes when I realized that the room was getting lighter now. Daylight filtered in from a crack at the top of the windows. Before I could do much more than wonder, the crack got wider and wider. Then I realized that I was hearing a continuous plop, plop, plop! I raced over to the door and pushed and shoved and finally managed to open the door, just enough to squeeze out. I pushed the snow back and trampled a path out of the shack. There was still a lot of snow about, but I had no problem finding the old woodpile. Nearly brought the whole pile into the shack; you never know when the weather will reverse itself. And besides, with most of my furniture gone up in flames, the room was mighty empty.

Well, now I had firewood, but the thought of boiled shoes still wasn't appetizing, so I waited an hour or so until the snow was at a passable level and then started walking into town. I had to pass by the cliff on the way to town, and just out of curiosity, I took a look down into the valley. I noticed that the acrobatics of my log had left a large trough on both sides of the mountain. Now this made me even more curious so I hiked down to see what had happened. I couldn't see my log at all until I got to the bottom. And there, still sliding back and forth ever so slightly, was my log! The continuous motion had whittled that tamarack down so nice and smooth it was the size of a toothpick! Now don't you laugh at me, I kept that toothpick with me all the time. Here look at it yourself!* Best toothpick I ever had.

---

* At this point in the story I always pull a round toothpick out of my pocket.

*Tantalus**
Retold by Gail de Vos

Zeus, the king of the Greek gods, was renowned for his power, his anger, his sense of justice, his jealous wife, and his philandering. Zeus begot numerous children of various goddesses, nymphs, and mortal women. One of his favorite children was Tantalus, son of the Titaness Pluto.

Tantalus was a wealthy king of Lydia and, like his father, he savored the pleasures of life. He was a generous host, enjoying the company of friends and lively conversation. A connoisseur of fine wine and gourmet food, Tantalus was frequently invited to dine with the gods on Mount Olympus. He was witty and clever in conversation, and Zeus relished his company.

Or, Zeus did, until Tantalus angered him threefold. You see, Tantalus felt that his position was so secure that he was invincible and therefore he could get away with anything, including murder. He began taking risks.

On Mount Olympus, Tantalus had been served food and drink that was fit for the gods. The best of all ingredients were used to prepare the numerous dishes that were mouth-watering and succulent. The most magnificent food of all was ambrosia, a dish that was so divine it was not found on earth at all. Tantalus was also especially fond of nectar, a drink made of the tiny droplets of sweetness gathered by the bees and butterflies from earth-bound flowers. On one occasion, Tantalus stole both a dish of ambrosia and a flask of nectar and returned with them to his kingdom in Lydia. The next evening he served his mortal friends food and drink of the gods. Zeus was furious but did not act.

Zeus became even more angry at Tantalus's next transgression. Zeus, as a god, was omniscient and therefore knew all that happened. He knew when the King of Miletus stole the golden dog from Zeus's shrine. He knew also that the dog was taken to Lydia and given to Tantalus to hide. Zeus sent his messenger, Hermes, to Tantalus and asked for the return of the dog with the golden fur. Tantalus pleaded ignorance of the whereabouts of the animal and denied ever having set eyes upon it. Again Zeus did not act.

But Tantalus's final betrayal was more than even a doting father could overlook. Tantalus knew that his recent behavior was frowned upon on Olympus: he had not been invited to dine with the gods for quite a long time. So he decided to invite the gods to dine with him at his earthly home. They accepted the invitation and Tantalus prepared a banquet.

Tantalus could not resist testing his father and the rest of the gods from Olympus. He knew that they were omniscient but he wondered if they could tell the difference between the flavor of the flesh of a human and that of some beast. Tantalus called his son, Pelops, his own flesh and blood, into the kitchen. There he slit Pelops's throat. He carved the boy's body into chunks and added the chunks to the vegetables that were cooking in a large cauldron on the hearth.

The gods sat down in the banquet hall, and Tantalus proudly carried in the large cauldron of stew. He served each of the gods a bowl and encouraged them to partake heartily of his feast. But the gods all knew what the meat was and ate very carefully, eating no portion of Pelops's body. I say all the gods, but one of

---

**Tantalize*, torment, tease, by sight or promise of desired thing withheld or kept just out of reach; *tantalus*, a spirit-stand in which decanters are locked up but visible.

them, the goddess Demeter, distraught with grief for the loss of her daughter Persephone, absentmindedly ate part of the shoulder blade, nibbling it clean.

The gods were appalled by both the meal and the lighthearted manner in which it was served, but they left the punishment of this heinous crime to the father, Zeus. This time, he could not forgive!

Tantalus was taken to the Underworld and tied forever to the gnarled vines that grew along the edge of a pool of sweet water. He stood there, punished for all eternity by a dreadful, devouring thirst. For although the water would at times be level with his chin, at his first movement to drink, the water would recede, flowing away to leave the ground dry at his feet.

Above Tantalus's head were tall trees, laden with fruit. The branches drooped down to him, offering juicy pears, radiant pomegranates, crimson apples, green olives, and luscious figs. But when, with a sudden grab, he tried to seize the fruit, the wind gently lifted the branches and the fruit high above his reach. Parched with thirst, Tantalus would reach for the water that once again tickled his chin, but once again it would recede. And as it receded, the trees would once more gently offer their delectable bounty to him. But as soon as he reached for it the wind lifted the branches high over his head. And the water would rise to his chin.

When Tantalus lifted his eyes above the treetops he could see a rock, teetering above his head. At any moment the rock could tumble down and crush the life out of Tantalus's body.

And that is the end, if end there can ever be, of Tantalus's story. But it is not the end of Pelops's tale. Zeus had gathered all the pieces of Pelops's body from the stew and boiled them once again in the cauldron. This time Zeus caused the pieces to become whole, and Pelops arose from the cauldron, alive and well. In fact he lived a long life, governing the kingdom his father had left behind. Demeter was so sorry when she realized what she had done to his shoulder, that she gave him a shoulder bone made of ivory. Pelops's descendants were all born with an ivory shoulder.

The Third Yawn
Retold by Gail de Vos

People have always made up stories to explain things that are hard to understand and that they fear. Many of humanity's fears are universal and the fear of wild wolves is one. The winter wind howling through a lonely forest could make a person speculate on the existence of extra-powerful wolves — wolves like gods or wolves like humans! Fear of werewolves is also a universal fear.

There have always been people, too, who are willing to exploit other people's fears for their own ends.

There was once a crafty thief who had depleted all his resources and was once again forced to purloin objects belonging to others. He chanced to stop overnight at a small inn. He was the only guest for the evening. His attention was immediately caught by the innkeeper's fine cloak. The garment was elegant, colorful, warm, and, most conveniently, just the thief's size. The only trouble was that the innkeeper never took it off. How could the thief liberate it without getting caught? After concentrating on the problem for the entire night, the thief hit upon a brilliant plan.

That morning the thief approached the innkeeper and started a friendly conversation. The inn was not busy and the two men continued talking throughout the entire day. They sat side by side on one bench, feet on the table, drinks in hand. After the evening meal the thief began to yawn. With the first yawn, he let out a long-drawn wolfish howl.

The innkeeper looked at his guest in amazement. "What on earth's the matter? Are you tired?"

"No, no," the thief responded. "I am not tired at all. Look, there is a full moon! Would you mind looking after my clothes for me? I have a slight problem and the clothes hamper me."

"Problem?" gulped the innkeeper. "What kind of problem?" The innkeeper tried to edge inconspicuously away from the thief.

"Oh, I feel wolfish," was the reply.

"Wolfish?" the innkeeper's voice quivered as he moved even further away.

"Yes," said the thief with another huge yawn. "It's happened a few times before. First, I start feeling peculiar, and then I yawn. A few moments later, I yawn a second time, and then a third time. After the third yawn, well, I turn into a wolf. Not the ordinary type of wolf, you understand, not the kind that eats livestock. No, the type that has to eat nice fleshy people, bones and all. I really don't understand why I have to be cursed with such an affliction, but there it is. You will hold my clothes for me?"

The innkeeper gave a strangled yelp and jumped to his feet, his glorious cloak surging about his rotund body. The thief grabbed hold of the cloak and said, "Oh please, guard my clothes for me." He started to undress and at the same time opened his mouth for the third yawn. In a complete panic, the innkeeper pulled free from the grip of the thief. He ran out into the night leaving the thief holding the precious cloak.

The Warning*
Retold by Gail de Vos

A cousin of mine, Joseph Blackwell, went visiting some friends for the weekend; they had just finished renovating an old three-story home out in the country and wanted to show it off. They had given Joseph fairly precise directions, and Joseph felt that he would have no trouble finding the house. He drove out of the city a little later than he had anticipated and by the time he turned off the highway onto the country road the sky was dark. There was very little light from the sliver of moon that hovered over the unfamiliar landscape. Joseph drove up and down countless roads before, with relief, he finally found their house and drove up the wide, circular, gravel drive that wound past the front of the house.

The hour was late. The friends visited for a short while and then they retired, Joseph in the guest bedroom on the third floor. Now usually Joseph did not have trouble sleeping, but that night he just could not fall asleep. Perhaps he was disturbed by the dark and the quiet around him; it never was that dark and silent in Edmonton! He was just on the point of getting a book to read when he heard the sound of horses. Curious about the sound, Joseph got out of bed and looked out the window. There, on the gravel driveway below his window, stood an old mail coach drawn by four black horses. A coachman was standing and peering into the night. The coachman was not much more than a skeleton but what Joseph noticed most was the cavernous eyes and the deep scar that slashed across the left side of his face. When he noticed Joseph at the window the coachman crooked a long, bony finger at him, and Joseph heard him whisper, "There's room for one more!" As Joseph stood dumbfounded, the coachman, coach, and horses faded into the night.

Needless to say, Joseph could not sleep for the rest of the night. By the time morning arrived Joseph decided that it must have been a nightmare. Just to be sure, he walked down the drive looking for tracks of the horses and coach in the gravel. There were none. He did not mention his experience to his friends. That night, however, the same thing happened again. The hideous coachman stood beside the coach and the four black horses. Once again he crooked a long bony finger and Joseph could hear him whisper, "There's room for one more!"

Again Joseph could not sleep. He still did not say anything to his hosts, but he left early in the morning and went back to Edmonton to his apartment on the twenty-third floor of a downtown highrise. Late that afternoon, after a long nap, he decided to go out to a movie. He got ready, went to the hall and stood waiting for an elevator. When it finally arrived it was very crowded. As Joseph stepped over the threshold he heard a familiar whisper. "There's room for one more!" Joseph quickly glanced up and saw the hideous face and beckoning finger of the coachman. Gasping, Joseph drew back with horror and the elevator door slammed shut in his face.

Joseph stood, shaken, in the hallway. Before he could move, the entire building shook as if an earthquake had hit it. The elevator had broken loose from its cables and plunged twenty-three stories to the basement. Everyone aboard was killed.

*Variation of *Room for One More*, see page 67.

Little Lem
By Marie Anne McLean

Old Charles McLean was a highlander by blood and by nature. His highland pride would never allow him to admit to hard times or private difficulties. He raised his children to believe in the same self-sufficiency that he had grown up with. The lessons he taught were hard, but his children remembered them well.

One day his wife, Flora, called out to Little Lem, their youngest boy, to go fetch his father. It was time to come home for dinner. Little Lem was told to hurry so that the dinner would not be cold.

Little Lem ran all the way to his father's blacksmith shop, excited with the importance of his task. When he arrived at the smithy it was filled with the usual crowd of gossips who stood around watching while Charles put shoes on MacDonald's miserable roan mare.

"Papa, Mama says that it's time to come home for our dinner," the little boy said.

"What's for dinner, boy?" the father said, frowning and lowering his eyebrows at Little Lem.

The boy announced, "Turnips and salt."

Charles said nothing as he tied up the roan and set his tools back on the shelf. He took Little Lem's hand and they set off down the road to the house.

As soon as they were around the curve and out of sight of the smithy, Charles turned and gave the boy a sharp cuff to the back of the head.

"What was that for?" Little Lem cried.

"When I ask you what we're having for dinner in front of all those people, you are to say something big," said Charles in most severe tones, "and don't forget this, boy."

Two days later, Little Lem was sent again to fetch his father home for dinner. Again he hurried to do a good job.

Again his father inquired what was for dinner. This time Little Lem looked carefully around at all the visitors in the smithy and then he announced in a clear voice, "Whale and salt!"

Author Index

Title Index

Note: Individual story titles are in roman type; collection titles are in italic.

Theme Index

Collections Index

Asterisk denotes single story volumes.

Library
Call Number

Aitken, Hannah. 1973. *A Forgotten Heritage: Original Folktales of Lowland Scotland*. Edinburgh, Scotland: Scottish Academic Press.

Anderson, Sherwood. 1962. *Sherwood Anderson: Short Stories*. Edited by Maxwell Geismar. New York: Hill and Wang.

Anderson, Sherwood. 1947. *The Sherwood Anderson Reader*. Boston: Houghton Mifflin.

Appiah, Peggy. 1967. *Tales of an Ashanti Father*. London: Andre Deutsch.

Appiah, Peggy. 1977. *Why the Hyena Does Not Care for Fish and Other Tales from the Ashanti*. London: Andre Deutsch.

Arbuthnot, May Hill. 1961. *Time for Fairy Tales: Old and New*. revised ed. New York: Scott, Foresman and Co.

Arbuthnot, May Hill, and Mark Taylor, comps. 1970. *Time for Old Magic*. Glenview, Ill.: Scott, Foresman and Co.

Asbjornsen, Peter Christen, and Jorgen Moe. 1960. *Norwegian Folk Tales*. New York: Viking.

Asian Cultural Centre for UNESCO. 1976. *Folk Tales from Asia for Children Everywhere, Book Four*. New York: Weatherhill.

Babbit, Natalie. 1974. *The Devil's Storybook*. New York: Farrar.

Bang, Garrett. 1973. *Men from the Village Deep in the Mountains and Other Japanese Folk Tales*. New York: Macmillan.

Bang, Molly. 1973. *The Goblins Giggle and Other Stories*. New York: Charles Scribner's Sons.

Battle, Kemp P., comp. 1986. *Great American Folklore: Legends, Tales, Ballads and Superstitions from All across America*. New York: Doubleday.

159

Bauer, Caroline Feller. 1977. *Handbook for Storytellers*. Chicago: American Library Association.

Berger, Terry. 1975. *Black Fairy Tales*. New York: Atheneum.

Bloch, Robert. 1986. *Midnight Pleasures*. Garden City, N.Y.: Doubleday.

Boccaccio, Giovanni. 1930. *The Decameron*. Translated by Richard Aldington. New York: Dell Publishing.

Bomans, Godfried. 1977. *The Wiley Witch and All the Other Fairy Tales and Fables*. Owing Mills, Md.: Stemmer House.

Bonnet, Leslie. 1963. *Chinese Folk and Fairy Tales*. New York: G. P. Putnam's Sons.

Bradbury, Ray. 1946. *Dandelion Wine*. New York: Alfred A. Knopf.

Bradbury, Ray. 1960. *A Medicine for Melancholy*. New York: Bantam.

Briggs, Katherine M., and Ruth L. Tongue. 1965. *Folktales of England*. Chicago: The Univ. of Chicago Press.

Brown, George Mackay. 1974. *The Two Fiddlers: Tales from Orkney*. London: Chatto & Windus.

Brunvand, Jan Harold. 1984. *The Choking Doberman and Other "New" Urban Legends*. New York: W. W. Norton.

Brunvand, Jan Harold. 1981. *The Vanishing Hitchhiker: American Urban Legends and Their Meanings*. New York: W. W. Norton.

Cerf, Bennett A. 1945. *Try and Stop Me: A Collection of Anecdotes and Stories, Mostly Humorous*. New York: Simon and Schuster.

Chase, Richard. 1971. *American Folk Tales and Songs*. New York: Dover Publications.

Chase, Richard. 1948. *Grandfather Tales*. Cambridge, Mass.: The Riverside Press.

Cohen, Daniel. 1980. *The Headless Roommate and Other Tales of Terror*. New York: M. Evans.

Cohen, Daniel. 1984. *The Restless Dead: Ghostly Tales from around the World*. New York: Dodd, Mead & Co.

Collier, John. 1980. *Fancies and Goodnights*. Alexandria, Va.: Time-Life Books.

Colum, Padraic. 1937. *Legends of Hawaii*. New Haven, Conn.: Yale Univ. Press.

Colwell, Eileen. 1978. *Humblepuppy and Other Stories for Telling*. London: The Bodley Head.

Colwell, Eileen. 1976. *The Magic Umbrella and Other Stories for Telling*. London: The Bodley Head.

Conford, Ellen. 1983. *If This Is Love, I'll Take Spaghetti*. New York: Four Winds Press.

Courlander, Harold, and George Herzog. 1947. *The Cow-Tail Switch and Other West African Stories*. New York: Holt, Rinehart and Winston.

Courlander, Harold. 1962. *The King's Drum and Other African Stories*. New York: Harcourt, Brace & World.

Courlander, Harold. 1959. *The Tiger's Whisker and Other Tales from Asia and the Pacific*. New York: Harcourt, Brace & Co.

Crossley-Holland, Kevin. 1977. *The Faber Book of Northern Legends*. London: Faber and Faber.

Dahl, Roald. 1982. *Roald Dahl's Revolting Rhymes*. London: Jonathan Cape.

Danaher, Kevin. 1970. *Folktales of the Irish Countryside*. New York: David White.

Davenport, Basil, ed. 1953. *Horror Stories from Tales to Be Told in the Dark: A Selection of Stories from the Great Authors Arranged for Reading and Telling Aloud*. New York: Ballantine Books.

Davenport, Basil, ed. 1962. *Tales to Be Told in the Dark: A Selection of Stories from the Great Authors, Arranged for Reading and Telling Aloud*. New York: Dodd, Mead & Co.

Dickinson, Peter. 1976. *Chance, Luck and Destiny*. Boston: Little, Brown and Co.

Dickinson, Peter. 1988. *Merlin Dreams*. London: Victor Gollancz.

Dorson, Richard M. 1975. *Folktales Told around the World*. Chicago: The Univ. of Chicago Press.

Erdoes, Richard, and Alphonso Ortiz. 1984. *American Indian Myths and Legends*. New York: Pantheon.

Fairies and Elves. 1984. Enchanted World series. Alexandria, Va.: Time-Life Books.

Fillmore, Parker. 1958. *The Shepherd's Nosegay: Stories from Finland and Czechoslovakia*. Eau Claire, Wis.: E. M. Hale and Co.

Foster, James R., ed. 1955. *Great Folktales of Wit and Humor*. New York: Harper & Brothers.

Fowke, Edith, ed. 1976. *Folklore of Canada*. Toronto: McClelland and Stewart.

Fowke, Edith. 1986. *Tales Told in Canada*. Toronto: Doubleday Canada Ltd.

Ghosts. 1984. The Enchanted World series. Alexandria, Va.: Time-Life Books.

*Ginsburg, Mirra. 1988. *The Chinese Mirror: Adapted from a Korean Folktale*. San Diego, Calif.: Harcourt Brace Jovanovich.

Godfrey, Thomas, ed. 1982. *Murder for Christmas*. New York: The Mysterious Press.

Gorog, Judith. 1982. *A Taste for Quiet and Other Disquieting Tales*. New York: Philomel.

Gorog, Judith. 1988. *Three Dreams and a Nightmare and Other Tales of the Dark*. New York: Philomel Books.

Graham, Gail B. 1970. *The Beggar in the Blanket and Other Vietnamese Tales*. New York: Dial Press.

Green, Roger Lancelyn. 1965. *A Book of Myths*. London: J. M. Dent & Sons.

Haines, Max. 1985. *The Collected Works of Max Haines. Vol. I*. Toronto: Toronto Sun Publishing.

Hamilton, Virginia. 1985. *The People Could Fly: American Black Folktales*. New York: Alfred A. Knopf.

Hardendorff, Jeanne B. 1970. *Clever-Clever-Clever: Folktales from Many Lands*. London: Macdonald.

Hardendorff, Jeanne B. 1971. *Witches, Wit, and a Werewolf*. Philadelphia: J. B. Lippincott.

Haviland, Virginia, ed. 1979. *The Faber Book of North American Legends*. London: Faber and Faber.

Hayes, Barbara. 1987. *Folk Tales and Fables of the World*. Buderim, Australia: David Bateman.

Hearn, Lafcadio. 1958. *Japanese Fairy Tales*. Mount Vernon, N.Y.: Peter Pauper Press.

Henry, O. 1906. *The Four Million*. New York: Doubleday.

Herriot, James. 1972. *All Creatures Great and Small*. New York: St. Martin's Press.

Hill, Kay. 1963. *Glooscap and His Magic: Legends of the Wabanaki Indians*. Toronto: McClelland and Stewart.

Hoke, Helen, ed. 1977. *Eerie, Weird, and Wicked*. Nashville, Tenn.: Thomas Nelson.

Hoke, Helen, ed. 1979. *Terrors, Terrors, Terrors*. New York: Franklin Watts.

Hoke, Helen, ed. 1978. *Terrors, Torments and Traumas*. Nashville, Tenn.: Thomas Nelson.

Hoke, Helen, ed. 1977. *Spectres, Spooks and Shuddery Shades*. London: Franklin Watts.

Hoke, Helen, ed. 1958. *Witches, Witches, Witches*. New York: Franklin Watts.

Hope-Simpson, Jacynth. 1964. *The Hamish Hamilton Book of Myths and Legends*. London: Hamish Hamilton.

Hughes, Richard. 1977. *The Wonder Dog*. New York: Greenwillow.

Ireson, Barbara, ed. 1973. *Haunting Tales*. London: Faber and Faber.

Jablow, Alta, and Carl Withers. 1969. *The Man in the Moon: Sky Tales from Many Lands*. New York: Holt, Rinehart and Winston.

Jacobs, Joseph. 1968. *English Fairy Tales*. London: The Bodley Head.

Jacobs, Joseph. 1892. *English Folk and Fairy Tales*. 3d ed. New York: G. P. Putnam's Sons.

Jaffrey, Madhur. 1985. *Seasons of Splendour: Tales, Myths & Legends of India*. New York: Atheneum.

Jagendorf, M. A. 1972. *Folk Stories of the South*. New York: Vanguard Press.

Jenkins, Peter. 1979. *A Walk across America*. New York: William Morrow.

Johnson, Edna et al. 1977. *Anthology of Children's Literature*. Boston: Houghton Mifflin.

Kelsey, Alice Geer. 1981. *Turkish Jokes: Once the Hodja, Nasr-ed-Din*. Taipei: Tung Fang Wen Hua ShuChu, Supplement of Asian Folklore and Social Life Monographs, 23.

Kendall, Carol, and Yao-wen Li. 1978. *Sweet & Sour: Tales from China*. New York: Houghton Mifflin.

*Kennedy, Richard. 1976. *Come Again in the Spring*. New York: Harper & Row.

*Kennedy, Richard. 1978. *The Dark Princess*. New York: Holiday House.

*Kennedy, Richard. 1977. *Oliver Hyde's Dishcloth Concert*. Boston: Little, Brown, and Co.

Kennedy, Richard. 1987. *Richard Kennedy: Collected Stories*. New York: Harper & Row.

Killip, Kathleen. 1980. *Twisting the Rope and Other Folktakes from the Isle of Man*. London: Hodder & Stoughton.

Knappert, Jan. 1971. *Myths & Legends of the Congo*. Nairobi, Kenya: Heinemann.

Le Guin, Ursula K. 1987. *Buffalo Gals and Other Animal Presences*. Santa Barbara, Calif.: Capra Press.

Le Guin, Ursula K. 1982. *Compass Rose*. New York: Harper & Row.

Leach, Maria. 1974. *Whistle in the Graveyard: Folktales to Chill Your Bones*. New York: Viking.

Leodhas, Sorche Nic. 1971. *Twelve Great Black Cats and Other Eerie Scottish Tales*. New York: E. P. Dutton.

Lester, Julius. 1972. *Long Journey Home: Stories from Black History*. New York: Dial Press.

Lester, Julius. 1987. *The Tales of Uncle Remus: The Adventures of Brer Rabbit*. New York: Dial Press.

Lines, Kathleen, ed. 1973. *The Faber Book of Greek Legends*. London: Faber and Faber.

Library
Call Number

*Lionni, Leo. 1964. *Tico and the Golden Wings*. New York: Pantheon.

The Lore of Love. 1987. The Enchanted World series. Alexandria, Va.: Time-Life Books.

Manning-Sanders, Ruth. 1968. *Stories from the English and Scottish Ballads*. London: Heinemann.

Manton, Jo, and Robert Gittings. 1977. *The Flying Horses: Tales from China*. London: Methuen.

Matsubara, Hisako. 1985. *Cranes at Dusk*. Garden City, N.Y.: Doubleday.

McCaughrean, Geraldine. 1964. *The Canterbury Tales*. Oxford: Oxford Univ. Press.

McCormick, Dell J. 1961. *Tall Timber Tales: More Paul Bunyan Stories*. Caldwell, Idaho: Caxton Printers.

*McDermott, Beverly Brodsky. 1976. *The Golem: A Jewish Legend*. Philadelphia: J. B. Lippincott.

*McDermott, Gerald. 1973. *The Magic Tree: A Tale from the Congo*. New York: Holt, Rinehart and Winston.

McKinley, Robin, ed. 1986. *Imaginary Lands*. New York: Greenwillow.

McManus, Patrick. 1989. *The Night the Bear Ate Goombaw*. New York: Henry Holt.

McManus, Patrick F. 1987. *Rubber Legs and White Tail-Hairs*. New York: Henry Holt.

McNeill, James. 1984. *The Double Knights: More Tales from Round the World*. Toronto: Oxford Univ. Press.

*Moeri, Louise. 1975. *Star Mother's Youngest Child*. Boston: Houghton Mifflin.

Night Creatures. 1985. The Enchanted World series. Alexandria, Va.: Time-Life Books.

Otten, Charlotte F., ed. 1986. *A Lycanthropy Reader: Werewolves in Western Culture*. Syracuse, N.Y.: Syracuse Univ. Press.

Phelps, Ethel Johnston. 1981. *The Maid of the North: Feminist Folk Tales from around the World*. New York: Holt, Rinehart and Winston.

Library
Call Number

Phelps, Ethel Johnston. 1978. *Tatterhood and Other Tales*. New York: The Feminist Press.

Picard, Barbara Leonie. 1964. *The Faun and the Wood Cutter's Daughter*. New York: Criterion Books.

Picard, Barbara Leonie. 1955. *French Legends and Fairy Stories*. New York: Henry Z. Walck.

Price, Susan. 1984. *Ghosts at Large*. London: Faber and Faber.

Ransome, Arthur. 1984. *The War of the Birds and the Beasts and Other Russian Tales*. London: Jonathan Cape.

Raskin, Joseph, and Edith Raskin. 1973. *Ghosts and Witches APlenty: More Tales Our Settlers Told*. New York: Lothrop, Lee & Shepard.

Riordan, James, translator. 1986. *Russian Gypsy Tales*. Collected by Yefim Druts & Alexei Gessler. Edinburgh, Scotland: Canongate Publishers.

Riordan, James. 1976. *Tales from Central Russia: Russian Tales, Volume One*. Harmondsworth, England: Kestrel Books.

Riordan, James. 1984. *The Woman in the Moon and Other Tales of Forgotten Heroines*. London: Hutchinson.

Roach, Marilynne K. 1977. *Encounters with the Visible World: Being Ten Tales of Ghosts, Witches and the Devil Himself in New England*. New York: Thomas Y. Crowell.

Roberts, Moss, ed. 1979. *Chinese Fairy Tales and Fantasies*. New York: Pantheon.

Roberts, Nancy. 1978. *Appalachian Ghosts*. Garden City, N.Y.: Doubleday.

Rochman, Hazel, ed. 1988. *Somehow Tenderness Survives: Stories of Southern Africa*. New York: Harper & Row.

Rugoff, Milton. 1949. *A Harvest of World Folktales*. New York: Viking.

Saki. 1982. *Storyteller: Thirteen Tales by Saki*. Boston: David R. Gooline.

Sanders, Scott R. 1985. *Hear the Wind Blow: American Folk Songs Retold*. New York: Bradbury Press.

Sawyer, Ruth. 1949. *The Long Christmas*. New York: Viking.

Library
Call Number

Schram, Peninnah. 1987. *Jewish Stories One Generation Tells Another*. Northvale, N.J.: Jason Aronson.

Schwab, Gustav. 1946. *Gods and Heroes: Myths and Epics of Ancient Greece*. New York: Pantheon.

Schwartz, Alvin. 1981. *Scary Stories to Tell in the Dark*. New York: Lippincott.

Schwartz, Howard. 1983. *Elijah's Violin and Other Jewish Fairy Tales*. New York: Harper & Row.

Serwer, Blanche Luria. 1970. *Let's Steal the Moon: Jewish Tales, Ancient and Recent*. Boston: Little, Brown and Co.

*Seuss, Dr. 1938. *The 500 Hats of Bartholomew Cubbins*. New York: Vanguard Press.

Sexton, Anne. 1971. *Transformations*. Boston: Houghton Mifflin.

Shedlock, Marie L. 1951. *The Art of the Storyteller*. 3d ed. New York: Dover Publications.

Smith, Jimmy Neil, ed. 1988. *Homespun: Tales from America's Favorite Storytellers*. New York: Crown Publishers.

Spalding, Andrea. 1989. *A World of Stories*. Red Deer, Alta.: Red Deer College Press.

Spellman, John W. 1967. *The Beautiful Blue Jay and Other Tales of India*. Boston: Little, Brown & Co.

Spretnak, Charlene. 1984. *Lost Goddesses of Early Greece: A Collection of Pre-Hellenic Myths*. Boston: Beacon Press.

*Stevens, Kathleen. 1982. *Molly McCullough and Tom the Rogue*. New York: Thomas Y. Crowell.

Stockton, Frank R. 1968. *The Storyteller's Pack*. New York: Charles Scribner's Sons.

Stone, Ted, ed. 1988. *13 Canadian Ghost Stories*. Saskatoon, Sask.: Western Producer Prairie Books.

Stratford, Philip, ed. 1974. *Stories from Quebec*. Toronto: Van Nostrand Reinhold.

Sullivan, Tom, and Derek Gill. 1975. *You Could See What I Hear*. New York: Harper & Row.

Library
Call Number

Switzer, Ellen, and Costas Switzer. 1988. *Greek Myths: Gods, Heroes and Monsters: Their Sources and Their Meanings*. New York: Antheneum.

Thurber, James. 1940. *Fables for Our Time*. New York: Harper & Row.

*Thurber, James. 1943. *Many Moons*. New York: Harcourt Brace Jovanovich.

Tolstoy, Leo. 1988. *The Lion and the Puppy and Other Stories for Children*. Translated by James Riordan. New York: Henry Holt.

Travers, P. L. 1976. *Two Pairs of Shoes*. New York: Viking.

Untermeyer, Louis, ed. 1946. *A Treasury of Laughter*. New York: Simon and Schuster.

Walker, Barbara, ed. 1975. *The Scared Ghost and Other Stories*. New York: McGraw-Hill.

Weinreich, Beatrice Silverman. 1988. *Yiddish Folktales*. New York: Pantheon.

Whitaker, Muriel, ed. 1980. *The Princess, the Hockey Player, Magic and Ghosts*. Edmonton, Atla.: Hurtig Publishers.

*Wieser, William. 1972. *Turnabout*. New York: Seabury Press.

*Williams, Jay. 1973. *Petronella*. New York: Parents' Magazine Press.

Williams, Jay. 1975. *The Wicked Tricks of Tyl Uilenspiegel*. New York: Four Winds Press.

Williams-Ellis, Amabel. 1981. *The Story Spirits and Other Tales from around the World*. London: Heineman.

Windham, Kathryn Tucker. 1977. *Thirteen Tennessee Ghosts and Jeffrey*. Huntsville, Ala.: The Strode Publishers.

Wolkstein, Diane. 1978. *The Magic Orange Tree and Other Haitian Folktales*. New York: Alfred A. Knopf.

*Wolkstein, Diane. 1977. *The Red Lion: A Tale of Ancient Persia*. New York: Thomas Y. Crowell.

*Wolkstein, Diane. 1979. *White Wave: A Chinese Tale*. New York: Thomas Y. Crowell.

Wood, Wendy. 1980. *The Silver Chanter: Traditional Scottish Tales and Legends*. London: Chatto & Windus.

Wyndham, Lee. 1970. *Tales the People Tell in Russia*. New York: Julian Messner.

Wyndham, Robert. 1971. *Tales the People Tell in China*. New York: Julian Messner.

*Yagawa, Sumiko. 1981. *The Crane Wife*. Translated by Katherine Paterson. New York: William Morrow.

Yep, Laurence. 1989. *The Rainbow People*. New York: Harper & Row.

Yolen, Jane. 1989. *The Faery Flag: Stories and Poems of Fantasy and the Supernatural*. New York: Orchard Books.

Yolen, Jane, ed. 1986. *Favorite Folktales from around the World*. New York: Pantheon.

Yolen, Jane. 1974. *The Girl Who Cried Flowers and Other Tales*. New York: Schocken Books.

Yolen, Jane. 1977. *The Hundredth Dove and Other Tales*. New York: Thomas Y. Crowell.

Yolen, Jane. 1988. *Sister Light, Sister Dark*. New York: Tom Doherty.

Young, Louise B. 1983. *The Blue Planet: A Celebration of the Earth*. Boston: Little, Brown and Co.